SUCCESSFUL TAX PLANNING

Kiplinger Books Also Publishes:
THE NEW AMERICAN BOOM
BUYING AND SELLING A HOME
MAKE YOUR MONEY GROW

KIPLINGER'S

SUCCESSFUL TAX PLANNING

By Kevin McCormally
Tax Editor, *Changing Times* Magazine

KIPLINGER BOOKS, Washington, D.C.

Published by
The Kiplinger Washington Editors, Inc.
1729 H Street, NW
Washington, D.C. 20006

Library of Congress Cataloging-in-Publication Data

McCormally, Kevin.
  Kiplinger's successful tax planning.

  Includes index.
  1. Tax planning--United States. 2. Income tax--
Law and legislation--United States. I. Title. II. Title:
Successful tax planning.   343.7305'2   88-13671
KF6297.Z9M3 1988   347.30352
ISBN 0-938721-06-2
ISBN 0-938721-04-6 (pbk.)

This publication is intended to provide guidance in regard to the
subject matter covered. It is sold with the understanding that the
author and publisher are not herein engaged in rendering legal,
accounting, tax or other professional services. If such services
are required, professional assistance should be sought.

First printing. Printed in the United States of America.

ACKNOWLEDGEMENTS

I am a reporter, not a tax attorney or accountant.

That's not a disclaimer but rather an indication of the debt I owe others for the completion of this book. During the decade I have covered federal income taxes for *Changing Times,* I have enjoyed and benefited from the generous counsel and advice of scores of accountants, attorneys, financial planners, tax preparers, members of Congress and their aides, and Internal Revenue Service employees from auditors to regulation writers to public affairs officers. I had the questions, they supplied the answers that fill this book, and I thank them.

Just as important are the source of those questions: the thousands of *Changing Times* readers who have showered the magazine with their questions about the federal income tax. Their demand for practical advice on real-life issues—a demand the Kiplinger organization vigorously encourages—gets the credit for this book's focus on down-to-earth realities rather than high-falutin technicalities.

My thanks to Steve Ivins, editor of the *Kiplinger Tax Letter,* and his associate Peter Blank for their patient tutelage over the years and for their valuable review of the manuscript. Their keen knowledge of the tax law and ability to cut through the intricacies has been an enormous benefit. Thanks, too, to David Harrison, director of Kiplinger Books for all of his help—particularly his editing and good-natured support—in getting this book to press. I am also grateful to Kristin W. Davis for her indefatigable copy-editing, proofreading and computer-coding of the manuscript, to Kim McClung who prepared the user-friendly index, to Nicholas Fasciano for his cheerful cover design and to Don Fragale and Millie Thompson who guided the book through printing and production. Oh, yes: Three cheers for the cartoonists whose work brightens the pages.

Special thanks to Lindy Spellman, research reporter at *Changing Times,* who devoted hundreds of hours chasing down facts to insure the accuracy of the manuscript. I am indebted to the enthusiasm and the skill she brought to this project.

Finally, my thanks to my children—Niamh Anna and Patrick Henry—for their patience during all the nights and weekends Dad worked on "The book." And, most of all, to my wife Anne, for her unwavering faith and encouragement, and more than a few good ideas.

Kevin McCormally
September 1988

CONTENTS

Introduction by **Knight A. Kiplinger**
Editor in Chief, *Changing Times*

INTRODUCTION

I ncome taxes: a civic duty, an annual ordeal, the butt of jokes and scorn, the lifeblood of government. Is there any other subject that evokes so much confusion and controversy in the public realm, year after year?

The tax-cutting decade of the '80s has seen more radical changes in taxes than any period since the Great Depression and World War II. In the 1930s and '40s, marginal rates were jacked up to historic highs. The top rate went to 63% during the Depression, and then into the 90% range by the mid '40s and early '50s.

The first wave of income tax cuts was initiated by President John Kennedy in the early '60s, when—to stimulate economic expansion in a sluggish economy—Congress reduced rates across the board, including dropping the top rate down to 70%. The first Reagan tax cuts of this decade cut it further, down to 50%, the lowest maximum rate since the early 1930s. Today, for most Americans, the top rate is 33%.

From the beginning of the personal income tax in 1913, it has been more than just a revenue-raising mechanism. It is a powerful tool for social change, enabling the government to discourage this or that activity, encourage others, and generally direct capital to "socially desirable" uses. Every tax deduction and credit, for whatever worthy purpose, is as much a government subsidy as a direct payment would be. Do you think homeownership is an essential ingredient of the American dream? Then subsidize it with a mortgage-interest deduction. Think people should give money to charity? Then subsidize it with a tax deduction. Think two-career families need help with their child-care costs? Then subsidize it with a tax credit.

That is the way the fairly simple tax system of 75 years ago became the extraordinary thicket of thorny rules and regulations it is today. Every tax break has its legions of beneficiaries and its zealous champions on Capitol Hill. Everyone wants to slash the other guy's tax breaks, but not his or her own. And the dominant beneficiary of tax munificence is America's gigantic middle class.

The legendary staying power of tax breaks makes it all the more remarkable that Ronald Reagan and Congress were able to achieve what they did over the past few years. For the first time in history, sharp rate reductions were adopted in exchange for a major cutback in deductions. Gone is the sales-tax deduction, once very popular in a high-consuming society. Gone is the open-ended, unlimited deductibility of mortgage interest (although the subsidy of homeownership survived pretty well for most Americans). Gone, too, is the tax break for capital gains, the full deductibility of real estate losses and, for millions of taxpayers, the deduction of IRAs.

But if you harbored any illusions that tax *reform* would be tax *simplification,* you got a rude awakening when it came time to tackle your first postreform tax return. Once again, tax reform looked like a full-employment program for accountants, tax attorneys and preparers. Granted, millions of lower-income taxpayers found their taxes slashed and their forms simplified, but for most people the headaches mounted. One of the chief foes of simplification is Congress's desire to cushion the shock by phasing in new rates and regulations over several years. It might be "fairer" to do it that way, but it sure makes a lot more work.

Just as tax reform shouldn't be confused with simplification, neither should it be mistaken for tax reduction. Upper-income Americans who had relied on a battery of exotic tax shelters, capital-gains preferences and income-shifting strategies found that the loss of these techniques more than offset the reduction of top marginal rates. Their bottom line: higher tax bills. But for most Americans, especially those who never made use of shelters in the first place, higher personal exemptions and lower marginal rates did, in fact, mean lower tax bills.

When Americans talk about taxes, they usually focus on the federal personal income tax. In the process, they often miss the significance of other things happening in taxes, both in Washington and throughout America. For decades, Americans have been paying a bigger and bigger chunk of their total income in taxes of all sorts—federal income taxes, social security, state sales and income taxes, local real estate taxes, etc. In recent years, the social security payroll tax has risen to the point where, for many Americans, it is a larger annual payment than the federal income tax. And soaring local property taxes have led to caps and rollback initiatives in several states.

This book may lead you indirectly to state income tax savings, since most state laws are tied to the federal system. You may also find here a way to hold down the social security tax on self-employment income. But our primary subject is the federal income tax, pure and not so simple. Our mission is to help you think through all the ways that you can organize your financial affairs to minimize Uncle Sam's bite. As eminent jurists have pointed out for years, you have no duty to pay the government one cent more than the law requires. You're entitled to every legal means at your disposal to determine that minimum amount.

Rather than a frantic, last-minute rush to unearth a few more deductions, tax planning should be a year-round activity. Not that anyone wants to think about taxes all year, but at least you should be aware of the tax angles of major financial decisions— saving for your children's education, buying life insurance, investing your money, planning career moves and retirement, and much more. As a result of tax reform, many taxpayers who thought they had a good grip on the rules of the game are now scurrying to reeducate themselves. Even before they sit down with tax experts, they want to become conversant with the new ways of doing things. And tax planning isn't just for the rich anymore. Anyone who itemizes will find that a little study will bear rewards.

At the Kiplinger organization, we've been advising Americans on their tax concerns for more than six decades. Tax planning tips are a regular feature of our *Changing Times,* the first magazine of personal-finance guidance, founded in 1947. And our biweekly *Kiplinger Tax Letter,* founded in 1925, is America's most widely read tax-advisory service, keeping readers posted of changes affecting both individual and business taxes.

Kiplinger's Successful Tax Planning was written by Kevin McCormally, senior editor of *Changing Times,* with research help from *Changing Times* reporter Lindy Spellman. McCormally, a veteran tax observer, authored a special report on the 1986 tax-reform law that won our magazine a consumer journalism award from the National Press Club. Valuable improvements to the manuscript were suggested by Steven Ivins and Peter Blank, tax attorneys who are, respectively, editor and associate editor of *The Kiplinger Tax Letter.*

Taxes aren't a laughing matter, but a little levity can often ease the pain of so weighty a subject. That's why we have sprinkled some of our favorite editorial cartoons about taxes throughout the text of *Successful Tax Planning.* We hope you enjoy them.

With so much tax tinkering going on all the time in Washington, it's impossible for any book to stay 100% current very long. We've tried to catch as many recent changes as possible, but events have a way of overtaking authors. For the latest changes, we recommend that you take a look at our regular publications, and by all means seek the counsel of tax professionals for more information about how the tax laws apply to your particular situation. Finally, we wish you the best of success with your own tax-planning program.

KNIGHT A. KIPLINGER
September 1988

1
THE LATEST TAX LAW AND YOU

I t has been said that the ten most feared words in the English language are: "I'm from the federal government, and I'm here to help." So it's no wonder taxpayers were skeptical when Congress served up a massive rewrite of the nation's tax laws in 1986, a revision wrapped in the promise of a simpler and fairer income tax system.

For millions of us, our worst fears were realized in the spring of 1988 as we struggled with the first set of reformed tax forms.

Fairness, of course, is in the eye of the beholder. Taxpayers who found the new rules resulting in lower tax bills undoubtedly were satisfied on that point. But the 20 million or so citizens who wound up owing more tax were apt to feel betrayed.

There was no split decision on the matter of simplicity. Unless you are one of those who under the new law no longer has to pay any federal tax—in which case you don't need to read any further—the law is more complex. We now face the confusion of the "kiddie tax," the "passive loss" rules, the phaseout of the deductibility of certain interest, complicated questions on the right to deduct mortgage interest and individual-retirement-account contributions, and too many other mind-boggling new twists and turns in the tax maze. One measure of the new complexity is that professional return preparers—the people we pay to figure out how much we must pay Uncle Sam—charged many clients 30% to 100% more to complete 1987 returns than they had charged the previous year.

Even where Congress succeeded in simplifying the law, the

changes are bittersweet. In many instances, simplification was accomplished by eliminating opportunities to save money. To relieve taxpayers of the burden of saving boxes of receipts to figure how much state sales tax they could deduct, for example, Congress just abolished that tax-saving write-off. To spare many of us from keeping track of our medical expenses, the new rules make it impossible for the vast majority of taxpayers to deduct such costs.

The confusion, consternation and outright anger that reigned in the spring of 1988 gave birth to this book. The aim is to help you understand the new law so you can arrange your financial affairs to take advantage of the rules rather than be victimized by a higher-than-necessary tax bill.

HOW WE GOT HERE

Despite the multitudinous shortcomings of the Tax Reform Act of 1986, no one denies that the income tax law was in desperate need of major surgery. It has taken a long, tortuous road since the income tax was legalized by the 16th Amendment:

> The Congress shall have power to lay and collect taxes on incomes, from whatever source derived, without apportionment among the several States, and without regard to any census or enumeration.

When it was ratified in 1913—six years before prohibition and seven years before women won the vote—Congress quickly went to work drafting an income tax law to take advantage of it. Now that was a simple law. The first $3,000 of a single person's income was tax-free; $4,000 for married couples. For perspective, if those amounts were adjusted for 75 years of inflation, the tax-free figures would be around $30,000 and $40,000 today. The basic tax rate was a whopping 1%, but there was a "super tax" on high incomes to claim as much as 7% of incomes above half a million dollars. The first Form 1040 was four pages—including a single page of instructions.

Very few Americans had to fool with the form at all. Less

than 1% of the population had to pay the tax. Fewer than half a million returns were filed for 1913, compared with around 100 million individual returns now filed each year. It was from that modest beginning that the income tax grew to the monstrosity that former President Jimmy Carter once called a "disgrace to the human race."

From a few pages tucked inside a tariff bill in 1913, the Internal Revenue Code has grown to over 2,000 pages—of the proverbial small print. There are thousands of pages of IRS regulations and volumes of public and private IRS rulings to explain what the law means and how it applies in various circumstances. The riddle of the tax law is further mystified by thousands of court decisions that support, contradict, expand or narrow the IRS view of the taxpayer's world. One former head of the IRS estimates that an attorney needs 33 feet of shelf space to hold the tax code and necessary official appendages.

From the straightforward 1040 form that made its debut for 1913 returns, the IRS now serves up an impressive arsenal of forms. The "principal" ones are gathered each year and pre-

REPRINTED WITH SPECIAL PERMISSION OF KING FEATURES SYNDICATE, INC.

sented in *Package X*. The 1987 edition was published in two volumes, crammed with nearly 100 forms and schedules and their instructions.

From the graduated rates of 1913—ranging from 1% to 7% on the theory that the higher one's income, the greater proportion of it he or she could afford to pay in tax—Congress has pushed the rate over the 90% mark. The top bracket was still 70% when Ronald Reagan became President in 1981 and hovered at 50% in 1986.

Over the years, the income tax has undergone a metamorphosis. . . from a simple means of raising revenue to the government's largest source of funds and, simultaneously, one of the central tools for manipulating and fine-tuning the economy. Over the years, one Congress after another has peppered the law with scores of exclusions, deductions, exceptions and credits—granting preferential treatment to encourage certain activities considered socially desirable or in the pursuit of the illusive goal of fairness.

Piece by piece, amendment by amendment, the Internal Revenue Code has become so complicated that 40 million Americans now have to pay someone for help with filing their annual returns. It has also spawned a massive industry of tax planners. Ingenious men and women spend their careers dreaming up ways to tie together seemingly unrelated nooks and crannies of the tax code. Excavating the tax law for nuggets that can save money has become a national pastime, and the higher the tax rates, the more incentive there is for finding ways to beat the IRS.

One of the goals of tax reform is that reducing tax rates—to a maximum of 33% in 1988—will encourage us to spend less time and worry on the tax ramifications of our financial decisions and pay more attention to the economic sense of our investments.

But don't let falling tax rates lull you into a false sense of security. The fact that federal income taxes remain one of the biggest annual expenditures of most families belies the idea that there's less need now for tax planning. In fact, even if you have never devoted much time or effort to planning, this is a superb time to start. The restructuring of the tax system brings opportunities to be exploited and dangers to be avoided.

It's a serious mistake to think of tax planning as the province of the wealthy. Consider this comment from a high-priced tax attorney:

> The best and finest tax planning is done by people who have more money than they'll ever spend or be able to give away to any meaningful purpose. The worst tax planning is done by nice middle-class people who have middle-class virtues, those who have to work hard and save and sacrifice.

If you are in the latter group, this book can help you. It is devoted to explaining how the law—with all its new rules—affects you and your tax strategies. The goal is to help you maximize your after-tax income. Although this is primarily a tax-planning handbook rather than a step-by-step guide to tax-return preparation, you should find answers here to most of the questions that will arise as you wrestle with your tax forms. Chapter 14 includes tips on preparing your return yourself or hiring someone to do the job for you.

As you move through the chapters ahead, keep in mind the clarion call of tax planning issued by Federal Judge Learned Hand in 1947. In a ruling in which he rejected the IRS's position that a taxpayer's maneuvers were part of a "reprehensible scheme to lessen" his tax bill, Judge Hand wrote these often-quoted comments that can be found framed in the offices of many accountants and tax attorneys:

> Over and over again courts have said that there is nothing sinister in so arranging one's affairs as to keep taxes as low as possible. Everybody does so, rich or poor; and all do right, for nobody owes any public duty to pay more than the law demands: Taxes are enforced exactions, not voluntary contributions. To demand more in the name of morals is mere cant.

DON'T GET MAD, GET EVEN

If you need extra incentive to invest time and effort to hold down your tax bill, consider this: Even if you take advantage of every possible break, you have to pay more tax than you should. Why?

Because millions of your fellow citizens cheat.

In the spring of 1988 the IRS estimated the income "tax gap" (the difference between what Americans owe in income taxes and what they pay voluntarily) for 1987 at $84.9 billion. That's $84,900,000,000!

Most of the cheating is blamed on individual taxpayers, not corporations. While the corporate tax gap was $21.4 billion, the IRS says individuals underpaid their 1987 income taxes by $63.5 billion. (See the box on the opposite page.)

Although the IRS ultimately collects some of that money through audits, if the full tax gap were spread evenly over the 100 million or so taxpayers who file individual returns, each of us would have to shell out about $635 extra just to make up for the shortfall.

That doesn't suggest you should join the cheaters, only that you should redouble your efforts to take advantage of every legitimate tax break.

THE REDESIGNED TAX LANDSCAPE

Throughout the two years of debate on the legislation that became the Tax Reform Act of 1986, we watched as lawmakers brewed a concoction that mixed the bitter with the sweet: the curtailment or elimination of tax breaks thought to be sacrosanct with the promise of significantly lower tax rates. The new law delivers both. Before going into detail about the changes and the opportunities they provide, consider an overview of the changing tax landscape.

Although the law passed in 1986, one of its key elements—significantly lower tax rates—didn't arrive until 1988. Rather than the promised top rate of 28%, rates as high as 38.5% applied in 1987, which is one reason so many taxpayers got a nasty surprise when they filed their 1987 returns.

HOW WE CHEAT THE IRS

SOURCE OF TAX GAP *(from individuals)*	AMOUNT OF UNPAID TAX *(in millions)*
Underreported income	
Wages and salaries	$1,417
Interest and dividends	3,227
Capital gains	6,650
Informal business (moonlighting)	7,739
Sole proprietorships	16,646
Farm income	1,904
Partnerships and small business corporation income	3,216
Pensions and annuities	123
Rents and royalties	3,141
Estate and trust income	64
State income tax refunds	86
Alimony income	173
Taxable unemployment and social security income	338
Other income	3,566
Subtotal	$48,292
Overstated subtractions	
Adjustments	545
Deductions	3,478
Exemptions	2,039
Subtotal	$6,062
Overstated credits	$899
Math "errors"	$1,049
Nonfilers of tax returns	$7,174
TOTAL TAX GAP, 1987	**$63,500**

The truth about tax rates. Even with the rate cuts now fully in effect, things aren't quite as advertised. What was promoted and hailed as a two-bracket tax system—with income taxed in either the 15% or 28% bracket—is actually a three-bracket system with rates as high as 33%.

The so-called "phantom" 33% bracket creates a bulge in the rate tables, as you can see on page 437. If your taxable income exceeds $43,150 on a single return or $71,900 on a joint return, you're in the "phantom" but costly 33% bracket. Note, though, that after a while the rate falls back to 28%.

The cause of the bulge is a 5% surtax designed to take away from higher-income taxpayers the right to have any income taxed in the 15% bracket. The surtax can also eliminate the tax-saving power of exemptions claimed for yourself and your dependents.

Before tax reform, no matter how much you made, the first $3,670 on a joint return was taxed at 0%; the next $2,270 was taxed at 11%; the next $2,260 at 12%; and so on until income over $175,250 fell in the 50% bracket.

Starting in 1988, the law extends the full benefit of the lower, 15% bracket only to those taxpayers whose income is below the trigger points for the 5% surtax. The amount of income that falls in the 33% bracket—the $77,350 between $71,900 and $149,250 on a joint return—is the amount on which a 5% surtax recoups the dollars the IRS "loses" because the first $29,750 was taxed at the 15% rate rather than in the 28% bracket.

Once the surtax has reclaimed the benefit of the 15% bracket, the 33% bracket continues for $10,920 of additional income for each exemption you claim for yourself, your spouse or dependents. That amount was chosen because in 1988 every $1,950 exemption you claim saves you $546 (28% × $1,950)—and, yes, a 5% surtax on $10,920 costs you $546 if you're affected by the phantom rate.

Although there are now fewer tax brackets, it's difficult to argue that the new system is simpler. You still need to know your bracket to assess the after-tax cost of tax-deductible items and the after-tax return on taxable investments. And the 33% bulge bracket brings new complications.

Starting in 1989, the tax brackets will be adjusted for inflation so that as dollars you earn decline in purchasing power so will the government's take. If, for example, the inflation rate in 1988 is 5%, the 15% bracket for 1989 will be extended by 5%. On a joint return that would push the top of the bracket from $29,750 to $31,200, so an extra $1,450 would be taxed at 15% rather than 28%. The savings would be $188. The top of the 28% bracket would also advance, delaying the imposition of the 5% surtax.

Escalating exemptions. Exemptions are worth $1,950 each in 1988, almost twice their pre-tax-reform value, and are $2,000 in 1989. After that they will be adjusted upward each year in step with inflation. If the cost of living increases by 5% in 1989, for example, exemptions will be worth $2,100 in 1990.

As discussed in Chapter 3, tax reform isn't all good news when it comes to exemptions. In the past, taxpayers age 65 and older and those who were legally blind were allowed to claim an extra exemption. That break is gone, although the loss is partially offset for taxpayers who do not itemize because they get a larger standard deduction than other taxpayers.

At the other end of the age spectrum, children no longer can claim a personal exemption. In the past, a child who was claimed as a dependent on his or her parents' return could also claim an exemption to shield investment income, for example, or earnings from a summer job. Congress put the kibosh on such double-dipping.

Swelling standard deduction. Tax reform brought back the old standard deduction and set it at a much higher level than the zero-bracket amount (ZBA) it replaced. The return of the standard deduction is an effort to simplify things by undoing an earlier, unsuccessful simplification effort. In the late '70s, Congress concocted the ZBA to save nonitemizing taxpayers the trouble of having to subtract a standard-deduction amount from their taxable income. Instead, a 0% bracket was built into the tax-rate tables: The first so many dollars—equivalent to the standard deduction for each filing status—was taxed at 0%. To prevent this change from giving an unintended benefit to itemizers, they had to reduce the total of their deductions by their ZBA before subtracting the leftover amount from their taxable income.

The disappearance of the standard deduction confused and angered many taxpayers who felt they were being cheated. Tax reform rights things for those taxpayers by abolishing the ZBA and restoring the standard deduction. The higher level will also save millions of taxpayers the trouble of itemizing.

If your standard deduction is higher than the total of your itemized deductions—which is more likely than in the past not only because the standard deduction is larger but also because of the curtailment of many deductions—your tax-filing chore is greatly simplified. Rather than keeping careful records of your spending during the year and adding everything up at tax time, you can simply use the standard deduction.

Beware, though: Don't detonate your record-keeping system prematurely. If you live in a home with a large mortgage or work in a state with high state income taxes, it's likely you'll still benefit handsomely by itemizing. If you are near the threshold, you'll still need to keep track of your expenses to determine whether itemizing can save you money. For taxpayers who find the bigger standard deduction the ticket from itemizer to nonitemizer status, there will also be heightened interest in the practice of "bunching": timing deductions to cram as many deductible expenses as possible into a year in which you'll itemize by depleting the supply from a year in which the expenses have no tax-saving value because you'll use the standard deduction. See Chapter 12 for details.

This table shows the standard deductions for 1988.

Type of Return Filed	Standard Deduction
Married filing jointly	$5,000
Single	3,000
Married filing separately	2,500
Head of household	4,400

Taxpayers age 65 and older or legally blind get a larger standard deduction. Married persons (filing either jointly or separately) and surviving spouses are permitted an extra $600 for either age or blindness, $1,200 for both. Singles and heads of household add $750 for age or blindness, $1,500 for both.

Consider, for example, a married couple in which both husband and wife are at least 65 and one is legally blind. They would qualify for three $600 allowances, adding $1,800 to their $5,000 standard deduction for a total write-off of $6,800.

Paying for the breaks. A battle cry of the politics of tax reform was that the final legislation would be "revenue neutral." Politicians facing a trillion-dollar national debt didn't want to plunge deeper into the sea of red ink by writing a tax law that would bring in less revenue. Billions of dollars of the nation's tax liability was shifted from individuals to business. But much of the "cost" of the lower individual rates and higher standard deductions and exemptions is being paid by base broadening— redefining things so the IRS has more income to tax at those lower rates. That was accomplished not only by slamming closed notorious loopholes but also by crimping some mom-and-apple-pie deductions—such as the right to deduct interest paid on car loans and write off contributions to IRAs.

Here's a rundown of some of the most significant changes. They are discussed in more detail in later chapters that address blending the new rules into your tax and financial strategies.

Medical expenses. One way to broaden the tax base is to limit the deductions allowed to reduce taxable income. With fewer or smaller write-offs, there's a bigger pool of money to tax at whatever rate applies.

That was the tack the lawmakers applied to medical expenses. Under the new rules, medical expenses are deductible only to the extent that the total exceeds 7.5% of your adjusted gross income—which is your income before reducing it by deductions and exemptions. Before tax reform the threshold was 5%, and as recently as 1982 it was only 3% of AGI. If your adjusted gross income is $35,000, for example, the 7.5% rule means you can't deduct your first $2,625 of medical and dental bills.

Taxes. Although Congress considered wiping out the deduction for state and local income taxes, tax reform preserved that write-off. The deduction for property taxes was also spared. But the right to write off state sales taxes paid didn't survive.

Interest deductions. In a move that stunned millions of taxpayers, Congress decided to phase out the deduction for personal interest—which includes what you pay on auto loans, credit cards, life insurance loans, student loans and debt-consolidation loans. For 1988, only 40% of such interest can be written off, and by 1991 these deductions disappear completely.

Tax reform generally preserved the deduction for mortgage interest on first and second homes, perhaps the most sacred of all write-offs. There are some restrictions, and this part of the law has already been rewritten once since the Tax Reform Act of 1986 became law. The latest rules—and how they can be used to skirt the crackdown on deducting personal interest—are discussed in Chapter 4.

The deduction of investment interest is also subject to new and increasingly tight restrictions. (See Chapter 5 for details.)

Charitable contributions. No longer can nonitemizers deduct charitable contributions, and for some wealthier taxpayers who do itemize, the tax benefit of donating appreciated property has been squeezed. See Chapter 10 for the details.

Miscellaneous deductions. Most taxpayers can no longer deduct expenses that fall into this category, including the cost of tax preparation and advice, union and professional dues, the cost of subscribing to professional journals and job-hunting expenses. As a base-broadener, Congress set a 2% floor for such expenses. You get a deduction only to the extent that your qualifying expenses exceed 2% of your adjusted gross income. AGI of $50,000, for example, wipes out the write-off for your first $1,000 of expenses.

Congress also shifted certain expenses that had been deductible as adjustments to income—and therefore of benefit to all taxpayers whether or not they itemized—to the miscellaneous category open only to itemizers. Among the affected write-offs are the costs of a job-related move and employee travel expenses. See Chapter 9 and Chapter 10.

Capital gains. One of the most astonishing, and painful, parts of the tax-reform package was Congress's decision to strip long-term capital gains of their preferential tax status. Long-term capital gains are the profit from the sale of such assets as stocks, bonds and real estate that are owned more than one year. Under the old law, 60% of that profit was tax-free. Now, 100% is taxed.

Those who search for silver linings note that, although profits will be taxed more heavily, investors will have more trading flexibility. With nothing to gain by holding on to property to meet the holding period, they will be more free to sell assets at what they consider the optimum time.

Capital losses remain deductible, first against gains and then up to $3,000 of other income. Tax reform helps a bit here. In the past it took $2 of net long-term loss to offset $1 of ordinary income. Now, capital losses will be able to offset other income dollar for dollar, up to the $3,000 annual limit, regardless of how long you owned the property that produced the loss. See Chapter 5 for more details.

IRAs and other retirement plans. Taxpayers made something of a mistake by enthusiastically accepting Congress's 1981 invitation to stash $2,000 a year tax-free into individual retirement accounts. So many of us took advantage of this tax-

© 1986 STAYSKAL—TAMPA TRIBUNE

shelter-for-all that when lawmakers were searching for ways to pay for tax reform, the money to be raised by curtailing the IRA was too seductive to be ignored.

Restrictions now apply if you are covered by a retirement plan at work and your adjusted gross income (before subtracting the IRA contribution) is more than $25,000 on an individual return or $40,000 on a joint return. See Chapter 7.

Tax reform also crimps other retirement plans, such as 401(k) plans, and denies most taxpayers the right to use ten-year forward averaging, a special tax-computation method that had saved substantial amounts for taxpayers who received qualifying lump-sum distributions when they quit their jobs or retired. The new law also imposes in almost all cases a 10% penalty tax on lump-sum distributions received by employees under age 59½, unless the money is rolled into an IRA. See Chapter 8.

Rental property. Real estate really took it on the chin, as property owners have already discovered. Tax reform created the fourth new depreciation schedule in six years—and this one is stingy. In 1986, real estate could be depreciated over 19 years according to a schedule that bunched bigger deductions into the earlier years. Now, write-offs are stretched over 27.5 years for residential buildings and 31.5 years for commercial property. The new law also calls for straight-line depreciation, meaning an equal percentage of the cost will be deducted each year.

In the crackdown on tax shelters, Congress severely limited the ability of investors in "passive activities"—a category that includes all real estate investments as well as limited partnerships—to deduct losses from those investments against other types of income. The rules are complicated, but basically the aim is to prevent losses from tax-shelter investments from wiping out the tax on other income, such as salary or profits from stock trading. See Chapter 6.

Self-employment. Tax reform sounded the death knell for the notorious three-martini business lunch. The law permits the write-off of only 80% of the cost of business meals and entertainment. (With the new restriction, to deduct the cost of three martinis, you have to drink four.) Probably of more consequence to most taxpayers who work for themselves, either full time or as a sideline, is a slower depreciation schedule that limits write-offs for business property. The so-called hobby-loss rules have also been tightened to make it tougher to qualify for deductions. See Chapter 9.

Corporate tax rates. If you operate your business as a corporation, you'll benefit from falling rates. But, as with individual rates, the new corporate schedule includes a bulge bracket. This one—the 39% bracket—is designed to obliterate the benefit of the lower corporate tax brackets for businesses with incomes exceeding $335,000. Businesses reporting more than that amount of taxable income effectively will be taxed at a flat 34% rate on every dollar.

Under the old law, corporate income over $100,000 was taxed in the 46% bracket. Here are the new rates:

First $25,000	15%
$25,001–$75,000	25
$75,001–$100,000	34
$100,001–$335,000	39
Over $335,000	34

The fact that corporate rates will be higher than individual rates—34% versus 28% in 1988, not counting the bulge brackets—has focused special attention on Subchapter S corporations, which provide a liability shield like other corporations but permit income to be taxed at individual rather than corporate rates.

Income shifting. Tried-and-true methods of intrafamily tax saving were blown out of the water by tax reform. For one thing, fewer and lower tax brackets make it less profitable to transfer ownership of property to children so that the income it earns will be taxed in their lower bracket. To make sure taxpayers got the message, Congress abolished Clifford trusts, long a favorite income-shifting tool, and created the "kiddie tax." See Chapter 3.

2
WHAT'S TAXABLE, WHAT'S NOT

Although a central premise of this book is to avoid legalese at all costs, it seems appropriate here to quote what must be the IRS's favorite part of the tax law, Internal Revenue Code Section 61(a). It is exceptionally straightforward in presenting the general definition of gross income:

> Except as otherwise provided in this Subtitle, gross income means all income from whatever source derived, including (but not limited to) the following items:
>   1) Compensation for services, including fees, commissions, fringe benefits, and similar items;
>   2) Gross income derived from business;
>   3) Gains derived from dealings in property;
>   4) Interest;
>   5) Rents;
>   6) Royalties;
>   7) Dividends;
>   8) Alimony and separate maintenance payments;
>   9) Annuities;
>   10) Income from life insurance and endowment contracts;
>   11) Pensions;
>   12) Income from discharge of indebtedness;
>   13) Distributive share of partnership gross income;
>   14) Income in respect of a decedent; and
>   15) Income from an interest in an estate or trust.

Whew!

Were it not for that glorious introductory phrase—*except as otherwise provided*—taxpayers might ruefully conclude that tax planning is a cruel, no-win game. Fortunately, though, our lawmakers have crammed "otherwises" into the law, provisions that spare certain kinds of income altogether and, just as important, opportunities to use deductions and adjustments to income to whittle away at the amount of income that actually will be taxed.

TAXABLE INCOME

Before looking at tax-free income and your options for squeezing down your tax bill with adjustments and deductions, review the principal kinds of earnings the IRS has in its sights. (Investment income and expenses are discussed separately in Chapters 5 and 6.)

Wages and salaries. This is the most common kind of income and the easiest to keep track of, for both you and the government. Just after the close of each year, you get a W-2 form from your employer showing how much you were paid. In addition to your salary, this includes commissions, bonuses, vacation pay, sick pay or severance pay. It also shows amounts that never find their way into your take-home pay, such as the 7.51% of earnings whisked away to pay your share of the social security tax. The IRS gets the same information.

Self-employment income. If you work for yourself, either full time or as a sideline to a job as an employee, the net profit from your activity is taxable.

Rental income. You pay tax on income in excess of your deductible expenses.

Alimony. Payments you receive are taxed, assuming your ex-spouse deducts the payment on his or her return.

Barter. You don't necessarily have to get cash to pique the IRS's interest. If you receive property or services in exchange for your work, you are taxed on the fair market value of what you get.

Awards. An award you receive for your work on the job is generally taxable. If you get goods or services—such as an all-expense-paid trip to Fargo, N.D.—you include the fair market value in your income. An exception permits tax-free gifts of property—such as a gold watch—worth up to $1,600 in recognition of length of service or safety achievement. Cash or gift certificates don't qualify for this exception.

Gambling winnings. This includes everything from multimillion dollar lottery winnings to the value of the basket of booze raffled off in the church hall, reduced by your gambling losses, which include the cost of raffle tickets.

IRA withdrawals. New rules permit a portion of the withdrawals to be tax-free if you make nondeductible contributions to your account, but the rest is taxable.

Jury fees. Payment you receive for doing your public duty is taxable.

Pension and annuity payments. These are generally taxed, although a portion of each payment may be tax-free as explained in Chapter 8.

Prizes. From the Nobel prize to the value of your winnings on *Wheel of Fortune,* the IRS expects a share of your good fortune.

Tips. All tips are taxable, and tip income of more than $20 a month is to be reported to your employer, who will withhold income and social security taxes and report the tips to the IRS along with your wages.

Unemployment compensation. A provision that had made some jobless benefits tax-free has been abolished.

TAX-FREE INCOME

The IRS does not stake a claim to every dime you receive. Some income gets a wink and a nod from the taxman.

Car-pool receipts. Payments you receive from fellow workers you drive to and from work are tax-free. Rather than income, these payments are considered reimbursement of your expenses.

Child-support payments. You are not taxed on the receipt of child support.

Casualty insurance proceeds. Reimbursements for a loss— after an auto accident or a home fire, for example—are almost always tax-free, although in certain circumstances they can result in taxable income. See Chapter 10 for an explanation of this paradox.

Damages. If you win damages as a result of a lawsuit, they are generally tax-free, except for any amount awarded to compensate you for lost income.

Dividends on a life insurance policy. Dividends are usually a tax-free refund of an overpayment of your premium. If the total of such dividends surpasses the total of premiums paid, however, the excess is taxable.

Employee death benefits. Up to $5,000 paid by the employer is tax-free.

Gifts. Whether it's a few dollars or tens of thousands, a gift is not taxed. To qualify, the gift must be given out of true generosity. A television given away by a bank as an incentive to deposit funds in a certificate of deposit, for example, doesn't count. Its value is income.

Don't be confused by the federal gift tax, which is one of Uncle Sam's most misunderstood levies. When that tax is owed—which is rare—payment is the responsibility of the giver of the gift, not the recipient, as discussed in Chapter 16.

"BUT THE NEW SIMPLIFIED FORMS ARE EASIER TO UNDERSTAND, SIR... IF YOU HAVE ANYTHING LEFT AFTER TAXES YOU FIGURED WRONG!"

© 1988 STAYSKAL—TAMPA TRIBUNE

Health and accident insurance benefits. Reimbursement compensation for medical expenses or compensation for permanent loss of use of part of the body or permanent disfigurement is tax-free.

Inheritances. Money or property you inherit is not taxed by the federal government, although your state may impose a tax.

Life insurance. Proceeds are tax-free, but if you choose to have the insurance company pay the proceeds in installments over a number of years, the part of each year's payment that represents interest earned on your account is taxed. The Tax Reform Act of 1986 abolished a provision, known as the "widow's exclusion," that had permitted surviving spouses to receive up to $1,000 of such interest tax-free each year.

Profits on the sale of a home. Qualifying individuals age 55 and older can exclude from tax up to $125,000 of profit on the sale of a principal residence. See Chapter 4.

Scholarships and fellowship grants. The value of tuition and such related expenses as books, supplies and required equipment is tax-free, but the value of room and board and any other perquisites is generally taxed. The details are in Chapter 3.

Social security. Most recipients receive these benefits tax-free, but the IRS may get a crack at up to 50% of your benefits if your earnings for the year plus half of your benefits exceed $25,000 or $32,000, depending on whether you file a single or joint return. See Chapter 8.

Veterans' benefits. Payments are tax-free.

Workers' compensation. Compensation for a job-related injury is tax-free. If your employer continues to pay your full salary in exchange for your turning over the workers' compensation payments, you are taxed only on the amount by which your salary exceeds the compensation.

FRINGE BENEFITS

Fringe benefits often deliver double benefits. Not only does your employer foot all or part of the cost, but the value of most of these benefits comes to you tax-free. Even when that value is included in your taxable income, you come out ahead.

Assume, for example, that your firm has a vacation resort that you can use free of charge. If you take advantage of such generosity, the law demands that you include in taxable income the fair market value of the accommodations. If the value is set at $1,000 for your two-week stay, for example, an extra $1,000 will show up on the W-2 form for the year and you must pay tax on the extra "income." For someone in the 33% tax bracket, the tax cost of the vacation would be $330 (33% of $1,000).

That's a good deal, compared to the $1,000 it would have cost you otherwise. But it's even better than it appears. If you had to pay the $1,000 out of pocket, it would really cost you more because you'd be spending after-tax dollars. In the 33% bracket you must earn $1,500 to have $1,000 left after the IRS gets its share.

The tax appeal of fringe benefits can even make it a smart move to *ask* your employer to cut your salary, with the pay cut being diverted to pay for fringe benefits. Assume your company has a plan that permits you to shift $300 a month into an account that will be used to pay $3,600 of annual child-care expenses. You more than break even by funneling money through the company plan. It would take $5,000 of taxable earnings, in the 28% bracket, to have the $3,600 after taxes you need to pay for child care.

Remember, too, that the tax-saving value of fringes is often boosted when you take state income taxes into account.

Medical and dental. Insurance premiums paid by your employer for you and your family are tax-free.

Educational assistance programs. Company-provided educational expenses are tax-free if the course is designed to maintain or improve skills for a job you already have—rather than to qualify for a new job—or is required by your employer. There's a chance that even non-job-related educational expenses may be tax-free. In mid 1988, Congress was considering reestablishing a program to allow a certain level of such benefits to be nontaxable, if the plan under which the benefits are provided meets IRS standards.

Company-provided car. This is a true sign that you have

arrived, and it usually carries a tax liability. You are taxed on the value of your personal use of the vehicle, but the value assigned to your business use of the car is tax-free.

There are different ways to set the value to be split between personal and business use. One, the lease-valuation rule, uses IRS-provided tables that show the annual lease value of cars worth various amounts. Here's a selection of the lease values assigned to automobiles. The full table is published in IRS publication 535, *Business Expenses*.

Fair Market Value of Auto	Annual Lease Value
$ 8,000–$ 8,999	$2,600
$12,000–$12,999	3,600
$15,000–$15,999	4,350
$20,000–$20,999	5,600
$25,000–$25,999	6,850
$30,000–$31,999	8,250

Assume your company provides you with a $20,000 car, which has an annual lease value of $5,600. If you use the car 60% of the time for business and 40% for personal driving, 40% of the lease value, or $2,240, would be included in your income. That would cost you $627 if you're in the 28% bracket.

Under the cents-per-mile method, your employer would include in your income an amount arrived at by multiplying the number of miles you drove the car on nonbusiness trips by 21 cents for the first 15,000 miles and by 11 cents for any mileage beyond 15,000. The rates drop 5.5 cents a mile if you have to buy your own gas. This method can be used only if the car is driven at least 10,000 miles during the year. It also applies only to relatively cheap cars—those worth $12,800 or less.

If you are not permitted to use the car for personal trips, but drive it to and from work, your personal use is assigned a flat $3-a-day value because commuting is considered personal use.

Your employer has to report to the IRS and include on your Form W-2 the annual value being assigned to your personal use of the car. The employer can, in fact, simply report the full lease value as income and leave it up to you claim employee-business-expense deductions to offset part of it. Try to talk your employer out of taking that course. Such deductions fall in the "miscellaneous" category and are deductible only to the extent that your total miscellaneous expenses exceed 2% of your adjusted gross income.

Group term life insurance. The cost of up to $50,000 of coverage provided by your employer is tax-free. Even though you must include in taxable income an amount for extra coverage, it's a real bargain. Here's the IRS method for figuring how much taxable income you will be assigned for more than $50,000 of coverage.

Your Age	Annual Rate per $1,000 Coverage
Under 30	$ 0.96
30–34	1.08
35–39	1.32
40–44	2.04
45–49	3.48
50–54	5.76
55–59	9.00
60 and older	14.04

A 50-year-old who gets $200,000 of company-provided insurance, for instance, would have to report as extra income the IRS-assumed cost of $150,000 of coverage. At $5.76 per thousand, that's $864, which in the 28% bracket would cost the employee $242 in taxes.

Employee awards are generally taxable, as mentioned earlier. But there's still an advantage. Assuming the award is something you otherwise would have purchased—a trip, say, or a car—you get the benefit of acquiring it with pretax dollars. A saleswoman of the year who wins a $17,000 car, for example, must pay tax on that amount, just as if she had received $17,000 in cash. In either case, the tax bill in the 28% bracket would be $4,760. But if she had won cash, after paying the tax bill she would have just $12,240, an amount that would buy much less car.

Child care. Expenses paid by your employer—whether for a care provider you hire or for the value of care at facilities provided by your employer—are tax-free, up to $5,000 a year. Even if you can't persuade your employer to institute a child-care-assistance program that offers this tax-free benefit, you may be able to garner tax help through a flexible spending account—discussed in the next section—that would let you pay the expenses with pretax dollars.

Cafeteria plans. Employees select from a menu of fringe benefits—which often includes the choice of cash as an entrée—to tailor a personalized package of benefits. The plans have become increasingly popular with the rise of two-earner married couples. Husbands and wives with duplicate benefits seek ways to trade in unnecessary items, such as double medical coverage, for more desired benefits, such as additional life insurance or dental coverage.

If you choose cash under such a plan, it is taxable income. If you choose tax-free benefits, their value is not included in your salary, and you therefore avoid the extra tax.

A popular selection on some employers' menus is a reimbursement account—funded through employee salary reduction—to pay certain expenses, such as medical and child-care costs. Say, for example, that your employer has a plan that permits you to divert $4,000 a year into a reimbursement account through which you will pay for child care. The advantage to giving up part of your salary is that you can pay necessary bills with pretax income.

Sometimes known as a flexible spending account, such a plan requires an employee to elect in advance how much salary to deflect for designated benefits. Another condition is that any amount left in the account at year-end must be forfeited. The use-it-or-lose-it stipulation makes using such an account for uncertain expenses—such as medical and dental bills—somewhat risky. But there's little danger for such predictable costs as child-care expenses.

Retirement plans. Often the most valuable and most important fringe benefit, money set aside for your retirement is not taxed until you actually get your hands on it. The ultimate taxation of retirement benefits is discussed in Chapter 8.

Vital to getting the most out of this tax-favored benefit is an understanding of exactly how your firm's plan works. A critical point is the rate at which your benefits are vested, that is, how quickly you earn an unforfeitable right to the money. New rules going into effect in 1989 will help. Through 1988, firms can require employees to work for ten years to become vested. If you quit one day short of ten years, you could lose all the benefits that had been socked away in your name.

Beginning in 1989, employers can choose between two vesting schedules: full vesting after five years or gradual vesting starting with your third year in the plan. Under the five-year schedule, you would not be vested at all until the end of your fifth year in the plan, at which time you would become 100% vested. Under the other option, your benefits would be vested gradually between years three and seven, according to this schedule:

Years on the Job	Nonforfeitable Percent of Benefit
1	0%
2	0
3	20
4	40
5	60
6	80
7	100

Although the new, speedier vesting schedule is not required to be in place until 1989, time you have put in on the job prior to that counts. Say, for example, that in 1988 you will have held a job for six years with an employer whose current pension plan requires ten years' vesting. If you quit before the new rules go into effect in 1989, you could lose all your retirement benefits. Stay on the job until 1989, though, and your previous six years will insure that you are either 80% or 100% vested, depending on which schedule your employer chooses. An extra few months on the job could be worth tens of thousands of dollars.

If your employer's plan permits employee contributions, give careful consideration to the tax value of signing up. See Chapter 8 for details.

Loans from retirement plans. You may be able to tap a retirement plan without triggering a tax bill by borrowing from the plan. Strict rules have to be followed, though. If your employer's plan permits such loans, you may borrow up to half of your vested benefit or $50,000, whichever is less. (The law permits loans up to $10,000 without regard to the half-your-benefits restriction.) In addition to the dollar limit, a retirement-plan loan must be repaid within five years unless the money is used to help you buy your home.

Despite the restrictions, these loans can be a good deal. Borrowing from your employer's plan may involve less hassle than going through a bank, for example, and since the loan is secured by your plan benefits, you may get a better interest rate than you would on an unsecured loan.

Interest-free or bargain-rate loans. The option to borrow from your employer—not from the pension plan—is a rare but sweet perquisite. To the extent that you get a break on the interest rate, though, the IRS says you have taxable income. In the past, that didn't matter because you also got to deduct as interest paid the same amount of interest that was reported as income. With the phaseout of the deduction for personal interest—discussed in Chapter 10—that offsetting deduction is disappearing.

Stock bonuses and bargain purchases. If your company gives you stock or permits you to buy it for less than the market value, you receive taxable income to the tune of the value of the stock minus what you paid for it. However, if there is a risk that you might have to forfeit the stock—such as a requirement that you return it to the company at the price paid if you quit your job within a certain number of years—you don't have to report any taxable income until those restrictions expire. At that time, you would report as income the difference between what you paid for the stock and its value when the restrictions expired.

Incentive stock options (ISOs). Often a part of executive compensation packages, ISOs offer the opportunity to buy company stock at a set price over a period of time as long as a decade. You can wait for the price to rise before exercising the option, thus locking in a sure profit. There is no taxable income when you are granted the option or when you exercise it to buy stock, even if the shares are worth more when you buy them than the option requires you to pay.

You are taxed only when you ultimately sell the shares. Prior to 1987 a key advantage of ISOs was that the appreciation between the time the option was granted and when you later sold the stock could qualify as a long-term capital gain, making it 60% tax-free. Now, the difference between what you pay for the shares and what you sell them for will be fully taxed. Since the tax bill comes due only when you sell the shares, however, ISOs still offer important flexibility.

Employee stock-purchase plans. Options granted under these plans, which are similar to ISOs, let employees buy company stock at a discount, often 15% below market value. You don't have to report any income when you get the option or when you exercise it to buy shares. When you sell the stock, you are taxed on the difference between what you paid and what you get.

Meals and lodging. Your employer can provide food and housing tax-free if specific conditions are met. Basically, to qualify as a tax-free fringe benefit rather than a noncash addition to your taxable compensation, the meals must be offered at your employer's place of business—a company cafeteria, say, or at the restaurant where you are a chef or waitress. The meals must also be for your employer's "convenience," a test that can be met if, for example, a short lunch hour or lack of local eateries makes it unreasonable for you to eat elsewhere. When housing is involved, there's an extra requirement: The lodging must be a condition of your employment—as it might be if you are a motel manager, for example, or a ranch foreman.

Special rules apply to members of the clergy who are given a house or a housing allowance as part of their pay. That value is not taxable.

There are specific guidelines for the tax treatment of on- or near-campus housing provided for professors and other employees of educational institutions. No amount is added to taxable income if the employee pays rent at least equal to either the average amount charged renters not affiliated with the institution for comparable housing or 5% of the appraised value of the housing unit.

The 5%-of-value test works like this: A professor who is provided a $100,000 home would be required to pay annual rent of $5,000 (5% of the appraised value of the house). Even if the house would otherwise rent for $12,000 a year, the professor would not have to include any part of the discount as income.

Employer-provided travel. The fact that your employer pays your way on business trips is no great shakes, but you may be able to squeeze a valuable benefit out of on-the-job travel. Of course, what your firm pays for airline tickets and hotel and restaurant bills while you're on assignment is not taxable income. That remains true even if you tack a vacation on to the end of your trip. If you go to the coast for a three-day meeting, your airfare is the same whether you rush back to the office or hang around for a holiday. If you take the family along, you have to pay for your spouse's fare and the kids', but working things

DRAWING BY M. STEVENS © 1986 THE NEW YORKER MAGAZINE, INC.

so you get a tax-free trip from the firm could save enough to pay a good share of that cost. Since many hotels let spouses and children stay for reduced or no cost, the time you're on business with your company footing the hotel bill can produce tax-free accommodations for the whole family.

Employee discounts. Discounts on goods or services sold by your employer can be as much as your employer's profit on products and as much as 20% on services and still be tax-free to you.

Working-condition fringe benefits. You are not taxed on such benefits as free parking provided by your employer, the value of a company car provided for business use and the cost of your subscriptions to professional journals paid for by your employer.

De minimis fringes. These are little things, the cost of which is so small that it's unreasonable to keep track. Included in this tax-free category: use of the office copying machine, supper money or taxi fare paid in connection with overtime work, the value of office parties and employer-provided sports or theater tickets. Another specifically included tax-free benefit: a subsidy of up to $15 a month for mass-transit passes for employees who take the bus or train to work rather than driving their own cars.

No-additional-cost services. You are not taxed on services that have value to you but don't cost your employer anything. Included are such benefits as free space-available air or train travel for airline or railroad employees.

If your employer operates a subsidized eating facility, the difference between what you have to pay for meals and what they would cost at an independent cafeteria or restaurant is a tax-free fringe as long as the employer charges at least enough to break even. And, apparently in an effort to encourage physical fitness, the IRS has included on its list of tax-free perks the use of an on-site athletic facility. It's nice to know Uncle Sam is concerned about your health.

3
YOUR FAMILY AND THE IRS

When it comes to family tax planning, Uncle Sam is an enigmatic relative—in some ways a kind and generous soul, in others a crotchety and demanding antagonist. Tax reform adds to the confusion by changing many of the rules you've grown up with. Congress has enhanced the worth of certain tax breaks while squeezing the value out of others. The changes affect the young and the old, the married and the single, the widowed and the divorced.

FILING STATUS

Like most relatives, Uncle Sam has his favorites, and the tax law treats different taxpayers differently. Begin with your filing status. As you can see on page 437, there are four separate sets of tax rates, and what you owe the government varies significantly, depending on which rate applies to you. Consider the tax bite on $50,000 of taxable income in each tax bracket.

Filing Status	1988 Tax on $50,000
Married/joint return	$10,132
Single	12,021
Head of household	10,893
Married/separate return	12,755

Glancing at the disparate bottom lines, you might conclude that the government will reward you for tying the knot. And seeing that a single taxpayer pays nearly 20% more tax on $50,000 income than a married couple, you may wonder about all the griping you hear about the "marriage tax penalty." But as with so much in the tax arena, things aren't necessarily as simple as they seem. There really is a marriage tax penalty, as discussed on page 53. First, though, consider the categories into which Congress places various taxpayers. Here, too, things aren't as straightforward as you may believe.

Married filing a joint return. If you are married on the last day of the year, you are entitled to file a joint return. This applies even if you are separated from your spouse and are pursuing a divorce. Unless the divorce is final by the end of the year, the IRS considers you married, and you can't file a return as a single taxpayer. (Discussion of the tax angles involved in the timing of marriage and divorce begins on page 55.) One exception to last-day-of-the-year status applies if your spouse died during the year. If you were married for any part of the year but were widowed at year-end, you may still file a joint return for yourself and your deceased spouse.

Unmarried individuals. You fall in the "singles" category if you aren't married at year-end and don't qualify to use the lower surviving-spouse or head-of-household rates.

Surviving spouse. For up to two years after the year in which your spouse dies you may be able to continue to use the joint-return rates rather than being shoved immediately into higher brackets. Not every widow and widower qualifies, though. Most, in fact, do not.

To be a surviving spouse in the eyes of the IRS, you basically have to have a child living with you. In fact, there are four tests:

• You must have been eligible to file a joint return for the year your spouse died.

• You must not have remarried. (If you did, of course, you can use the joint-return rates by filing with your new spouse.)

• You must have a child, stepchild or foster child who qualifies as your dependent (which is explained on page 37).

• You must have paid more than half the cost of keeping up your home, which is the principal residence of the child for the entire year (except for temporary absences).

In other words, if your children are grown and have moved

out of the nest when your spouse dies, you're out of luck.

Head of household. This category causes some confusion, particularly among young people starting out on their own. If you're the only member of your household, you must be the "head," right? Not as far as the IRS is concerned.

To earn the head-of-household title and the right the use the lower-than-single tax rates you basically have to be providing a home for a child or other relative. To qualify:

• You must be unmarried at the end of the year. (Even if you're legally married at year-end, you can pass this test under a special "abandoned spouse" rule if your spouse didn't live with you during the last six months of the year.)

• You must pay more than half the cost of keeping up the principal home for you and a child or other relative you can claim as a dependent. If the child (including a grandchild, stepchild or adopted child) is unmarried, he or she doesn't have to qualify as your dependent to earn you head-of-household status. Any other relative living with you, however, must pass the dependency tests, which are outlined beginning on page 37.

In most cases, you and the child or other relative must share the same house for more than six months of the year. There is an exception, however, if you are paying more than half the cost of maintaining a home for your dependent mother or father for the entire year. In that case, he or she does not have to live with you for you to qualify for head-of-household tax status. If you are paying more than half the cost of a nursing home for your dependent parent, for example, you can qualify.

When figuring whether you pay more than half the cost of maintaining the house in which you live with a child or other relative, count such expenses as rent, mortgage interest, taxes, insurance on the home, repairs, utilities, domestic help and food eaten in the home. Don't count what you pay for clothing, education, medical treatment, vacations, life insurance or transportation.

If you qualify as a surviving spouse, you may be able to meet the head-of-household test once your two-year use of the joint rates runs out. Although higher than joint rates, the head-of-household rates are lower than those that apply to singles.

Married filing separately. This filing status almost never makes sense. The rare circumstances in which it can pay off usually involve spouses with similar incomes who by splitting the income on separate returns rather than combining it on a joint one can claim deductions that would otherwise elude the couple. One often-cited reason for filing separate returns, for example, is if one spouse has significant medical bills. Such expenses are deductible only to the extent that they exceed 7.5% of adjusted gross income. Splitting income on separate returns might squeeze out a bigger medical deduction for one spouse, but only in very special circumstances would the tax savings offset the cost of skipping the advantages that come by filing a joint return.

There are plenty of disadvantages to filing separately:
• One spouse can't claim the standard deduction if the other itemizes. If one itemizes, both must.
• On separate returns, you can't claim the child-care credit.
• The $25,000 passive-loss allowance for active rental real estate investors (Chapter 6) is forfeited if you file separate returns.
• If you receive social security benefits, filing separately guarantees that half your benefits will be included in taxable income. On a joint return, benefits are partially taxable only if income exceeds $32,000 (Chapter 8).
• Don't think filing separately lets you short-circuit the phase-out of individual-retirement-account deductions for joint-return filers with income between $40,000 and $50,000 who are covered by a company retirement plan (Chapter 7). On a separate return, the IRA write-off is phased out between $0 and $10,000 rather than in the $25,000–$35,000 range that applies to single returns.
• Some of these separate-return disadvantages don't apply if you and your spouse don't live together during the year for which you file separate returns.

(Although filing separate returns seldom makes sense at the federal level, don't assume the same applies to your state-tax return. In some states, choosing married-filing-separately status can cut your tax bill significantly. Check the instructions with your state return carefully.)

EXEMPTIONS

Although there may be flecting fame attached to the first baby born in a new year, tax-savvy expectant parents are likely to prefer a New Year's Eve birth to a New Year's Day baby. After all, a child considerate enough to arrive before the year ends delivers unto his or her parents a nice tax break, valuable enough to go a long way toward outfitting the nursery. A baby born anytime before midnight December 31 earns the folks a full year's dependency exemption. Thanks to tax reform, that's now worth more than ever. One of the major tax-saving changes voted by Congress was the near doubling of the value of the personal exemption: from $1,080 in 1986 to $1,950 in 1988 and a nice, round $2,000 in 1989. (After that the exemption amount will continue to climb to keep up with inflation.)

Each exemption you claim on your return shelters income from the IRS. A baby born in 1988 knocks $1,950 off her folks' taxable income. In the 28% bracket, that's worth $532. A half-dozen exemptions in 1988 will shield $11,700 of otherwise taxable income—a savings of $3,276 in the 28% bracket.

The new rules aren't all good news on the exemption front, however. In its exercise of give-and-take, Congress also:

● Eliminated the extra exemption that had been granted to senior citizens and blind taxpayers;

● Denied children who are claimed on their parents' return—and older parent's who are claimed as dependents on their children's return—the chance to claim their own personal exemptions; and

● Devised a "recapture" system to wipe out the value of all personal exemptions for upper-income taxpayers.

The new rules come at a time when the value of exemptions and the importance of making sure you take maximum advantage of them is at an all time high. It's up to you to claim all the exemptions you have coming.

Regardless of what kind of return you file, you can claim a personal exemption for yourself—unless you can be claimed as a dependent on someone else's return, as explained on page 41. On a joint return, both husband and wife claim a personal exemption.

Beyond that, you've got to earn these valuable tax savers by meeting a series of tests to determine whether someone qualifies as your dependent. That's not difficult when it comes to a minor child who lives with you. It's almost taken for granted, in fact, and it's doubtful you'd ever be asked to produce records to back up your claim. It's not so simple as children grow older or when you try to claim adult relatives—your parents, say—or unrelated people as your dependents.

Kiddie cards. Before considering the rules for claiming dependents, note that children age 5 and older must have a social security number. No more waiting until his or her first job to sign up with that government agency. For the parents to claim a little one as a dependent, the child's social security number must be listed on the parents' return. Failure to provide the number triggers a $5 fine.

If you need a number for a child, contact your local social security office for a Form SS-5. (The forms might also be available at a local post office.) In addition to completing the SS-5, you'll have to provide evidence of the child's age, identity

© 1988 GORRELL—RICHMOND NEWS LEADER

and U.S. citizenship. The easiest proof of age and citizenship is the child's birth certificate. The Social Security Administration demands the original, though. Not even a notarized copy will do. A religious certificate showing date and place of birth, such as a baptismal certificate, is acceptable.

In addition, you'll need one other proof of identity. If your child is precocious enough to have a driver's license or work ID, that's fine. Otherwise, you'll need something like a nursery school or vaccination record or a Cub Scout or Brownie identification card. Check with the local office for specific demands. Once you apply for a card you should receive the child's number within two weeks.

As you're running around to meet this new congressional directive, keep in mind that the aim is to prevent taxpayers from claiming dependents they don't deserve—like puppies and parakeets. And remember that as the law stands now, you don't need to apply for a social security number before leaving the hospital with your baby. As this book went to press, however, Congress was considering lowering the kiddie card requirement to age 2.

CLAIMING DEPENDENTS

There are five hoops you must jump through to win the right to claim someone as a dependent on your tax return:
- Member-of-household or relationship test.
- Citizenship test.
- Joint-return test.
- Gross-income test.
- Support test.

The last two are the ones most likely to trip you up, but you should review all five. Each and every requirement must be met for you to claim someone as your dependent.

Member of household or relationship. Perhaps the most important thing to note about this test is that someone does not have to be related to you to qualify as your tax dependent. For example, if you pass the other four tests, a friend you are supporting can be your tax dependent.

When an unrelated person is involved, the IRS demands that he or she be a member of your household, which means he or she must live with you for the entire year. When it comes to relatives, the IRS doesn't demand that they live under your roof for you to qualify for the tax break. And the IRS is relatively broad-minded when defining relatives. Included are:

• Children, grandchildren or other lineal decendents;

• Stepchildren;

• Brothers, sisters, half brothers, half sisters, stepbrothers, stepsisters;

• Parents, grandparents or other direct ancestors (but not foster parents);

• Stepfathers, stepmothers;

• Brothers or sisters of your mother or father (your dad's brother—your uncle—counts, for example, but not his wife—your aunt);

• Sons or daughters of your siblings; and

• Fathers-in-law, mothers-in-law, sons-in-law, daughters-in-law, brothers-in-law, sisters-in-law.

The list probably contains about everyone you think of as a relative—except your cousins. To claim a cousin as your dependent, he or she must live with you for the entire year.

Citizenship. Simple enough. To be a tax dependent, a person must be a U.S. citizen, resident or national, or a resident of Canada or Mexico.

Joint return. This test usually raises its ugly head only in the year a son or daughter you've been supporting gets married. The law prohibits claiming a dependency exemption for someone who files a joint return. Thus, if the new bride or groom files a joint return, you can lose out an a dependency exemption—even if you meet all the other tests. In such cases, it may pay off if you can persuade the young marrieds to file separately so that you can use the dependency exemption one last time on your return. Particularly with the new, higher value of exemptions, you may save more than the couple stands to lose by filing separately rather than jointly.

There's an exception to the joint-return rule. If the couple owes no taxes but files jointly simply to reclaim pay withheld during the year, the joint return doesn't scotch your right to claim the dependency exemption.

Gross income. This test can deny you an exemption you may feel you deserve. If a person earns more than the exemption amount—$1,950 in '88 or $2,000 in '89—he or she cannot be your dependent. Say your elderly mother lives with you and the value of the food and lodging you provide and medical bills you pay amount to far more than 50% of her support. If she earns more than the exemption amount—say from interest on her life's savings—you can't claim her as your dependent.

There's an important exception here. The income test does not apply to a child under 19 years old or an older child who is a full-time student for at least five calendar months of the year. That means you usually don't have to worry about the gross-income test until your kids are out of college. Regardless of how much a child under 18 or a full-time student earns, you can claim him or her as a dependent if you pass the other tests.

Because too much income can obliterate your right to a dependency exemption, it's important to know what is included in gross income—and more important to know what is not. Essentially, gross income is all income that's not exempt from tax. Earnings from a job or taxable investments count; social security benefits don't, unless they are taxed under the rules discussed in Chapter 8. Gifts and insurance proceeds are not included, either; nor is tax-free interest.

If someone's investment income is tripping you up here, consider whether it would make sense to suggest a switch to tax-free investments. Although there may be little or no tax benefit to a low-bracket investor, the exemption could be worth more to you than the amount of income lost to a lower yield.

Support test. To claim someone as a dependent, you must provide more than half of his or her support. With children living at home, there's generally no question that the parents pass this test. However, as the kids get older and get jobs to generate their own spending money, the 50% test can topple your right to the exemption.

When figuring the support you provide for someone living with you, include the fair rental value of the housing you provide: That means what you could expect a stranger to pay for it. Count what you spend for the person's food, clothing, transportation, education, medical bills and wedding costs. That's right, you can include what you pay for your child's wedding—another reason you may want to persuade him or her not to deny you the exemption by filing a joint return. If you buy your son a state-of-the-art stereo system for his birthday, the cost is included in what you paid for his support.

You get the idea. A person's total support is what it cost for him or her to live during the year; your share is the amount of the total that came out of your pocket. If you are fortunate enough to have a son or daughter who received a scholarship, you don't have to count its value as support provided by someone else, so it can't tip the support-test scales against you.

When you tote up what the person paid for his or her own support, don't assume it includes everything earned during the year. Money that is saved—whether it's summer job earnings put in a college account or social security benefits set aside in a rainy-day account—does not count as support.

The savings rule can trip you up, however, if a frugal child saves for several years and then spends a bundle all at once. Assume your son has saved $7,500 over several years and upon graduation from high school blows it all on a car. The full amount counts as his own contribution to his support. Unless you've provided more than $7,500 worth that year, the IRS says you lose the exemption.

Special rules apply to the children of divorced parents. Generally, the parent with custody gets the exemption. For more details, see the discussion of divorce starting on page 55.

Multiple-support agreement. There is a bend in the hard-and-fast rule that a taxpayer provide more than half of someone's support to claim that person as a dependent. When two or more persons together provide more than half of someone's support—and pass all the other dependency tests—one of the providers can claim the exemption if the others agree not to claim it.

The multiple-support agreement generally comes into play when two or more adult children are supporting a parent.

Assume a brother and sister each provide 40% of their mother's support and that either one could claim her as a dependent if it weren't for the 50% test. Form 2120, *Multiple Support Declaration,* will permit one of them to claim the tax-saving exemption. That form is filed with the tax return of the person claiming the exemption and must be signed by the other provider, certifying that he or she provided more than 10% of the dependent's support and could have claimed her on his own return except for the 50%-support stipulation.

If more than two persons are involved in the multiple-support agreement, the one claiming the exemption must have 2120 forms signed by each person who provided more than 10% of the dependent's support. The providers can decide which one will claim the exemption—it doesn't have to be the one who provided the greatest share of support. You can assign it to the provider in the highest tax bracket—to whom the exemption is worth the most—or rotate the tax break from year to year. You have to file 2120 forms each year you claim a dependent under the multiple-support agreement.

Death of a dependent. If a person who qualifies as your dependent dies during the year, you may claim the exemption on your return for that year. As long as the various requirements were fulfilled during the part of the year the person was alive—even if it was just part of one day—you qualify to claim the full exemption.

Senior citizens. Until tax reform, the IRS delivered a birthday present to senior citizens. When a taxpayer turned 65, he or she earned an extra personal exemption. Now, senior citizens—like everyone else—get only one. (Those who do not itemize deductions, however, do get a larger standard deduction than allowed younger taxpayers, as explained in Chapter 10.)

No more double-dipping. Tax reform also eliminated the long-standing rule that permitted every taxpayer to claim a personal exemption. Now, a person who can be claimed as a dependent on someone else's return can't claim a personal exemption on his or her own return.

This primarily affects children claimed on their parents' returns, but it also applies to anyone who can be claimed as a dependent, such as elderly parents who are being supported by their children. The loss of the exemption means more of their income is subject to tax. It also means children who in the past didn't have to file tax returns may have to under the new "simplified" system.

Taking it back. Congress also decided that once your income reaches a certain level, you don't need the tax-saving assistance delivered by exemptions. Tax reform introduced a system to recapture the benefit of exemptions. The method is similar to that which creates the "phantom" 33% tax bracket, as explained in Chapter 1.

When your taxable income goes above the top of the 33% bracket, the 5% surtax stays in effect to eat away the benefit of your exemptions. In 1988, the 33% bracket is extended by $10,920 for every exemption you claimed on your return. That figure was chosen because an extra 5% tax on that amount collects $546 for Uncle Sam—the exact amount a $1,950 exemption saves in the 28% bracket. In 1989 when the exemption amount rises to $2,000, the 33% bracket will extend by $11,200 for each exemption you claim on your return—to recapture the $560 a $2,000 exemption is worth to you.

KIDDIE TAX

Before tax reform families had a golden opportunity to save on income taxes by spreading the wealth among family members. Such "income splitting" was at the heart of many college savings plans and is most easily explained with an example.

Assume you have $25,000 to invest and can buy bonds yielding 10% to produce $2,500 income a year. Under the old tax law, if you were in the 50% tax bracket the IRS would claim $1,250. However, if you transferred ownership of the bonds to your son or daughter—either with an outright gift or in a trust— that $2,500 of annual income would have been taxed to him or her. The tax bill would have been a paltry $156. The family saved $1,094. Multiplied over a number of years, the tax savings delivered by income splitting could make a significant dent in tuition bills.

Congress isn't against higher education, but with the Tax Reform Act of 1986 lawmakers came flat out against using this type of tax maneuvering to get Uncle Sam to help pay for it.

The power of income splitting was greatly diluted by the reduction of tax rates and the narrowing of tax brackets—from steeply progressive rates ranging from 11% to 50% to the new three-rate 15%/28%/33% system. Although pushing income from the 33% to the 15% bracket slashes the IRS's take by more than 50%, it's not as significant as the impact of slicing the tax bite from 50% to 11%.

Denying children the chance to claim their own personal exemption also trims the tax-saving potential of income splitting. The inability to shelter income with the exemption translates to a higher tax bill.

Although those changes indirectly diminish the value of income splitting, Congress took direct aim at it by introducing a set of rules immediately dubbed the "kiddie tax." Basically, in the post-tax-reform world income reported by children under age 14 can be taxed in their parents' tax bracket.

The kiddie tax applies only to unearned income of children who are 13 years old or younger at the end of the year. If your child has his or her 14th birthday anytime during the year—even on New Year's Eve—the new rules don't apply.

The distinction between *earned* and *unearned* income turns on whether the income is compensation for work performed. Salary, tips and self-employment income, for example, are considered earned income. Almost all other kinds of income—including interest, dividends, capital gains, rents, and trust income—fall in the unearned income category and are vulnerable to the kiddie tax.

Note this: Income hit by the kiddie tax is not taxed on the parents' return. It is taxed on the child's return, but at the parents' top tax rate.

Not all of a child's unearned income is covered. Only investment income over $1,000 can be taxed in the parents' bracket. The first $500 is tax-free, because up to $500 of a child's standard deduction can be used to shelter unearned income. The next $500 is taxed at the child's 15% rate. Excess unearned income is nicked by the parents' rate.

If your son or daughter has earnings from a job, that earned income is always taxed in the child's bracket. Here are some examples of how the kiddie tax applies to the income of dependent children under age 14 at year-end.

• Melody's only income is $400 of interest. The federal tax bill is $0. No tax—kiddie or otherwise—is due because $500 of the standard deduction is available to shelter the income.

• James has $900 of dividend and interest income and no earned income. The first $500 is tax-free thanks to the standard deduction. The remaining $400 is taxed at James's 15% rate.

• Jennifer receives $1,300 of interest and dividends and has no earned income. The first $500 is tax-free and the next $500 is taxed at 15%. Then the kiddie tax kicks in, taxing the remaining $300 in her parents' bracket.

• Tony has $700 earned income from a paper route and $300 from interest on a savings account. His standard deduction is $700—the higher of earned income or $500—and is applied first to the $300 of unearned income. The remaining $400 of Tony's standard deduction shelters $400 of earned income. The remaining $300 of earned income is taxed in Tony's tax bracket. The kiddie tax doesn't come into play.

• Anne has $700 of earned income and $1,200 of unearned income. Of her $700 standard deduction (based on earned income), $500 is allocated to unearned income and the remaining $200 shelters earned income. Of the remaining $700 of unearned income, $500 is taxed in her bracket, along with the remaining $500 of earned income. The leftover $200 of unearned income—$1,200 minus the $500 standard deduction minus $500 taxed in Anne's bracket—is hit by the kiddie tax and taxed at her parents' top rate.

The IRS has dutifully designed a new form for figuring the kiddie tax. Form 8615, *Computation of Tax for Children Under Age 14 Who Have Investment Income of More Than $1,000,* must be filed with the return of each of the half a million or so "kiddies" to whom the new rules apply. Although children's returns once were among the easiest to complete, those that involve the kiddie tax are now among the most difficult. When developing the Form 8615, the IRS estimated that completing the single-page form will add nearly a full hour to the return-preparation chore.

The government has also already come up with rules for some unusual situations. If the parents of the child to whom the kiddie tax applies are divorced, for example, the tax bracket of the custodial parent is used to calculate the tax on the child's excess investment income. If the parents are married but file separate returns, guess what? The IRS says the kiddie tax is figured with the rate of the parent in the higher tax bracket. What happens when more than one child in a family is subject to the kiddie tax and part of the investment income falls in one tax bracket and part in a higher bracket? First, find the difference between the parents' tax bill with and without the addition of the kids' income. Then prorate the extra tax among the children according to each one's share of the kiddie-taxable income.

Killing Clifford. The Clifford trust used to be a key element of many family income-splitting plans. These short-term trusts—named for the taxpayer whose battle with the IRS won the tax breaks—permitted parents to transfer income-producing assets to their children temporarily. As long as the trust lasted for at least ten years and one day, all the income earned by the trust was taxed at the child's lower tax rate. When the trust terminated, the parent got assets back. A decade's worth of tax savings was a powerful incentive.

No more. You can still set up a short-term trust, but don't count on any income tax savings. Income from such trusts is now taxed to the grantor, usually the parent, who transferred the assets to the trust and will reclaim them when the trust terminates. If you had set up a Clifford trust before the March 2, 1986, the effective date of the new provision, trust income is still taxed to the beneficiary. However, it is subject to the kiddie tax if the beneficiary is under 14 when he or she receives the income.

INCOME SPLITTING LIVES

Despite all the new rules, income splitting can still save your family money. If you're planning to help pay for your children's college education, starting to give them the money for tuition long before the first bill comes due can still get Uncle Sam to help pay the bill.

Remember that the first $1,000 of unearned income escapes the kiddie tax. A child could have $10,000 in an account yielding 10% without having to worry about the new tax. If that $1,000 was the child's only income in 1988, the tax bill would be just $75. The same $1,000 taxed in the parent's top bracket could cost $330. The $255 savings is the IRS contribution to the college fund.

Since the kiddie tax disappears when a child reaches age 14, consider giving your kids investments that defer income until that time.

U.S. savings bonds are a natural choice because income can be deferred until the bond is cashed. If that's after the child reaches 14, even the interest that accrued during his or her younger days is taxed at the child's own rate.

Growth stocks, which generally throw off little if any current income in the form of dividends, are another way around the kiddie tax. There is no tax due as the stock appreciates. If the stock is sold after the child is 14, the profit is taxed in his or her bracket. Note that if a child invests in growth-stock mutual funds, rather than individual stocks, the fund will pay out capital-gains distributions each year based on trading within the fund. Such income would be subject to the kiddie tax if the child's unearned income exceeded $1,000.

For income splitting to work, the child must actually own the assets that generate the income. If you want your son to pay taxes in his bracket on $1,000 of interest income generated by a $10,000 savings account, you can't simply give him the $1,000. You've got to give him the $10,000 account itself. Only then will the income it produces be his for tax purposes.

The easiest way to make such a gift to a minor child is to set up a custodial account under your state's Uniform Gift to Minors Act (UGMA) or Uniform Transfer to Minors Act (UTMA). Banks, savings & loans, credit unions, mutual funds and brokerage firms offer such accounts. All you need is a social security number for the child and a custodian to manage the account until the minor comes of age. You can name yourself custodian, but if you are also the donor and you die before the child reaches majority, the gift will be considered part of your estate for federal estate-tax purposes.

An important point about custodial accounts is that your gift is irrevocable—you can't get it back. Once the child reaches the age set by your state's UGMA or UTMA law—typically 18 or 21—adult supervision of the account ends and the child can do anything he or she wants with the money. If sandy beaches are more enticing than ivy-covered walls, well. . .

You don't need a custodial account if you invest the child's money in U.S. savings bonds. Just buy the bonds in the child's name. Don't name yourself co-owner, though, or the income will still be taxed to you when the bonds are cashed.

Another move with income-splitting potential is to give your child appreciated securities. The tax bill on the increase in value of the stocks or bonds is passed on to the recipient along with the gift. Assume that stock you bought for $2,500 is now worth $5,000 and that you have a tuition bill coming due. If you sold the stock, you'd owe tax on the $2,500 gain in your top bracket. That would cost $825 in the 33% bracket.

Alternatively, you could give the shares to your college student. When sold, the same $2,500 would be taxed, but at the child's rate (assuming he or she isn't a prodigy who has started college before age 14). In the 15% bracket, the tax on the profit would be $375. Bottom line: a $450 tax savings. And if you didn't really want to part with the stock, you could buy it back with the cash that otherwise would have gone for tuition.

All this attention to generosity demands a brief mention here about the federal gift tax. The law permits you to give up to $10,000 each year to any number of people without having to worry about the gift tax. If you're married, you and your spouse can give up to $20,000 each year to each person on your gift list. Gifts above those levels are subject to the gift tax—which is imposed on the giver of gifts, not the recipient—but there's a substantial tax credit that makes it doubtful you'll ever have to pay a dime in gift taxes. See Chapter 16 for more on the gift tax.

Hiring the family. If you have your own business—either full- or part-time—you have another income-splitting opportunity. Put your children on the payroll, working in the evenings and on weekends during the school year and during the summer. What you pay them is a business deduction for you and earned income for them. That shifts income out of your tax bracket and into the child's. Because it's earned income, the kiddie tax doesn't come into play. Although a child can use only $500 of the standard deduction to shelter unearned income, the full deduction— $3000 in 1988—can offset earned income. If your child's only income during the year was $2,000 earned working in the family business, for example, the child's tax bill would be zip. The $2,000 business deduction could save you $660 if the income would otherwise have been taxed in the 33% bracket.

To be deductible, the wages paid have to be reasonable and for real work your child performs for your business. Claiming a deduction for paying your 8-year-old $100 an hour to clean your office on Saturday mornings would be asking for a fraud charge. But paying a reasonable wage for cleaning, being your answering service, filing documents, making deliveries or performing other necessary services is a legitimate way to save on taxes and help build a college fund. If your child is a computer whiz, you might have no problem finding chores for him or her to do.

To protect your deduction you need to handle the employment of your child in a businesslike manner. Keep careful records of the work done, the number of hours worked and the hourly wage. Pay with a check drawn on the business account. If you pay a child $600 or more during the year, you must file a form W-2 reporting the earnings to the IRS.

In addition to trimming your income tax bill, putting your kids on the payroll can save you a substantial amount of social security tax. As discussed in Chapter 15, that tax claims 13.02% of the first $45,000 of net self-employment income in 1988. Because you get to deduct as a business expense the amount of wages you pay, you avoid the social security tax on that amount. Every $1,000 of income you shift to a child via wages saves you $130 in social security taxes. Assuming you operate your business as a sole proprietorship rather than a corporation, wages you pay your children under age 18 are not subject to the social security tax.

If you own rental property, consider hiring your children to mow the grass or help with other maintenance or repairs. What you pay them would shave the amount of rental income taxed in your bracket, and up to $3,000 of their earned income will be sheltered by the standard deduction starting in 1988.

Here's another income splitting/real estate combination that some parents have found a valuable help in paying for a child's college education. They pull together the down payment for a house or condo in the college town. The child gets a roommate or two and they all pay rent to the parents, who report it as income but also get to deduct mortgage interest, property taxes and depreciation. The parents also hire their child to manage the apartment—finding tenants, collecting rents, taking care of maintenance and repairs. What they pay him or her is deductible from the rental income. If the rental property shows a loss, and if the parents qualify for the $25,000 exception to the passive-

DANA SUMMERS © 1988 ORLANDO SENTINEL/
WASHINGTON POST WRITERS GROUP

loss rules discussed in Chapter 6, that loss can shelter other income. Any profit when the home is sold after graduation is an added sweetener.

SCHOLARSHIPS AND FELLOWSHIPS

There's more bad news on the paying-for-college front. Tax reform put a big dent in the tax-free status of scholarships and fellowships.

First, the good news: For degree students, the value of grants for tuition and course-related expenses for books, supplies and equipment remains tax-free. However, any part of a grant that goes for room, board or incidental expenses is taxable.

Nondegree students, who in the past could qualify for a limited tax break, now will be taxed on the full value of any scholarship, including the amount that covers tuition.

The new law also taxes amounts received for teaching, research or other services. In the past, those amounts could be tax-free if the activity was required as a condition for receiving the scholarship or fellowship. The new rule applies whether the student is paid in cash or through a tuition-reduction program. If tuition is discounted in exchange for a graduate student serving as a teaching assistant, for example, the amount that's shaved off tuition is considered taxable income.

The taxable part of a scholarship or fellowship is considered earned income, so at least students can use their standard deductions to offset part of it.

Congress did provide relief for students who were granted scholarships or fellowships before August 17, 1986. If you qualify, your grant retains the tax benefits extended by the old law. To qualify, before that date you must have received notice of a firm commitment for a multiyear scholarship for a definite period.

Say, for example, that on May 1, 1986, just before your son graduated from high school, he was notified by his college that he would receive a four-year scholarship, covering tuition, room and board. Because the notification beat the August deadline, the scholarship falls under the old law and remains entirely tax-free.

New rules phasing out the deduction of personal interest also retract the government's helping hand in paying for college. Only 40% of such interest paid in 1988 is deductible, 20% in 1989, and 10% in 1990. After that, personal interest will be nondeductible (see Chapter 10). Interest on student loans falls in the personal interest category, which means it is shedding its deductibility. Even if you racked up thousands of dollars of student debt in the past, when the tax law's promise to subsidize the cost was in effect, the right to write off the interest is evaporating.

FAMILY LOANS

With soaring house prices, this is an increasingly probable scene: Your son and his wife come over for dinner, fill the air with friendly chitchat and finally mumble sheepishly what's really on their mind: They've found their dream house and need help with the down payment.

No, they're not so brash as to ask for a $20,000 gift. Just a loan. A loan with *very* lenient terms—like no interest and an extremely flexible repayment schedule.

As you discuss the request, be aware that Uncle Sam may want to horn in on this congenial family scene. The government's interest in intrafamily loans stems from having been burned by no-interest loans designed to dodge taxes. Wealthy parents could "lend" money to a child in a low tax bracket and, in the best of income-splitting traditions, the child would invest the money so the income was now taxed at the child's lower rates. Congress has closed that loophole.

The law now treats such loans as though the lender is charging interest on the deal and simultaneously making a gift to the borrower of the amount needed to pay that interest. This fiction has a very real tax consequence: The lender has to report as taxable income the phantom interest the loan did not produce, and the borrower gets to deduct on his tax return the amount of "imputed" interest he didn't pay. That can leave a bad tax taste all around because the lender is often in the higher tax bracket.

What's more, if the amount of forgone interest—for each year on a demand loan or over the entire term on a loan with a set repayment schedule—exceeds $10,000, the lender may be liable for federal gift taxes.

Don't turn down your kids' request straightaway, though, because—as usual—there are exceptions that can protect your intrafamily loan from the IRS.

As long as the amount of the loan outstanding at any time is $10,000 or less, the IRS will ignore it. Under that test, husband and wife are considered to be one lender and the $10,000 limit applies.

The second exception protects even bigger low-interest or even interest-free loans. For loans up to $100,000, the IRS won't get involved as long as the borrower's investment income is less than $1,000. If it goes over $1,000, the forgone interest to be reported by you and deducted by the borrower is limited to the amount of the borrower's investment income.

In other words, you can go ahead and lend your children $20,000 interest-free for their down payment, but they'd better use most of their own savings, too. If their investment income for the year surpasses the $1,000 threshold, your friendly arrangement could be stung by the imputed-interest rules.

Both the $10,000 and the $100,000 exceptions are voided if the purpose of the loan is to save taxes. If the borrowed funds are used to acquire income-producing assets, for example, the loan automatically falls victim to the imputed-interest rules. That doesn't hold you back from making a loan for such purposes as a house down payment, college tuition or to help a child start a business.

If you make a loan that fails to meet one of the exceptions, the amount of imputed interest on the deal is based on IRS-set rates that reflect what it costs the government to borrow money. These "applicable federal rates" are adjusted periodically. Call your local IRS office to learn the current AFR. If you charge a low interest rate, rather than no interest, the imputed interest is the difference between what you actually charge and the amount due using the prevailing applicable federal rate.

Bad debts. What if the family loan goes sour? Sure, you can count on your daughter the scholar to repay your loans after she gets her Ph.D., but what about your brother-in-law the taxidermist? If he stiffs you, can you write off the bad debt and thereby get Uncle Sam to subsidize your loss?

Perhaps, but the IRS is particularly suspicious of bad-debt deductions when the transaction involves relatives. Whether the borrower is your child or someone else, however, you can earn a bad-debt deduction if you can prove a true debtor/ creditor relationship existed and you fully expected to be repaid. That means you should go through the formalities of drawing up a note specifying repayment terms. If the borrower stops payments, you have to make an effort to collect, enough of an effort that you can convince an IRS auditor that there is no hope of collecting. You also have to be able to show that the debt became worthless in the year that you're claiming the deduction. Did the borrower file for bankruptcy, for example, or skip the country?

Clearly, it's difficult to qualify for a bad-debt deduction growing out of an unpaid family loan. If you can pass the tests, the bad debt is treated as a capital loss and deducted on Schedule D. As with other capital losses, bad debts are deducted first against capital gains and then against up to $3,000 of ordinary income.

MARRIAGE TAX PENALTY

You might as well add Uncle Sam to the guest list for your wedding because the government has a financial stake in your nuptials. You and your bride or groom will wind up owing either more or less tax after the ceremony. Whether matrimony is for better or for worse on the bottom line of your tax return depends on how much each of you earns.

If your spouse has little or no income, marriage is sure to cut the family tax bill. But if you have similar incomes, you're likely to pay more tax as a couple than if you didn't tie the knot.

Enter the marriage penalty. It's simple to understand, if not to accept. On a joint return, a husband's and wife's income are combined. Since our graduated tax system applies higher tax rates to higher incomes—under the theory that the more you earn, the more you can afford to pay—your combined income can be nudged up into a higher tax bracket. This is so even though the tax brackets are wider for joint returns than for single returns. The extra tax you pay on a joint return, compared to the combined bill if you and your spouse were filing individual returns, is the marriage tax penalty.

In 1988, for example, the 15% bracket covers taxable income up to $17,850 on single returns. If you and your betrothed each reported that much, you'd each owe $2,677 in tax, for a total of $5,356. On a joint return, the 15% bracket covers income up to $29,750.

Although that's much higher than on a single return, it's not twice as high. Combining the two $17,850 incomes gives you a total of $35,700, shoving $5,950 into the 28% bracket and pushing the tax to $6,128—$772 more than the combined levy on two single returns.

That's the marriage penalty.

Moving from single filing status to a joint return doesn't always work to your disadvantage. In the example above, assume one of the engaged couple had a taxable income of $35,700 and the other had no income. On a single return, the breadwinner would owe a tax of $7,675. Marriage to a nonearning spouse would slash that bill. On a joint return, the tax would be $6,128, for a marriage bonus of $1,547.

Although far from romantic, cranking the income tax consequences of marriage into your wedding plans could pay off handsomely. If it's a toss-up whether you'll go to the altar around Christmas or just after New Year's, take a look at how Uncle Sam views your union.

If you and your soon-to-be spouse each have $40,000 of taxable income in 1988, for example, you'll save more than $1,000 in taxes if you put off the wedding until 1989. As the example in the previous paragraph shows, though, under different circumstances getting married sooner rather than later would be rewarded by the IRS.

DIVORCE

As if divorce were not difficult enough, the changing tax laws complicate matters and demand your attention, too.

At the simplest level, of course, getting a divorce switches your filing status. If the divorce is final anytime before the end of the year, the IRS considers you single for the whole year. You can't file a joint return with your ex-spouse even if you were married for the first 364 days of the year. It's your marital status on December 31 that matters to the IRS.

More importantly, the way the IRS treats various parts of the financial arrangements that accompany the split can play a major role in the structure of those arrangements. Careful tax planning can produce a settlement with the most favorable tax consequences for both parties—leaving more for each of you by limiting the government's share. If your differences keep you from addressing the tax issues, the only winner on this front will be the IRS.

Alimony/child support. The tax distinction here is enormous. Payments that qualify as alimony are deductible by the ex-spouse who pays them and taxed as income to the one who receives the money. Child support, on the other hand, is neither deductible nor taxed.

Tax reform didn't alter those basic rules, but changing tax brackets may have a significant effect on settlements. Falling tax rates mean that alimony is more expensive for the paying spouse and more valuable, after taxes, to the recipient. For someone in the 50% tax bracket under the old law, for example, paying $1,000 a month in alimony really cost just $500 after considering the tax savings of the deduction. Now, assuming the payer is in the 33% bracket, the after-tax cost is $670 a month. At the same time, if the recipient was in the 23% bracket but is now taxed at the 15% rate, after-tax monthly income rises from $770 to $850.

Although their tax-saving power has been diminished, payments that qualify as alimony still have a real advantage over payments that don't. Generally, to qualify for the deduction alimony must be paid in cash and be required by a written divorce agreement. If you and your ex just amicably decide that one will pay the other "alimony," forget the deduction. The payer must be obligated to make the payments to earn the tax deductions.

There are special rules to prevent transfers that should be classified as child support or property settlements—neither of which is deductible—from sneaking through as deductible alimony.

Until a few years ago, support payments from one spouse to the other could be treated as alimony unless the payments were specifically called child support. Now, regardless of how payments are classified in the divorce agreement, they are treated as nondeductible child support if the payment is contingent on a future occurrence involving the child. If the payment will be reduced or eliminated when a child reaches a certain age or completes school, for example, that part of the payment can never be claimed as alimony.

In the past, alimony was usually a long-term obligation to pay an ex-spouse, often until he or she remarried or died. The trend now, however, is toward so-called rehabilitative maintenance for only a few years. Such payments are often designed to help the recipient get training and then a job.

Although the government has nothing against such arrangements, there is concern that big payments in the first few years after a divorce may really be an attempt to disguise a nondeductible property settlement as deductible alimony. To prevent that, the law provides for "recapture" of alimony deductions under certain circumstances.

This is another area in which tax reform brought change. The old rules basically demanded that payments of more than $10,000 a year had to continue for at least six years to qualify as alimony. If payments during any of those six years fell by more than $10,000 from the amount paid in the previous year, part of the previous year's deduction would be recaptured by requiring the payer to report that amount as income.

The new recapture rule is easier to apply—and avoid—than the old, and it extends for just three years, rather than six. You don't have to worry about recapture at all if alimony payments are $15,000 or less a year. As long as you meet the other requirements for alimony, the payments are fully deductible. A single $15,000 cash payment can qualify as deductible alimony under the new law. When larger payments are involved, however, the recapture rules may be triggered. If the payment in the first year exceeds the average payment in years two and three by more than $15,000, the excess is recaptured. Also, if the payment in the second year exceeds the payment in the third by more than $15,000, the excess is recaptured.

One Solution

Schedule X - Feelings   1984
▶ Attach to Form 1040

Did You Feel This Was Fair?	1. ☐ Yes ☐ No
If You Had Your Druthers, On What Would You Spend All the Money You Owe Us?	2. 3. 4. 5. 6.
What Was Your Least Favorite Section of This Tax Return?	7.
What Section Did You Have the Most Fun Filling Out?	8.
Now Are You Still Hot Under the Collar?	9. ☐ Yes ☐ No

R. Chast

The impact is best explained with illustrations.

Assume a divorce settlement calls for a $50,000 payment in the first year and no payments in years two or three. If the entire $50,000 was deducted as alimony in the first year, $35,000 of it would be recaptured in the third year—the amount by which $50,000 exceeds by more than $15,000 the average payment in the second and third years ($0 in this example). Under the rules, the payer would have to report the $35,000 as taxable income. And the recipient—who had to report the entire $50,000 in year one—gets to claim a $35,000 deduction to even things up.

Now assume that the payments are $50,000 the first year, $20,000 the second and $0 in the third. In this scenario, a total of $32,500 would be recaptured: $5,000 from the second year and $27,500 from the first. The second-year recapture is the amount by which that $20,000 payment exceeds by more than $15,000 the $0 paid in year three.

The first-year recapture is complicated by the fact that when figuring the average second- and third-year payments, you must reduce the total for any second-year recapture before dividing by two. In this example, the $5,000 recapture reduces the total second- and third-year payments to $15,000, for an average of $7,500. That amount is subtracted from the first-year payment, leaving $42,500. The alimony to be recaptured is the $27,500 by which that amount exceeds $15,000.

Because the new rules cover just three years, it is possible to cram a substantial cash settlement into just 13 months and treat the full amount as deductible alimony. You could make the first payment in December of 1988, for example, the next sometime during 1989, and the third and final payment in January of 1990. If all three payments were equal, there would be no recapture.

Also, there is no recapture if payments drop off in the second or third year because the recipient dies or remarries.

Although conventional wisdom suggests that support payments should be classified whenever possible as alimony—because traditionally the payer was in a higher tax bracket than the recipient—it's not necessarily so these days. With more working couples and fewer tax brackets, it's more and more likely both spouses will be in the same tax bracket—no more writing off alimony in the 50% bracket and reporting it in the 20% bracket. If there is no overall tax advantage to classifying payments as alimony, the recipient may be particularly resistent to having to pay tax on the support payments.

The law gives divorcing taxpayers the leeway to declare that qualifying payments will not be considered alimony. That means the payer can't deduct the payments and the recipient doesn't have to report them as income. The recipient, of course, may be willing to accept smaller payments if they're tax-free. Since the deduction is worth less to the payer in a lower tax bracket, a profitable compromise may be attainable. You need to work out the best overall deal with your attorneys.

Reporting requirements. If you do pay alimony during the year, you can deduct it whether or not you itemize your other deductions. You must include your ex-spouse's name and social security number on your tax return. That demand is designed to insure that if you're claiming a deduction, somebody is reporting the same amount as income. There's a $50 fine if you fail to include your ex's social security number.

Property settlements. Thanks to the tax law, in a divorce settlement one piece of property can be worth far more than another with exactly the same market value. The reason is that when property changes hands as a result of a divorce—whether it is the family home, a portfolio of stocks or other assets—the tax basis of the property also changes hands. The basis is the amount from which gain or loss will be figured when the property is sold. Because the new owner gets the old owner's basis, he or she is responsible for the tax on all the appreciation before as well as after the transfer.

This rule means you have to look carefully at the tax basis of property that may be part of a settlement. For example, $100,000 worth of stock with a basis of $90,000 is worth significantly more than $100,000 worth of stock with a $50,000 basis. The maximum tax on the sale of the first stock would be $3,300 (33% of the $10,000 profit). The tax on the sale of the second block of stock could be as high as $16,500 (33% of the $50,000 gain).

Exemptions for children. For years, the question of which spouse should claim the exemption for dependent children of divorced parents caused nothing but trouble. Often, the custodial parent would claim the exemption, and so would the noncustodial parent who was providing child support.

To simplify things, the law now generally gives the exemption to the custodial parent named in the divorce decree. If neither parent is named, the custodial parent is the one with whom the child lives for the greater part of the year.

It's possible, however, for the noncustodial parent to claim the exemption. That could be beneficial if he or she is in a higher tax bracket than the custodial parent, particularly since tax reform nearly doubled the value of the dependency exemption.

The noncustodial parent may claim the exemption if the custodial parent signs a waiver pledging that he or she won't claim it. Form 8332, *Release of Claim to Exemption for Child of Divorced or Separated Parents,* is provided for waiving the right to the exemption. That form must be signed by the custodial parent each year the exemption is shifted. And the form must be attached to the return of the noncustodial parent who is claiming the exemption.

For taxpayers divorced before 1985, if the divorce decree awarded the right to claim the dependency exemption to the noncustodial parent, he or she need not file a Form 8332 each year. Instead, there is a box on the tax return to check to indicate that the dependency exemption is controlled by a pre-1985 agreement.

Whether or not a divorced parent can claim a child as a dependent, the amount he or she pays for the child's medical care counts when the parent totes up medical costs to see if they are deductible. (Such costs can be written off only to the extent that they that exceed 7.5% of adjusted gross income, as discussed in Chapter 10.)

Legal fees. Although legal fees and court costs involved in getting a divorce are generally considered nondeductible personal expenses, the part of your attorney's bill attributable to tax advice is deductible. If you are receiving alimony, you can deduct the portion of the fee the lawyer ascribed to setting the amount. It's tougher than ever to get any tax savings here, though, since these costs fall into the category of miscellaneous expenses that are deductible only to the extent that the total exceeds 2% of your adjusted gross income. Still, be sure your attorney provides a detailed statement that breaks down his fee so you can tell how much of it may qualify for a deduction.

DEATH IN THE FAMILY

Death and taxes may be equally inevitable, but the taxman demands the last word. Death does not excuse a final accounting with the IRS. In fact, taxes can further complicate the lives of survivors. Federal estate taxes are discussed in Chapter 16. At issue here is the final income-tax return.

When a taxpayer dies, a new taxpaying entity—the taxpayer's estate—is born to make sure no taxable income falls through the cracks. Income is taxed either on the taxpayer's final return, on the return of the beneficiary who acquires the right to receive the income, or, if the estate receives $600 or more of income, on the estate's income tax return.

The chore of filing the taxpayer's final return usually falls to the executor or administrator of the estate, but if neither is named, a survivor must do it. The return is filed on the same form that would have been used if the taxpayer were still alive, but "deceased" is written after the deceased taxpayer's name and the date of death entered on the name-and-address space. The filing date remains the same: April 15 of the year following the taxpayer's death.

Only income earned between the beginning of the year and the date of death should be reported on the final return. For taxpayers who use the cash method of accounting, as most do, income is considered earned as it is actually received or at least made available to them. Taxpayers who use the accrual method of accounting, on the other hand, count income as earned when they actually earn it, regardless of when it is received.

The distinction is important because some income that might logically seem to belong on the decedent's final return is considered "income in respect of a decedent" and is taxable either to the estate or to the person who receives it. Consider these examples.

• Joe Jones owned and operated an orchard. He used the cash method of accounting. He sold $2,000 worth of fruit to a customer but did not receive payment before his death. That amount is not reported on Joe's final return. When the estate was settled, payment had still not been made and the right to receive it went Joe's niece. When she collects the money, she will report it as taxable income.

If Joe had used the accrual method of accounting, the $2,000 would have been considered earned on the date of the sale and therefore included on his final return. His niece would not have to include the money on her return when the payment was actually received.

• Mary Smith was entitled to a large salary payment at the date of her death, to be paid in five annual installments. Her estate collected two payments and then gave the right to the remaining three payments to her grandson. None of the income would be included on Mary's final return. The estate would include in its taxable income the two payments it received. Her grandson would include the other three payments in his taxable income—as income in respect of a decedent—on the returns for the years he received the money.

Income in respect of a decedent encompasses only income that the decedent had a right to receive at the time of death but that is not reported on the final return. It does not include, for example, earnings on savings or investments that accrue after death.

Say a taxpayer who has a substantial amount in money-market mutual funds dies June 30. Only interest earned up to that date would be reported on the final tax return. Earnings after that date are taxable to the beneficiary of the account or the estate. That can create some hassles since the payer—a mutual fund, bank or broker, for example—will report income to the IRS on a 1099 form. Although you should try to get ownership of the account changed as quickly as possible after the death of the owner, the 1099 income report may well show more income assigned to the decedent than it should. In such cases, you must report the entire amount on Schedule B of the decedent's return and then deduct the amount that is being reported by the estate or other beneficiary who actually received the income.

Remember that money you inherit is not subject to the federal income tax. If you inherit a $100,000 certificate of deposit, for example, the $100,000 is not taxable. Only interest on it from the time you become the owner is taxed. If you receive interest that accrued but was not paid prior to the owner's death, it is considered income in respect of a decedent and is taxable on your return.

There's a special rule for U.S. savings bonds, income on which generally accrues tax-free until the bonds are cashed. When the bond owner dies, the accrued interest may be treated as income in respect of a decedent. In that case, the new owner of the bonds becomes responsible for the tax on the interest accrued during the life of the decedent. (The tax isn't due, however, until the new owner cashes the bonds.) Alternatively, the interest accrued up to the date of death can be reported on his or her final tax return. That could be a tax-saving choice if the decedent will be in a lower tax bracket than the beneficiary. If that method is chosen, the person who gets the bonds includes in his or her income only interest earned after the date of death.

On the deduction side of the ledger, all deductible expenses paid before death can be written off on the final return. In addition, medical bills paid within one year after death may be treated as having been paid by the decedent at the time the expenses were incurred. That means the cost of a final illness can be deducted on the final return even if the bills were not paid until after death.

If deductions are not itemized on the final return, the full standard deduction may be claimed, regardless of when during the year the taxpayer died. Even if the death occurred on January 1, the full standard deduction is available. The same goes for the taxpayer's personal exemption.

If the taxpayer was married, the widow or widower may file a joint return for the year of death, claiming both personal exemptions and the full $5,000 standard deduction and using the lower joint-return rates. A joint return is usually filed by the executor, but the surviving spouse can file the return if no executor or administrator has been appointed.

If an executor or administrator is involved, he or she must sign the return for the decedent. When a joint return is filed, the spouse must also sign. When there is no executor or administrator, whoever is responsible for filing the return should sign the return and note that he or she is signing on behalf of the decedent. If a joint return is filed by the surviving spouse alone, he or she should sign the return and write "filing as surviving spouse" in the space for the other spouse's signature.

If a refund is due, there's one more step. You must also complete and file with the final return a copy of Form 1310, *Statement of Person Claiming Refund Due a Deceased Taxpayer.* Although the IRS instructions say you don't have to file Form 1310 if you are a surviving spouse filing a joint return, you probably should file the form anyway to head off possible delays.

If the person filing the final return is the decedent's court-appointed representative, he or she must attach a copy of the form certifying the appointment. When a return calling for a refund is filed by anyone other than a court-appointed representative or a surviving spouse filing a joint return, Form 1310 must also be accompanied by a copy of the taxpayer's death certificate or other proof of death.

4
HOME SWEET TAX SHELTER

Your home—probably the biggest investment of your life—is likely to be the best tax shelter you'll ever enjoy. Uncle Sam is standing by to serve as a generous partner in your investment, ready to subsidize your mortgage payments and willing to turn a blind eye to the profit you make when you sell the place—so long as you buy another home that costs at least as much as the one you sell.

Given the favored status of homeownership in America, it was no surprise that the sacrosanct deductions for mortgage interest and local property taxes survived the onslaught of tax reform. Homeowners not only held their own at a time when many tax breaks were sacrificed on the altar of lower rates, we actually won a valuable new tax-saving right: the opportunity to use our homes for protection against the elimination of the deduction of consumer interest. The new limits on mortgage-interest deductions and the new opportunities open to homeowners are discussed later in this chapter. First, though, consider the basic tax picture.

If you are considering buying your first house, you can be confident that doing so will cut your tax bill. As veteran homeowners know, it will just as surely complicate your tax life.

If you don't itemize deductions already, you're almost sure to once you buy a home. After all, the mortgage-interest portion of the first 12 monthly payments on a $100,000, 10%, 30-year mortgage come to nearly $10,000. That's almost twice the $5,000 standard deduction amount for married couples filing jointly. You'll also get to deduct state and local property taxes.

Once you begin itemizing, other expenses that are of no value to nonitemizers—such as state income taxes, charitable contributions and, possibly, medical bills—are transformed into tax-saving write-offs.

The deductions you earn by paying mortgage interest and property taxes just scratch the surface of the tax benefits attached to owning a home. The better you understand the law, the better able you will be to take full advantage of it.

HOME BUYER'S SUBSIDY

The opportunity to trade nondeductible rent payments for mostly deductible mortgage payments is a powerful lure to pull tenants out of their apartments and into the housing market. Whether you are looking for your first home or planning to move up, the number crunching necessary to determine how much house you can afford demands two sets of books: one for your actual monthly outlays; the other for the true, after-tax cost.

In the early years of a home mortgage nearly *all* of *every* monthly payment you make is interest. That's disappointing from the standpoint that it means you are paying off just tiny bits of loan principal. But it's terrific in terms of tax savings.

Look again at a $100,000, 30-year, 10% mortgage. The monthly payment would be $877.57, and the table below shows the breakdown in various years between principal repayment and deductible interest.

Year	Annual Payments	Principal	Interest
1	$10,530.84	$ 555.88	$9,974.96
2	10,530.84	614.10	9,916.74
3	10,530.84	678.39	9,852.45
4	10,530.84	749.44	9,781.40
5	10,530.84	827.91	9,702.93
10	10,530.84	1,362.16	9,168.68
15	10,530.84	2,241.18	8,289.66
20	10,530.84	3,687.44	6,843.40
25	10,530.84	4,971.33	4,463.90
30	10,530.84	9,981.07	548.84

In the first year, $9,974.96 of your monthly payments—fully 95%—would be deductible as mortgage interest. Even in the 15th year, 79% of your payments would be deductible. In fact, only in the unlikely event that you live in the house for 24 years would the scales tip so that less than half of the total paid during the year would be tax-deductible.

Just what the deductions are worth to you depends, of course, on your tax bracket (see the appendix). If you are in the 28% bracket, every $1,000 of deductible interest and taxes translates to a $280 subsidy from Uncle Sam. In our $100,000 mortgage example, assume that in addition to the $877.57 monthly mortgage payment you also pay $150 a month for local property taxes. During the first 12 months, you pay a total of $12,330.84—just over $1,000 a month.

But $11,774.96 is deductible. In the 28% bracket that generates tax savings of $3,296.99 and pulls the after-tax cost to $9,033.85, or about $750 a month. The tax savings built into the home-buying equation is why you can afford to make higher mortgage payments than your current rent payments without squeezing your budget. As disgruntled renters often complain, there is no similar tax subsidy for tenants. In this example, the after-tax cost of home payments of $1,000 a month are the equivalent of rent at $750 a month. Of course, owning the house could present you with repair bills a renter doesn't have to worry about, but on the other hand, as an owner you reap all the appreciation on the value of your abode.

Adjust withholding. What good is the tax subsidy if you're worrying about coming up with the cash needed each month to make the mortgage payment? Fortunately, you don't have to wait until the following year when you file a tax return to cash in on the savings. As soon as you purchase your first home or buy a new house that carries higher deductible expenses, you can direct your employer to begin withholding less from your paychecks. If you are self-employed, it's likely you will be able to scale back your quarterly estimated tax payments beginning with the next one due. In either case, your cash flow can increase almost immediately to help cover the mortgage payments. Chapter 13 discusses how to adjust estimated payments or file a revised W-4 form with your employer to trim withholding. (If you have problems coming up with the down payment, see the section on equity-sharing arrangements that begins on page 98.)

RECORD KEEPING

Buying a home may be your introduction to the endearing term "tax basis." That's the home's value for tax purposes. Keeping track of it is as demanding as it is important. The basis of your home is the figure you'll compare to the amount you get when you sell the place to determine whether you have a taxable profit that piques the interest of the IRS.

Although the basis of a home begins simply enough—as what it costs you to buy the house—it will change often between the time you buy and the time you sell. As discussed later, the basis of each home you own affects the basis of the next one you buy. You must keep track of all adjustments to the basis—for your entire homeowning career—to ensure that you are not overtaxed.

The record-keeping chore begins with sorting out the tax consequences of the closing costs you pay at settlement. Although a few of these expenses may be deducted in the year of the purchase, most are considered part of the cost of acquiring the house and are therefore included in the basis.

First, consider the deductible closing expenses because they have the most immediate financial impact.

Points you pay to get a mortgage. A "point" is a fee—1% of the loan amount—that the mortgage lender charges up front. Assuming the charge is for the use of the borrowed money—as it clearly is when the number of points charged affects the interest rate on the mortgage—rather than a fee to cover loan-processing costs, the point is considered prepaid interest. As long as the home you're buying will be your principal residence, these points are fully deductible in the year paid.

Assume, for example, that to get a 10%, $100,000 mortgage you have to pay the lender three points, or 3% of the loan amount. You can write off that $3,000 on the tax return for the year of the purchase. The IRS even provides a special line for the deduction on Schedule A, in addition to the space for deducting the interest paid on the mortgage. The deduction effectively serves as a rebate of part of the costs. In the 28% bracket, $3,000 in points translates into $840 in tax savings.

Keeping the special tax status of points in mind can come in handy when you're negotiating the purchase of a home. A buyer often suggests, for example, that the seller pay part of the buyer's points. From the seller's point of view, the effect of paying $1,000 in points is identical to accepting a $1,000 reduction in the price of the house.

Not so for the buyer. Knocking $1,000 off the sales price is worth *more* to the buyer than sloughing off $1,000 in points. Because the buyer can write off the points, the $1,000 out of pocket has an after-tax cost of just $720. In this example, cutting the price by $720 would give the buyer the same advantage as avoiding $1,000 in points. Uncle Sam could effectively be called on to help close the deal.

To lock in your deduction the year you buy, get a written statement from the lender listing the points separately from fees for specific administrative services. *Also, write a separate check to pay the points, rather than having the charge rolled into the mortgage proceeds.* If you borrow extra money from the same lender to pay the points, the IRS can block the deduction.

The right to deduct points fully in the year paid applies only to points paid on a mortgage to buy or improve your principal residence. Points paid on a loan to buy a vacation home or rental property don't get this special treatment. Neither does the loan-processing fee charged on VA mortgages because it is assumed by the IRS to be for services rather than for the use of the borrowed funds. And special rules apply if you refinance your mortgage, as discussed on page 79.

When points are not fully deductible in the year paid, the expense is deducted ratably over the life of the loan. On a 30-year mortgage, for example, one-thirtieth of the points generally would be deducted each year. In the first year, though, an even smaller amount would be deductible, based on the month you bought the house. If the house is sold before the mortgage is paid off, the undeducted points are fully deductible in the year of the sale.

Prepaid interest and property-tax adjustments. If your settlement costs include reimbursing the seller for interest or taxes he or she paid in advance for a period you will actually own the house, you may deduct those amounts as though you paid the bills directly. Such adjustments ought to be spelled out on your settlement sheet.

If the seller made such payments and you do not reimburse him at settlement, the prepayments are considered to be built into the price you are paying for the house. In that case, you still write off the prepaid interest and taxes as itemized deductions on your return and reduce your basis in the house by the same amount.

Other closing costs and acquisition expenses are generally not deductible unless you qualify to write them off as job-related moving expenses, as discussed in Chapter 10. Instead, many such out-of-pocket costs are added to the purchase price to hike your tax basis. Since additions to basis don't produce any immediate tax savings, you might be tempted to dismiss them. But that would be a costly mistake. Sooner or later you are going to have to know the adjusted basis of your home, and the higher you can prove it to be, the better. The higher the basis when you sell, the smaller any potential taxable profit you have to report to the IRS.

Maintaining detailed records from the beginning is the best way to assure accuracy. It's also a lot easier than trying to reconstruct the basis later on. As you begin the running tab on your adjusted basis, add the following costs to the purchase price:

- Appraisal and credit-report fees.
- Attorney and notary fees.
- Recording and title-examination fees.
- State and county transfer taxes.
- Property inspection fees.
- Title insurance premiums.
- Utility connection charges.
- Amounts owed by the seller that you agree to pay, such as

part of the real estate agent's selling commission or back taxes and interest.

The cost of an option to purchase under a rent-with-option-to-buy arrangement. It is also possible that part of the rent payments made prior to closing may be added to the basis if they were applied to the purchase price.

Claiming your annual deductions. It's easy to take advantage of the basic tax benefits—the write-offs for mortgage interest and property taxes. If your mortgage is held by a financial institution, you will receive a statement early each year showing how much deductible interest you shelled out in the previous year. (The IRS gets a copy, too.) The statement will also show how much you can deduct for property taxes if you make those payments through your lender. Otherwise, copies of tax bills and your canceled checks provide the information you need to claim that deduction.

Your tax situation is more complicated if your mortgage is held by an individual or you are buying with the help of some sort of "creative financing." The specifics of your arrangement control what part of your payments qualify as tax deductions.

Assume, for example, that in addition to a first mortgage at a bank, the seller holds a $10,000 second mortgage that calls for

BY JIM BORGMAN FOR THE CINCINNATI ENQUIRER

"OH COME ON, HOWARD...THE NEW TAX FORM CAN'T BE THAT BAD..."

monthly interest-only payments for three years and then a balloon payoff of the entire principal. All of your payments on the note during the three years would be deductible as interest.

With a shared-appreciation mortgage (SAM), the home buyer gets a lower-than-market-rate loan in exchange for promising to share with the lender the future appreciation in the value of the house. As far as the IRS is concerned, the part of the appreciation that winds up in the lender's pocket is interest, too, and is deductible when paid. That can result in a huge interest deduction in the year a SAM-financed home is sold.

Say, for example, that a $125,000 home is purchased with a SAM that entitles the lender to 40% of the appreciation. If the home is sold three years later for $165,000, the borrower owes the lender $16,000 (40% of the $40,000 profit). In the year that is paid, the taxpayer can deduct the full $16,000 as mortgage interest, in addition to the interest portion of any regular monthly payments made before the sale.

What about a "zero-interest" deal involving seller financing at the best of all interest rates: 0%? Although you might find such a deal, beware that the IRS does not believe such generosity exists. The law assumes the financing costs are actually built into the price of the home, so the buyer's basis is reduced by subtracting the value of interest-free financing from the purchase price.

The law also demands that the seller report as interest income each year an amount that reflects what would have been charged if the note carried a reasonable rate of interest (see Chapter 6). And the buyer can deduct as interest paid the amount the government demands the seller report as interest, even though the buyer doesn't make those payments. If you consider a zero-interest deal, be sure the price you pay reflects the tax consequences.

Other special rules apply to graduated-payment mortgages and other financing plans. The more you stray from conventional financing, the more you need to consult with an attorney or accountant to discuss the tax twists and turns involved in your home-buying pursuits.

Local assessments. In addition to real estate taxes, it is not unusual for local governments to assess homeowners for services or benefits provided during the year. Such bills need to go in your home file because, depending on what the charge is for, the cost may be either a deductible expense or an addition to your basis.

In general, assessments for benefits that tend to increase the value of your property—sidewalks, for example—should be added to the basis of your property. Special charges for repairs or maintenance of local benefits, such as sewers or roads, however, can be deducted as additional local taxes. Fees for specific services, such as garbage collection, are neither deductible nor additions to basis.

IMPROVEMENTS AND REPAIRS

Monthly payments are just the beginning of the costs of owning a home. You can count on spending plenty of money over the years maintaining, repairing and improving your property. Here, too, Uncle Sam gets involved.

For tax purposes, work around the house is divided between projects considered *repairs* and those constituting capital *improvements* that enhance rather than just maintain the value of your home. The distinction is critical. The cost of repairs is a nondeductible personal expense. What you pay for improvements is nondeductible, too, but such expenses add to your basis.

The idea here is that although you will use and enjoy the improvements, they also are likely to boost the amount a buyer will pay for the place. Because you can add 100% of the cost of improvements to your basis, every $100 of such expenses will cut $100 of the potentially taxable profit when you sell. An improvement is anything that adds value to your home, prolongs its life or adapts it to new uses. There is no laundry list of what the IRS considers an improvement. On page 74, though, is a checklist of items and projects that can qualify. (When appliances or other items that can be removed are involved, the items can add to basis only if they are sold with the house.)

Repairs, on the other hand, merely maintain the home's

condition. Fixing a gutter, painting a room or replacing a window pane are repairs rather than improvements. In some cases, though, the cost of projects that ordinarily fall in the repair category—such as painting a room—can be added to basis if the work is done as part of an extensive remodeling or restoration of your home. Also, some major repairs—such as extensive patching of a roof—may qualify as basis-boosting improvements.

BASIS-BOOSTING IMPROVEMENTS

- Addition or conversion of unfinished attic, basement or other space to living area.
- Air-conditioning: a central system or window units that will be sold with the house.
- Attic fan, furnace, furnace humidifier, heat pump, thermostat, hot-water heater, radiators and radiator covers.
- Bathroom: bathtub, jacuzzi, shower, shower enclosure, faucets, toilet, sauna, medicine cabinets, mirrors, towel racks.
- Built-in bookcases.
- Doorbell, burglar- and fire-alarm system, smoke detector, intercom and telephone outlets.
- Electrical: new or upgraded power lines, replacement of fuse box with circuit breakers, additional outlets or switches, floodlights.
- Fireplace, mantel, chimney, built-in fireplace screen.
- Insulation, weather stripping and caulking.
- Kitchen: refrigerator, freezer, garbage disposal, dishwasher, stove, cupboards, countertops, exhaust fan.
- Landscaping: trees, shrubs and underground sprinkler systems.
- Outdoors: aluminum siding, skylight, deck, garage, garage-door opener, carport, shed, fences and gates, lamppost, walls, screen and storm doors, porch, new roof, gutters, termite-proofing, waterproofing, paving and resurfacing of a driveway or sidewalks, barbecue pit, birdbath, hot tub, swimming pool.
- Plumbing: new pipes, sump pump, septic system, solar-heating system.

- Rooftop TV antenna and wiring.
- Washer and dryer.
- Windows: screens, storm windows, shutters, awnings, weather stripping.

Keep detailed records of any work done around the house, including receipts for items that might qualify as improvements. The pack-rat habit can pay off handsomely for homeowners. It's better to save papers you might not need than to toss out evidence that could save you money. In addition to receipts and canceled checks, keep notes to remind yourself exactly what was done, when and by whom.

When toting up the cost of improvements, be sure to include any incidental costs. If you pay to have your lot surveyed as part of installing a fence, for example, the cost of the survey can be added to your basis. Although you can count what you paid hired workers, you are not allowed to add anything for your own time and effort if you do the work yourself.

HOME-EQUITY LOANS

This is an area of great opportunity and great confusion. To understand the new rules so that you can take the most advantage of them, some background is necessary.

When Congress drafted the Tax Reform Act of 1986, the lawmakers decided to put an end to the deduction of "personal interest." As discussed in Chapter 10, that category includes interest on car loans, credit card accounts, student loans, personal loans and about every other kind of borrowing most taxpayers do. Only 40% of such interest is deductible in 1988, 20% in '89, 10% in '90 and nothing after that.

But the lawmakers didn't dare take away the deduction for home mortgage interest. However, by creating different classes of interest—some deductible and some not—Congress immediately created problems. How would one type be distinguished from another and, more importantly, how could the law discourage ever-ingenious taxpayers from rearranging their financial affairs to sidestep the intent of the law? If you use a second mortgage on a house to buy a car, for example, would the interest be deductible mortgage interest or nondeductible personal interest?

To answer such questions, the lawmakers drafted a ferociously complex set of rules—so bad, in fact, that within a year Congress reformed this part of tax reform, throwing out the first set of rules and concocting a new one.

The latest rules, which apply in 1988 and later years, are both easier to understand and a better deal for most homeowners. Best of all, they offer an enormous opportunity to dodge the crackdown on deducting interest on personal borrowing.

Acquisition debt. Congress couldn't bring itself to return to the good old days when mortgage interest was mortgage interest and every dime of it was deductible. But for most taxpayers, the new law comes close to doing just that.

You can deduct all the interest you pay on up to $1 million of "acquisition debt." That's money you borrow to buy, build or substantially improve your principal residence or a second home. For the interest to be deductible, the loan must be secured by the house.

Yes, $1 million is an almost inconceivable amount of mortgage debt. (At 10% interest on a 30-year loan, the monthly payments would be close to $9,000.) But the amount of debt on which you can deduct mortgage interest is likely to be far less.

Your personal ceiling is set by the size of the original loan used to buy or build your first or second home, plus amounts borrowed for major improvements. As you pay off those loans, the amount of tax-favored acquisition debt declines. Under the rules that applied in 1987, the deduction limit was tied to the *cost* of the homes, plus the *cost* of improvements. The switch from cost to acquisition debt may seem insignificant, since you pay interest only on what you borrow. But this change can throw you a curve if you refinance the mortgage.

(There is an exception to the general definition of acquisition debt. If your mortgage debt on October 13, 1987, exceeded the amount borrowed to buy, build or substantially improve your home, you can count that higher amount as acquisition indebtedness.)

Home-equity debt. Here's the end-run around the elimination of write-offs on personal loans. In addition to deducting interest on acquisition debt, homeowners can deduct interest on up to $100,000 of home-equity debt. The interest on such debt is fully deductible—whether you tap your equity via refinancing, a second mortgage or a home-equity line of credit—as long as the loan is secured by your principal residence or second home.

Another restriction—unlikely to come into play because it's doubtful any lender will let you use your home as security for a loan for more than your house is worth—blocks the deduction of interest if the combination of home-equity debt and acquisition debt exceeds the fair market value of the house.

Refinancing. The restrictions also come into play if you refinance your home mortgage. The amount of the new loan qualifying as acquisition debt is limited to the debt outstanding on the old loan, plus any part of the new money used for major home improvements. This tale is best told with an illustration:

Assume that several years ago you bought a $150,000 home with $30,000 down and a $120,000 mortgage. The debt is now paid down to $90,000 and you decide to refinance for $150,000. What's the tax status of the new loan?

Interest on $90,000—the remaining balance on the old loan—is sure to be deductible because that amount qualifies as acquisition indebtedness. The IRS's stand on the other $60,000 depends on how the money is used.

Any part spent for major home improvements also earns the status of acquisition debt. Plunge $20,000 of the new loan into a swimming pool, for example, and your tax-favored debt jumps from $90,000 to $110,000. Any part of the new loan that neither replaces the old mortgage nor pays for improvements—$40,000 in this example—is not acquisition debt.

That doesn't automatically mean you can't deduct the interest, however. Because the debt is secured by your home, the interest may be deducted as home-equity interest, subject to the $100,000 rule. If the extra funds are used in a business, the interest can be written off as a business expense. If you use the cash for an investment, the interest on that portion of the loan may be deductible as investment interest, within the limits discussed in Chapter 5.

If none of those options protects you, however, the interest falls in the category of personal interest, the deduction for which is disappearing.

Although the rules are complicated, the opportunity is extraordinary. To the extent that you can exchange nondeductible personal borrowing with deductible home-equity borrowing, you can continue to have Uncle Sam help pay the interest on your debts. The dwindling deductibility of personal interest has made home-equity loans the debt of choice for millions of homeowners. These loans offer a line of credit—which you can usually tap simply by writing checks—secured by your home. In addition to preserving the deductibility of interest charged, these loans often carry lower interest rates than unsecured borrowing.

That makes a home-equity line of credit a powerful tool. Beyond considering this source for your future borrowing needs, you may want to tap a home-equity line to pay off higher-priced debt on credit cards, auto loans and personal notes. Trading $10,000 of 12% nondeductible debt for $10,000 of 9% deductible debt would slice the after-tax carrying costs from $1,200 to $648 a year for a taxpayer in the 28% bracket.

Although the tax law encourages consumers to borrow against their homes, a note of caution is necessary. To qualify for the tax deduction, these loans must be secured by your home, which means if you find yourself unable to repay, your home is at stake. Don't let the siren song of deductible interest pull you into a deal if you don't fully understand the terms.

If you shop for a home-equity loan, shop carefully. The cost of setting up the line of credit varies widely and can be stiff. Interest rates and repayment schedules also differ substantially.

When you buy a home, the rules on acquisition indebtedness may encourage you to hold down your down payment. Remember that the size of your tax-favored debt is based on your original mortgage—not the price of the house. Assume, for example, that you can choose between (1) adding $10,000 to your down payment and later borrowing $10,000 to pay for new furniture and (2) cutting the down payment by $10,000, using the cash to pay for the furniture and adding $10,000 to your

mortgage. The second course would be more advantageous—
for tax purposes—because interest on the higher mortgage
debt would be fully deductible, but interest on a personal loan to
buy furniture would not.

The new rules can also encourage you to borrow to pay for a
home improvement rather than pay cash. As long as the debt is
secured by the home, the amount that pays for the improvement counts as acquisition debt. The tax subsidy of the interest
cost could make borrowing cheaper than the amount you'd lose
by pulling cash out of an investment to pay for the improvement.

It's important to keep reliable records of your borrowing to
back up the deductions you claim. If you use a home-equity line,
carefully distinguish between borrowing that pays for major
home improvements and loans used for other purposes. The
amount that goes for improvements is added to your acquisition
debt, rather than eating away at your $100,000 home-equity
allowance.

REFINANCING

There are two important tax points regarding refinancing—the
transaction that involves trading in one home mortgage for
another. The goal is usually either to reduce monthly payments
via a lower interest rate or to tap the equity in a home with a
larger first mortgage rather than adding a second trust or
home-equity line.

First, consider the tax status of the points you pay to get the
new mortgage. In a controversial 1986 decision, the IRS
announced that points paid on refinancing are not fully deductible in the year paid, except to the extent that the funds are
used for home improvements.

Here's an example of the IRS's position: A homeowner with
a $100,000 mortgage refinances at $120,000 and uses $20,000
to build a swimming pool. Assume that two points (2% of
$120,000, or $2,400) were charged. Because one-sixth of the
money went for a home improvement, one-sixth of the points,
or $400, may be deducted in the year paid. The rest must be

deducted evenly over the life of the loan. On a 30-year mortgage, that would mean one-thirtieth of the remaining $2,000, or $66.66, would be deducted each year, assuming the homeowner remembers to do so. If the house is sold and the mortgage paid off before the end of the term, any remaining portion of the points could be deducted as interest at that time.

The second issue growing out of refinancing has to do with prepayment penalties. If the lender holding the original loan slaps you with a penalty for paying it off early, the amount is considered interest and is fully deductible in the year you pay it.

But what if the lender is willing to cut the amount due to encourage you to pay off the mortgage early? That's not as unlikely as it may appear. In times of soaring interest rates, lenders sometimes offer sweet deals to get out of long-term loans at low, fixed interest rates. But if you're on the receiving end of such an offer, beware. The amount of such a discount is considered taxable income to you.

Consider this example: You still owe $60,000 on a 7% mortgage and market rates have risen far above that level. To get that low-rate loan off its books, the lender offers to let you pay off the debt in full for $50,000. If you agree to such a deal, the IRS wants a share of your windfall. The $10,000 discount is considered taxable income—costing you $2,800 in the 28% bracket. If you are offered such a deal, be sure to take the tax consequences into account.

SELLING YOUR HOME

You don't have to file any forms with the IRS when you buy a home or when you make improvements that add to the tax basis. When you sell, though, the government wants to know the details. After all, there may be a tax to be collected. There's a good chance, though, that the sale won't add a dime to your tax bill.

When you sell, you will see how clever you have been to keep meticulous records of every improvement to your home over the years. To determine the tax consequences of the sale, you have to know the adjusted basis of your home, a value easily computed with the information in well-kept files.

Your adjusted basis is what you paid for the house plus the cost of all improvements, minus any casualty losses on the property you claimed while living there—for fire or storm damage, for example. (Casualty-loss deductions are explained in Chapter 10.) The basis is also reduced by any gain from a previous home you rolled over into the house being sold, as discussed later.

Your profit or loss on the sale is the difference between that adjusted basis and the amount you realize on the sale. As nothing involved with taxes is easy, the amount realized is not simply the selling price. That's the beginning point from which you subtract costs connected with the sale. Common selling expenses include real estate commissions, advertising and legal fees, points paid for a buyer, the cost of termite inspection and any other costs you incur to sell the place. Not included, however, are amounts you spend for repairs or other efforts to make the place more attractive to buyers.

If your adjusted basis is more than the amount realized, your loss is not deductible. In the more likely event that the bottom line shows a profit, the gain may be taxable in the year of the sale, sometime in the future, or perhaps never at all.

The opportunity to put off or completely avoid tax on the profit has long been one of the most valuable tax benefits enjoyed by homeowners. It's more important than ever now that Congress has abolished the special break for capital gains. Before 1987, 60% of the profit on a house was tax-free. Now, such gain is fully taxable.

Rolling over the gain. Fortunately, it's easy to defer the tax bill almost indefinitely. To do so, all you have to do is buy a new principal residence—costing at least as much as you get from the sale of the one sold—within a specified time period.

To qualify, you must buy or build *and* occupy the new home within two years—before or after—the sale of the old one. (If you are in the armed forces or living outside the United States when your home is sold, you may qualify for a longer replacement period allowing up to four years to buy and occupy a new principal residence.)

Be warned that the IRS is inflexible about the replacement period. In a case in which a serious illness prevented a taxpayer from occupying the new home before the deadline, the IRS prohibited the rollover. What if you're building a new home and it burns down just before you're planning to move in? Again, the IRS says you forfeit the rollover privilege.

To defer the tax on all the gain on the sale of one home, the replacement home must cost at least as much as you realized from the sale of the old one. Assume, for example, that the adjusted basis of your home is $70,000 and you sell it for $100,000. Within the replacement period, you buy and move into a new home that costs $125,000. The tax bill on your $30,000 profit is deferred. Rather than report it as income in the year of the sale, you reduce the basis of the new home by that amount. The basis of the new home becomes $95,000—the $125,000 purchase price minus the $30,000 of deferred gain.

If you later sell that house for $150,000, in the eyes of the IRS the profit would be $65,000, the combination of the $30,000 gain from the first house and $25,000 from the second. Of course, you could put off the tax bill again by buying a replacement home within two years that costs $150,000 or more. Its basis would be reduced by the $65,000 of rolled-over gain.

You don't have to invest the actual proceeds of the sale in the new home to qualify to defer tax on the gain. Say you sold a house for $200,000 and bought a new one for $210,000. You can roll over all the profit from the first house, even if you made a minimum down payment on the new house and used the remaining proceeds for some other purpose. The key is that the new home cost at least as much as the one you sold, not how you pay for the new house.

What if you and your fiancé each own a home, sell both of them and together buy a new home? You can defer the gain on both of the old homes if the price of the new house exceeds the combined sales prices of the old ones. Any profit left out of the rollover, though, would be taxable in the year of sale. What if one taxpayer sells a home to move in with a new husband or wife in a home the spouse already owns? Sorry, no chance to defer tax on the gain in this situation. But if the seller is over age 55, he or she might qualify for the exclusion discussed on page 87.

The law does provide for a situation in which a jointly owned home is sold in connection with a divorce and each spouse buys a separate home. If each spouse invests his or her share of the proceeds of the sale in a new principal residence—within the rollover deadline—the tax bill on the profit is deferred.

Say that you and your spouse divorce and sell your jointly owned home for $150,000, including $40,000 profit. Assuming that each of you is entitled to half the proceeds of the sale, each has a $20,000 gain. Either of you can defer tax on the gain by buying a new home that costs at least $75,000, your half of the amount realized on the sale.

In any situation, if you choose a replacement home that costs less than the one you sold, you will owe tax on the profit to the extent that the adjusted sales price of the old home exceeds the cost of the new one.

The adjusted sales price is usually the same as the amount realized on the sale, but it can be less if prior to the sale you incurred qualifying fix-up expenses, such as the cost of painting or repairs to make the home more attractive to buyers. Those are costs that can't qualify as improvements to boost your basis. They come into play for tax purposes only if your replacement home costs less than the one you sold. Although real estate agents encouraging you to spruce up the place may suggest that such costs are deductible, they are not. If you don't buy a replacement home, or if you buy one that costs enough that you can roll over all your profit, fix-up costs have no tax power.

Consider this example: You sell your home for $100,000. Your adjusted basis was $70,000 and your new home costs $90,000. Of the $30,000 profit on the sale, $20,000 can be rolled into the new house, giving it a basis of $70,000. The other $10,000 of profit would be subject to tax. However, if you had $1,000 of qualifying fix-up expenses, that amount is subtracted from the amount realized to arrive at the adjusted sales price. That means you can defer the tax on an extra $1,000 of the profit. As a result, of course, the basis of the new home would fall to $69,000 so that at some time down the pike, Uncle Sam would get that $1,000 in his sights.

To qualify for this limited tax benefit, fix-up expenses must be for work done during the 90 days before you sign a contract to sell your house and must be paid for within 30 days afterward.

Trading down without tripping up. It is possible to buy a less expensive home without winding up with taxable profit in the year of the sale. Anything you spend on the new place that qualifies as an improvement—such as the cost of renovation or adding an addition or a swimming pool—can serve to raise the new home's "price" for rollover purposes. The key here is that the expense must be incurred and the bill paid within the two-year replacement period.

This provision can prove especially rewarding if you're transferred from an area of the country with high home prices to an area of more modestly priced homes.

Say the "adjusted basis" of your old house is $100,000. You sell it for $150,000, after expenses. Thanks to a transfer to a less expensive part of the country, your new home costs just $120,000—the amount that sets the ceiling for rolling over the proceeds of your home sale. That leaves $30,000 of profit out in the cold, taxable in the year of the sale. In the 28% bracket, the bill is $8,400.

You can hold down or eliminate that tax bill, though, by investing more in the new place. If you spend $30,000 or more on improvements within two years after the sale of the first house, the entire profit could be rolled over.

The rollover provision applies only to your principal residence, not to a second home, say, or rental property. And if you use part of your principal home for business—by renting out a room, say, or having a home office for which you claim deductions—part of the profit from the sale will not qualify for rollover treatment. If you claim 10% of your home as a home office (under the rules described in Chapter 9), for example, 10% of the gain on the sale won't be eligible for the deferral. Fortunately, however, there's a way around paying tax on the gain attributed to the home-office part of the house. If the home office does not exist in the year of the sale, the IRS will let you treat the entire house as a principal residence.

There is no limit on the number of times or the amount of profit you can roll over from one home to the next. In fact, the profit from the first home you own is likely to affect the tax basis of the last place you live, a point that emphasizes the importance of detailed record keeping.

"*I'm pleased to say, Mr. Mulrooney, that all your tax data—checks, vouchers, W-2s, and 1099s—from 1928 through 1984 have been forwarded to us.*"

DRAWING BY H. MARTIN
© 1985 THE NEW YORKER MAGAZINE, INC.

There is a restriction, however, that generally prevents you from using the rollover provision more than once every two years. If during the replacement period you buy or build more than one new principal residence, only the last one can be treated as your new home for figuring the rollover. Assume, for example, that you sold one house in January 1988 and deferred the gain by buying another home the same month. Then in August 1988 you sold the new house and bought another one. The rules prohibit postponing tax on the gain from the sale of the intermediate house. Rather, the profit from the first home is considered to be rolled over into the third. Any profit that built up during the time you owned the middle house is taxed.

That restriction does not apply if the sale of your home is connected with a job-related move that qualifies you to deduct moving expenses (Chapter 10). In that case, in the example above you could roll over the profit from house one to house two and then from house two to house three.

Reporting home sales. In the year of the sale, you must file a Form 2119, *Sale or Exchange of Principal Residence,* with your tax return. The form must be filed whether or not you owe tax on the sale. It's a relatively simple form, and it includes a section for determining the adjusted basis of your new home by subtracting from its cost any rolled over profit from the sale. Since each sale will affect the basis of your next home, you'll want to hang on to a copy of every Form 2119 you file throughout your homeowning career.

What if you plan to buy a replacement home but haven't closed the deal by the time your tax return is due for the year of the sale? You can still postpone the gain. Just file a Form 2119—reporting only the date your old home was sold—with your return. If the replacement home you buy costs enough to defer all of your gain, just notify the IRS Service Center where you filed your return and file a completed Form 2119 at that time. If the new house doesn't cost enough to permit a rollover of all the profit—or if the replacement period expires before you buy—you'll have to file an amended tax return (see Chapter 14) for the year of the sale. In addition to the tax on the profit, you'll have to pay interest on the tax due.

You'll also have to file an amended return if you report the profit from the home sale—under the assumption that you won't replace the house—and later decide to buy a new home. If you occupy the new place within the replacement period, you can retroactively defer the gain and reclaim the tax you paid on the original sale.

THE $125,000 EXCLUSION

So over the years you keep packing your profit with you from one home to another, holding the IRS at bay by purchasing more and more costly homes. But what happens when you finally decide to cash in on all that profit that has built up tax-free? When you retire or for some other reason decide not to buy another house, is the IRS going to swoop down and demand a healthy share of your nest egg?

Not if you qualify for the homeowners' icing on the cake: the right to escape tax entirely on up to $125,000 of profit. The same $125,000 exclusion is available whether you're married filing a joint return or single filing an individual one. If you are married filing separate returns, the limit is $62,500 for each spouse.

The value of this tax break is enhanced by the fact that it usually comes around retirement time, when extra cash often comes in particularly handy. In the 28% tax bracket, sheltering $125,000 of gain saves you $35,000! Perhaps that's the real American dream.

With such a rich reward at stake, it's essential that you know how to claim it.

You qualify if you are at least 55 years old when you sell a home you have owned and lived in for at least three of the five years leading up to the sale. If you are married and the house is jointly owned, you can qualify as long as either you or your spouse meets the age, ownership and residency tests.

Unlike the rollover rule, which applies only if the house sold is your principal residence at the time of the sale, you don't have to be living in the house when it is sold to qualify for the exclusion. If you move before the place is sold, you can still dodge tax on the profit as long as the sale occurs before so much time has passed that you no longer meet the three-out-of-five-year residency test.

Assume, for example, that you are at least age 55 and have owned and lived in your home for at least three years. You retire and move to an apartment. As long as your home is sold within two years of the move, you will meet the three-of-five-year test and qualify for the exclusion. That applies whether you rent your old home or leave it vacant prior to the sale.

Married couples are limited to a single $125,000 exclusion, and if one spouse used the exclusion before marriage, that scotches the other spouse's right to it as long as they are married. That restriction can give rise to tax-planning opportunities. Say that you own a home and plan to marry someone who also owns a home. Assume, too, that both of you meet the age, ownership and residency tests. If each of you sells your house before marriage, you each qualify for up to a $125,000 exclusion. Wait until after the ceremony, though, and together you can exclude only $125,000. Similarly, if you plan to marry someone who has already used the exclusion, selling your home before the wedding can protect your right to the exclusion.

The exclusion can also come into play in divorce. If you're planning a divorce, in some circumstances it may make sense to hold off selling the family home until after the split. If the profit will exceed $125,000, postponing the sale until you are both single co-owners of the place can permit each ex-spouse to exclude up to $125,000 of gain.

You don't necessarily want to use the exclusion the first time it is available to you. In fact, that can be a costly mistake. This is a once-in-a-lifetime opportunity. You can't use part of the exclusion to shelter $50,000 of profit on one home, for example, and later use the rest of it to avoid tax on the sale of another. Use any part of the exclusion and you use it all.

Your best bet will usually be to hold off using the exclusion until you sell what you expect to be your last home or until you can take advantage of the full $125,000. Don't worry about shortchanging your heirs by forfeiting the tax break if you die before using it; the tax on all profit that builds up during your life is excused when you die.

You claim the exclusion on Form 2119, the same form you use to report home sales and the deferral of gain.

OWNER FINANCING

Sometimes, particularly when mortgage rates are high, the sale of a home goes through only because the seller helps finance the deal. If you wind up holding a note of some sort, your tax picture can be more complicated.

The selling price of your home—for purposes of determining the gain to be rolled over, excluded or taxed—includes the face value of any mortgage or note you receive, as well as cash. If you are deferring tax on the gain or using the exclusion to shelter it from the IRS, however, you basically report the sale just as you would if you received all cash.

Payments on the note may be a combination of return of your basis (nontaxable), part of your gain (deferred or excluded) and interest on the loan (taxable). You should report the interest as income on Schedule B, the same form you use to report interest on a bank account.

If gain is taxable in the year of the sale and you help finance the deal, you may report the profit on an installment basis. That permits you to pay tax on the profit as you receive it over the years. Installment sales are discussed in Chapter 6, as are the rules demanding that you charge a reasonable interest rate on the loan.

What if you can't sell? It's a homeowner's nightmare: You move to a new home but can't find a buyer for the old homestead. Not only might you have to get a bridge loan to finance the new home, you also face the prospect of making two mortgage payments month after month. Few family budgets can handle that financial burden.

One solution is to rent your former residence to generate cash to help pay the bills. But that can lead you into a maze of tax complications.

The part of the tax law that permits homeowners to defer the tax on the profit from one house by rolling it over into a new home applies only to your principal residence. Can a house that's being rented to someone else when you finally sell it qualify as *your* home? If not, the vagaries of the housing market could force you to pay tax on the profit rather than roll it over.

The good news is that if you can show the rental was temporary, the house still qualifies as your principal residence and the gain can be rolled over—as long as you sell the old house within two years of the time you buy the new home. If the old home hasn't sold within the rollover-replacement period, you're out of luck.

Things get complicated, though, when it comes to writing off your expenses on the temporary rental property.

As you would expect, the IRS demands that you treat the rent you receive as income. Temporary or not, you become a landlord in the eyes of the IRS. You may be able to completely offset the tax bill on the rental income, however, with deductions for rental expenses including the continued mortgage interest and tax payments on the house, the cost of repairs and even depreciation.

The big question is whether the arrangement can produce a tax loss if expenses exceed rental income—as they often will under these circumstances. Such a loss, of course, could shelter from tax other income, such as your salary, assuming you actively manage the rental and don't run afoul of the passive-loss rules explained in Chapter 6.

But the IRS says you can't have it both ways—treating the house as a principal residence for rollover purposes and as a rental property for tax-loss purposes. According to the IRS position, you can deduct rental expenses up to the amount of your rental income, but no more.

The issue is up in the air, however, because courts have disagreed on that point. In a key case in which the taxpayers beat the IRS, the court ruled, basically, that because the taxpayers charged fair-market rent for their home they deserved the same write-offs available to other landlords, even if that meant they had a tax loss to shelter other income. At the same time, because the taxpayers continued their efforts to sell the place—and in fact did sell it before the replacement period ran out—the rollover provision also applied.

The IRS is sticking to its position, though. If you find yourself in this situation and claim a rental loss, the IRS may challenge your deductions if your return is audited.

Permanent rental. If you are unable to sell your old house within two years, you may want to consider making the rental arrangement permanent. After the replacement period ends, any profit on a sale—including any gain from previous homes that had been rolled over into the house—will be taxed. Neither the rollover nor the $125,000 exclusion provision will protect you.

Some homeowners plan from the outset to hang on to their old homes, a move that can be among the easiest ways to become a real estate investor and latch on to the tax benefits discussed in Chapter 6.

There's one potential catch to converting your home to a rental property, however. Its value for figuring depreciation deductions—a key write-off for real estate investors—is your adjusted basis or the fair market value of the house, whichever is less. The basis may be far less than what the house is worth when you convert it, particularly if you have pushed it down by rolling over profit from previous homes.

Assume, for example, that your house is worth $150,000. You bought it for $100,000 several years ago and, at that time rolled over $30,000 in profit from your previous home. If you convert the house to a rental property, your basis for depreciation purposes is a skimpy $70,000. Because you cannot depreciate the value of land, you must subtract its value to determine the amount on which to base your depreciation write-offs. (If someone else bought your home for $150,000 and turned it into a rental property, the new owner's basis for depreciation purposes would be $150,000—minus the value of the land—and he or she would enjoy depreciation deductions more than twice as large as you are allowed.)

Until recently, homes that were converted to rental use were depreciated under the rules in effect when the house was acquired, not when it was changed to rental use. When writing the Tax Reform Act of 1986, however, Congress realized that that rule could force taxpayers who bought their homes between 1981 and 1986 to use the more generous depreciation schedules in effect during those years rather than the new, slower timetable for write-offs. To prevent that outcome, the law requires that homes purchased during that period use the 27½-year depreciation schedule set by tax reform. Homes purchased before 1981 are depreciated under the rules in effect at the time, which generally require a write-off period of 30 years or more.

Selling your home for a loss. Although profits from the sale of your home are taxable—except to the extent that you can defer or exclude the gain—losses are not deductible. You may have heard, however, that there's a way to write off such losses. Often promoted as a great tax scheme, promoters say home-sale losses can be deducted if prior to the sale you convert your house to a rental property.

That's true, but there's a catch that usually makes that tactic worthless. The basis for figuring your loss begins as the lower of the adjusted basis or fair market value at the time of the conversion. (The basis is increased for any improvements after the conversion and reduced for any depreciation claimed.) In other words, any loss in fair market value that occurs while you're living in the house can't be deducted.

VACATION HOMES

Taxes take no holiday at your vacation getaway. In fact, the rules that apply have been declared "exasperatingly convoluted" by no less than an authority in the U.S. Tax Court.

Strictly personal. First, look at the bright side. If your home away from home is only that, a second residence that's never rented out, the tax benefits come with few complications. Even after tax reform, you can fully deduct mortgage interest on a second home just as you can on your principal residence.

If you own a third house, however, you're out of luck. Congress apparently figures that anyone who can afford more than two homes can handle the mortgage interest without the help of a tax deduction. Interest on any additional homes—and on any debt on the first and second homes that exceeds the $1 million cap discussed on page 76—falls in the category of personal interest, the deduction for which is being phased out between now and 1991. Although there has been talk to the contrary, a motor home or boat can qualify as a second residence for purposes of this deduction. (However, if you are subject to the alternative minimum tax, discussed in Chapter 15, interest on a loan for a boat you use as a second home can't be deducted as mortgage interest.) Property taxes are deductible too, regardless of how many homes you own.

However, points paid to get a mortgage on a vacation home are not deductible in the year paid. Rather than being able to write off that expense right away, as you can when a principal residence is involved, the points are deducted proportionally over the life of the loan, as discussed on page 79.

Mixed personal and rental use. It's when you start renting the vacation home—as many owners do to help pay the freight— that things get tricky.

In an uncharacteristic display of generosity, the IRS does not care about any rental income you receive if you rent the place for 14 or fewer days during the year. That nugget in the tax law has prompted some homeowners who find themselves in a temporarily hot rental market—say the Super Bowl or a major college bowl game occurs in your area—to rent their homes briefly when they can command especially high rents. (The rule offers the opportunity for tax-free income from a principal residence as well as a second home.) There is no limit on how much you can charge for the use of your home. As long as your temporary tenants stay no more than two weeks during the year, the rent you receive is tax-free. Rent for more than 14 days and you become a landlord in the eyes of the IRS. You have to report rental income and qualify to deduct rental expenses.

How much time tenants use the property versus how much time you enjoy it yourself controls whether the house is treated as a personal residence or a business property. The distinction is the key to the tax ramifications.

If your personal use accounts for more than 14 days during the year or more than 10% of the number of days the place is rented (26 or more personal days compared to 250 rental days, for example), the house is considered a personal residence.

Hold personal use below the 14-day/10% threshold, however, and the house is considered a rental property.

Because the tax consequences turn on the amount of personal use, it's important to know that the IRS takes a broad view of what counts. It includes:

• Any day the property is used by you or anyone who is a part-owner (unless it is rented as a principal residence to a part-owner under a shared-equity arrangement, as discussed on page 98).

• Any day it is used by a member of your family, whether or not rent is paid. For this test, a member of your family includes your spouse, brothers and sisters, parents and grandparents and children and grandchildren.

• Any day it is rented to anyone else who pays less than fair market rent.

• Any day the property is used by someone in connection with an arrangement that gives you the right to use another dwelling, such as if you trade a week at your beach home for a week at a mountain resort.

Note that time you spend at the place doing repairs or general maintenance does not count as personal use. As long as that is the primary purpose of staying at the vacation home, the day is not counted as personal use. You must keep detailed records showing the dates of personal use, rental use and repair and maintenance days.

Before the Tax Reform Act of 1986, many vacation-home owners went out of their way to pass the 14-day/10% test so the rental activity qualified as a business. Doing so meant that if expenses—including mortgage interest and property taxes attributable to the time the place was rented, plus operating costs, repairs and depreciation—exceeded rental income (as they usually did), the owners could claim a loss on their tax returns. Not only was the tax on the rental income wiped out, but that loss could protect other income.

When personal use exceeded 14 days or 10% of the rental time, rental deductions were limited to the amount of rental income. Any excess expenses were of no tax value. That restriction effectively ruled out depreciation write-offs in many cases. Without the tax shelter, the vacation villa became much more expensive.

Tax reform's tangled web. The 14-day rule survived the latest version of tax reform, but the consequences of passing or failing the test have changed.

Limiting personal use no longer automatically opens the door to big tax losses. As discussed in Chapter 6, the law now limits the deduction of "passive" losses, a category that includes all losses on rental property. There is an important exception, though, that will protect many vacation-home owners. If your adjusted gross income is less than $100,000, you can deduct up to $25,000 of rental losses each year. The $25,000 allowance is gradually phased out as AGI rises to $150,000. To qualify for this exception to the passive-loss rules, you must "actively" manage the property, but you can probably meet that requirement so long as you're involved in such decisions as approving tenants, rental terms and repairs.

If the exception doesn't help you, there is a phase-in of the new rules to ease the pain for taxpayers who had the rental property in service as of October 22, 1986. The law permits 40% of otherwise nondeductible passive losses to be deducted in 1988, 20% in 1989 and 10% in 1990.

Expenses you can't deduct because of the passive-loss rules aren't lost forever. Unused losses are held over to future years when they can be used to offset income from the vacation home or other passive investments. Also, any passive losses that are unused at the time you sell the property can be deducted against the profit on the sale or any other income.

Even if the $25,000 exception will protect your rental write-offs, there's another potential trap. Limiting personal use to qualify a vacation home as a business property may mean giving up the right to some mortgage-interest deductions.

Remember that the law now permits mortgage-interest deductions for loans secured by your first and second *residence*. If your vacation place is a business property, the mortgage isn't covered. Part of the interest would still be deductible—the portion attributable to the business use of the property—and the rest would be considered personal interest, which is losing its deductibility.

That rule has led some tax advisers to recommend that taxpayers intentionally flunk the 14-day/10% test by increasing their personal use of vacation property. That way, you preserve the full interest write-off. Part of the interest would be deducted as a rental expense and the rest as personal mortgage interest. What you give up, of course, is the opportunity to claim a tax loss.

With the phase-in of the passive-loss rules and the phaseout of the deductibility of personal interest, the after-tax cost of owning a vacation home may change substantially over the next few years. If you are in a situation to choose whether to pass or flunk the 14-day/10% test, you'll have to do a lot of number crunching to figure out which one will produce the best overall result. As you work through the various scenarios, remember that tax reform stretched out the depreciation period for rental real estate to 27.5 years. But, as explained in Chapter 6, the longer timetable applies to homes purchased after 1986. Vacation homes purchased earlier continue to enjoy the faster depreciation periods in place when the houses were first rented.

TRICK OR TREAT?

Allocation of expenses. To figure your vacation-home deductions, you have to allocate expenses between personal and rental use. According to the IRS, you begin by toting up the total number of days the house was used for both purposes. Your deductible expenses are the same proportion of the total as the number of rental days is to the total number of days the place was used.

For example, assume you have a cabin in the mountains that you use for 30 days during the year and rent out for 100 days. The 100 days of rental use equals 77% of the total 130 days the cabin was used during the year. Using the IRS formula, 77% of your expenses—for interest, taxes, insurance, utilities, repairs and depreciation—would be rental expenses.

The government is also particular about the order in which you deduct those expenses against your rental income. You deduct interest and taxes first, then expenses except for depreciation, and then depreciation. The sequence is important, and detrimental, because of the rule that limits rental deductions to the amount of rental income when personal use exceeds 14 days or 10% of total use. Remember that the property taxes and a declining portion of the interest assigned to rental use could be claimed as regular itemized deductions if they are not used to offset rental income. By demanding that those costs be applied against rental income, the law can limit or eliminate the value of deductions for other out-of-pocket expenses and depreciation.

By using a different allocation formula, though, you can limit the interest and tax deductions and thereby boost the write-off of other expenses. Courts have allowed taxpayers to allocate taxes and interest over the entire year rather than over just the total number of days a property is used. In the example above of 100 days of rental use, that method would allocate just 27% (100 ÷ 365) of the taxes and interest to rental income. That would leave more rental income against which other expenses can be deducted. The extra taxes and a portion of the "personal" interest (40% in 1988, 20% in 1989 and 10% in 1998) can be deducted as regular itemized deductions.

Although the court-approved formula can pay off when the

14-day/10% test makes the property a personal residence, the IRS version can be more appealing if the place qualifies as a business property. Consider, for example, the result if you use your vacation place for ten days out of the year and rent it for 75 days.

The court-approved method would allocate 21% (75 ÷ 365) of the interest to rental use. Under the new law, that would make 79% of the interest personal interest subject to the phaseout. Using the IRS formula, though, 88% of the interest would be assigned to rental use (ten days personal use divided by 85 days total use). That would throw just 12% into the vulnerable personal-interest category.

Even if the bigger rental-interest deduction converts some of your other expenses and depreciation into nondeductible passive losses, the tax value is not lost forever. Those losses are stored for use in future years—unlike nondeductible personal interest, which has no tax value.

EQUITY SHARING

Despite all the advantages of homeownership, rising home prices and the shrinking tax subsidy of falling rates can make it tougher than ever to afford a home, particularly that first house. Coming up with the cash for the down payment is often a family affair, with parents helping their children buy into the American dream of homeownership. The tax consequences of making a low- or no-interest loan to help your children buy a house are discussed in Chapter 3.

Here's a look at another path to the same goal that may make more sense for you: equity sharing.

The parties in a shared-equity arrangement don't have to be related, but this discussion will focus on parents and children. Basically, rather than making a loan or gift to your child, equity sharing involves becoming his or her partner. You become part-owner and rent your share of the place to the child. As an investor, you share in the appreciation of the house. As a landlord you also get rental income and the tax deductions that go along with rental real estate.

Assume the equity is split 50/50, although the property does not have to be divided equally. You and your child each put up half of the down payment and agree that you will each pay half of the mortgage interest, property taxes and other expenses such as insurance and repairs. Your child would also have to agree to pay you fair market rent for your half of the house.

The child, as the owner-occupant of the house, gets all the tax advantages of homeownership, on a scaled-down level. The mortgage interest and property taxes he pays are deductible, just as if he owned the house outright. (Like any tenant, of course, the rent he pays you is not deductible.)

You, as the owner-investor, get all the tax advantages of owning rental real estate. You report the rent you receive as income and deduct the mortgage interest and property taxes paid as a rental expense. You also deduct your share of the insurance bills, for example, and the cost of repairs. In addition, you can claim depreciation deductions based on the cost of your half of the house. Under current tax law, residential real estate is deductible over 27.5 years and straight-line depreciation is used. If your expenses outstrip the rent you receive, you may be able to qualify to deduct up to $25,000 of your losses against other income. See Chapter 6 for the details.

When the house is sold, you and your child will split the proceeds. As an investor, your profit is taxable in the year of the sale. Since the house is the child's principal residence, however, he or she may defer the tax bill by rolling the profit into a new home, as explained on page 81.

Setting a fair rent for your share of the house is a key to whether a shared-equity arrangement will pass muster with the IRS. If you charge a bargain rent, the deal can fall under the vacation-home rules (page 92). That would prohibit you from deducting any expenses that exceed the rental income.

Remember that the owner-occupant has to pay rent only on the part of the house you own. In a 50/50 deal, if similar homes in the area generally rent for around $1,000 a month, for example, you wouldn't need to set the rent above $500. You could probably set it somewhat lower, in fact, since you can count on the owner-occupant to be a particularly good tenant.

Presented with such arguments a few years ago, the U.S. Tax Court said that "fair rent" for a relative can be as much as 20% lower than fair rent for a stranger.

The law requires that these arrangements be set up under a written "shared-equity financing agreement" that spells out the conditions of the deal, including each partner's share, which one will make the house a home, how expenses will be split and the fact that the owner-occupant will pay rent to the other owner. Because of the complexities, if you're interested in equity sharing, find a lawyer, real estate agent or mortgage-company official who is familiar with these arrangements. It may take some effort, but the tax savings could be well worth the trouble.

5
INVESTMENT INCOME AND EXPENSES

O ne of the goals of tax reform was to get Uncle Sam to back out of your investment decisions, so that your deployment of funds would turn on economic factors rather than tax consequences. But although many incentives favoring certain investments have disappeared, the shake-up of the investment/tax landscape means some investments that had been disadvantaged now look better. Face it: Uncle Sam still has an abiding, pecuniary interest in your investments, and even after tax reform profit from different investments is treated differently by the taxman.

That means after-tax return—what you get to keep in your pocket after April 15—is still a critical element to consider as you weigh the increasing number of choices in the investment marketplace. Knowing how the IRS treats various investments and how to use the tax rules to your best advantage can be as valuable as a hot stock tip.

CAPITAL GAINS

First a brief eulogy on the passing of one of the investors' best friends: the capital-gains exclusion.

Before tax reform, investment profits were divided into two classes distinguished by the calendar. Gains on such assets as stocks and bonds, real estate and collectibles owned six months or less before selling were considered short-term. Profit on the sale of property owned more than six months earned the tax-favored status of long-term capital gains.

The difference was enormous.

Although 100% of short-term profits was taxed, only 40% of long-term gains fell victim to the IRS. The glorious capital-gains exclusion made the other 60% of those profits tax-free. Back when tax rates soared to the 50% level, a $10,000 short-term gain, like $10,000 of salary, could cost up to $5,000 in extra tax. The same amount of profit from an asset held long-term could add no more than $2,000 to the tax bill. For someone in the 50% bracket, the top rate on long-term gains was 20% (40% of 50%). The lure of lower taxes kept investors' eyes on the calender and perhaps sometimes persuaded them to hold on to an asset longer than their investment sense told them was smart. There was even a formula for figuring how much you could afford to lose to falling stock prices and still come out ahead thanks to gentler tax treatment.

Tax reform put an end to such preoccupation, but in a painful way. The capital-gains exclusion was abolished. Now, 100% of investment profit—whether short-term or long-term—is taxable. One reason Congress felt comfortable abolishing the exclusion was that basic tax rates were being slashed. But although the top tax rate on other kinds of income—including salaries, interest and dividends—has fallen from 50% to 33%, the top rate on long-term gains has actually leaped from 20% to 33%. That jump in Uncle Sam's take demands that investors rethink their portfolios.

The end of the capital-gains exclusion does not mean you can forget about the calendar. Congress did not abolish the law's distinction between short- and long-term gains. At some point in the future, it would be easy to reestablish tax-favored status for long-term profits.

Keep this in mind: The holding period that distinguishes short-term gains from long-term gains changed in 1988, thanks to a law passed several years ago. Assets acquired from 1988 on must be held for more than one year for the profit or loss to be categorized as long-term.

There is a retroactive flavor to the change in capital-gains rules if you engaged in an installment sale before 1987 and are still receiving payments. When you made the sale you expected the portion of the long-term profit received over the years to be 60% tax-free. But tax reform made no provision to grandfather installment-sales profits. Gain received is now fully taxable.

On the plus side, the law is now more generous when it comes to deducting long-term capital losses. There continues to be a $3,000 annual limit on the amount of capital losses that can be deducted against other kinds of income, such as your salary. Any extra loss can be carried over indefinitely until it is used up. In the past, only 50% of long-term losses could be deducted, so it took $6,000 of loss to reach the $3,000 limit. Now, just as long-term gains are fully taxable, long-term losses are 100% deductible up to the annual cap.

SAVINGS ACCOUNTS

Ho, hum. Boring old savings accounts and certificates of deposit. Not much opportunity for tax savings here. On the bright side, the tax treatment is fairly simple and straightforward: The interest you earn is fully taxable. There are a few twists, though.

Interest earned by a savings account is taxable in the year it is credited to your account, whether or not you withdraw the money. Even if a savings and loan or credit union labels the income on your account as dividends, the IRS says it's interest, and that's how you should report it.

With certificates of deposit that mature in a year or less, the interest income is taxable in the year the deposit matures. This rule permits you to shift taxable income from one year to the next and hold off Uncle Sam from one April 15 to the next. Buy a six-month CD in July, for example, and the interest will not be taxable until the following year when it matures.

Interest paid on time deposits with maturities of more than a year is taxable as it is credited each year. The institution where you invest should send you a notice of how much you should report each year on your tax return.

If you withdraw funds early from a CD, the bank or s&l is likely to exact an early-withdrawal penalty. You can deduct that charge even if you do not itemize your deductions.

What about "gifts," such as the ubiquitous toasters offered by savings institutions to induce you to make a deposit? The value of the gift is included in the amount the bank tells the IRS it paid you during the year. The extra tax would be insignificant if a toaster is involved. But if you receive a pricey inducement—cars have been offered on multiyear, jumbo deposits—you could face a hefty tax bill up front. If you eschewed such a "gift" in favor of receiving higher interest over the term of the certificate, the tax bill would be spread out, too.

Children's accounts. If you set up custodial accounts for your minor children, the interest earned should be reported on the child's tax return if the interest and any other income exceeds $500 for the year. Worries that parents were dumping funds into kids' accounts—so the interest would be taxed in the child's low tax bracket rather than the parents' higher one—prompted the enactment of the "kiddie tax" discussed in Chapter 3. Basically, investment income in excess of $1,000 a year earned by a child under age 14 is taxed on the child's return but at the parents' tax rate.

Joint accounts. When married couples who file joint returns own joint accounts, there's no tax problem. All the interest is simply reported on the joint return. When unmarried taxpayers share an account, though, things can be complicated.

Say you have a joint account with your sister. The bank or s&l will report income to the IRS in the name of the owner whose social security number is listed first on the account. That means you could be paying tax on interest that really went to your sibling. You can avoid that, but it will take some effort.

Here's how to do it. Assume that you receive a Form 1099-INT from the bank showing $1,500 of interest but that you and your sister have agreed to share the income in proportion to the amount invested in the account. You each have deposited half the funds, so $750 of the interest is yours, $750 hers. Because it was all reported to you, you're considered the "nominee recipient" of your sister's $750.

To shift the tax bill where it belongs, you need a blank 1099-INT form, which you can get at a local IRS office. Fill it out, showing $750 of interest income for your sister. Give your sister a copy of the form—by the February 2 after the year for which the income was reported—and file another copy, along with a Form 1096 (also available from the IRS), with the IRS service center for your area by March 2. With those forms, you show yourself to be the payer of the interest and your sister to be the recipient.

When you file your own tax return, you report the full $1,500 of interest as income on Schedule B, but also subtract the $750, labeling it as a "nominee distribution." It's much easier to maintain separate accounts.

But what if you have signed on as a joint owner of a savings account belonging to a parent, for example, simply as a convenience so you can withdraw funds for them if necessary? The key is to be sure that the beneficial owner of the account— your mother or father in this example—is the one whose social security number is listed first. The interest will be reported in her or his name, not yours. If things get fouled up and the income is reported in your name, you'll have to go through the nominee-distribution rigmarole.

U.S. SAVINGS BONDS

These used to be such lousy investments that the tax angles were among the least of the concerns of people who bought the bonds. Now, however, savings bonds have a lot to commend them. They have shed the fixed, well-below-market interest rate of the past. Series EE bonds are sold for half of their face value and guarantee a minimum interest rate—now 6%—if held for at least five years. But the rate actually earned fluctuates with market interest rates. Bondholders are paid 85% of the average yield on five-year Treasury notes. The rate has reached as high as 11%. A bank or other institution selling the bonds can tell you the current rate.

Series EE savings bonds have two special tax appeals. First, the interest earned is exempt from state and local income taxes, which means the earnings are worth somewhat more to you than interest that would be taxed by your state or local government. Second, you can put off the federal tax bill on the interest until you cash the bonds. Such tax-deferred interest is advantageous because funds that otherwise would go to the IRS can remain invested for further growth. (Series HH bonds enjoy a similar freedom from state and local income taxes, but the interest is taxable as it is paid out semiannually.)

The tax-deferred nature of Series EE bonds makes them an appealing tool for a child's educational savings plan. You, or some other generous soul, can buy bonds for your children and the investment will be permitted to grow unmolested by the IRS until the bonds are cashed, perhaps to cover tuition bills. As long as the child is named owner of the bonds, he or she will be responsible for the tax bill, even if the parent or other purchaser is named the beneficiary. If you name yourself co-owner of the bond, however, you will be liable for the tax bill even if the child cashes the bond.

Because tax on the bonds is deferred until they are cashed, the income does not count when figuring whether the child is subject to the "kiddie tax" discussed in Chapter 3. As long as the bonds are not cashed before the year the child reaches age 14, the interest will be taxed in the child's bracket rather than the parents'.

In some cases, though, it may make sense to skip the tax deferral and report the income each year as it builds up. If your child has a limited amount of income, this maneuver may effectively make part or all of the savings-bond interest completely tax-free. Annual reporting of the interest could be advantageous if the child's total income is so low that no tax would be due. A child can have up to $500 of tax-free investment income each year, and an additional $500 is taxed at his or her own rate without triggering the kiddie tax.

To report the interest annually, simply file a tax return for the child and show the amount of interest that accrued during the year. A bank or other institution that sells bonds should have a table showing how much was earned by bonds purchased at different times during the year. You wouldn't have to file another tax return until the child's income was high enough to require one.

If you have been using the annual reporting method but are

tripped up by the new kiddie tax—because income you thought would be taxed in your child's low bracket is now being taxed in yours—you have to get IRS permission to switch back to deferring the tax bill until the bonds are cashed. File Form 3115, *Application for Change in Accounting Method.*

When savings bonds are cashed, the owner will receive a 1099-INT form showing as income the difference between the purchase price of the bond and its redemption value. If you have reported some or all of the interest annually, however, you don't have to pay tax on that amount. You do have to report the full amount of interest on your tax return but should also list the amount as "U.S. savings-bond interest previously reported" and subtract it from the interest total. Clearly, you must maintain careful records over the years to prevent you, or your child, from overpaying the tax bill.

What if you inherit Series E or EE bonds? The IRS demands that someone pay tax on the interest that has built up but doesn't care whether you or the deceased owner foots the bill. Even if the bonds are not redeemed, the untaxed interest can be reported on the decedent's final tax return. In that case, you would be responsible for the tax only on the interest earned between the date of death of the previous owner and when you redeem the bonds.

If the interest isn't reported on the deceased's final tax return, you assume the tax liability along with ownership of the bonds. When you cash in the bonds, you will report and pay tax on all the interest. The choice turns on the tax rate that would apply if the interest were reported on the decedent's final return as opposed to yours and on how long you are likely to hold on to the bonds—and therefore how long you will hold off the tax bill if you assume the liability.

STOCKS

Despite the demise of the capital-gains exclusion, stocks retain a special tax advantage. Profits are not taxed as they build up. The IRS gets a crack at your appreciation only when you sell your shares and thereby transform paper profit to real dollars in your pocket. Whether you're just getting your feet wet in the market or you're a seasoned investor, it's important to keep an eye on the tax angles if you want to share as little as possible of your portfolio success with Uncle Sam.

Unlike a savings account—in which someone else keeps track of exactly how much you earn and must pay tax on—investing in stocks demands that you be a meticulous bookkeeper. It's up to you to be able to pinpoint the tax basis of your investment. *Basis* is a key word in tax lingo. It is, in brief, your investment in the property—the amount you will compare to the sales proceeds to determine the size of your profit or loss. Sounds simple, but it isn't necessarily so. For one thing, it depends on how you got the property in the first place.

Purchase. The tax basis of stock you purchase is what you pay for it, plus the commission you pay the broker. Say you buy 100 shares of XYZ Inc. at $40 a share, and you pay a $100 commission. The total cost is $4,100, and your tax basis in each share is $41.

Gift. The basis of securities you receive as a gift depends on whether your ultimate sale of the stock will produce a profit or loss. If you sell for a profit, your basis is the same as the basis of the previous owner. If you sell for a loss, though, the basis is either the previous owner's basis or the value of the stock at the time of the gift, whichever is lower.

For example, say your aunt gives you 100 shares of stock for which she paid $5,000 but which are worth only $2,500 at the time of the gift. If the stocks turns around and you sell for $6,000, the basis for determining gain is $5,000. If you sell for less than $2,500, however, the basis for figuring your loss is the $2,500 value at the time you received the gift. The loss in value while your aunt owned the stock is ignored. What if the selling price falls between $2,500 and $5,000? You have neither gain nor loss. (If the gift is big enough to require the donor to pay federal gift tax—see Chapter 16—that cost can increase the basis.)

Inheritance. When you inherit stock or other property, your basis is usually the value of the asset on the date of death of the previous owner. The income tax on any profit that built up while he or she was alive is forgiven. You are responsible only for the tax on appreciation after you inherit the stock. If the stock price falls before you sell it, you can claim a tax loss. (An exception to the general rule sets the basis of inherited property at its value six months after the owner died. If the executor of the estate chooses that value for estate-tax purposes, it becomes your basis in the stock.)

If you own stock with someone as joint tenants or tenants by the entirety—forms of ownership that insure that on the death of one co-owner the survivor becomes the sole owner—the basis is adjusted upward on the death of the co-owner. Basically, the survivor is treated as though he or she inherited half of each share of stock, with its basis increased to current market value. For example, assume you and your spouse jointly own stock with a basis of $20 a share and your spouse dies when the shares are worth $40 each. Your basis in the shares would become $30: half of the original basis plus half of the fair market value at the time of your spouse's death.

If you live in a community-property state, the entire basis of community property—not just half—may be increased to date-of-death value upon the death of one spouse. Since that could have a major impact on the taxes due when the stock is sold, check this point carefully if you live in one of these states: Arizona, California, Idaho, Louisiana, Nevada, New Mexico, Texas, Washington or Wisconsin.

Divorce. Stocks or other property received as part of a divorce settlement retain the same basis they had when owned by your ex-spouse. In other words, the paper gain or loss that built up while your spouse owned the property and the tax liability for it are transferred to you.

Stock splits. When a company in which you own stock declares a stock split, your basis in the shares is spread across both the new and old shares. Say you own 100 shares with a basis of $10 each in a firm that declares a two-for-one split. Your total basis of $1,000 (100 × $10) would be spread among the 200 shares, giving each share a basis of $5.

Dividend-reinvestment plans. Your basis in shares purchased through a dividend-reinvestment plan is the stock's cost. Thus, if you have $500 in dividends reinvested in additional shares, your basis in each share would be $500 divided by the number of shares you received.

Strategies. Keeping track of the basis of all your shares might sound like a hassle, but it is essential for successful tax planning. It is particularly important when you buy the stock of the same company at different times and at different prices. When you decide to sell some of the stock, being able to identify which shares to part with will permit you to control the tax consequences of the deal.

Consider this example. You bought 100 shares of ABC stock in January 1986 for $2,400, giving you a basis of $24 per share. In January 1987, you purchased 100 more shares, this time for $2,800. Your basis in each share is $28. In January 1988, you purchased another 100 shares for $3,000, giving each share a basis of $30.

When the stock hits $40 a share, you decide to sell 100 shares. If you simply tell your broker to sell 100 shares, the IRS FIFO rule—first in, first out—will come into play. It will be assumed that the first shares you purchased—the 1986 group with their $24 basis—were the first ones sold. That would create a taxable profit of $16 a share or $1,600. But if you direct your broker to sell the shares purchased in 1988, with a $30 basis, the taxable profit will be $10 a share or just $1,000.

In either case you would get $4,000 from the sale of the stock, but your tax bill would be significantly different. In most cases, you'll probably want to structure the sale to produce the smallest taxable profit. It's possible, though, that circumstances will warrant selling the shares with the lowest basis first—if you have sufficient losses to offset the larger gain, for example, or if you need higher investment income to permit you to write off investment expenses.

In any case, only if you have conscientiously maintained records do you have the flexibility to insure the best after-tax outcome. Records of what you own, your basis and the paper profit or loss are especially helpful at the end of the year when you review your portfolio for tax-motivated sales, as discussed in Chapter 12.

Short sales. What if you sell stock you don't own, which is exactly what happens in a short sale? An investor borrows stock from a broker in order to sell it, usually with the hope that the stock price will fall. If it does, the investor profits by repaying the loan with shares purchased at the lower price. If the stock price increases, the investor loses and has to repay the loan with shares that cost more than those sold.

As far as the IRS is concerned, the transaction doesn't count for tax purposes until the investor delivers the stock to the lender to close the sale. If you sell stock short in 1988 and close the deal in 1989, for example, the gain or loss will be reported on your 1989 tax return. The premium you pay the broker to borrow the stock used in the short sale is considered investment interest, deductible to the extent of your investment income, as explained on page 140.

Sometimes an investor who owns stock will sell the same stock short, a maneuver called selling "short against the box." This technique can be attractive at year-end because it permits you to lock in profit on a stock in an uncertain market while postponing recognition of the taxable gain until the following year. You sell borrowed stock at the current price, but the transaction doesn't count for tax purposes until the following year when you deliver your shares to repay the loan. The short sale shields you from market risk in the meantime.

Wash sale. The IRS doesn't like being made the chump, which explains the existence of the wash-sale rule. It is most easily explained by outlining the maneuver it aims to prevent: Assume you own stock showing a substantial paper loss. Although you have every confidence the shares will recover their value, you sell the stock to realize the loss and trim your tax bill and then you rebuy the shares so that you can profit if the expected rebound occurs.

It will work, but only if you wait at least 30 days after the sale before you rebuy the shares. Otherwise, the IRS will ignore the sale and deny the tax loss. It sees the deal as a wash because you wind up with the same stock in your portfolio.

The wash-sale rule applies if within 30 days *before or after* the sale of stock or other securities showing a loss you buy "substantially identical" stock or securities. There's no precise definition of "substantially identical," but the wash-sale rule clearly puts the kibosh on buying and selling shares of the same company.

Although you can't claim the tax loss on a wash sale, it's really postponed rather than forfeited. You get to add the disallowed loss to the basis of your newly purchased shares. For example, say you bought 100 shares of XYZ stock for $1,000 and later sell them for $750. Within 30 days of that sale, however, you purchase 100 shares of the same stock for $800. Your $250 loss on the sale is disallowed, but you get to add that amount to the $800 cost of the new stock, giving it a basis of $1,050.

Note that the wash-sale rule applies only to losses. It's okay with the IRS if you want to sell securities to realize a taxable profit and then turn around immediately and reinvest in the same issues. Such a move isn't necessarily always a blunder, either. If you have enough other losses to absorb the gain, for example, you'd owe no tax on the sale/repurchase, but your basis in the stock would be bumped up to the higher, new-cost price. That, in turn, would hold down the tax bill when you later dispose of the stock.

Dividends. Ordinary dividends are your share of the earnings and profits of the company whose stock you own. And, like interest on a savings account, such dividends are fully taxable. But not all dividends are considered ordinary and, therefore, different tax rules apply. As an investor, it's up to you to study carefully the 1099-DIV form you receive reporting corporate distributions and to make certain you pay tax on no more than you must.

If you are in a dividend-reinvestment plan, for example, your income for the year includes dividends that are reinvested in additional shares even though you never put your hands on the cash. When a plan permits you to buy shares at a discount from current market value, the amount of the discount is included in your taxable dividend income for the year. Assume that you use your dividends to buy 50 shares of stock at a $2.50-per-share discount. That would give you an extra $125 of dividend income. Your basis in the new shares would be their market value, that is, what you paid plus the discount amount you had to include in your income.

Many reinvestment plans let shareholders buy extra shares, with cash, at a discount, too. If you take advantage of such an offer, the amount of the discount on the extra shares is considered dividend income.

What if the corporation decides to pay dividends on its common stock with extra shares of common stock rather than in cash? Generally, such stock dividends are not taxable. Rather, as with the stock split discussed earlier, the new shares simply dilute your basis in the stock, meaning you'll wind up paying tax on the dividend when you ultimately sell the stock. Say you have 100 shares of stock with a basis of $5,000 and you get a stock dividend of ten shares. The $50-a-share basis in the stock ($5,000 ÷ 100) becomes a $45.45-a-share basis ($5,000 ÷ 110).

If shareholders are given the option of taking the dividend in stock or in cash, the dividend is taxable even if you take the shares. You are taxed on the market value of the stock you receive. In this case, however, the basis of your original shares does not change and your basis in the new shares is the amount you have to include in income.

Companies sometimes make cash payments to shareholders that don't come out of earnings and profits but rather represent a return of part of the investors' original investment. Such returns of capital distributions are not taxable. Instead, they reduce your basis in the stock. That will hike your profit or reduce your loss when you eventually sell the shares but has no immediate effect on your tax bill.

Although taxpayers are often confused, dividends paid on life insurance policies are not dividends as far as the IRS is concerned. Rather, the payments are simply considered a refund of part of the premium you paid for the policy. Such dividends are not taxable, whether you receive them in cash or have them applied to reduce the premium the following year. (As usual, there's an exception: In the unlikely event the dividends surpass the total of premiums paid, the excess would be taxed.)

CORPORATE BONDS

On the face of it, the taxation of interest earned on corporate bonds is simple. These company-issued IOUs generally pay interest every six months, and it is taxable in the year you receive it. Fair enough. And it can work that way if you buy a bond at par—that is, face value—and hold it until maturity. Interest will be taxed as it is received, and when you redeem the bond for exactly what you paid for it, there will be no taxable gain, no taxable loss.

But things often don't work out so neatly.

For one thing, you can buy bonds at a premium (more than face value) or a discount (less than face value). Neither is necessarily a bargain, but both complicate your tax picture.

And the value of bonds can fluctuate wildly while you own them. Because the interest rate paid on the bond is set, the value of the bond rises and falls as market interest rates change. If interest rates spike after you've bought bonds, the value can plunge. No one wants to pay full price for a bond paying 5%, say, if the going rate on newly issued bonds is 10%. If you sell, you'll suffer a loss. Similarly, if in that same 10% environment you own 14% bonds with call protection for several years, you can count on a hefty profit if you sell.

Bond investors need to bone up on the tax rules. Only by understanding the government's take can you choose the investment that gives you the best after-tax return.

Bonds sold between interest dates. Because interest generally is paid every six months, the price of bonds sold between interest dates includes an amount for interest accrued since the last payment date. If you're the seller, that amount is considered interest income—and should be reported as such rather than as part of the price of the bond—for purposes of figuring whether you have a gain or loss on the sale.

If you're the buyer, this "purchased interest" is not part of your basis in the bond. Rather, when you receive your first payment on the bond, part of it is considered a nontaxable return of your investment rather than taxable interest.

For example, assume that you buy a $10,000, 10% bond midway between semiannual $500 interest payments. You pay

$10,250, for the bond and its $250 of accrued interest. When you receive the $500 interest payment on the bond, half of it is considered return of your investment. Although you must report the full $500 on your tax return—on Schedule B—you also get to subtract the $250 "accrued interest." Your basis in the bond is $10,000.

Bonds purchased at discount. Generally, when you sell such property as stocks and bonds for more than you paid for it, the difference is a capital gain. That rule doesn't always apply, however, to bonds purchased at a discount from face value. Different tax rules apply to different types of discounts and to bonds issued at different times.

Some bonds are originally issued at a discount price, which basically means part of the interest won't be paid over the life of the bond but rather in a lump sum when it matures and is redeemed for more than the purchase price. On such original-issue-discount (OID) bonds, the IRS doesn't mind if you put off receipt of the interest, but it won't hold off on the tax bill. Each year that you own the bond you have to report—as interest income—a portion of the discount. There are different methods for figuring how much to report, depending on whether the bond was issued before or after July 1, 1982. Fortunately, though, the issuer should send you a 1099-OID form showing how much to include in your taxable income.

Keep careful records. The original-issue discount reported as income increases your basis in the bond, which will affect the taxable gain or loss when you dispose of the bond.

Bonds issued at par—face value—often sell at a discount, too, due to market forces. As mentioned above, when interest rates rise, the value of bonds carrying yesterday's lower rates fall. Until a few years ago, gain on a market-discount bond held long-term was a capital gain. For bonds issued after July 18, 1984, however, at least part of the gain will be taxed as interest income.

Basically, the difference between what you pay for the bond and its redemption value is considered to be interest that will accrue between the time you buy the bond and when it matures. Unlike the OID rules, you are not required to report the interest annually as it accrues. You can wait until you dispose of the bond—via sale or redemption—and figure what part of the proceeds is interest.

Here's how the calculation works. You divide the market discount by the number of days between your purchase of the bond and its maturity. Multiply the result by the number of the days you held the bond before selling. Say you buy a bond that matures in four years and the market discount is $500. You sell the bond after two years. To determine the amount of the proceeds to report as interest income, divide $500 by 1,461 (the number of days in four years). That gives you 34.22 cents. Multiply that amount by 730 (the number of days in two years). In this example, $250 of the proceeds from the sale of the bond would be treated as interest.

Although not required, you may choose to treat market-discount bonds the same way the law demands that OID bonds be treated. That is, you may report part of the market discount as interest each year as it accrues, paying the tax and increasing your basis as you go along. Beware, though, that you can't use the annual reporting method for some market-discount bonds

"You cannot deduct last year's taxes as a bad investment!"

and not for others. Once you make the election, it applies to all market-discount bonds you own.

Zero-coupon bonds. Take the idea behind original-issue discount to the extreme and, voila, you have the zero-coupon bond. These debt instruments pay no interest over their lifetime but overcome that handicap because they are issued at steep discounts from their redemption value.

How steep? A 30-year zero-coupon bond—with a face value of $10,000 and a yield to maturity of 10%—would cost you just $535. That's $535 today for $10,000 thirty years down the road. The difference is interest that builds up along the way.

A key disadvantage, though, is that the IRS won't wait 30 years to get its cut. The interest is taxed as it accrues. Each year you own zeros, you must report and pay tax on the interest your investment is assumed to have earned that year. It's not as simple as dividing the discount by the number of years until maturity and reporting the result as your annual interest. If that were the case in the example above, you'd divide the $9,465 discount by 30 and report $315 interest a year.

The method required by the IRS is much more complicated but, believe it or not, more advantageous to the taxpayer. Basically, interest is taxed as it would actually accrue. In the example of a $535 investment yielding 10%, the first-year interest would be closer to $55 than the $315 figured under the simpler method. The rate of accrual accelerates over the life of the bonds, so each year you'll have more to report.

Fortunately, you don't need a computer to figure out how much to report. Each year you should receive from the bond issuer or your broker a 1099-OID showing how much interest you must report on your return. As usual, record keeping is essential. All zero-coupon-bond interest you report increases your basis in the bond, which will affect the gain or loss if you sell it before maturity.

The taxability of accruing interest on zeros makes them particularly attractive for funding retirement accounts, such as IRAs and Keoghs, in which the tax bill is deferred. Before tax reform, zeros were also a popular means of saving for a child's education. Purchased in the child's name, the bond's interest was taxable in the child's lower tax bracket or perhaps not at all. Although this can still be an advantageous way to save, you must beware of the effects of the "kiddie tax," discussed in Chapter 3.

Investors can buy tax-free zeros issued by municipalities, an investment that dodges the annual federal tax liability. Because the interest would be tax-free if it were paid periodically, there's no tax problem in having the accruing income assigned to you annually. Even though you face no annual tax bill, the accruing interest does hike your basis in the zero-coupon municipal. You must keep track to hold down the tax bill when you dispose of the bond. (Beware that although the IRS doesn't tax accruing interest on municipal zeros, your state might.)

Bond premiums. The IRS has special rules, too, if you buy a bond for more than face value, as you might if the bond pays higher interest than current market rates. You get your choice of amortizing the premium over the life of the bond—claiming a tax-saving deduction each year—or dealing with the premium when you dispose of the bond. If you hold the bond to maturity and redeem it for face value, the extra amount you paid for it can be claimed as a capital loss.

If you choose to amortize the premium, you have to figure how much to deduct each year. You use IRS Form 4562, which you attach to your tax return. The method for figuring how much of a premium to deduct each year depends on when the bond was originally issued. For those issued before September 28, 1985, you can determine the annual deduction by dividing the premium amount by the number of years to maturity (or to the call date if that option would produce a smaller deduction). For bonds issued after September 27, 1985, the amortization deduction must be based on your yield to maturity on the bond. The amount will change each year. You may well need an accountant's help to figure out how much to deduct.

As you amortize the premium, your basis in the bond decreases in step with the deductions you claim. (If you buy a tax-exempt bond at a premium, you must amortize the premium over the life of the bond, but you get no deduction. Your basis falls each year, though, in accordance with the amount of the premium allocable to the year.)

The alternative to amortizing your bond premium is to report the interest income as you receive it and wait until you dispose of the bond to collect the tax savings you're due. If you don't amortize, you don't have to reduce your basis. If you redeem the bond at par, you'll have a capital loss to the tune of the premium. Basically, since you didn't write off the premium over the years, you get to deduct it all at once.

Convertible bonds. These are bonds that can be exchanged for a specified number of shares of stock in the same company. Promoters call them the best of both worlds because they let you lock in the steady income of a bond and still have the chance to enjoy the appreciation of a stock. The IRS is willing to go along. The bond interest you receive is taxable, just as on any bond. If you opt to convert to the stock, that transaction is not taxable. Your basis in the bonds simply shifts to the stock, so your basis in the shares is what you paid for the bonds plus any extra you shelled out to convert. Only when you later sell the stock will the tax bill come due.

U.S. government obligations. The tax treatment of Uncle Sam's IOUs is similar to that of corporate bonds. An important exception, though, is that interest on Treasury bills, notes and bonds is exempt from state and local income taxes—just as is interest on U.S. savings bonds.

Say, for example, that you live in a state with an 8% state income tax and have your choice between investing $10,000 in a fully taxable corporate bond yielding 10% and a state tax-exempt Treasury note yielding 10%. Either investment will generate $1,000 of interest income, and if you're in the 28% federal tax bracket, the IRS will demand $280 of your earnings. On the T-note, that's all you'd have to pay. With the corporate bond, however, your state would get a bite of your income, claiming $80. (Because that state tax bill would be deductible on your federal return—saving you 28% of that $80—the actual extra cost would be $57.60.)

T-bills, which are issued with 13-week, 26-week and 52-week maturities, also offer investors the chance to defer income from one year to the next. The bills are issued at discount, with the interest paid when they are redeemed at face value. The tax isn't due until the year the bills mature.

If you sell a T-bill before maturity, part of the sales price is considered accrued interest and must be reported as interest income rather than taken into account when figuring capital gain or loss. The amount counted as interest is determined by dividing the number of days you owned the T-bill by the number of days in its term and multiplying the result by the discount. For example, assume you buy a six-month T-bill at a discount of $500 from face value and sell it after four months. Divide 120 (the number of days in four months) by 180 (days in six months). Multiply the result (0.66) by the $500 discount to find that $333 of the sales proceeds should be reported as interest.

Treasury notes and bonds. These are similar except that notes have maturities ranging from one to ten years and bonds are issued with maturities in excess of ten years. Both pay interest every six months, and the interest is taxable each year as you receive it. Basically, when these obligations are purchased at a discount or premium price, the same rules apply as for corporate IOUs.

Ginnie Maes. Investors in Ginnie Maes buy into a pool of government-backed home mortgages. Although payment of both principal and interest is guaranteed by a federal agency—the Government National Mortgage Association (GNMA)—the income is not automatically exempt from state taxes. However, part of each payment will be totally tax-free. That's because you're really just getting back some of your own money.

Remember, Ginnie Maes represent an investment in home mortgages. As homeowners make their monthly payments, your share of the interest and principal is passed on to you. The principal portion is a return of your investment and therefore is not taxable. With each payment, you should get a statement showing what part is taxable interest income and what part nontaxable return of principal. Keep careful records to insure you don't pay tax on the return of your own money.

Municipal bonds. Just as U.S. government securities are exempt from state and local income taxes, IOUs issued by states and municipalities escape the grasp of federal revenuers. Known generically as municipal bonds, these tax-exempt issues usually carry a lower interest rate than fully taxable bonds. Investors make up the difference—and sometimes more—via tax savings.

By pulling down federal tax rates, tax reform diluted the value of tax exemptions. When investors could pay as much as 50% of their taxable income to Uncle Sam, for example, a 5% tax-free yield was worth as much as a 10% taxable yield. Now, with the top rate at 33%, the tax appeal of municipal bonds is somewhat tarnished.

Tax-exempts can still be good investments, however. For one thing, as the tax benefits change so does the spread between tax-exempt and taxable interest rates. With less of a subsidy from Uncle Sam, municipalities have to offer higher yields to attract investors.

To know whether municipals make sense for you, you need to compute the taxable-equivalent yield—that is, how much you would have to earn on a taxable investment to have as much left over after taxes. The table on page 122 shows the taxable equivalents for tax-free bonds issued at various interest rates. Here's the formula for figuring the precise taxable-equivalent rate for any bond you consider:

$$\frac{\text{tax-free rate}}{1 - \text{federal tax bracket}} = \text{taxable-equivalent rate}$$

For example, assume you are in the 33% tax bracket and are offered a 5.75% tax-free bond. You would divide 5.75 by 0.67 (1 − 0.33) and find that the taxable-equivalent yield is 8.58%. In other words, you'd need a taxable investment paying more than 8.58% to beat the return on the 5.75% tax-exempt.

There's a similar formula for figuring things the other way, to find the tax-exempt equivalent of a taxable yield:

taxable rate × (1 − federal tax bracket) = tax-free rate

Assume you are considering a taxable investment yielding 10%. If you are in the 33% tax bracket, multiply 10 by 0.67 (1 − 0.33). The result is 6.7, telling you that a 6.7% tax-free yield will put the same amount in your pocket after tax as a 10% taxable yield.

TAXABLE-EQUIVALENT YIELDS

This table shows the taxable-equivalent yield of tax-exempt investments for investors in various tax brackets. If you are married and file a joint return, for example, and your taxable income for 1988 falls between $29,751 and $71,900, you're in the 28% tax bracket. If you're considering a tax-exempt investment paying 5%, find the figure at the point where your 28% tax bracket intersects with the 5% tax-free yield. It's 6.94%, meaning you'd need a taxable investment paying 6.94% to match the after-tax yield on the tax-exempt offering.

The formula for determining the taxable-equivalent yields for bonds offered at rates not shown in the table is shown on page 121.

1988 TAXABLE INCOME	TAX BRACKET	TAX-FREE YIELD						
		4%	5%	6%	7%	8%	9%	10%
SINGLE RETURN		TAXABLE EQUIVALENT						
Up to $17,850	15%	4.71%	5.88%	7.06%	8.24%	9.41%	10.59%	11.76%
$17,851 to $43,150	28	5.56	6.94	8.33	9.72	11.11	12.50	13.89
$43,151 to $89,560*	33	5.97	7.46	8.96	10.45	11.94	13.43	14.93
Over $89,560	28	5.56	6.94	8.33	9.72	11.11	12.50	13.89
JOINT RETURN		TAXABLE EQUIVALENT						
Up to $29,750	15%	4.71%	5.88%	7.06%	8.24%	9.41%	10.59%	11.76%
$29,751 to $71,900	28	5.56	6.94	8.33	9.72	11.11	12.50	13.89
$71,901 to $149,250*	33	5.97	7.46	8.96	10.45	11.94	13.43	14.93
Over $149,250	28	5.56	6.94	8.33	9.72	11.11	12.50	13.89

* See Chapter 1 for circumstances under which the 33% bracket can extend to higher incomes.

Taxable equivalents get a boost when you buy tax-exempts issued within the boundaries of your own state if your state, like most, exempts income on such bonds from state as well as federal tax. If you happen to face a city income tax, municipals can brag of triple tax-free status—shielded from federal, state and local income tax.

Figuring taxable-equivalent yields gets more complicated if your investment dodges both state and federal tax. Because state income taxes paid are deductible on your federal return (if you itemize) you can't simply add the state rate to the federal rate in the formulas above. First, you must find the effective state tax rate—what you pay minus the tax savings of deducting that amount. For example, if you pay a 10% state tax and deduct it in the 33% federal bracket, your effective state tax rate is 6.7% (the 10% state tax rate minus 33% of that rate). Thus, in the formula given on page 121 for figuring taxable equivalents, the divisor would be 1 minus the combination of your federal rate (33%) and your effective state rate (6.7%), or 1 − 39.7%, or 60.3%. If you are considering a 7% municipal that is exempt from both state and local taxes, you would divide 7 by 0.603 and find that the taxable equivalent is 11.61%.

If you live in one of the following states, there's an advantage to buying in-state municipals because these states tax the income on out-of-state bonds but give the tax-free nod to in-state obligations.

Alabama	Maine	North Carolina
Arizona	Maryland	North Dakota
Arkansas	Massachusetts	Ohio
California	Michigan	Oregon
Colorado	Minnesota	Pennsylvania
Connecticut	Mississippi	Rhode Island
Delaware	Missouri	South Carolina
Georgia	Montana	Tennessee
Hawaii	Nebraska	Vermont
Idaho	New Hampshire	Virginia
Kentucky	New Jersey	West Virginia
Louisiana	New York	

In the rest of the states and the District of Columbia your after-tax yield will be the same on either in- or out-of-state bonds, but for different reasons. Kansas, Illinois, Iowa, Oklahoma and Wisconsin tax the income on both kinds of bonds while the following tax neither:

Alaska	Nevada	Utah
District of Columbia	New Mexico	Washington
Florida	South Dakota	Wyoming
Indiana	Texas	

Taxable tax-exempts. Call it an oxymoron if you want, but some tax-exempt bonds generate interest that can fall victim to the alternative minimum tax (AMT). Worried that some municipalities were taking unfair advantage of the federal tax exemption to raise "nonessential" funds at below-market rates, Congress made interest on "private purpose" bonds a preference item for the AMT, as discussed in Chapter 15.

Although interest from these bonds remains tax free for the vast majority of taxpayers—who are not subject to the AMT—such interest is taxed at 21% for those who fall under the AMT. Only certain bonds issued after August 7, 1986, are affected, and your bond dealer should be able to tell you whether bonds you are considering fall in the AMT shadow. This rule creates a potential benefit for some taxpayers. The AMT threat pushes up the yield slightly on affected private-activity bonds, and that's a bonus for investors who don't have to worry about the AMT.

Tax-exempts and social security. Taxpayers who receive social security benefits could argue that the new alternative minimum tax threat isn't the first time Uncle Sam decided to tax tax-exempt income. Since 1984, tax-exempt interest has been included in the calculation to determine what part, if any, of social security benefits are taxed. Since that could trigger a tax on otherwise tax-free benefits, many investors have seen this as a back-door way to tax their municipal-bond income.

Social security benefits are taxable only if your modified adjusted gross income for the year exceeds a certain base amount—$25,000 if you file a single return, $32,000 if you file jointly. The catch is that in this case, modified AGI includes tax-free bond interest. Basically, if your adjusted gross income for the year plus your tax-free income plus one-half of your social security benefits exceeds the base amount, up to 50% of your benefits can be taxed. See Chapter 8 for more details.

Whether or not your tax-free income may be nipped either by the tax on social security or the alternative minimum levy, the IRS now wants to know just how much tax-exempt income you receive. There is a line on the tax forms to report this income. **Gains and losses on municipal bonds.** Although interest from municipal bonds is exempt from the federal income tax, the IRS doesn't ignore the gain or loss that results when you sell the bonds. If you sell a bond for more than your basis, the profit is a capital gain; if you sell it for less, it's a deductible capital loss.

In general, your basis is figured the same way as for taxable corporate bonds. However, if you buy a tax-exempt bond at a premium, you must amortize the premium over the period you own the bond. This amortization reduces your basis in the bond, but unlike a taxable bond, you get no annual deduction for the amortized amount. Because the interest you earn is tax-free—and you paid the premium to get a higher-than-current-market, tax-free rate—the premium amortization is not deductible.

If you buy a bond originally issued at a discount, you increase your basis each year as is required with taxable bonds, but you don't have to report the annual amortization of the discount as income. It, like interest paid on the bond, is tax-free.

Buy a municipal bond at a market discount, however, and different rules apply. You don't amortize the market discount. Rather, your basis remains stable, and when you redeem the bond at face value, the difference between what you paid and what you receive is a taxable capital gain.

Bond swaps. If you own bonds showing a significant paper loss, which is quite possible if market interest rates are higher now than when you purchased the securities, you may want to consider a bond swap. With this maneuver, you simply sell the bonds to realize your loss and then reinvest the proceeds in other bonds. Depending on the quality and maturity of the replacement bonds, it's possible to wind up with bonds paying higher income than the ones you unloaded. In addition, you get the tax savings generated by deducting the capital loss. The wash-sale rule discussed on page 111 would disallow the tax savings if the replacement bonds are "substantially identical" to the ones you unloaded. Your broker should be able to help you select replacement bonds that don't run afoul of this rule.

You can avoid most of the tax headaches associated with bonds by investing in them via mutual funds or unit trusts that give you a share of a diversified portfolio of bonds. You get professional managers who not only choose the bonds for the portfolio but worry about the tax ramifications. In most cases, you'll get a year-end report including the information you need to file your tax return. You must keep track of your basis in your investment in the mutual fund or trust, as discussed in the next section, but you don't have to worry about such details as amortizing bond discounts or premiums.

If the funds invest in tax-free issues, the income that is passed on to you retains its tax-exempt status. Some unit trusts are available, in fact, that invest only in bonds issued by an individual state—insuring investors a double tax exemption.

MUTUAL FUNDS

When you invest in a mutual fund, you buy a sliver of a huge collection of stocks or bonds. It's a convenient way to buy into a diversified portfolio with professional management, but don't think it relieves you of record-keeping chores or income-tax considerations.

Except for money-market funds, in which the value of shares remains constant, the price of mutual-fund shares fluctuates, just like the price of individual stocks and bonds. When you sell shares, you need to know exactly what your tax basis is to pinpoint the taxable gain or loss. Set up a separate file for each fund you invest in and faithfully keep it up to date. Beyond simplifying your life at tax-return time, there's a good chance thorough records will save you money.

Your basis in the shares begins as what you pay for them. If you invest in a no-load fund—one free of a sales commission—your basis is the same as the share's net asset value on the day you buy. If you buy into a load fund, your per-share basis is the total investment divided by the number of shares you receive.

For example, consider two funds: Fund A has no load, Fund B has an 8.5% load. Assume that when you invest, the shares in each fund have a net asset value of $20. If you put $1,000 in the no-load fund, you get 50 shares, each with a tax basis of $20. Invest in the load fund, however, and $85 of the $1,000 will go to pay the commission. The remaining $915 buys 45.75 shares, each with a basis of $21.86.

Assume you later redeem the shares for $21 each. Your investment in Fund A will result in a $50 gain ($1,050 proceeds minus $1,000 basis). The investment in Fund B leaves you with a $39.25 loss ($960.75 proceeds minus $1,000 basis).

Your basis in the shares can change while you own them, too. On rare occasions, funds declare capital gains but retain the profits and pay tax on them rather than distribute the profit to shareholders. Such undistributed capital gains increase your basis in fund shares and complicate your tax return.

If your fund does this, you'll receive a Form 2439 showing your share of the undistributed gain and your portion of the tax bill the fund paid on the gain. You have to report the undistributed gain as taxable income—even though you didn't get it— but you also get to claim a tax credit for the amount of tax paid by the fund on your behalf. You also increase the tax basis by the difference between the undistributed gain you report and the credit you claim.

For example, say you own 100 shares of a mutual fund that reports an undistributed gain of $100 and a tax paid of $34. You'd report the $100 of income, take a credit for the $34 of tax paid and increase your basis in the shares by $66—or 66 cents a share. That might appear to be a hassle, but remember that hiking your basis will trim the tax bill due when you ultimately sell your shares.

Just as you may have to report mutual fund income you don't receive, it's possible to get a payment from the fund that's not taxable. Funds occasionally make a payment that doesn't come out of earnings or profits. Such return of capital distributions are sometimes called tax-free dividends or nontaxable distributions, but they should not be confused with tax-free income passed through to owners of tax-exempt bond funds. Instead, they are a return of your investment and reduce your basis in the mutual fund shares. Although you don't have to pay tax on these distributions, there is a place on Schedule B to report them so the IRS can remind you to adjust your basis.

It's likely you'll be buying shares at different times, too, which guarantees to complicate your tax picture. If you sign up for a dividend-reinvestment plan—so that fund earnings are reinvested in additional shares rather than paid out to you in cash—you'll be buying new shares each month or however often the fund distributes income. Say, for example, that you earn $87.50 in dividends that are reinvested in shares that on the date of the distribution are selling for $18.77 a share. You get 4.66 shares, each with an $18.77 basis.

You need to keep a running tally of your investment in the fund. If you liquidate your entire investment at once, your gain or loss will be determined by comparing how much you get with how much you paid for every share you own, whether purchased outright or via dividend reinvestment. By keeping track of all those dividend reinvestments, you'll be sure not to pay more tax than you owe.

If you sell only some of your shares, your record keeping can pay off handsomely. In choosing which shares to sell, you can pick the ones with the basis that produces the best tax result. Assuming all your shares have appreciated, if you sell those with the highest basis, you will wind up with the lowest taxable gain. If your other investments have produced capital losses, however, you may want to sell low-basis shares to take a bigger profit for the losses to offset.

Since your shares are pooled in a single account by the mutual fund, who knows which shares are sold and which retained? You do, if you have the records and direct the fund to sell shares you can specifically identify. If you have records showing you told the fund to sell specific shares—a note identifying the shares by the date you acquired them and the price you paid, for example—it's the basis of those shares that determines the tax consequences of the sale.

If you simply call or write the fund and ask that a certain number of shares be redeemed without specifying which ones, however, the same FIFO rule that applies to individual stocks and bonds comes into play. It is assumed that the first stocks sold are the first ones you bought.

The IRS does permit mutual fund investors to use an "average" basis for figuring gain or loss on the sale of fund shares. Basically, you divide your total investment in the fund by the number of shares you own and compare that average basis to the proceeds of the sale. (IRS Publication 564, *Mutual Fund Distributions,* explains this procedure.) Although that might sound simpler than specifically identifying shares, it means forfeiting important flexibility. You're much better off keeping the records you need to identify shares and controlling the tax consequences of the sale.

Mutual fund shareholders sometimes get an unpleasant surprise at tax time when they learn belatedly that switching among mutual funds—even funds in the same "family" of funds—is a taxable transaction. Inside a fund family, for example, a telephone call can send your money from a stock fund focusing on a specific sector of the market to a bond fund invested heavily in low-grade securities or a money fund investing in only rock-solid U.S. Treasury securities. It's so easy that the tax consequences can be overlooked.

Remember, though, that such a switch means selling shares in the fund you're leaving. Unless you're moving funds out of a money-market fund, the switch usually produces a taxable capital gain or a tax-saving loss.

The wash sale discussed on page 111 applies to mutual-fund shares just as it does to stocks and bonds. If you sell shares for a loss and within 30 days before or after the sale buy back into the fund, your loss is disallowed for tax purposes.

Annual fund income. Even in years you don't sell shares, the IRS is interested in your fund investments, as they are likely to be generating taxable income. In January you should receive a 1099-DIV form from each fund in which you own shares, showing income received during the year. Many funds have their year-end statement do double duty, serving as the 1099-DIV as well as the regular report to shareholders.

Income from money-market and taxable bond funds is considered dividend income for tax purposes, even though the source of the income is interest. The fact that it is being funneled through the fund changes its tax status. (If you goof and report this income as interest, you may hear from the IRS demanding tax on the dividends and a penalty for failing to report them.)

If you invest in a tax-free municipal-bond fund, the income passed through to you retains its shield from federal income tax. Although dodging Uncle Sam, the income may well be taxed by your state. However, the percentage of the income representing interest from bonds issued within your state may be state-tax-free, too. (See the discussion of municipal bonds on page 121.) Your fund should tell you what portion of the income you received was attributed to such homegrown issues. Many tax-exempt funds also hold "private-activity" bonds, the interest from which can be hit by the alternative minimum tax. If you're subject to the AMT, check the mutual fund's portfolio carefully. You may do better investing in a fund that spurns bonds potentially subject to the AMT.

Some funds invest only in U.S. government securities, the interest from which would be free from state tax if the investor owned the obligations directly. Many states allow income from such funds to retain that state-tax-free status. Other states take the position that citizens who choose this type of fund are investing in the fund rather than in the U.S. obligations. With that rationale, those states tax the income. If you invest in this kind of fund, check with state tax authorities about the tax status of the income. In mid 1988, the following states did not tax dividends paid by mutual funds that invest in federal obligations:

Alabama	Kentucky	Oregon
Alaska	Louisiana	Rhode Island
Arizona	Maine	South Carolina
California	Massachusetts	South Dakota
Colorado	Michigan	Texas
District of Columbia	Missouri	Utah
Florida	Montana	Virginia
Georgia	Nebraska	Washington
Hawaii	Nevada	West Virginia
Idaho	New York	Wyoming
Kansas	North Carolina	

In other states, either such dividends were taxed or the tax status was uncertain. Unless you are absolutely certain your state taxes such income, be sure to check before you report it on your state return.

Ordinary dividends—basically your share of the fund's dividend or interest income—are taxable in the year paid, whether you have the dividends paid out in cash or have them reinvested in new shares.

A Form 1099-DIV may report to you a capital-gains distribution, which is your share of the profits fund managers scored by trading within the portfolio during the year. Regardless of how long you owned the mutual fund shares, this income is considered a long-term capital gain.

Even a tax-exempt municipal-bond fund can show a taxable capital-gains distribution. That's not back-door taxation because the payout doesn't come from tax-free interest earned by the fund. Rather, it is your share of the profit realized when the fund manager sold bonds from the portfolio.

In recent years, the top-performing mutual funds have included funds that invest in foreign securities. If you own shares in such a fund, you may be in line for a foreign tax credit. If so, your 1099-DIV will show the amount of foreign tax paid on your behalf. You have to include that amount with your taxable income for the year, but you also get the choice of either deducting it along with the other taxes you write off as itemized deductions or tackling the two-page Form 1116 to compute the foreign tax credit to claim on your tax return. Despite the hassle, your best bet is to figure the tax benefit both ways to determine which will be more advantageous.

Phantom income. Here's one of tax reform's real crowd pleasers: Congress decided that investors should pay tax on mutual fund income they never receive. Funds were to include in income reported to shareholders the management fee charged by the fund. Even investors in tax-exempt funds were to be stuck with a tax bill on this "phantom income."

Those management costs are normally subtracted from gross income before the net is distributed to shareholders. Congress decided that, for tax purposes, investors should be treated as though they received extra income equal to their share of the management fees and then paid that amount back to the fund. This bookkeeping sleight of hand would leave investors with no more in their pockets but would give Uncle Sam more to tax.

Although this rule was supposed to go into effect in 1987, numerous complaints led Congress to postpone it until 1988. As this book went to print it was all but certain that new legislation would rescind the phantom-income provision altogether.

PASSIVE-LOSS RULES

For years, Congress chipped away at tax shelters, those investments with more tax appeal than economic sense. The 1986 law dealt shelters a grievous blow with the hope of bringing an end to deals that thrive on the seemingly daffy promise of huge losses.

The latest antishelter weapon is a new category in the tax lexicon: passive activity. It includes investments in a business in which you don't "materially" participate—including all limited partnerships. Practically all rental activities fall in the passive category, too, regardless of how involved you may be. (A valuable exception applies to owners of rental real estate who are "actively" involved. The details are in Chapter 6.) The material-participation test is a tough one, demanding that you be regularly and substantially involved in the business year-round.

The killer is that losses from investments branded passive can't be used to shelter income from other activities, such as your job or investments in stocks and bonds. For example, the law now prevents paper losses generated by a limited partnership—via the pass-through of oil depletion write-offs, perhaps, or real estate depreciation deductions—from wiping out part of the tax bill on your salary or portfolio income. Most passive losses come from limited partnerships and real estate, but the crackdown can affect businesses that generally aren't labeled tax shelters.

Consider the case of two brothers who jointly own a tobacco store. One brother actually runs the store, working in it 40 hours a week and making most of the purchasing and hiring decisions single-handedly. The other brother's interest is mostly financial, and although he has a voice in major decisions, he is seldom involved in the day-to-day operations. The brother who works in the store would pass the material-participation test and wouldn't have to worry about the passive-activity rule. His brother, however, would be tripped up by the rule and would be forbidden to use his share of the store's losses to shelter his other income.

IRS-issued regulations outline what's required to pass the material-participation test and thus qualify to write off business losses against nonbusiness income. You pass the test if:

• You work in the business 500 or more hours during the year;

• You are the primary person involved, virtually to the exclusion of everyone else, even if you put in less than 500 hours; or

• You put in at least 100 hours during the year and it's more time than anyone else has put in, including employees.

The IRS also came up with a "significant participation" test, which involves working in the business more than 100 hours during the year but not up to the 500-hour threshold. If you earn "significant" status for two or more businesses, and the combined time you work exceeds 500 hours, you pass the material-participation test for each activity.

You also avoid the passive classification if you have met any of the above requirements during five of the previous ten years. However, if the business is a personal-service activity—such as a legal, accounting or medical practice—it is not branded as passive if any of the material-participation tests were passed during any three years in the past. Although that might sound like a break, it's actually aimed at blocking a possible end-run around the passive-loss rules.

For example, assume that you have a profitable business in which you materially participate and also have investments in a limited partnership that is throwing off significant losses. Under the rules, you can't use those losses to shelter the business income. However, some advisers thought that if you scaled back your hours to purposely flunk the material-participation tests, the business income could be reclassified as passive income and be sheltered from tax by the limited partnership losses. The five-out-of-ten and three-year tests put the kibosh on such strategies.

(There is an exception to the passive-loss rules that lets investors in certain oil- and gas-drilling ventures write off losses against other income even if the investor doesn't materially participate. Although this exception got a lot of attention when Congress passed tax reform—as a loophole fashioned by powerful lobbyists—it is a tight loophole. It applies only to investors with a "working interest" in an oil or gas venture. That entails far more personal liability than a typical limited partnership. The trade-off for not materially participating is to take on much more risk.)

Passive losses you can't deduct immediately are not rendered worthless. For one thing, any deductions you deserve for passive-activity-related expenses—such as interest payments or depreciation—can still offset income from that investment. Any excess loss can be used to shelter income from other passive activities, such as a profitable rental or partnership.

Beyond that, any leftover loss will be suspended until a future year when you have passive income to offset. When you dispose of an investment that has generated unused losses, those losses are unleashed to shelter any income, whether passive or not.

Much to the chagrin of tax-shelter investors, the passive-loss rules apply even to deals entered into during the good old days before tax reform. To ease the pain, however, Congress provided a phase-in period during which a portion of otherwise suspended passive losses may be deducted against nonpassive income. Here's the schedule:

Year	Percent of Passive Loss Allowed
1988	40%
1989	20
1990	10
1991 and later	0

The phase-in period applies only to investments entered into on or before the Tax Reform Act of 1986 was signed into law on October 22, 1986. For investments made after that date, the passive-loss rule is fully effective now.

A potentially painful curve is thrown to taxpayers liable for the alternative minimum tax (Chapter 15). They don't get the advantage of the phase-in period. When figuring the AMT, no passive losses may be deducted.

Investors in passive activities must assess the damage inflicted by these rules. First, net the results of your various passive activities. Only if the total loss exceeds total passive income do you have a loss that may be suspended. Look ahead, too. In the past, some limited partnerships were designed specifically to throw off heavy losses in the early years and then become income producers. The closer you are to the turn-around, the less you have to worry about the passive-loss rules.

If it's clear the new rules will cause you financial pain, you have several choices. One is to ditch the investment. That may be much easier said than done. You may have to take a distress-sale price that could be worse than the suspension of the tax benefits. You could try to restructure the investment to curb the tax loss—refinancing debt on rental property, perhaps, or raising rents.

Another choice is to seek out investments that produce passive income. Such passive-income generators—affectionately known as PIGs—could give you the income you need to absorb passive losses. With the general crackdown on shelters, many real estate limited partnerships are being designed as income producers—with less debt and therefore less in mortgage interest deductions to be passed on to investors. One kind of partnership often mentioned as a PIG is one that invests in parking lots: As there are no buildings to depreciate, such deals are more likely to throw off income.

Another point to keep in mind: The new rules create new planning opportunities along with the headaches. Losses suspended under the new law could wind up being worth more to you in the future when you get to use them—to shelter a big profit when you finally dispose of the passive investment, for example. That's particularly true if the alternative to generating unusable passive income now is an investment offering only mediocre return or if future tax laws raise tax rates. Who knows, a loss suspended when you're in the 28% bracket might be triggered when you're in a much higher bracket.

Whatever you do, don't let the quest to preserve passive write-offs lead you into a lousy investment. Remember, you'd have to invest $100,000 in a passive activity yielding 10% to absorb $10,000 of threatened losses. One of the goals of tax reform was to get investors to spend less—not more—time finagling their portfolios for tax purposes.

LIFE INSURANCE

As Congress has squeezed the tax benefits out of many investments, life insurance has taken on a special glow. Policies that combine investments with insurance—including whole life, universal life and single-premium life policies—enjoy tax-favored status. Part, and sometimes a very substantial part, of the premiums go not to pay for insurance but into investments that build cash value. The tax break is that earnings on the cash value are protected from the IRS. The tax bill is deferred until you cash in the policy, or if it is in force when you die, the proceeds go to your beneficiary completely free of any federal income tax.

There are even ways to get at those earnings—tax-free—without dying for the privilege. Policyholders are permitted to borrow against the cash value in their policies. They are very special loans, too, since they never have to be paid back. Any outstanding loan at the time of death is simply deducted from the proceeds paid to beneficiaries. Although borrowers have to pay interest on the policy loan, in the sweetest deals the cash value in the policy earns just as much as the interest charged.

For a glimpse of the advantages, consider the most extreme example: single-premium life policies that are mostly investment, with barely enough insurance veneer to qualify for the tax breaks. As the name implies, you pay the premium only once and that buys you a paid-up policy. The death benefit is small, but the key here is the investment.

With most policies, the entire premium immediately starts earning interest—or may be invested in your choice of various stock and bond funds—and starts building cash value. The cost of insurance comes out of your earnings.

Because the investment is wrapped inside an insurance policy, the earnings accumulate tax-free, just as money in an individual retirement account grows without annual interruption from the IRS. A $100,000 investment in a single-premium policy yielding 10% annually, for example, would grow to over $672,750 in 20 years. The same amount in a taxable investment would reach just $335,838 in two decades if you're in the 33% tax bracket.

Although the original investment is not deductible, as it can be with an IRA, the insurance policy has an advantage over the IRA. It's possible for the earnings to be completely tax-free. With an IRA, although the earnings grow tax-deferred, the money is taxed when withdrawn, and if you tap the account before you reach age 59½, you'll also be hit with a penalty.

If you cash in the life insurance policy, your earnings will be taxed, too. But you can dance around the tax bill by borrowing against the policy. Most single-premium policies are designed so that in most cases there is effectively no charge for the loan. Interest on the loan is offset by earnings that continue to be credited to your cash value. Although structured as a loan, it works like a withdrawal in that it doesn't cost you anything, and as mentioned above, you don't have to pay the money back.

These policies have been promoted as investments to enhance your retirement nest egg—particularly if the new IRA rules (discussed in Chapter 7) deny you the right to deduct annual contributions. An extra advantage as part of a retirement savings plan is that money borrowed from a policy won't count as income for purposes of figuring out what part, if any, of your social security benefits are taxable.

Crackdown coming. If this sounds too good to last, you are hearing right. The tax shelter side of insurance was promoted so heavily in the aftermath of tax reform, in fact, that as this book went to press it seemed certain that Congress would crack down. A proposal that appeared to be on its way to becoming law would tax distributions—including loans—and hit policyholders under age 59½ with a 10% penalty similar to the early-withdrawal penalty on annuities, discussed below. Single-premium policies would be affected, as would any policy funded at a rate faster than seven annual premiums.

Watch this area closely if you consider this kind of invest-ment. It appeared likely to grandfather policies funded before a certain date—probably around mid 1988—meaning owners would continue to enjoy the tax benefits promised when they made the investments. In addition to keeping an eye on the lawmakers, watch for ingenious insurance companies to cook up new policies to take advantage of whatever tax advantages survive.

Annuities. These are also life insurance products sporting tax advantages. But there's no life insurance involved. You invest in

© 1988 MIKE LUCKOVICH
NEW ORLEANS TIMES-PICAYUNE

the annuity, and earnings accumulate tax-free until you begin to withdraw the funds. Holding off the IRS in the interim super-charges the power of compounding and leaves you well ahead even after paying the deferred tax bill.

Annuities come in two basic flavors: fixed and variable. With a fixed annuity, your investment earns interest at a rate set by the insurance company, a rate that can change periodically in line with market interest rates. A variable annuity gives you investment options much like a family of mutual funds. The insurance company offers you the choice of several funds—stock, bond, money-market, etc.—and your return depends on the success of the investments in which you deploy your money.

Unlike bank CDs and mutual funds, however, the annuity contract serves as an impenetrable wrapper that keeps the tax collector's hands off your earnings. No tax is due until you pull funds out of the contract, presumably in retirement, either in a lump sum or by annuitizing the contract and having the company make payments to you for life.

Such tax-deferred growth gives funds invested in an annuity the same advantage as cash stashed in an individual retirement account, discussed in Chapter 7. Unlike an IRA, though, you can't deduct amounts put into an annuity.

If you cash in the annuity before retirement, you'll pay dearly. For one thing, most contracts impose surrender charges during the first several years. Any earnings pulled out of the annuity are taxable, and if you're under age 59½, you'll be hit with a 10% penalty tax. What portion of the withdrawal represents earnings that are taxable and penalty-prone? If you cash in the annuity and pull out all the funds, the difference between your original investment and what you get is taxable. But if you pull out only part of the money, what part is taxable turns on when you made the annuity investment. If it was on or before August 13, 1982, the IRS considers the first money pulled out of the annuity to be a tax-free return of your investment. Only after you have recovered your full investment is any further withdrawal taxed. For investments after that date, however, the rule is turned around. The first money out is considered earnings—taxable and potentially subject to the 10% penalty.

Say, for example, that you now invest $10,000 in an annuity and its value grows to $25,000 in ten years. If you were to cash in the contract, $15,000 would be taxed, and if you were under age 59½, the 10% early-withdrawal penalty would apply to that portion. The other $10,000 would be a tax-free return of your original investment. If you simply withdrew $10,000 from the contract, it would all be taxed and penalized. If this investment had been made on or before August 13, 1982, however, that $10,000 withdrawal would be a nontaxable return of your investment. (If you choose to receive lifetime payments, a portion of each one is tax-free, as discussed in Chapter 8.)

The 10% penalty does not apply to payouts to taxpayers under age 59½ who are disabled. Nor does it apply to any payment that is part of a series of periodic payments based on your life expectancy. If you decide to annuitize a contract at age 50 and receive equal payments over the rest of your life, for example, you wouldn't be hit with the early-withdrawal penalty.

A key to shopping for an annuity is to watch that the fees charged by the insurance company don't devour a good portion of the tax breaks.

INVESTMENT INTEREST

If you borrow money to make an investment, the interest on the loan is deductible—in most cases. As usual, the law includes exceptions and limitations to keep you on your toes.

First, the exceptions. For the interest to be deductible, the investment has to be designed to produce taxable income. Interest on a margin loan from your broker to invest in stocks or taxable bonds qualifies. But if the borrowings are used to invest in tax-exempt securities, the interest is not deductible. Ditto if you borrow to buy a single-premium life insurance policy or annuity. Congress doesn't want the IRS subsidizing loans to help you purchase tax-favored investments.

If you borrow to invest in a passive activity, the interest is an expense of the passive activity (see page 132)—and thus is deductible only to the extent of passive income.

There is a limit to how much investment interest you can deduct, too, and the ceiling is falling. Before tax reform, you could deduct investment interest up to the amount of your investment income plus $10,000. That was plenty high to insure that most investors' interest expenses would be fully deductible. Tax reform is phasing out that extra $10,000 so that beginning in 1991 investment-interest write-offs will be limited to investment income reported.

For 1988, the limit is investment income plus 40% of up to $10,000 of interest that exceeds the income level. That's not the same as saying investment income plus $4,000. An investor whose investment interest comes to $5,000 over investment income would be permitted to write off just 40% of that $5,000 ($2,000) in addition to an amount equal to his or her investment income. In 1989, the limit is investment income plus 20% of up to $10,000 of excess interest, and in 1990 the cap is investment income plus 10%.

The investment-interest deduction cap is the same whether you are single or married filing a joint return. If you're married and file separate returns, however, the limit is your investment income plus half of the declining excess amount. For 1988, for example, on a married-filing-separately return, the limit would be investment income plus 40% of up to $5,000 of extra investment interest.

The investment income on which the interest limit is based includes income from interest, dividends, rents and capital gains. For 1988, 1989 and 1990 investment income for this purpose is reduced by the amount of any otherwise disallowable passive losses you are permitted to claim under the phase-in of those rules. (Note, however, that at press time Congress was expected to eliminate this requirement.)

Any interest you are unable to deduct because of the investment-income cap is not lost forever. It may be carried over to future years and deducted as soon as there is sufficient investment income to offset it, or on the final tax return after your death.

OTHER EXPENSES

Even if you don't borrow to help finance your investment portfolio, there are plenty of expenses associated with trying to make money with your money. Generally, the most important costs are those that affect your basis in the property, as discussed throughout this chapter. The importance of maintaining meticulous records to verify your basis cannot be overemphasized. Record keeping is the key to insuring that you're not overtaxed when you sell the investment.

There's a whole series of other expenses that can be deductible in the year you pay them, although, once again, tax reform squeezed these write-offs.

Typical deductible expenses include the following:

• Rental of a safe-deposit box used to store taxable securities.
• Investment counselor or management fees.
• Subscriptions to investment-advisory newsletters.
• Cost of books and magazines purchased for investment advice.
• State and local transfer taxes on the sale of securities.
• Fees paid to a broker or other agent to collect bond interest or stock dividends. (Unlike commissions paid brokers on the purchase of stock—a cost which is added to basis—this type of fee is deductible.)
• Cost of travel to see your broker to discuss investments. (This does not include simply dropping by the broker's office to check on the general condition of the market or to watch the ticker tape.) If you drive your own car, you can deduct the actual cost (see Chapter 9) or the IRS standard rate, which was 22.5 cents a mile in 1988. In either case, add what you paid for parking or tolls.

If some of those expenses seem to fall in the nickel-and-dime category, you may appreciate what Congress has done to relieve you of the burden of keeping track. In a move to "simplify" your tax life, the law now allows such expenses to be deducted only to the extent that they—when added to all your other "miscellaneous" expenses—exceed 2% of your adjusted gross income. Chapter 10 discusses what other expenses fall in the miscellaneous cauldron for purposes of passing the 2% threshold.

This is supposed to simplify matters because if you're sure you're not going to rack up enough expenses to garner any tax benefit, you theoretically don't need to keep track of any of the costs. The flaw in the logic, of course, is that you won't know whether you'll pass the 2% barrier unless you keep track of qualifying expenses throughout the year.

There is no such uncertainty about one kind of investment expense that used to be deductible: The cost of attending an investment convention, seminar or similar meeting. As discussed in Chapter 9, such write-offs are now forbidden.

6
INVESTING IN REAL ESTATE

Portions of the Tax Reform Act of 1986 read like an obituary for real estate investments:

• Congress created the fourth new depreciation schedule in six years, and the latest version is the most stingy.

• The new law introduced a set of rules to prevent losses on rental property from sheltering income from other sources, such as your salary or investments.

• The losses you do get to take aren't worth as much because tax rates are lower.

• The elimination of the capital-gains exclusion means you'll owe more tax when you ultimately sell your property.

But tax reform didn't ruin real estate as an attractive investment vehicle. Real estate still has the powerful allure of leverage: For a relatively small down payment, you can buy the appreciation on the entire value of a building. Say you put $15,000 down on a $100,000 building. If it appreciates 15% over two years and you sell it for $115,000, you've earned a 100% return (not counting transaction costs.)

And although the tax benefits have been scaled down, Uncle Sam still stands by to help you in your business as a landlord. Whether you're a veteran investor in rental property or just considering your first real estate investment, the changing tax angles may be pivotal to your success.

DEPRECIATION

This is a noncash expense that can put money in your pocket. The law lets you depreciate rental property, claiming deductions that are supposed to reflect how the building is being "used up." You depreciate your basis in the building. The basis is basically what you paid for the property minus the value of the land. Depreciation is a key to many real estate investments because even if rental income fails to cover all out-of-pocket expenses, the tax savings of depreciation—by sheltering other income from the IRS—can make up much, if not all, of the difference.

Before tax reform, buildings could be depreciated over 19 years (never mind the fact that a building would probably last much longer) using a method called the Accelerated Cost Recovery System (ACRS). It was "accelerated" because the write-off schedule bunched bigger deductions in the earlier years.

Now the law demands that you use the straight-line method and stretches the write-offs over 27.5 years for residential real estate and 31.5 years for commercial buildings. (Note this: The new rules apply only to buildings put into service in 1987 and later years. If you put rental property into service earlier, you continue to use the more favorable depreciation rules in effect at the time.)

Under the new law, the first-year depreciation deduction depends on the month you put the property into service and is based on what accountants call the midmonth convention: Regardless of what day of the month you start depreciating the building, you get credit for half of the first month. Put a rental house into service on July 1, for example, and your first-year depreciation write-off would be for 5½ months—half of July plus the rest of the year.

The calculations are fairly simple. You begin with the depreciable basis—which is the cost of the building itself. (You have to reduce what you pay for the property by the value of the land, which is not depreciable.) Divide the basis by either 27.5 or 31.5—depending on whether it is residential or commercial property—to find the annual depreciation amount. Divide that by 12 to get the monthly figure, and multiply that amount by the number of months it was available for rent, whether or not you actually had a tenant.

On a residential property with a $100,000 basis a full year's depreciation would be $3,636 ($100,000 ÷ 27.5). One month's worth would be $303. Thanks to the midmonth convention, the first-year depreciation deduction for a property put into use anytime in July would be $1,667 ($303 × 5.5).

Here are the percentage amounts to apply to your original tax basis to determine first-year write-offs, depending on what month you put the property into service:

| Month Put Into Service | First-Year Depreciation | |
	27.5-Year Residential Property	31-Year Commercial Property
January	3.48%	3.04%
February	3.18	2.77
March	2.88	2.51
April	2.58	2.25
May	2.27	1.98
June	1.97	1.72
July	1.67	1.45
August	1.36	1.19
September	1.06	0.92
October	0.76	0.66
November	0.45	0.40
December	0.15	0.13

After the first year, you deduct 3.64% of your basis for residential property and 3.17% for commercial property each year, until the final year. In the 29th year, assuming you still own the building, the write-off would be slightly smaller depending on the first-year deduction.

Remember this about depreciation: Each deduction you take reduces your adjusted basis in the property. When you sell the property, the reduced basis will be subtracted from the sales proceeds, giving you a larger profit.

If you make improvements to your rental property, the cost is added to your tax basis and can therefore trim the taxable profit when you sell. Such capital improvements should be depreciated separately from the building. Say, for example, that four years after you begin renting a duplex you add a $20,000 addition. You would depreciate that $20,000 over its own 27.5-year tax life rather than simply including that amount when figuring future depreciation write-offs for the building.

OTHER RENTAL EXPENSES

You can still deduct the costs of producing rental income. Uncle Sam demands a share only of your net income, so it's clearly in your best interest to tote up all the tax-saving expenses that can trim that figure. Be sure to count the following:

- Mortgage interest.
- Property taxes.
- Insurance premiums you pay.
- Fees paid to a management company.
- Cost of newspaper ads advertising the availability of the property.
- Legal or accounting costs connected with drafting a lease or evicting tenants.
- Cost of repairs to the property.
- Any utilities you pay for your tenants or while the place is vacant between renters.
- Salary or wages you pay to others to take care of the property, for cleaning or gardening, for example. This includes what you pay your child if he or she really works on the rental. The tax advantages of employing family members are discussed in Chapter 3.
- The cost of travel to look after your properties. This can include the cost of driving across town to repair a leaky faucet or the expenses—including travel, meals and lodging—of visiting out-of-town rental property. The key to including such costs is that the principal purpose of the trip be to inspect or work on your property. Taking a two-week vacation to Florida and spending an afternoon checking on a rental condo won't qualify. A week-long visit, five days of which are spent on painting and repairs to prepare the place for a new tenant, would qualify.

SURVIVING THE PASSIVE-LOSS RULES

As part of the crackdown on tax shelters, discussed in Chapter 5, Congress severely limited the ability of investors in "passive activities" to deduct losses from those investments against other kinds of income. Rental real estate is specifically labeled a passive activity.

That could have been the death knell for a lot of landlords who count on claiming tax losses to make their real estate investments financially feasible. However, Congress included a major exception to the passive-loss rules that makes rental real estate an oasis in the otherwise barren tax-shelter landscape. If you qualify for this special exception, you can continue to deduct up to $25,000 of rental real estate losses against other income, such as your salary or interest and dividends.

To qualify you must *actively participate* in the management of the property. Fortunately, the demands for passing that test aren't particularly onerous. You don't have to be on call for middle-of-the-night repairs, cut the grass and collect rents. The IRS rules don't say exactly what you do have to do, but even if you hire a management firm to handle day-to-day matters, you can be actively involved as long as you approve tenants, set the rent and okay capital improvements.

The $25,000 exception isn't for fat cats, though, no matter how actively they're involved. It is phased out as adjusted gross income (which is your income before subtracting itemized deductions, exemptions and rental losses) moves between $100,000 and $150,000. The $25,000 loss allowance is reduced by 50% of your AGI over $100,000. This is how the tax break evaporates as your income rises:

If AGI Is	You May Deduct Rental Losses up to
up to $100,000	$25,000
110,000	20,000
120,000	15,000
130,000	10,000
140,000	5,000
150,000 or more	0

The $25,000 allowance and the phaseout schedule are the same whether you are married filing a joint return or single filing an individual return. If you are married filing separately, however, and you and your spouse lived together at any time during the year, neither spouse gets a loss allowance. In other words, although filing separately might pull AGI on one or both returns below the $150,000 level, the maneuver won't work to revitalize passive losses that would be denied on a joint return.

The $25,000 allowance doesn't protect losses generated by a limited partnership or any rental property in which you own less than 10%. As discussed in the previous chapter, losses not protected by the active-participation exception are not useless. They can be deducted against passive income, if you have any, and otherwise are suspended rather than obliterated. You can deduct such suspended losses in future years when you have passive income to shelter, and when you sell the rental property, any unused losses are liberated to be deducted against any type of income, including your salary.

CONVERTING YOUR HOME TO A RENTAL PROPERTY

This is how many taxpayers get into the landlord business—by deciding to hold on to their house when they move to a new home. That may sound like an easy way to do it; after all you know the property and the neighborhood and probably have a good idea of what would be a reasonable rent. If you can afford it, why not turn the old homestead into a rental property? That way you could enjoy the rental income and tax benefits, not to mention the continued appreciation on the place.

Uncle Sam has a few special twists for homeowners-turned-landlords. You do qualify to write off all the basic rental expenses, and if those expenses exceed your rental income, you can use the loss to shelter up to $25,000 of other income as long as you pass the active-participation and income tests. But you fall under a unique rule when it comes to figuring depreciation and calculating the gain or loss when you sell the property.

Although your home probably appreciated—perhaps quite

significantly—while you lived in it, you don't get to use the higher value for depreciation purposes. Your tax basis in such a converted residence is the lower of the house's value when you convert it to rental property or your adjusted basis. That means you're usually stuck with adjusted basis, which is generally what you originally paid for the place, plus the cost of improvements.

That rule can make a big difference in your depreciation write-offs. Say you bought your home several years ago for $50,000, $40,000 of which was the value of the building. Although you've made no improvements, it's now worth $120,000, $100,000 of which is the value of the building. If you convert it to rental use, you're depreciation is based on the $40,000 basis.

Back in the days when the congressional penchant was to liberalize deprecation rules—that is, change the law to permit quicker write-offs—there was another rule to hold down depreciation on residences transformed to rentals. Basically, you had to use the depreciation rules in effect when you bought the property, not the possibly more-liberal method in force when you converted.

Now that Congress has done a turnaround by slowing down depreciation schedules, there's a new rule. If the depreciation method in effect when you bought the property would deliver bigger annual deductions—as it certainly would if you bought the house while ACRS was in effect from 1981 through 1986— you can't use it. Instead, you're stuck with the new law's 27.5-year depreciation period. Heads you lose, tails the IRS wins.

Special vacation-home tax rules apply to a property you rent part-time and use personally, and these are discussed in Chapter 4.

TAX-FREE EXCHANGES

You may have heard of a "tax-free exchange" of real estate, a concept that has definite appeal. This maneuver allows you to dispose of rental property without triggering an immediate tax bill on the gain. What it demands is that you find an amenable owner of similar property. Although that's not easy, some brokers specialize in real estate exchanges.

If you trade property for property of a "like kind," the IRS does not treat your disposal of your property as a sale. Like kind is liberally defined. Clearly, exchanging a rental house for another rental house is covered, but so is trading raw land for an apartment building. The advantage is that you hold off the tax bill on your profit from the first property.

Consider an example. Say you have a rental house with an adjusted basis of $50,000 and that it is now worth $150,000. You'd like to expand your rental activities by buying a duplex with a price tag of $250,000. If you sell the first house, you'll owe tax on $100,000 of profit. That will cost you $33,000 if you're in the 33% bracket. Instead, assume you persuade the owner of the duplex to trade—his $250,000 duplex for your $150,000 house plus $100,000 in cash. As long as the deal qualifies as a tax-free exchange, you avoid that $33,000 tax tab.

Avoid is really too strong a term. Defer is more accurate. Your basis in the new building would not be its $250,000 price but rather your old $50,000 basis plus the $100,000 cash you had to put into the deal. When you later sell the duplex— assuming you don't work another tax-free exchange—the gain would be based on your $150,000 basis. That would give the IRS its delayed shot at the $100,000 of profit that built up in the first house.

Since, in this example, the owner of the duplex received cash as well as like-kind property, it's not a totally tax-free exchange for him. Part or all of his profit—the difference between his basis in the property and the $250,000 value of your building plus cash—would be taxable. He would owe tax on the lower of his total profit or $100,000 (the amount of cash received). His basis on the rental house would be reduced by any part of the $100,000 that wasn't taxed in the year of the trade.

Although holding off Uncle Sam is always an appealing prospect, like-kind exchanges have disadvantages. For one thing, your depreciation deductions on the new property will be held down because you carry over the basis from old property. Also, if you use a like-kind exchange in a year you have suspended passive losses (discussed in Chapter 5) you'll miss the chance to absorb some of those losses.

To qualify as a tax-free exchange, the trade must take place within a specified time frame. You must identify the property you're going to receive within 45 days of transferring your property, and the trade must generally be completed within 180 days.

INSTALLMENT SALES

Installment sales are a popular method for selling property, particularly rental real estate, because the seller can help grease the deal by providing at least part of the necessary financing for the buyer. Rather than demanding the full price up front, with an installment sale you agree to have the buyer pay at least part of the price in the future. And, wonder of wonders, the IRS doesn't tax your profit on the sale until you actually get the money.

If you will receive at least one payment in a year after the sale, you can use the installment method to report and pay tax on the profit as you receive it. Each year, the payments you receive will have three components:

• Return of your basis, which is nontaxable.
• Profit, which thanks to tax reform's elimination of the capital-gains exclusion is fully taxable.
• Interest on the "loan" you made by financing the sale. The IRS demands that you charge interest on the unpaid balance. This, too, is taxable.

The interest portion should be easy to identify and segregate. To determine how much of the rest of the payments is taxable, you must first figure the "gross profit percentage" on the sale.

If the sale isn't plagued by depreciation recapture, discussed next, the gross profit percentage is determined by dividing gain on the sale (proceeds minus basis) by the contract price. Assume that you sell for $150,000 a rental house that had a tax basis of $75,000. You receive a $25,000 down payment and the contract calls for $25,000 payments (plus interest) for each of the next five years.

The gross profit percentage on this sale would be 50%: $75,000 profit divided by $150,000 contract price. That means 50% of the down payment and each subsequent payment you receive is taxable gain. The other half is the nontaxable return of your basis.

Depreciation recapture. This is a complication—one of many— that may make you wonder whether the benefit of delaying the tax bill is worth the hassle. As mentioned earlier in this chapter, because depreciation reduces your basis, it translates into higher gain when you sell. And if you used an accelerated depreciation method—as most residential real estate investors who bought their property before 1987 do—you claimed more depreciation over the years than you would have been allowed under straight-line depreciation. Although the law encourages that, it also calls for that extra depreciation to be "recaptured" when you sell. The part of the profit that results from that extra depreciation is taxed as ordinary income rather than as capital gain. Now that capital gains are 100% taxable, just like ordinary

© STEVE KELLEY—THE SAN DIEGO UNION

income, that might seem an insignificant distinction.

But it's not when it comes to installment sales. The law demands that all depreciation recapture be taxed in the year of the sale, regardless of when the income is received. When considering an installment sale, consider the impact of depreciation recapture. You'll probably want to be sure the down payment on the sale is at least enough to cover the tax bill that's due on the sale.

Depreciation recapture also affects the gross profit percentage on the deal. When figuring that ratio, you reduce your gross profit on the sale by the amount of depreciation recapture taxed in the year of the sale.

In the example above, if the seller had to report $5,000 of depreciation recapture, the gross profit percentage would be 46.6% ($70,000 ÷ $150,000) rather than 50%. Because some of the profit has to be reported up front, there's less of it to be taxed as part of the installment payments.

Minimum interest. The law requires that you charge an "adequate" amount of interest on the installment sale, and it's not because the IRS is worried that you'd otherwise have an unfair advantage over banks and other lenders. The rationale is to prevent the price from being set artificially high to make up for interest-free or below-market financing. The IRS cares about the price of the sale, of course, because it affects the seller's gain or loss and the buyer's basis for depreciation in the building. (Although you might think the IRS wouldn't mind if you reported an inflated gain, remember that in the prereform days when these rules came into being, the profit would have been a long-term capital gain. That means 60% of it would have been tax-free, while 100% of interest income was taxable.)

To meet the IRS definition of adequate, your installment sale must provide for interest at least equal to the "applicable federal rate" (AFR) at the time of the sale. The AFR is determined by the IRS and is basically what it costs the government to borrow money. Regardless of how high the AFR goes, however, you don't have to charge more than 9%, compounded semiannually, on your installment sale.

If the contract fails to provide for adequate stated interest, the IRS has ways—very complicated calculations—for figuring what part of each payment is "imputed" interest—that is, what part will be treated as interest no matter what you call it. This affects not only your gain or loss and the buyer's basis but also the amount of interest income you report each year and the amount the buyer gets to deduct. It's much easier to check with the IRS before finalizing a deal to be sure you include an adequate interest rate.

7

INDIVIDUAL RETIREMENT
ACCOUNTS

The promise of longer life spans brings with it the guarantee that you'll need more money to sustain a comfortable life-style in your retirement. The tax law is filled with incentives to encourage and help you save for your golden years. This chapter focuses on the most popular do-it-yourself retirement plans: individual retirement accounts. Chapter 8 addresses other types of plans, including Keogh plans, 401(k)s and simplified employee pensions as well as company pension and profit-sharing plans and social security.

First, IRAs. It's no wonder they are so attractive since they strike a blow for two of our most cherished goals: avoiding taxes and providing for a financially secure retirement. When Congress opened the door to IRAs to nearly everyone in 1981, the accounts were immediately dubbed "everybody's tax shelter." Money deposited in an IRA could be deducted on your tax return, and all earnings inside the account were sheltered from the IRS.

Back then, the decision of whether or not to use an IRA was a cinch—the epitome of a "no-brainer" investment decision. You put $2,000 into an IRA and, in the days of the 50% tax bracket, could automatically knock as much as $1,000 off your tax bill: an immediate return as high as 50%. You didn't have to be a financial wizard—or pay one for advice—to understand the value of an IRA deduction or the power of tax-deferred earnings inside the tax shelter. Promoters promised us the chance to retire as IRA millionaires, and millions of us believed. The threat of a penalty if you tapped your IRA before age 59½ seemed a small price to pay.

With tax reform, however, the beautiful simplicity of the IRA vanished for millions of taxpayers. Although everyone who qualified for an old IRA can still make contributions, some taxpayers can't deduct those deposits. After years of luring us into the ranks of tax-shelter junkies, Congress decided to change the rules.

The restrictions are explained in detail after a review of the basic IRA rules, which still apply to most taxpayers. You have to concern yourself with tax reform's twists and turns only if your modified adjusted gross income exceeds $40,000 on a joint return or $25,000 on an individual return *and* you are covered by an employer-provided retirement plan. If you don't have a plan at work or your income is below the $25,000 or $40,000 level, you're still eligible for full-fledged IRA benefits.

WHO CAN HAVE AN IRA?

The IRA tax shelter is open to anyone under age 70½ who receives compensation, which is earnings from a job rather than income from investments.

Income that counts for IRA purposes includes:
- Wages, salaries and tips;
- Sales commissions;
- Professional fees;
- Bonuses;
- Self-employment income; and
- Alimony.

Income that doesn't count as compensation includes:
- Interest and dividends;
- Profit from the sale of stocks or other property;
- Rental income;
- Pension or annuity income; and
- Deferred compensation.

The annual limit on IRA contributions is $2,000 or 100% of your compensation, whichever is less. Thus, if you earn just $1,000, your IRA limit for the year is $1,000.

There is no minimum age for IRA participation. If your 10-year-old has compensation—from a paper route, say, or from working in a family business, as discussed in Chapter 3— he or she can stash up to $2,000 of that pay in an IRA. (The extended period of time such a contribution would have to grow inside an IRA accentuates the power of this tax shelter. A single, $2,000 investment at age 10 would grow to more than $375,000 by age 65, assuming an average 10% annual yield and to more than $1 million with a 12% average yield.)

As explained later, the law demands that you begin withdrawing from your IRA by April 1 of the year after you reach age 70½. That age also brings an end to your IRA deposits. By that time you're supposed to be enjoying your retirement nest egg, not continuing to build it up.

For taxpayers born between July 1, 1917, and June 30, 1918, the final year for IRA contributions is 1988. The following table shows the last year of IRA eligibility for taxpayers with certain birthdays.

Birthday Between	Last Year for IRA Contribution
7/1/18 to 6/30/19	1989
7/1/19 to 6/30/20	1990
7/1/20 to 6/30/21	1991
7/1/21 to 6/30/22	1992
7/1/22 to 6/30/23	1993
7/1/23 to 6/30/24	1994
7/1/24 to 6/30/25	1995

Spousal IRAs. There is an exception to the $2,000 annual limit for couples in which one spouse does not have a job. In addition to your own IRA, you can open an account for a nonworking spouse and contribute a total of $2,250 to the two accounts. The money can be split however you wish, as long as neither account gets more than $2,000. Also, you may continue contributing up to $2,000 of your compensation to a nonworking spouse's account even after you reach age 70½, assuming he or she is under that age.

When both spouses have jobs, each may have his or her own IRA with a $2,000 contribution limit. That means a working couple can sock away as much as $4,000 in IRAs each year, as long as each spouse has at least $2,000 in compensation.

Putting in too much. The government is serious about the annual limits. Excess contributions are hit with a 6% penalty tax. Assume you work part-time and, expecting to earn more than $2,000 for the year, you deposit $2,000 in your IRA at the beginning of the year. Because you have a bad year, though, your earnings total just $1,500. Your deduction is limited to $1,500, and the extra $500 is considered an excess contribution subject to the 6% penalty. That will cost you $30. The penalty applies each year until the excess is either withdrawn or absorbed by the unused portion of a future year's contribution. If you qualify for a $2,000 contribution the following year, for example, depositing just $1,500 would absorb the $500 excess contribution and avoid another 6% penalty. You'd get to deduct the extra $500 in the second year.

It's possible to dodge the first-year penalty, too, by withdrawing the extra money before you file your tax return for the year involved. Because you had not yet deducted the IRA deposit, you don't have to report the withdrawal as income. Any earnings on the extra $500 should be withdrawn from the account, too. That amount would be taxed, and if you are under age 59½ at the time, the earnings would also be hit with a 10% early-withdrawal penalty, discussed later.

A matter of timing. The deadline for making your IRA contribution each year is the day your tax return is due for that year. That's usually April 15, of course, but can be a day or two later if the 15th falls on a weekend. This rule means you can make your 1988 contribution anytime from January 1, 1988 until April 17, 1989. If you mail your IRA contribution, you meet the deadline if it's postmarked on the due date.

Although you may be tempted to hold off as long as possible to make sure you have the spare cash to lock up in an IRA, making your deposits sooner rather than later can pay off handsomely. The earlier you make your contribution, the sooner your money begins earning in the supercharged environment of the IRA, as the table below indicates. In each case, an annual deposit of $2,000 and a yield of 10% is assumed.

Total at End of Year	If Annual Deposit Made at End of Year	If Annual Deposit Made at Beginning of Year
5	$ 12,210	$ 13,431
10	31,875	35,062
15	63,545	69,899
20	114,550	126,005
25	196,694	216,364
30	328,988	361,887
35	542,049	596,254
40	885,185	973,703

THE POWER OF THE IRA

The tax incentives to sign up for an IRA are compelling. Unless you're tripped up by the new restrictions, every dollar you deposit can be deducted on your tax return. If you're in the 28% bracket, a $2,000 deduction saves you $560 immediately—money that would otherwise go to the IRS. An added bonus is that most states bestow similar tax benefits on IRAs. If you live in a state with an 8% income tax and you get to deduct the $2,000 IRA deposit on your state return, you save another $160.

The IRA has a tax advantage even if you can't deduct your contributions. As long as funds are tucked inside the IRA tax shelter, earnings accumulate tax-free. Holding off the IRS gives the power of compound interest added magic.

Consider this example. You put $2,000 aside each year in a taxable investment yielding 12%. Each year, the IRS demands 28% of the earnings, money that would continue to earn 12% if it didn't go to the IRS. At the end of 20 years, your series of $2,000 investments would be worth a total of $106,769.

Now, put that same $2,000 a year in an IRA in which growth won't be interrupted annually by Uncle Sam. Assuming the same 12% yield, at the end of 20 years your account will total

$161,397. The $50,000-plus difference is the power of the IRA tax shelter. Although all the IRA earnings would be taxable when withdrawn—while the tax bill has already been paid on the non-IRA investment—you still come out well ahead.

The table below shows how a series of $2,000 annual contributions made at the beginning of each year will grow inside an IRA, assuming various investment results.

Balance at End of Year	Compound Annual Yield				
	6%	8%	10%	12%	15%
5	$ 11,951	$ 12,672	$ 13,431	$ 14,230	$ 15,507
10	27,943	31,291	35,062	39,309	46,699
15	49,345	58,649	69,899	83,507	109,435
20	77,985	98,846	126,005	161,397	235,620
25	116,313	157,909	216,364	298,668	489,424
30	167,603	244,692	361,887	540,585	999,914
35	236,242	372,204	596,254	966,926	2,026,691
40	328,095	559,562	973,703	1,718,285	4,091,908

Early-withdrawal penalty. If the tax breaks are the carrot Congress uses to encourage you to save for your retirement, penalties for early withdrawal are the sticks that make sure you keep at it. Make no mistake: IRA money is different from funds you are saving on your own for, say, a child's college education or a retirement cushion. You may think of those accounts as sacrosanct, but you know you can put your hands on the cash in an emergency.

It's different with an IRA. When you accept the tax breaks, you sign the government on as a partner—and a stern one at that. Dip into the account early—as far as the law is concerned, generally anytime before you're 59½ is early—and you'll be hit with a 10% penalty for premature distribution. Take $5,000 out at age 50, for example, and you probably will be slapped with a $500 penalty. In addition, the full $5,000 will be included in your income for the year and taxed in your top tax bracket. If part of the withdrawal is attributed to nondeductible IRA contributions—discussed in the next section of this chapter—that part is neither taxed nor subject to the 10% penalty.

The premature-distribution penalty is waived if you become permanently disabled. To qualify for this exception, the IRS says you must be unable to do any substantial gainful activity and that the mental or physical disability must be expected to last longer than a year or lead to death. The 10% penalty also does not apply if an IRA is distributed after the death of the owner, regardless of how old he or she was at the time of death.

In addition to those exceptions, the Tax Reform Act of 1986 added another penalty-free way to get at some of your IRA money early. It is discussed in the section on IRA distributions on page 180.

Break-even point. The threat of the early-withdrawal penalty can be a major deterrent for younger workers with years, perhaps decades, to go before age 59½. But letting the potential penalty scare you away from an IRA could be a costly mistake. The advantage of this tax shelter is so powerful that the 10% penalty can wind up seeming pretty puny in comparison.

Consider a worker who makes deductible $2,000 contributions to an IRA each year, beginning at age 25. Ten years later, our 35-year-old needs cash for a down payment on a house and liquidates the IRA to get the money needed. Assuming the IRA has grown at a compounded annual rate of 10%, it holds $35,062. The tax—in the 28% bracket—takes $9,817, the 10% penalty another $3,506. After tax and penalty, the early-out investor has $21,739.

Despite the $3,500 penalty, that's still more than our investor would have had if the IRA was ignored. If the investor had saved $1,440 each year ($2,000 minus the 28% that would go to the IRS without the IRA deduction) and earned a 7.2% compounded return (10% minus 28% for the IRS), the total after ten years would have been $21,531.

The point is not that the 10% penalty should be ignored. Far from it. The penalty is a stiff one, designed to prevent you from using the IRA as a short-term tax shelter. But you don't necessarily have to leave your money in the account until you're

59½ for the IRA to pay off. The higher your tax bracket and the higher the return inside the IRA, the sooner you'll reach the break-even point. And each year you stay in the IRA, the benefits of the tax shelter chip away at the pain of any early-withdrawal penalty. If you are prevented from deducting IRA contributions, the break-even point will still arrive, but it will be much delayed.

RESTRICTED IRA WRITE-OFFS

As one of many ways to raise revenues while cutting tax rates, the Tax Reform Act of 1986 wiped out the right of millions of taxpayers to deduct their IRA contributions. There are two tests for determining whether you're among the losers.

First, are you an "active participant" in a company pension plan? You are, as far as the law is concerned, if you are eligible to participate in any of the following types of plans, whether or not your benefits are vested:

- Pension, profit-sharing or stock-bonus plan.
- 401(k) plan.
- Simplified employee pension plan (SEP).
- Qualified annuity plan.
- Retirement plan for state and federal employees, including civil service and the Federal Employees Retirement System.
- Keogh plan.
- Tax-sheltered annuity (403(b) plan).

If you are eligible for such a plan during any part of the year, you are considered covered for the entire year as far as the IRA test goes. (If you are in a profit-sharing plan but no contribution is made to your account for the year, however, you are not considered covered for that year.) The W-2 form you receive from your employer should indicate to you—and the IRS— whether you are considered to be an active participant in a company plan.

Note this: If you are married and file a joint return and either you or your spouse is covered by an employer-sponsored plan, both of you are regarded as covered for purposes of this test and your IRA deductions may be in jeopardy.

If you aren't tripped up by the company-plan test, you can continue to deduct your IRA contributions regardless of how high your income is.

Income test. If you are covered by a plan, however, a second test will determine whether you can write off your IRA contributions. The IRA deduction is phased out for active participants in company plans whose adjusted gross income (AGI)—before subtracting IRA contributions—exceeds $25,000 on an individual return or $40,000 on a joint return. If your AGI is below the threshold, your full IRA contribution can be deducted. As AGI surpasses the $25,000 or $40,000 level, however, the maximum deduction is reduced by $10 for each $50 of additional AGI.

For example, AGI of $5,000 over the threshold—either $30,000 on an individual or $45,000 on a joint return—would knock your maximum annual deduction down to $1,000. You could still contribute up to $2,000 to your IRA, but only $1,000would be deductible. (The introduction of nondeductible contributions gives rise to all sorts of complications, which are discussed later.) On a joint return reporting AGI of $45,000, each spouse could write off up to $1,000 of IRA contributions,

assuming husband and wife each had compensation of at least $1,000 during the year.

There is a $200 floor under the deductible IRA. When your AGI is between $9,000 and $10,000 over the threshold, the permissible deduction stays at $200, rather than sliding to a laughably low $10 before disappearing. The table below shows how rising AGI diminishes the allowable IRA deduction.

Adjusted Gross Income		Top IRA Deduction*
Single Return	**Joint Return**	
up to $25,000	up to $40,000	$2,000
25,500	40,500	1,900
26,000	41,000	1,800
26,500	41,500	1,700
27,000	42,000	1,600
27,500	42,500	1,500
28,000	43,000	1,400
28,500	43,500	1,300
29,000	44,000	1,200
29,500	44,500	1,100
30,000	45,000	1,000
30,500	45,500	900
31,000	46,000	800
31,500	46,500	700
32,000	47,000	600
32,500	47,500	500
33,000	48,000	400
33,500	48,500	300
34,000	49,000	200
34,500	49,500	200
35,000	50,000	0

On a joint return, each spouse who earns at least this much may deduct this amount.

When you contribute to a spousal account—so the top unrestricted deduction is $2,250 instead of $2,000—the deduction is also phased out as your AGI exceeds the $40,000 threshold for a joint return. Here's an example of how it works:

When AGI is $45,000, the $5,000 of excess AGI is 50% of the $10,000 phaseout range. Your combined deduction for regular and spousal accounts would be limited to 50% of $2,250, or $1,125. You could split that amount however you wish, as long as neither account receives more than $1,000—half of the customary $2,000 limit.

Does filing separate returns offer a two-earner married couple the chance to preserve IRA deductions that would be prohibited on a joint return? Probably not, although this issue was still somewhat murky in mid 1988. It is clear that on separate returns the deduction phaseout range for taxpayers covered by a company plan is $0 to $10,000; the right to any IRA deduction disappears when AGI on the separate return hits $10,000.

The unresolved question is whether a spouse not covered by a company pension plan can avoid the IRA phaseout altogether by filing separately from the spouse who is covered. On 1987 returns that was possible because of the way the law was written. At the time this book went to press, however, it appeared likely that Congress would amend the law to eliminate this invitation to file separate returns. There will probably be an exception, though, to permit IRA write-offs for a noncovered spouse who files separately and did not live with his or her spouse at all during the year. Under the proposal, each would be treated as single, so one's coverage by a plan could not thwart the other's right to an IRA deduction.

Should you make nondeductible contributions? That's the big question, and expert opinion runs the gamut from an emphatic yes to an absolute no.

One thing is certain: Without the write-off, the IRA's appeal is tarnished. But don't sell the wounded shelter short. Indeed, if you were planning to retire a millionaire based on annual $2,000 contributions, the same $2,000 deposits will still make you a millionaire. The money will grow just as fast in a nondeductible IRA as in a deductible one. The difference is that each contribution will cost you more because Uncle Sam will no longer subsidize your retirement savings with the instant gratification of a tax deduction.

If you face the loss of the write-off, you should at least take a look at alternative tax-favored investments before pressing ahead with your IRA.

Accounting headaches. The creation of nondeductible IRAs brings new accounting headaches. Under the old law, the rules were straightforward. Just as every dime you put into an IRA was deductible, every dime withdrawn was taxed as ordinary income. That's still the way it is for taxpayers who never make a nondeductible contribution. However, if you make nondeductible deposits, part of each withdrawal will be a return of your already-taxed investment. Congress doesn't want to tax you twice on that money, so that part will be tax-free.

But the lawmakers didn't make it easy. Rather than let taxpayers set up separate accounts—and then choose whether to withdraw taxable funds from a deductible IRA or tax-free money from a nondeductible account—the law says that an ever-changing percentage of each withdrawal will be taxed. You have to determine what's what. Here, step by step, is how you do that:

1. Find the total amount in all of your IRA accounts at the end of the year.

2. Find the total that you withdrew from the accounts during the year.

3. Add (1) and (2).

4. Find your basis in your IRAs—the total of your nondeductible contributions over the years minus any tax-free withdrawals you've taken in previous years.

5. Divide (4) by (3). That's the percentage of your withdrawals during the year that is tax-free. The rest is taxable.

Here's an example. In a few years, your IRA accounts hold $50,000 at year-end. Your basis is $10,000, reflecting your nondeductible contributions. During the year, you withdrew $10,000 from your accounts. Adding that amount to the year-end balance brings the total to $60,000. Dividing $10,000 by $60,000 tells you that your basis represents 16.66% of the total. That means 16.66% of your $10,000 in withdrawals ($1,666) would be tax-free. The other $8,334 would be taxed in your top bracket.

In the following year, your basis would be $8,334—the

original $10,000 minus the $1,666 you recovered tax-free.

Investors who make nondeductible IRA contributions must file an extra form with their tax returns—showing the the nondeductible amount. You have to keep copies of the form—number 8606—for as long as you have an IRA (perhaps for the rest of your life) so you can prove what part of your distributions are a tax-free return of those nondeductible investments. **The aggravation of aggregation.** The demand that taxpayers aggregate deductible and nondeductible IRAs—for purposes of determining what part of a withdrawal is taxable—has convinced some advisors that investors should shun the nondeductible variety. Although getting to treat at least part of a withdrawal as tax-free may appear to be an advantage, consider the problems the new rule could cause.

Say you have $98,000 in an IRA made up of deductible contributions and earnings. Caught by the new restrictions, you make a $2,000 nondeductible contribution, and shortly after you report it on your tax return you decide to withdraw the $2,000. Thanks to the aggregation rule, you can't treat the $2,000 as a return of that nondeductible investment. Rather, you would have to pay tax on 98% of it. In the 28% bracket, that would cost you $549. The taxable part would also be hit with the 10% early-withdrawal penalty if you were under 59½. Had you invested the $2,000 outside the IRA, you could have retrieved it without being taxed or worrying about that penalty.

Just how significant this potential problem is to you depends on several factors, including the size of your IRA and how soon you will want to pull funds out. It's something to keep in mind, though, if you choose between nondeductible IRA contributions and alternative investments.

Should you open a separate account for any nondeductible contributions? The aggregation rule would seem to make separate accounts superfluous, but keeping the money separate may simplify your bookkeeping chores. Your choice may turn on whether using an additional account will involve extra costs. **The hindsight rule.** If your income is close to the new IRA thresholds, you may not know until year-end whether your contribution will earn you a deduction. If your decision on whether to continue using an IRA turns on its deductibility, should you wait until you're certain? Remember, it's best to put your cash in early in the year. The deductible/nondeductible twist to the equation doesn't alter that.

Fortunately, you don't have to make an irreversible decision. You can put your contribution in at the beginning of the year and start earning tax-deferred income. If it turns out that your AGI is so high that you can't deduct the contribution—or you discover a better investment for the money—you can withdraw the funds. As long as the contribution and any earnings on it are out of the IRA by the time your tax return is due, there will be little or no penalty. If you are under 59½ when you pull the funds out, the IRS will impose the 10% early-withdrawal penalty to the investment income earned on the now-withdrawn deposit. If you contribute $2,000 in January and it earns $200 by the time you change your mind, for example, you would withdraw $2,200. The $200 of earnings would be taxable and the 10% penalty would apply to that amount, costing you $20. If you are at least 59½, you avoid that charge.

INVESTMENT OPTIONS

If you've been to an international food bazaar where the delicacies of many nations are spread out before you, you have an idea of the temptation, confusion and wonderment presented by the IRA menu. You have almost unlimited choice of where to put your retirement dollars, and as the table on page 162 demonstrates, a slight difference in investment performance can make a major difference in how comfortable your retirement will be.

You can choose a bland—but predictable—investment, such as a bank account, or go for spicy, speculative stock in a new company. You can buy high-grade corporate bonds, zero-coupon bonds or junk bonds. You can choose all sorts of mutual funds, buy into a shopping center or sign up for an annuity contract. About the only place you can't put your money is in collectibles, which the law defines to include art work, antiques, gems, stamps and precious metals.

Where you put your money depends in part on your temperament or, put another way, how much risk you can take and still sleep at night. Another factor is how the IRA fits into your overall retirement planning. If you're counting on it to provide a significant portion of your retirement income, you may be more conservative in your investments than someone whose IRA is relatively less important thanks to expected benefits from social security, company retirement plans or outside investments.

Your age comes into play, too. Someone with decades to go before retirement may choose more volatile investments, figuring there's plenty of time to make up any loss in the early years. One nearing retirement, on the other hand, may be drawn to investments with guaranteed yields.

Changes brought by tax reform may affect how some investors deploy their IRA funds. In the past, for example, many advisers steered IRA investors away from stocks, stock mutual funds and other investments designed to generate long-term capital gains. The reasoning was that because every dime coming out of the IRA would be taxed, such profits would forfeit the gentle tax treatment afforded by the law that, at the time, made 60% of capital gains tax-free. That matter is now moot because those gains are now fully taxed, whether made inside or out of an IRA.

One thing that hasn't changed is that any losses suffered inside an IRA are not deductible.

Tax reform did create a new investment option with an exception to the general prohibition against investing IRA money in precious metals. You can now invest contributions in gold and silver American Eagle coins issued by the government.

However you decide to invest your IRA money, you must do it through a trustee or custodian approved by the IRS. You cannot be the trustee of your own IRA, but you can retain total control over the investments inside the account.

There's no shortage of qualified trustees.

You can set up your IRA at a bank, savings and loan or credit union, where your funds are likely to be invested in certificates of deposit or money-market deposit accounts.

You can choose a mutual fund where your retirement cash

will go into a professionally managed portfolio of stocks or bonds or into a money-market fund.

Insurance companies offer IRAs, too, with funds invested in either fixed or variable annuities. Some advisers shun annuities for IRAs because earnings on an annuity are sheltered from the IRS whether they're in an IRA or not. However, others say that if earnings outstrip those on alternative IRA investments, you can ignore tax peculiarities outside the IRA and focus only on the performance inside.

For the ultimate in IRA investment flexibility you can set up a self-directed account. Offered by full-service and discount brokers, these IRAs let you pick the exact stocks, bonds and other investments you want in your account. The brokerage firm serves as the trustee, but you're the boss. You need a self-directed account to invest in gold or silver coins, real estate investment trusts and limited partnerships.

When choosing a trustee for your IRA, pay particular attention to the fees charged. Some IRA sponsors offer IRA accounts free, others impose annual fees. In the past, those

OLD TAX SYSTEM SIMPLIFIED TAX SYSTEM

charges could be deducted as miscellaneous itemized deductions as long as you paid the fee directly rather than permitting the trustee to deduct the amount from your IRA balance. Now, however, such expenses can be written off only to the extent that your total costs in that category exceed 2% of your adjusted gross income.

You can have as many IRA accounts as you want. You can use a single IRA for all your contributions over the years, open a different account with each year's deposit or split each investment among several accounts. Although the IRS doesn't care how many IRAs you open, trustee fees and bookkeeping chores put a damper on having too many.

MOVING YOUR MONEY AROUND

Although a key trade-off for the IRA tax breaks is the threat of the 10% early-withdrawal penalty, you are not locked into the same IRA investment from the time you put your money in the tax shelter until you retire. You may move your money around freely to take advantage of changes in market conditions or your investment philosophy. There are, of course, rules to be followed. And you don't want to be switching your IRA around willy-nilly. Some investments, such as CDs and annuities, can carry stiff early-withdrawal penalties that have nothing to do with the IRS.

When you decide to transfer your retirement funds from one trustee to another, you have two ways to do it.

Direct transfer. This involves telling your current IRA sponsor to transfer the funds to a new account. The sponsor you are switching to should be able and willing to help expedite the move. The first step is to set up a new account for your money to go to.

You may have to stay on top of the transfer because institutions giving up IRAs are sometimes less than speedy. Before you begin the process, be sure you are clear on how long it's likely to take and that you understand any exit or setup fees involved.

You can use the direct-transfer method as frequently as you

wish, and it is usually the most convenient way to go.

Rollover. The alternative is to use a rollover. This choice may be quicker, and time may be of essence if you're moving your funds to lock in a certain investment.

With a rollover, you actually cash in one account and personally serve as the go-between, shepherding the funds to the new IRA. Within 60 days of the date you receive the money, it must be reinvested in the new IRA; miss the deadline and you forfeit the right to a rollover. As far as the IRS is concerned, you have liquidated the IRA and the full amount is taxable. If you are under 59½, the 10% early-withdrawal fine will be due, too.

If you use a rollover, be sure to tell the sponsor you are leaving not to withhold any part of your money for income taxes. Otherwise, 10% of the amount withdrawn will be withheld and sent to the IRS, as though a taxable distribution rather than a tax-free rollover was involved.

The rollover method can be used only once every 12 months, but that limit applies to each account you have. If you have three separate IRAs, for example, you may roll over each of them once each year.

Although the law forbids borrowing against your IRA—doing so is considered a taxable distribution—the rollover provision offers an opportunity to use IRA money temporarily. You can withdraw funds from the account and use them for whatever purpose you choose—as a bridge loan when buying a new home, for example. As long as the same amount you withdrew is safely tucked back into another IRA within 60 days, there is no adverse tax consequence.

GETTING THE MONEY OUT

Sooner or later, you will want to get to the money you have squirreled away in your IRAs. There are three basic sets of rules for IRA withdrawals, each tied to the owner's age.

• Until you reach age 59½, withdrawals are usually subject to the 10% penalty. (A penalty-free way to tap an IRA at an earlier age is discussed on page 180.)

• Between the day you reach age 59½ and the year in which

you reach age 70½, you may withdraw as much or as little from the account as you like.

• Once you reach age 70½, you must begin to take a minimum amount out of your IRAs each year or face a stiff penalty.

At any time, money coming out of the IRA is taxable, except to the extent that it represents a return of nondeductible contributions, as discussed earlier. The tax deduction you take when you put money in really just puts off the tax bill on the deposit until the money comes out. Also, when the tax-deferred earnings are withdrawn, the IRS finally gets a crack at them.

You can cash in your IRA all at once, but doing so could subject you to an enormous tax bill. You'll probably do better taxwise by taking out as little as necessary each year during the 59½-to-70½ period. Not only does that hold down the tax bill you owe each year, but you also extend the benefit of tax-deferred growth.

But the IRA shelter does not last forever. These tax-favored accounts were created to help you accumulate money for your retirement—not build up a pile of money for your heirs to inherit—so the law demands that you begin pulling money out when you reach age 70½. The minimum withdrawal schedule is designed to get all your money out—and taxed—by the time you die, or at least by the time your designated IRA beneficiary dies. If you don't take out the minimum required each year, the government will relieve you of 50% of the amount you fail to withdraw.

The first mandatory distribution must be made by April 1 following the year you reach age 70½. If your 70th birthday falls in January through June, you will be 70½ before the end of that year and must begin tapping your IRA by the following April. If your 70th birthday is July 1 or later, the first required distribution would be for the next year.

Minimum withdrawals are based on your life expectancy as estimated in tables published by the IRS. To find the required IRA distribution each year, you divide the amount in your IRA at the end of the previous year by the number of years you are expected to live. A 70-year-old, for example, has a life expectancy of 16 years according to the IRS tables. If you had

$200,000 in an IRA, the first required withdrawal would be one-sixteenth of that amount, or $12,500. If you have named a beneficiary for your IRA, your minimum withdrawal would be based on the longer joint life expectancy of your and your beneficiary. (Life expectancy figures for various ages are shown on pages 178 and 179.)

That may not sound bad, but here's the kicker: The IRS demands that you figure the minimum distribution for each IRA you own. If you have diversified into several accounts and have named beneficiaries of different ages, the life expectancy divisors will mean a different percentage has to come out of each account.

Once you determine the minimum withdrawal demanded from each account, add them together to find the total you need to withdraw for the year. You may then decide which account or accounts to tap to meet the minimum distribution requirement. Say, for example, that you have five accounts and you determine you need to withdraw a total of $15,000. If you want to take the full amount out of a single IRA—say the one returning the lowest return on your investment—that's okay. You don't have to take money out of every IRA you own. (A short-lived requirement that a withdrawal be made from each IRA was revoked in 1988.)

Stretching it out. When figuring minimum withdrawals, you are permitted to recompute your life expectancy each year, a move that will let you stretch IRA distributions—and therefore extend the tax shelter—over a longer period of time.

Consider again someone who is 70 years old at year-end. Assuming no beneficiary, the IRA owner's life expectancy is 16 years and one-sixteenth of the account must be withdrawn. If life expectancy is not recomputed, the following year one-fifteenth of the remainder of the account would have to be withdrawn, then one-fourteenth, one-thirteenth and so on.

However, the longer you live, the longer the actuaries expect you to live. Notice in the table on pages 178 and 179, for example, that although a 70-year-old is expected to live 16 years—to age 86—a 75-year-old is given a life expectancy of 12.5 years—to age 87½. The minimum withdrawal rules let you take advantage of that fact of life. Rather than base the payouts on a steady one-sixteenth/one-fifteenth/one-fourteenth stream, you can figure it using your extended life expectancy each year. The first payout would still have to be one-sixteenth of the amount in the account. But the next year the divisor would be 15.3 rather than 15; the following year 14.6 rather than 14, and so on. You can recalculate joint life expectancies, too, to hold down minimum withdrawals.

If your goal is to keep as much as possible as long as possible inside your tax shelter, you can accomplish that by naming the youngest beneficiary possible. The joint life expectancy of a 70-year-old with a 5-year-old beneficiary, for example, is a whopping 76.7 years. But there are a couple of problems with that approach. First, naming a beneficiary ties your hands in an important matter: When you die, your beneficiary gets what's left in the IRA. In other words, don't name a grandchild beneficiary to hold down the minimum withdrawals if you really want your spouse to inherit the account.

Also, starting in 1989 a new rule kicks in to prevent hoarding cash in an IRA by naming a youngster as the account beneficiary. Basically, regardless of the age of your beneficiary, he or she won't be considered to be more than ten years younger than you for purposes of figuring joint life expectancy. This rule won't apply if your beneficiary is your spouse. You can use his or her actual age, no matter how young.

As sweet as the IRA shelter is, it doesn't always make sense to hold down withdrawals. You may simply need more money than the IRS says you have to take. Also, if a future Congress raises tax rates—as many experts believe inevitable—pulling out funds early may let you dodge a bigger tax bill.

In the year you reach age 70½, you have until April 1 of the following year to actually make the first mandatory withdrawal. If your 70th birthday fell in the first half of 1988, for example, you will be required to make a withdrawal for 1988. But you get until April 1 of 1989 to do it. Putting off the withdrawal would let you put off the tax bill on the money until you file your 1989 tax return.

After the first year, required withdrawals must be made by
continued on page 180

MINIMUM IRA WITHDRAWALS

To determine how much you must withdraw from your individual retirement account after age 70½ to avoid the 50% penalty tax, divide your IRA balance at the end of the previous year by a life expectancy figure from the tables below. If you have not named a beneficiary for your account, use the figure in the single-life column. If you have a beneficiary, find the joint-life figure at the point where your age intersects with the age of your beneficiary.

For example, if you are 72 at the end of 1988 and your beneficiary is 65, the joint life expectancy is 22.5 years. To determine the minimum mandatory IRA withdrawal for 1988, you would divide the account balance at the end of 1987 by 22.5. For Life expectancies not shown here, see IRS Publication 590. *Individual Retirement Arrangements.*

JOINT-LIFE EXPECTANCY

YOUR AGE	SINGLE LIFE EXPECTANCY	Beneficiary's Age															
		60	61	62	63	64	65	66	67	68	69	70	71	72	73	74	75
70	16.0	26.2	25.6	24.9	24.3	23.7	23.1	22.5	22.0	21.5	21.1	20.6	20.2	19.8	19.4	19.1	18.8
71	15.3	26.0	25.3	24.7	24.0	23.4	22.8	22.2	21.7	21.2	20.7	20.2	19.8	19.4	19.0	18.6	18.3
72	14.6	25.8	25.1	24.4	23.8	23.1	22.5	21.9	21.3	20.8	20.3	19.8	19.4	18.9	18.5	18.2	17.8

JOINT-LIFE EXPECTANCY

YOUR AGE	SINGLE LIFE AGE EXPECTANCY	Beneficiary's Age															
		60	61	62	63	64	65	66	67	68	69	70	71	72	73	74	75
73	13.9	25.6	24.9	24.2	23.5	22.9	22.2	21.6	21.0	20.5	20.0	19.4	19.0	18.5	18.1	17.7	17.3
74	13.2	25.5	24.7	24.0	23.3	22.7	22.0	21.4	20.8	20.2	19.6	19.1	18.6	18.2	17.7	17.3	16.9
75	12.5	25.3	24.6	23.8	23.1	22.4	21.8	21.1	20.5	19.9	19.3	18.8	18.3	17.8	17.3	16.9	16.5
76	11.9	25.2	24.4	23.7	23.0	22.3	21.6	20.9	20.3	19.7	19.1	18.5	18.0	17.5	17.0	16.5	16.1
77	11.2	25.1	24.3	23.6	22.8	22.1	21.4	20.7	20.1	19.4	18.8	18.3	17.7	17.2	16.7	16.2	15.8
78	10.6	25.0	24.2	23.4	22.7	21.9	21.2	20.5	19.9	19.2	18.6	18.0	17.5	16.9	16.4	15.9	15.4
79	10.0	24.9	24.1	23.3	22.6	21.8	21.1	20.4	19.7	19.0	18.4	17.8	17.2	16.7	16.1	15.6	15.1
80	9.5	24.8	24.0	23.2	22.4	21.7	21.0	20.2	19.5	18.9	18.2	17.6	17.0	16.4	15.9	15.4	14.9

December 31. If you delay your first withdrawal until April 1, you will be required to take two distributions during that calendar year.

If you have a good reason for failing to make the mandatory withdrawal—say the IRA sponsor provided you with incorrect balance information or you didn't understand the life-expectancy method—the IRS can (but doesn't have to) excuse the 50% penalty on the amount you should have withdrawn. You figure any penalty due on Form 5329, *Return for Individual Retirement Arrangement and Qualified Retirement Plan Taxes*. If you think you have a good enough excuse to get the IRS to waive the penalty, attach your explanation to the form. If the IRS agrees, you'll get a refund of the penalty tax.

There is a way to get around having to annually recalculate the minimum withdrawal, too. You can use your IRA funds to buy an immediate-pay annuity. Unlike the annuities offered as IRA accumulation investments, these contracts guarantee to pay you (and perhaps a designated beneficiary) a certain amount for the rest of your life. Because the insurance company figures those payments based on your life expectancy, these contracts will meet the minimum distribution requirements.

Getting your money early. The life-expectancy tables also play a key role in a new exception to the 10% penalty for withdrawals prior to age 59½. Thanks to tax reform, the penalty is waived if the withdrawal is part of a series of roughly equal payments tied to your life expectancy.

To use this loophole to crack an IRA nest egg early, you must stick with the lifetime payout schedule for at least five consecutive years *and* until you're at least 59½. Violate either of those requirements and the 10% penalty would be applied retroactively to your pre-59½ withdrawals.

Here's how the new rule works. If you are 55 and have no IRA beneficiary, your life expectancy is 28.6 years. Although that won't permit you take a big chunk out of your IRA, if you have $100,000 in the account, you could reclaim $3,500 in the first year without penalty. Over the next four years, your penalty-free payouts would probably increase slightly, as life expectancy shortens and the growth of investments inside the

IRA probably outpaces the withdrawals. Once you reach age 60—and pass the age and five-year tests—you can withdraw as much or as little as you desire without worrying about penalty-tax recapture.

Death and the IRA. What if the IRA owner dies while there's still money in the tax shelter?

First, the 10% early-withdrawal penalty does not apply to distributions after the owner's death. The beneficiary of the account can cash in the IRA without worrying about that penalty, regardless of how old the owner was at the time of death or how old the beneficiary is when he or she claims the cash.

The potential problem, however, is that the money pulled out of the IRA is taxable to the beneficiary (except to the extent that it represents a return of nondeductible contributions). That could present you with a substantial tax bill. You may be better off leaving the money in the IRA to continue taking advantage of the tax shelter for as long as possible. Of course the IRS has something to say about that, too.

The rules for inherited IRAs require that if the owner was old enough to have begun making required withdrawals, distributions must continue to the beneficiary at least as fast as if the original owner were still alive.

If the owner was younger than 70½ and required distributions had not yet begun, the payout rules depend on the beneficiary's relationship to the IRA owner.

If you are the surviving spouse, you have the greatest latitude. A widow or widower may cash in part or all of the account without worrying about the early-withdrawal penalty. Or you may roll over the funds into an IRA of your own, in which case the money would be covered by the basic rules: You would be penalized if you withdrew funds before age 59½, and you must start withdrawals when you reach age 70½. If the spouse-beneficiary chooses not to roll over the money into a personal IRA, the funds can remain in the account until the year the original owner would have reached age 70½, at which time withdrawals would have to begin, based on the life expectancy of the beneficiary.

If the beneficiary is not the surviving spouse, the new owner has two basic choices: To withdraw everything from the IRA within five years of the death of the owner or to begin withdrawals within one year of the death of the owner, based on the life expectancy of the beneficiary. The second choice could permit you to extend the tax shelter far longer than five years— exactly how long depends on your age.

If you are not the named beneficiary of the IRA—but inherit it under the original owner's will, for example—your only choice is to cash in the entire IRA within five years.

8
OTHER RETIREMENT PLANS

Keoghs, Simplified Employee Pensions, 401(k)s, Company Pension and Profit Sharing, Social Security

Long before individual retirement accounts became the darlings of taxpayers, Congress provided an array of tax incentives for setting aside today's income for tomorrow's needs. Some of the alternatives have a do-it-yourself appeal. Others are open to you only if your employer offers them. Here's the rundown.

KEOGH PLANS

If you earn any self-employment income—from your own full-time business, a sideline business or free-lance or consulting work—consider setting up a Keogh retirement plan to shelter some of that income. Keoghs are sometimes called H.R. 10 plans. (The first appellation credits the congressman who sponsored the legislation creating the plans; the second refers to the number of the bill that authorized them.)

Funds you contribute to a Keogh are deductible, and earnings inside the account grow without interruption from the IRS—just as in IRAs, discussed in Chapter 7—until you withdraw the funds, presumably in retirement. There are many differences between IRAs and Keoghs, though, and most of them benefit the taxpayer.

For example, rather than an annual $2,000 limit on contributions, the most popular Keogh plans permit deposits of up to $30,000 a year. Payouts are taxable, but there are special methods to ease the tax bite. Also, Keogh plans are not affected by the new restrictions on IRA deductions. You can deduct every dollar you are permitted to put in a Keogh, regardless of how high your income is or whether you or your spouse is covered by another retirement plan.

If you have employees, establishing a Keogh plan requires that you make contributions for them as well as yourself. The discussion here, however, focuses on taxpayers who don't have employees and who therefore are the only participants in the retirement plan.

To qualify for a Keogh, you must have self-employment income. That means money you earn working for yourself rather than someone else. Investment income doesn't count.

How much self-employment income you can deposit in your Keogh and write off on your tax return depends on which kind of plan you choose.

The most flexible is a profit-sharing defined-contribution Keogh. It lets you decide each year how much to contribute. You can even forgo deposits altogether if you decide to skip a year. The maximum annual contribution to a profit-sharing plan is 13.0435% of your self-employment income, up to a top pay-in of $30,000.

That weird figure—13.0435%—results because the law permits you to contribute 15% of your *net* self-employment income. For this purpose, though, net income is defined as the amount left after your Keogh contribution has been subtracted. Say, for example, that your self-employment income for the year is $20,000. Fifteen percent of that would give you an annual contribution of $3,000. However, $3,000 works out to a too-high 17.65% of $17,000—your net income after the $3,000 Keogh deposit. To get the proper Keogh contribution, take 13.0435% of your income (before the contribution). On $20,000 of self-employment income, that sets the contribution limit at $2,609—15% of $17,391 ($20,000 minus the $2,609 contribution).

You can also choose a money-purchase defined-contribution

plan. This plan has the same $30,000 annual limit but permits you to sock away up to 20% of your self-employment income toward that goal. (Actually, the law permits contributions of up to 25% of net self-employment income, but 20% of after-contribution income is the same as 25% of precontribution income.) With a money-purchase plan, a taxpayer with $20,000 of self-employment income could save up to $4,000 in a Keogh.

Although that gives you the potential of a bigger deduction, it comes at a price: You're required to make the fixed-percentage-of-income contribution each year.

One way to boost the percentage of your earnings eligible for a Keogh without locking yourself into a 20% money-purchase plan is to set up both kinds of defined-contribution plans. You could commit 7% of earnings to a money-purchase plan, say, and use a profit-sharing plan to shelter up to 13% more of your self-employment income. You can contribute a total of 20% of your pre-Keogh self-employment income to the two plans, up to the $30,000 annual limit.

The third variety, the defined-benefit Keogh, is the most demanding but also offers the greatest potential tax shelter. With it, you decide how much you want to receive from the plan each year after you retire. Your contributions—up to 100% of your self-employment earnings—are based on how much you must set aside each year before retirement to build a fund sufficient to pay the desired level of benefits.

There is a restriction on how big your Keogh retirement benefit can be, though. The limit is the average of your self-employment earnings during your three highest-earning years or $94,023, whichever is less. (That dollar limit applies in 1988; it will increase each year to keep up with inflation.)

Defined-benefit plans are particularly attractive to older taxpayers—age 50 and older, say—who want and can afford to build up a big retirement fund quickly. Because this type of plan involves complicated actuarial computations, you'll probably need a lawyer or an accountant to help you set it up and figure the required contribution each year.

You can have a Keogh plan in addition to an IRA. However, a Keogh counts as an employer-provided retirement plan for purposes of the IRA restrictions that are discussed in the previous chapter. Basically, if you have a Keogh plan and your adjusted gross income for the year is more than $35,000 on a single return or $50,000 on a joint return, you can't deduct IRA contributions.

Keogh plans are offered by the same types of sponsors that handle IRAs—banks, savings and loans, mutual funds, insurance companies and brokerage firms—and the same kinds of investments are available. (See Chapter 7.) Unlike trustee fees for IRAs, which are deductible only if you pass the 2%-of-AGI threshold for miscellaneous deductions, trustee fees for a Keogh plan are deductible as a business expense, assuming you pay the expense separately rather than have it deducted from the account.

As with IRAs, your Keogh contribution can be made as late as April 15 of the following year. (Keogh contributions can be made even later, in fact, if you get an extension for filing your

"*I suppose one could say it favors the rich, but, on the other hand, it's a great incentive for everyone to make two hundred grand a year.*"

tax return, as discussed in Chapter 14.) There is an important difference on the issue of timing, however. The Keogh plan to which the contribution is made must be set up by year-end for you to claim a deduction. Even if you're not certain exactly how much you can put in the Keogh, the plan must be established by December 31. Any contributions made as late as the filing deadline could then be deducted on your return. With an IRA, you can set up a new account as late as April 15 and still get a deduction.

Penalties and payouts. Tapping an Keogh before age 59½ will generally trigger a 10% early-withdrawal penalty, but as with an IRA there are several exceptions. The penalty does not apply if the owner is disabled or if the funds are distributed after the owner's death. Also, you can get at the money early if funds are withdrawn periodically over your life expectancy, as under the IRA rules discussed on page 180. The Tax Reform Act of 1986 added an extra exception to the early-withdrawal penalty, too. If you pull funds out of your Keogh to pay catastrophic medical bills, the 10% penalty does not apply. This exception applies only to funds used to pay medical bills that exceed 7.5% of your adjusted gross income. Another exception lets you get at your money without penalty as early as age 55 if you have closed the business that has generated the self-employment income going into the Keogh.

The threat of the penalty does not mean your Keogh funds are locked in a single investment until you retire. As with an IRA, you can move your money around using the direct trustee-to-trustee transfer or rollover method, discussed on pages 173 and 174. The once-in-12-month limit on rollovers applies to Keoghs as well as IRAs.

When you reach age 59½, you can withdraw funds from your account without penalty. Between that time and the year you reach age 70½, you can withdraw as much or as little as you want from your Keogh. Once you reach 70½, though, the law demands that the Keogh tax shelter begin disappearing—just as with an IRA. At that time, the law demands annual payouts based on your life expectancy or the joint life expectancy of you and your beneficiary. Failure to withdraw funds fast enough subjects you to a 50% excess accumulation penalty: The IRS will relieve you of half the amount you should have pulled out of the Keogh.

Note this additional difference between IRAs and Keoghs. With an IRA, not only are withdrawals required to begin after age 70½, but that age also brings an end to your right to contribute to the account. With a Keogh plan, however, there is no prohibition against continuing tax-deductible contributions. Regardless of your age, if you continue to have self-employment income, you can continue to stash part of it in your Keogh tax shelter.

Lump-sum distribution. There is a special, often favorable, taxing method available to Keogh investors. If you have had the plan for at least five years and cash in the entire account at once, the withdrawal may qualify as a lump-sum distribution. If you are over age 59½, part of the payout could be totally tax-free and the rest taxed under the special five- or ten-year averaging method. The details of those methods—which are also available to trim the tax on lump-sum distributions from company plans—are presented beginning on page 199. In brief, if you qualify for five-year averaging, the tax is figured as though you were receiving the Keogh money over five years rather than all at once. That, plus the potentially tax-free portion, can hold Uncle Sam's take to far less than it would be if the payout was simply taxed in your top tax bracket.

Beware, though, that the Tax Reform Act of 1986, sets a stingy limit on use of the averaging method. It's available only once in your lifetime. You wouldn't want to "waste" the tax benefits by applying averaging to a relatively small Keogh payout, for example, if it is likely you would want to apply it later to a larger company-plan distribution.

Reporting requirements. Just as the tax benefits can be greater, there's more paperwork involved with a Keogh plan than with an IRA.

If you have a defined-contribution plan, you must file Form 5500EZ each year, a one-page form that's fairly simple to complete. If you have a defined-benefit plan, however, you must also file a Form 5500 Schedule B, a complicated two-page form showing how you arrived at the required contribution. That schedule must be signed by an actuary attesting to the accuracy of the information provided.

If your Keogh plan covers employees as well as yourself, you generally must file the much more complicated Form 5500-C. One bright spot: The Keogh report for the year isn't due April 15 of the following year. The deadline is generally July 31.

SIMPLIFIED EMPLOYEE PENSIONS

This is another do-it-yourself retirement-plan option if you have self-employment income. Although designed as an easy-to-administer retirement plan for small businesses, you can open an SEP if you have self-employment income, from a sideline business or free-lancing, for example. As with a Keogh plan, if you have full-time employees, you must make contributions for them as well as yourself. This discussion, though, assumes no employees are involved.

Sometimes called SEP-IRAs or Super IRAs, these plans are a hybrid between Keogh plans and individual retirement accounts. You must have self-employment income to use an SEP, and the annual contribution limit is the same as for profit-sharing Keoghs: 13.0435% of self-employment income up to a top deposit of $30,000 a year. You also have the flexibility to alter the percentage of income deposited in the SEP or to skip contributions altogether some years.

Contributions go into a special individual retirement account set up at a bank, mutual fund, brokerage or other sponsor. You have the same investment and transfer options as with a regular IRA. When you set up the account, be sure the trustee knows it is an SEP instead of a garden-variety IRA. Otherwise you might run into some resistance if you try to deposit more than $2,000 a year.

SEPs are covered by many of the same rules that apply to IRAs. Your contributions are deductible, and earnings compound tax-deferred. The 10% early-withdrawal penalty hits payouts before age 59½, and distributions are required starting the year you reach age 70½.

The big differences are that you can sock much more in an SEP—up to $30,000 a year—and you can write off SEP contributions without regard to the new restriction on IRA deductions for high-income taxpayers who are covered by company retirement plans.

SEPs are not burdened by the annual reporting requirements that apply to Keogh plans. All you have to do is claim the deduction for your contribution. Another advantage is that, unlike the December 31 deadline for opening a Keogh plan, taxpayers who choose this plan can open the account as late as April 15 and still deduct contributions for the previous year. If you miss the deadline for opening a Keogh, you can use the SEP as a last-minute tax shelter, and if you decide you would rather have the 20%-of-income contribution limit of a money-purchase Keogh, you can establish such a plan and use a tax-free rollover to transfer your SEP funds into it.

Note this, too: The SEP is considered an employer-provided plan for purposes of the new IRA-deduction restriction. If you have such a plan and your AGI for the year is over the IRA income thresholds, you won't be able to write off contributions to your regular IRA.

401(k) PLANS

Unlike IRAs, Keoghs and SEPs, 401(k) plans must be set up by your employer. This isn't a do-it-yourself tax shelter. But that's not necessarily bad. When the employer is involved, some of the company's cash—rather than just your own—is usually being set aside for your golden years.

With 401(k) plans, there's some volunteerism on your behalf involved, too. In fact, these plans—named after the section of the tax code that permits them—involve employees taking a voluntary pay cut in order to cut their tax bills.

What's going on here? Has the obsession to beat the IRS added financial hara-kiri to the arsenal of tax-saving strategies?

Not at all. Also known as "salary reduction plans" and "cash or deferred arrangements," 401(k) plans give employees the option to divert a portion of salary to a tax-sheltered savings account set up by the employer. The IRS agrees to postpone taxing the portion of the pay you agree to postpone receiving.

Say, for example, that you earn $50,000 a year and your company's plan permits you to divert as much as 10% of your salary to the 401(k). That means you could request a $5,000 pay cut, with the cash that would otherwise be in your paycheck going into the 401(k). The advantage is that only the remaining $45,000 would be taxed—saving $1,400 in the 28% bracket. The result is that for an after-tax cost of $3,600, you have set aside $5,000 in a tax-sheltered retirement account.

As with an IRA, earnings accumulate tax-free, so you have the power of compounding working on 100% of your earnings. The tax bill doesn't come due until you tap the account.

Although tax reform restricted the amount of salary that can be diverted to a 401(k) plan, the new limit is still far above the $2,000 IRA cap. For 1988, the cap is $7,313, an amount that will increase in the future to keep up with inflation. Your personal limit depends on your salary and what percentage of it the company permits to go into the retirement plan. Most firms allow contributions of between 2% and 15% of compensation.

The company match. A special attraction of 401(k) plans is that most firms offering them sweeten the pot by matching part of the employee's contribution. Companies often kick in 50 cents for each dollar an employee sets aside. Some firms match 25% or less and others match dollar for dollar. Matching contributions do not count toward the $7,313 annual contribution cap.

If your firm offers matching contributions, learn how the company funds are vested, that is, when the money is yours to take if you leave the firm. Your own money is automatically 100% vested. The company's contributions, however, may be progressively vested over the years so that if you quit after just a few years in the plan you may forfeit part or all of the matching deposits. This point is controlled by the blueprints of your employer's plan.

Getting your money out. Like IRAs, the aim of 401(k) plans is to encourage saving for retirement. So along with the tax breaks come restrictions aimed at keeping you away from your nest egg until retirement.

Basically, salary funneled to a 401(k) account is locked up until you reach age 59½, unless you die, become disabled or quit the company.

To qualify for a hardship payout, the employee must need the money—to buy a house or pay tuition or medical bills, perhaps—and not have other resources available to meet that need. The IRS imposes other restrictions, too, and it's up to your company whether or not to permit hardship withdrawals and, if so, under what circumstances.

Even if your plan provides for such withdrawals, though, you're not home free. Hardship withdrawals made before age 59½ are subject to a 10% early-distribution penalty. Starting in 1989, the most you can pull out for hardship expenses is the total of your personal contributions to the account. You won't be able to touch company deposits or earnings.

Note that a key difference between IRAs and 401(k)s is that, except in limited circumstances, you *can't get money out* of a 401(k) early—even if you're willing to pay the 10% penalty. Plan rules control whether you can tap the account early. When you can, you still have to worry about the 10% IRS penalty.

There are several exceptions to that penalty. It is waived, for example, if the pre-59½ distribution is:
• Made after your death;
• Made because of your disability;
• Part of a series of roughly equal payments based on your life expectancy or the joint life expectancy of you and a beneficiary;
• Made after you leave the job in the year you reach 55 or later; or
• Used to pay deductible medical expenses.

If you leave your job before age 55, you can still avoid the penalty on a 401(k) payout by rolling the funds into an IRA.

There may be a way to tap your account early without being burned by the 10% penalty. Company plans can permit employees to borrow from their accounts. Government restrictions on such loans are detailed on page 196. Basically, you can borrow no more than half of your account, up to a maximum loan of $50,000, and the loan must be repaid within five years, unless the money is used to buy a principal residence. Although the law permits such loan provisions, it's up to your company whether you can borrow from the plan.

After age 59½, distributions from the plan are taxed as ordinary income. If you receive a lump-sum distribution, it can qualify for five-year averaging to trim the tax due, as discussed on page 201.

These plans are company retirement plans for purposes of the IRA deduction restriction, but it's possible that deferring salary into a 401(k) will boost the size of your allowable IRA deduction. Because 401(k) contributions reduce your taxable salary, they may pull your AGI down to a level that permits IRA deductions.

403(b) plans. Continuing in the alphanumeric soup, 403(b) plans (also named after the section of the tax code that authorizes them) are tax-sheltered retirement programs for public-school teachers and employees of nonprofit organizations. Also known as tax-sheltered annuities or tax-deferred annuities, 403(b) plans are similar to 401(k)s in that they are generally funded through salary deferral. Earnings that are diverted to this type of savings plan don't show up in your taxable pay.

The percentage of salary that can be contributed annually to a 403(b) plan is limited by a complicated formula that involves how long you have been employed and how much you have contributed in previous years. The 1988 dollar limit is $9,500, compared to $7,313 for a 401(k).

The rules for early withdrawals—including the 10% penalty on distributions prior to age 59½—are also similar to those that apply to 401(k) plans. These plans can also include provisions for hardship withdrawals and loans.

COMPANY PENSION AND PROFIT-SHARING PLANS

These retirement programs don't require employee contributions. Qualified plans—so called because they must adhere to government standards—let the employer claim an immediate tax deduction for funds set aside for the employees, although employees aren't taxed until they actually get their hands on the retirement benefits. Just how those benefits are taxed is discussed on page 196.

Faster vesting. First consider how you earn nonforfeitable rights to the money that is being set aside for you. Companies usually require that you work for a certain number of years before you are guaranteed retirement benefits. Quit or get fired before putting in the required time and you kiss part or all of your benefits good-bye.

When you have worked long enough to have an unqualified right to your benefits, you are considered fully vested. Through 1988, companies could require employees to work for ten years to meet the plan's vesting requirements. Leave before passing the required threshold and you could leave empty-handed.

The Tax Reform Act of 1986 demanded that retirement plans speed up the process as of 1989. Companies can choose between two schedules. Under one, known as cliff vesting, you will lock in benefits after five years in the retirement plan. Leave before five years, though, and you forfeit all your benefits. Or, companies can use a seven-year gradual vesting schedule under which you earn a nonforfeitable right to 20% of your benefits after three years and an additional 20% each year until you are 100% vested after seven years. Here's how the schedules work:

	Percent Vested	
Years in Plan	**Cliff**	**Gradual**
1	0%	0%
2	0	0
3	0	20
4	0	40
5	100	60
6		80
7		100

(The new mandatory vesting schedules do not apply to participants in multiemployer pension plans established through collective bargaining.)

Although the new vesting schedules are not mandatory until 1989, time you put in on the job prior to the effective date will count toward the five- or seven-year requirement. Of course, employers can provide for speedier vesting if they wish.

Early-distribution penalties. Tax reform made sure you earn rights to your benefits sooner, but also hiked the cost of withdrawing funds early. The same 10% penalty that hits early withdrawals from individual retirement accounts now also generally applies if you receive company retirement benefits before reaching age 59½—as you might if you quit your job. When you leave a company, some plans will hang on to your vested benefits until you reach retirement age; others will simply cash you out—that is, pay you whatever your vested benefit is worth.

Since the whole point of the tax benefits for retirement plans is to help make sure you'll have money to live on in retirement, the 10% penalty is designed to encourage you to roll over such payouts into an IRA. Such a rollover lets you dodge the 10% penalty because, once inside the IRA, the money is still tied up until you're at least 59½.

There are, of course, the inevitable exceptions to the early-withdrawal penalty. It does not apply if one of these conditions exists:

• You are disabled.

• The distribution is made to your beneficiary after your death.

• The payments are made in roughly equal installments over your life expectancy or the life expectancy of you and your beneficiary. (These payments must continue for at least five years and until you are at least 59½ for this exception, as discussed in the previous chapter.)

• The payout comes after you leave the job in a year you are at least 55 years old.

• The money is used to pay catastrophic medical expenses in excess of 7.5% of your adjusted gross income.

Even if you qualify for one of the exceptions, the funds you receive will be taxed as ordinary income in the year you receive them. As noted above, however, you can avoid the penalty by rolling the payout into an IRA. That choice also puts off the tax bill on the benefits and permits continued tax-deferred growth of your nest egg. That triple benefit gives the rollover route almost irresistible appeal.

Plan loans. Although you usually can't withdraw funds from a company plan early without penalty, you may be able to borrow from the plan. Check with company officials to see if your pension or profit-sharing plan permits you to borrow against your vested benefits.

To make sure loans aren't used as a loophole around the early-distribution rules, there are restrictions. You have to pay interest on the loan. But since it is secured by your interest in the plan, the rate may be below what you would have to pay on other borrowing. If the loan is for any purpose other than to buy a principal residence, it must be repaid within five years. There's no time limit for repaying home loans, but these must include a regular repayment schedule with payments required at least quarterly. Note, too, that if you borrow from a plan loan to buy a home, the loan must be secured by the house for the interest to qualify to be deducted as mortgage interest.

There's also a limit on how much you can borrow. Basically, you can't borrow more than half of your vested benefit in the plan, up to a maximum loan of $50,000. There's an exception, though, that permits loans of up to $10,000 without worrying about the half-the-benefit limit.

TAXATION OF BENEFITS

The point of all these retirement plans, of course, is to provide you with money to spend after your regular paychecks stop. When you begin receiving your benefits, the IRS is standing by to tax all the money that has built up in your retirement tax shelters. Although some people seem to believe there is an enchanted age somewhere between 65 and 80 after which they are excused from the burden of paying taxes, there's no such luck. As long as you're receiving income, the government wants a share of it.

Benefits under a company retirement plan are usually paid out either as a lump sum (see page 199) or as an annuity, with regular payments for a set number of years or for the rest of your life.

If the company fully funds the annuity, every dime you receive is taxable. When you have contributed after-tax funds to the plan, however, part of the payments will be tax-free because they are simply a return of your already taxed investment.

Figuring out what's what is quite complicated. The tax-free portion depends on how much after-tax money you have invested and the total you are expected to receive in retirement payments. Because annuities usually guarantee payment for the rest of your life, the amount you are expected to receive depends on how long you're expected to live after payments begin.

YOUR AGE	**SINGLE LIFE EXPECTANCY**	**JOINT-LIFE EXPECTANCY**										
		Beneficiary's Age										
		60	**61**	**62**	**63**	**64**	**65**	**66**	**67**	**68**	**69**	**70**
60	24.2	29.7	29.2	28.8	28.4	28.0	27.6	27.3	27.0	26.7	26.3	26.2
61	23.3	29.2	28.7	28.3	27.8	27.4	27.1	26.7	26.4	26.1	25.8	25.6
62	22.5	28.8	28.3	27.8	27.3	26.9	26.5	26.1	25.8	25.5	25.2	24.9
63	21.6	28.4	27.8	27.3	26.9	26.4	26.0	25.6	25.2	24.9	24.6	24.3
64	20.8	28.0	27.9	26.9	26.4	25.9	25.2	25.1	24.7	24.3	24.0	23.7
65	20.0	27.6	27.1	26.5	26.0	25.5	25.0	24.6	24.2	23.8	23.4	23.1
66	19.2	27.3	26.7	26.1	25.6	25.1	24.6	24.1	23.7	23.3	22.9	22.5
67	18.4	27.0	26.4	25.8	25.2	24.7	24.2	23.7	23.2	22.8	22.4	22.0
68	17.6	26.7	26.1	25.5	24.9	24.3	23.8	23.3	22.8	22.3	21.9	21.5
69	16.8	26.5	25.8	25.2	24.6	24.0	23.4	22.9	22.4	21.9	21.5	21.1
70	16.0	26.2	25.6	24.9	24.3	23.7	23.1	22.5	22.0	21.5	21.1	20.6

Life expectancies for other ages and other age combinations can be found in IRS Publication 575, Pension and Annuity Income.

Say, for example, that you have contributed $10,000 to a

company retirement plan that beginning at age 65 will pay you $200 a month for the rest of your life. According to IRS life-expectancy tables, a 65-year-old is expected to live for 20 years. Assuming you receive $200 a month for 20 years, you will receive payments totaling $48,000. Your $10,000 investment is 21% of that total, so 21% of each payment you receive would be tax-free.

If you choose a joint-and-survivor annuity—with payments guaranteed during your life and, if you die before your beneficiary, through his or her life, too—the expected return would be based on your joint life expectancy.

See page 197 for the life-expectancy table the IRS uses for determining the expected returns from annuities for taxpayers of various ages.

Determining what part of your monthly checks is tax-free is even more complicated if you have a variable annuity—one in which the payments can change depending on the return on the funds invested on your behalf—or one that, for example, pays you a certain amount during your life and then a different, usually lower, amount to your survivor. If you have contributed to your company plan, be sure you get the advice you need to determine what part of the payments you receive is tax-free.

Playing the Grinch. Before tax reform, if you outlived your life expectancy, you could continue to exclude the set percentage of each payment even though you had already recovered your entire investment in the contract. Now, once you have recovered your investment—the $10,000 of after-tax contributions in our example above—100% of all future payments is taxed.

To be fair, the new law also allows a tax deduction on your final tax return if you die before recovering all of your contributions. That won't help you, but it may be important to your heirs if you are receiving partially tax-free annuity payments and die before the age assumed by the life-expectancy tables.

Commercial annuities. If you buy a commercial annuity—perhaps to supplement your company pension—payments are taxed in the same manner as benefits under a company plan. A portion of each payment, based on the ratio of your cost to your total expected return, is tax-free.

When figuring your tax-free portion, you can't count as part of your investment funds from an IRA or Keogh plan or pretax contributions you made to a 401(k) or other tax-sheltered retirement plan. Because those funds and the earnings on them have not yet been taxed, they will be taxable when they are withdrawn—whether directly or via annuity payments.

LUMP-SUM DISTRIBUTIONS

When you retire, you may be offered a chance to take your retirement benefits in a lump sum. Temper your excitement about the prospect of getting a big hunk of cash with the thought of the huge tax bill it will trigger. The tax law gives you several options on how to handle such a payout, and the choice you make can have a lot to do with how financially comfortable you are in retirement. This is another area where tax reform added complications to an already tough decision.

When you get a lump-sum payment, the first thing you do is subtract from the distribution any after-tax contributions that you made to the plan. That's your money, tax-free. As for the taxable part:

• You can simply take the cash and pay tax on it in your top tax bracket. That's sure to be the worst choice taxwise.

• You can roll over the funds into an IRA, a move that postpones the tax bill until you later withdraw the funds from that tax shelter. This choice is attractive if you won't need the bulk of the money for at least a few years.

• You may be able to apply a special computation formula—known as five- or ten-year forward averaging—to the payout and perhaps treat part of the distribution as tax-favored capital gains. This could be your best bet if you plan to spend a substantial part of the payout fairly soon.

The rollover. To qualify to be rolled over into an IRA, the payout must:

• Represent at least 50% of your vested interest in the plan;

• Be received within a single tax year; and

• Be paid because you quit, retired, became disabled or died.

To use the rollover option, you have to act within 60 days of the time you receive the distribution: That's the deadline for having the money safely ensconced in an IRA. Once you meet the 60-day test, you can move the money around as often as you like, using the procedures discussed in the previous chapter. If you want to diversify your investment, you can roll the money into several IRA accounts.

The advantage of the rollover is that you continue to hold the IRS at bay. Funds that otherwise would go to pay taxes stay in the account and enjoy tax-sheltered growth.

You don't have to put all the money in an IRA. You could keep some of the cash out—paying taxes on it right away—and roll the rest into an IRA to preserve the tax shelter. Assuming you receive the distribution after you reach age 59½—so you don't have to worry about the 10% early-withdrawal penalty for tapping the IRA—you would have penalty-free access to the rest of the money as you need it. Only as you withdraw cash from the IRA is it taxed.

Choosing an IRA rollover does prevent you from using the special averaging methods discussed next. Whether that's a significant loss would depend on how quickly you'll need access to your funds. Holding off the tax bill by using an IRA for just a

few years could more than compensate for skipping the chance to pay a somewhat reduced tax bill now.

If you have a Keogh plan—set up with self-employment income—you can hold off the IRS *and* retain the right to averaging. The company-plan distribution can be rolled over tax-free into the Keogh. If you later take a lump-sum distribution from the Keogh, it could qualify for averaging.

Five- or ten-year averaging. These special computation methods tax the distribution all at once, but the bill is figured as though you received the money over a number of years. Although you must actually pay the tax right away, the amount due will be significantly less than if the full amount was heaped on top of your other taxable income.

This is one of the many areas that tax reform complicated rather than simplified. Congress decided to abolish the old ten-year averaging method for most people and replaced it with a five-year method. If you were at least 50 years old before January 1, 1986, you still have the option of using ten-year averaging. Making the right choice involves some hair-raising calculations.

First consider the five-year method, then the options for older taxpayers.

To use either type of averaging, your lump-sum distribution must:

● Come from a qualified plan in which you have participated for at least five years before the distribution;

● Represent your entire interest in the plan and be paid to you within a single tax year;

● Be paid after you leave your job; and

● Be paid after you reach age 59½. (The age test does not apply if you were born before January 1, 1936.)

If your payout passes the test, what's the prize?

First, if the distribution is less than $70,000, part of it is absolutely tax-free, thanks to the "minimum-distribution allowance." This break can exempt from tax 50% of the first $20,000 of a lump-sum distribution. As the payout rises above $20,000, the tax-free portion shrinks. The maximum allowance of $10,000 is reduced by 20% of the amount by which the distribution exceeds $20,000. This table shows how the minimum-distribution allowance is phased out:

Distribution	Tax-Free Amount
$10,000	$ 5,000
20,000	10,000
30,000	8,000
40,000	6,000
50,000	4,000
60,000	2,000
70,000 and more	0

The tax on the rest of the distribution is figured this way:
• Divide the total by 5.
• Find the tax on the resulting amount using the rates for single taxpayers. (Your actual filing status and your other income for the year don't matter.)
• Multiply that tax by 5 to find the tax bill on your lump-sum distribution.

Consider this example. Say you receive a lump-sum distribution of $250,000. That's too big to benefit from the minimum-distribution allowance. But you benefit from averaging. One-fifth of $250,000 is $50,000. Although part of it falls in the 33% tax bracket in 1988, most of it is taxed at either 15% or 28%, and the tax bill is $12,019. Multiplying that by 5 gives you a tax bill of $60,095.

A stiff bill to be sure, but it's more than $10,000 less than it would be if averaging weren't available. A key privilege of averaging is that you get to take quintuple advantage of the lower tax brackets. Each fifth is treated as though it were your only income for the year.

There's another twist that can further complicate your decision making—but that might save you money.

Benefits accrued before 1974 can be taxed at a flat 20% rate rather than included with the rest of the lump-sum distribution when the averaging calculations are done. (That 20% rate applies because it was the top tax applied to capital gains before Congress abolished the tax-favored treatment for such gains.)

Your employer should report to you how much of your distribution qualifies for capital-gains treatment. It's based on the years you participated in the retirement plan before 1974 compared with the total time you were in the plan. It's up to you whether or not to use the flat 20% rate or apply averaging to your entire distribution. You'll have to figure the tax bill both ways to know which is better.

Congress is simplifying this decision, however, by gradually eliminating the option to treat pre-1974 benefits as capital gains. Starting in 1988, the following phaseout schedule applies:

Year	Percent of Pre-1974 Gains Qualifying as Capital Gains
1988	95%
1989	75
1990	50
1991	25
1992	0

Assume you receive a lump-sum distribution in 1989 and the statement from your employer reports that $50,000 qualifies as pre-1974 benefits. Thanks to the phaseout, the most to which you could apply the 20% tax rate would be $37,500, 75% of $50,000. That's still advantageous if that $37,500 would otherwise be taxed in either the 28% or 33% bracket.

Special rules for older taxpayers. Now for the advantage of age. If you were born before 1936, you have the option of applying ten-year averaging to your distribution.

It works basically the same as its five-year cousin. You first subtract any after-tax contributions—your tax free portion of the payout. If the remainder is less than $70,000, you get the advantage of the minimum-distribution allowance.

Divide the remainder by ten and find the tax on that amount, using the rates for single taxpayers, and multiply it by ten.

Sounds great, but there's a catch. To use the ten-year version, you must apply the tax rates that applied in 1986—regardless of when you actually receive the distribution. Those rates, shown on page 204, are much higher and the tax brackets much more steeply progressive than current rates. (One reason Congress compressed the averaging period was that the lawmakers figured special relief was not as necessary under the new, lower tax rates.)

1986 Tax Rates for Single Returns

These are the tax rates that applied to single taxpayers in 1986; they must be used if you apply ten-year averaging to a lump-sum distribution.

Taxable Income	Tax
Up to $ 2,480	
$ 2,481 to 3,670	11% of amount over $ 2,480
3,671 to 4,750	$ 131 + 12% of amount over 3,670
4,751 to 7,010	261 + 14% of amount over 4,750
7,011 to 9,170	577 + 15% of amount over 7,010
9,171 to 11,650	901 + 16% of amount over 9,170
11,651 to 13,920	1,298 + 18% of amount over 11,650
13,921 to 16,190	1,706 + 20% of amount over 13,920
16,191 to 19,640	2,160 + 23% of amount over 16,190
19,641 to 25,360	2,954 + 26% of amount over 19,640
25,361 to 31,080	4,441 + 30% of amount over 25,360
31,081 to 36,800	6,157 + 34% of amount over 31,080
36,801 to 44,780	8,102 + 38% of amount over 36,800
44,781 to 59,670	11,134 + 42% of amount over 44,780
59,671 to 88,270	17,388 + 48% of amount over 59,670
Over 88,270	31,116 + 50% of amount over 88,270

Consider the effect on a $250,000 lump-sum distribution, which, using five-year averaging and 1988 rates, produces a tax bill of $60,095.

The payout is too big to benefit from the minimum-distribution allowance, so divide the full amount by ten. To the $25,000 result, you must add $2,480 (an amount known as the zero-bracket amount, which is already built into the 1986 tax tables). The tax on $27,480, using 1986 rates, is $5,077. Multiply that by ten and your tax on the quarter-of-a-million-dollar payout is $50,770.

The $10,000 savings over five-year averaging is the bonus you receive because of your age.

The tax could be even less if you qualify to treat part of the payout as capital gains taxed at the flat 20% rate. And if you're old enough to use ten-year averaging, you don't have to worry about the phaseout of capital-gains treatment. Taxpayers born before January 1, 1936, can treat 100% of the pre-1974 benefits as capital gains if they use either five- or ten-year averaging. Whether doing so makes sense, however, depends on the size of your distribution. You need to crunch the numbers both ways to see if electing capital-gains treatment can save you money. It's up to you whether to carve out pre-1974 benefits or apply averaging to your full distribution.

Considering how complex this area of the law is and how important it is that you make the right choice, you may well need professional help sorting through your options. There is a rule of thumb to help with the five- or ten-year averaging decision. For lump-sum distributions of about $470,000 or less, ten-year averaging is the better bet. Larger distributions will benefit from five-year averaging using the lower 1988 rates. Since Congress has a penchant for changing tax rates, though, you'll have to do your own number crunching for later years, using the tax rates in effect when you get your payout.

TOO MUCH OF A GOOD THING

Although Congress has been more than happy to help taxpayers save for their retirement, in 1986 the lawmakers decided to put a limit on that generosity.

On one front, tax reform scaled down the maximum benefit you can receive from a company plan if you retire early. Most employees have nothing to worry about, though. The new rule is aimed primarily at preventing business owners from socking away enormous amounts for themselves in tax-qualified plans.

Under the old law, a plan could provide for benefits as high as $90,000 a year for an employee retiring at age 62 or older. Quitting earlier reduced that top benefit, but not below $75,000.

Now you must be at least 65 to collect the top benefit, which has increased to $94,023 for 1988 and will rise in the future in step with inflation. For each year you are younger when you retire, the maximum annual payment is reduced—falling to around $40,000 if you retire at age 55. The reduction is actuarially based—that is, the younger you are when you begin receiving benefits, the longer you are expected to live to collect them and, therefore, the less you can get each year. The maximum benefit from a qualified plan can be further trimmed if you participate in the plan for fewer than ten years before retiring. Benefits accrued before 1987 escape this crackdown.

Another change may affect far more taxpayers. The law now includes a 15% penalty tax if you receive "too much" in retirement benefits in any year. As far as Congress is concerned, too much is anything over $150,000.

That's not $150,000 from any single plan. It's $150,000 in total taxable retirement benefits (social security benefits don't count). If you held several jobs during your career and enjoy several pensions, the limit applies to the combined amount you receive, plus any IRA or Keogh withdrawals during the year. The 15% tax applies to any excess over $150,000, and it's in addition to the regular income tax you must pay on the benefits.

There is an exception if you receive a lump-sum distribution and elect to use five- or ten-year averaging. In that case, your annual limit jumps to $750,000 for the year of the distribution. Another exception can protect benefits accrued before August 1, 1986, from this new rule. If you believe this new penalty may apply to you, check with a specialist before you file your 1988 return. To qualify to protect benefits accrued before August 1, 1986, you must elect to do so with your 1988 return.

When figuring whether your are threatened by the $150,000 limit, don't count benefits you roll over tax-free into an IRA. Only when you pull that money out does it fall under the rule.

SOCIAL SECURITY BENEFITS

Not so long ago, the tax rules for social security benefits were the epitome of simplicity: Benefits were tax-free. Period.

No more, and this complication can't be blamed on the Tax Reform Act of 1986. Social security benefits lost their tax-free status in 1984. Now as much as half of your benefits can be taxed in your top tax bracket. And the formula for figuring whether any of your benefits are hit can effectively impose a back-door tax on income from otherwise tax-free bonds.

Your benefits are vulnerable if your adjusted gross income plus tax-exempt interest plus 50% of your social security benefits exceeds a particular amount based on your filing status.

If you file a joint return, the threshold is $32,000; if you are single and file and individual return, the base amount is $25,000; if you are married and file a separate return, the threshold is $0.

When your income—as defined above—exceeds the threshold, half of the excess or half of your benefits, whichever is less, is the amount of benefits to be included in your taxable income.

Assume you and your spouse file a joint return. Your AGI for the year is $30,000, and you have an extra $4,000 of tax-free interest from municipal bonds and $5,000 of social security benefits. Adding your AGI ($30,000), your tax-exempt interest ($4,000) and half of your benefits ($2,500) gives you $36,500. That's $4,500 over the $32,000 threshold for joint returns. Since half of that amount ($2,250) is less than half your benefits ($2,500), the smaller amount is the part of your social security that is taxed. In the 28% bracket, that will cost $630.

If you're affected by this tax, some planning can help limit the bite. If your AGI will include amounts withdrawn from an IRA, for example, you may be able to stagger your withdrawals and vary your income so that your social security benefits are taxed only in alternate years. The same goes for the sale of stocks or other appreciated property. By timing your sales, you may be able to boost your income in years when half your benefits will be taxed anyway and limit income in intervening years to reduce the amount of your benefits that fall victim to the IRS.

If you have municipal bonds, you may consider unloading them now that this "tax-free" income can trigger a tax on your social security benefits. That could backfire, however, because switching to a comparable taxable investment would probably give you a higher yield that could push even more of your benefits into the taxable range. Even though tax-exempt income is taken into account in the social security formula, the income itself is still not taxed.

9
DEDUCTIBLE BUSINESS AND EMPLOYEE EXPENSES

It takes money to make money. That axiom is normally associated with investments, but you often have to spend money to earn money on the job, too, whether as an employee or in your own business. And, believe it or not, the IRS is reasonable enough not to tax you on the *outgo* necessary to produce taxable *income*.

This chapter is devoted to ways to make those expenses pay off in tax savings. Even with tax reform's rate cuts fully in place, every $100 worth of deductible expenses can put as much as $33 in your pocket. To be sure, people who are self-employed have more opportunities to shift their expenses to Uncle Sam than do those who work for others. But employees make a costly mistake if they *assume* there's nothing in the way of write-offs for them. The deductions may be rare, but they are precious.

One new impediment for employees is that several write-offs that had been adjustments to income—and therefore deductible whether or not you itemized—are now treated as miscellaneous expenses and are deductible only to the extent that the total exceeds 2% of your adjusted gross income. If your AGI is $75,000, for example, the first $1,500 of miscellaneous expenses are not deductible.

Employees shouldn't feel singled out by Congress, though. The self-employed were clobbered by tax reform, too, and only now are some of the changes hitting home.

Whether you are an employee or self-employed, your chore is to make the most of the write-offs left open to you.

AUTOMOBILE EXPENSES

If you use your car on business, either as an employee whose job requires it or in your own business, the cost is a deductible expense. Sounds simple enough. But the IRS is so worried about taxpayers inappropriately charging off the cost of personal driving, and so intent on thwarting those who try, that business use of a car drives you smack into a Pandora's box of rules and regulations.

In fact, Congress and the IRS seem intent on making you do more work for fewer and less-valuable write-offs. Gone, for example, is the investment tax credit that served as a cash rebate of up to 6% of the cost of your business car. Gone, too, is the rapid, three-year depreciation of automobiles. Since 1987, depreciation write-offs stretch over at least six years. Employees who rack up deductible mileage on the job find their deductions threatened by the 2%-of-AGI threshold that applies to miscellaneous deductions.

Although a "woe is me" reaction to such deprivation is natural, preserving any business-car deductions you have coming is well worth the hassle.

The first step is to maintain thorough records of your business driving to pinpoint what portion of your costs qualify as business expenses rather than nondeductible personal expenses. Keep track of all your business mileage and compare it to the total mileage driven during the year.

It's almost impossible to use a car 100% of the time for business because commuting to and from the office is considered personal driving, just as are trips to the grocery store or the kids' school. If you have more than one office, either for the same employer or for more than one job, include as business mileage the trips you make between the two.

Standard mileage rate. Once you have determined your business use of your car, you may choose between two methods of calculating your deduction. One—the standard mileage rate—is by far the simpler. And, as you would expect, it's also likely to be the less valuable.

Each autumn the IRS announces its standard mileage rates for the year. These are fixed per-mile rates you can use to find your deduction. For 1987, the IRS standard rates were 22.5 cents a mile for the first 15,000 business miles traveled and 11 cents a mile for additional miles. Any change for 1988 is likely to be minor.

At 1987 rates, for example, 18,000 business miles translated to a deduction of $3,705, which is 15,000 miles times 22.5 cents ($3,375) plus 3,000 miles times 11 cents ($330).

If you hold on to the vehicle long enough to deduct 60,000 business miles at the higher rate, the deduction for all additional miles is limited to 11 cents a mile. That's because the higher rate includes an allowance for depreciation, and after 60,000 miles the car is considered fully depreciated.

If you use the standard rate, you can add to your deduction all parking fees and tolls paid in connection with your business use of the car.

To use the standard mileage rate, you must choose it for the first year you use the car for business, and once you use it you're pretty much stuck with it. Although the IRS will permit you to switch to the actual-cost method discussed below, originally using the standard-rate technique blocks the use of accelerated depreciation to boost your write-offs.

Actual-cost method. This system also requires you to keep track of business and personal mileage, and it demands a whole lot more. To complicate things, different rules apply depending on whether the car is used predominately for business or personal driving.

As the name suggests, this method requires that you keep track of the actual expenses of owning and operating your car, including the cost of gas and oil, lubrication, tune-ups, repairs, tires, washing and waxing, auto-club memberships, license tags and auto insurance.

To determine how much of your expenses is deductible, you figure what percentage of the mileage driven during the year qualifies as business mileage. If you drove 15,000 miles during the year, with 10,000 being on business and 5,000 personal, for example, 66.6% of your expenses would be deductible.

Don't shy away from the actual-cost method because of the paperwork and calculations involved. Thanks to congressional crackdowns aimed at blocking undeserved auto deductions, a lot of record keeping is required for any deductions, as discussed later in this chapter. In any event, the rewards for your efforts can be high.

One tax-reform change that has received a lot of attention—the phaseout of the deductibility of interest on car loans—applies to cars used by employees on the job, but not to autos used in your own business. Thus, if you are self-employed, interest on a loan for a car used in your business can be included in your overall costs. The business portion of those costs would be fully deductible, but the part of the interest assigned to the personal use of your car would be subject to the deduction phaseout discussed in Chapter 10.

In addition to out-of-pocket expenses, your deduction includes an amount for depreciation. That's how you recover the cost of the car. Depreciation could easily produce the largest of all your auto write-offs.

The first step in determining your depreciation deduction is to find the car's *basis*. That is its value for tax purposes and starts out, easily enough, at what you pay for the car. Although tax reform abolished the personal deduction for state sales taxes paid, you may include the sales tax in the basis and therefore write off the business portion in your depreciation deductions.

Finding the basis is much more complicated if you trade in one business car for another, particularly if you use the auto for personal as well as business driving, as is almost always the case.

First, consider the simpler calculation: trading in a car used 100% of the time for business for another used 100% of the time for business. The tax basis of the new car is the adjusted basis of the old one—generally that's what you paid for it minus the depreciation deductions you claimed in previous years—plus the extra money you had to pay on top of the trade-in value. Say you bought a car for $10,000, claimed depreciation deductions totaling $6,300 over the first two years, and traded it in on a new car in the third year. If the new car cost $12,000 more than the trade-in value of the first car, its basis would be $15,700, which is $12,000 plus the $3,700 adjusted basis ($10,000 − $6,300) of the old car.

Now, consider the more prevalent scenario: trading in one mixed-use car for another. (Assume the car being traded in was put into service after June 18, 1984, when the rules that apply here went into effect.) The basis of the new car would be the adjusted basis of the old one—it's cost minus whatever depreciation deductions you have claimed—*plus* the amount you paid in addition to the trade-in value, *minus* the difference between the depreciation claimed and what you could have claimed if the old car had been used 100% for business. The result of this convoluted calculation is to pull down the starting basis of the new car to the same level as if you had used the trade-in 100% for business.

Here's how the rule works. Say the trade-in in the previous example had been used 60% for business instead of 100%. During the first two years, your depreciation deductions would have been $3,780 (60% of the $6,300 write-off earned by the 100% business user), which would pull your adjusted basis down to $6,220 ($10,000 cost minus $3,780 depreciation). The $6,220 would be added to the $12,000 you paid for the new car, for a total of $18,220. But that amount would be reduced by $2,520—the difference between depreciating 60% and 100% of the old car over two years—giving the new car a basis of $15,700. That extra squeeze curbs the depreciation write-offs you'll get on the new car.

Deductions are also restricted by a tax-reform change that stretches out the tax life of business cars. Before 1987, cars used in business could be depreciated over three years. Now, business autos have a five-year depreciation life, and because of the accounting procedures used, write-offs actually stretch over six years. Generally, no matter when during the year you purchase depreciable property, the law gives you credit for half a year's worth of depreciation. Because you can't get more than half a year's worth the first year, you are forced to extend write-offs into the sixth year to completely depreciate the full business cost.

Here's the schedule for writing off the cost of an auto, assuming the vehicle is used more than 50% of the time for business:

Year	Deduction
1	20.00%
2	32.00
3	19.20
4	11.52
5	11.52
6	5.76

To see how the change affects business deductions, consider how the depreciation write-offs differ for a $12,000 car used 80% for business. The depreciable basis is $9,600 (80% of $12,000).

Year	Write-off Under	
	Old Law	Current Law
1	$2,400	$1,920
2	3,648	3,072
3	3,552	1,843
4	—	1,106
5	—	1,106
6	—	553

The car would be depreciated even more slowly if business use slips below 51%, as discussed later. (If you bought your business car before January 1, 1987, you continue using the faster depreciation schedule allowed at that time.)

There is also an exception to the general rule that permits a half-year's depreciation for the first year. If more than 40% of all the depreciable property you buy during the year is purchased in the final three months, the write-off for each asset is figured assuming it was put into service in the middle of the quarter in which it was purchased. If you buy a new business car in October, November or December and its depreciable basis is more than 40% of the total basis of all the property purchased during the year, for example, your write-off would be greatly reduced. You would qualify for just six weeks' worth of depreciation for the first year. In the example of the $12,000, 80% business-use car, the first-year write-off would fall from $1,920 to $480. Keep that in mind if you consider buying a new car late in the year. Buying before October 1 could mean a much larger depreciation deduction.

Expensing. One change introduced in 1987 seems to offer business-car buyers a real bonus, but it's illusive. Tax reform doubled (to $10,000) the amount of otherwise depreciable property that can be "expensed" each year. Known as the Section 179 deduction, after the part of the tax law that permits it, expensing lets you treat up to $10,000 of expenditures that normally would be depreciated over a number of years as current expenses that can be written off in full immediately.

Sounds great: Buy a new car with a depreciable basis of $10,000 or more and automatically deduct $10,000. But there's a hitch. Another section of the tax law—known as the luxury-car rule—limits business-car deductions to no more than $2,560 in the first year. If your depreciable basis is $12,800 or more, the regular depreciation schedule racks up the maximum deduction, leaving you no use for expensing. (The $12,800 figure increases yearly starting in 1989 to keep up with inflation.)

Luxury-car rule. This is what short circuits the potential advantage of expensing for business cars and clamps down on depreciation deductions for "expensive" autos. Back in 1984, Congress fretted that the tax law was being exploited by some businesspeople to subsidize opulent vehicles. Although getting from point A to point B on business was certainly a legitimate deductible expense, the argument went, it really wasn't *necessary* to do the traveling in a Rolls or a Ferrari—or, considering how low Congress has set the threshold, even a nice Chevy.

To make their point, the lawmakers enacted the luxury-car rule. At first, it affected cars costing more than $16,000, but in 1985 Congress knocked the price of luxury down to $12,800. The Tax Reform Act of 1986 left the $12,800 alone, but the slower depreciation schedule further impedes your write-offs.

Regardless of an auto's cost, deductions are limited to the amount of depreciation allowable on a vehicle with a $12,800 tax basis. Here are the annual limits on business car depreciation:

Year	Depreciation Cap
1	$2,560
2	4,100
3	2,450
4	1,475
5	1,475
additional years until fully depreciated	1,475

Despite the new five-year tax life for cars, the luxury-car restriction means it will take 14 years to fully depreciate a $25,000 business car.

Because this rule thwarts the use of expensing, it affects cars that cost even less than $12,800. If it weren't for the luxury-car rule, for example, the buyer of a $7,500, 80% business car could use expensing to deduct the full $6,000 business cost in the first year. The luxury-car rule, though, puts a $2,560 first-year cap on the combination of expensing and first-year depreciation.

If you use your car for both business and personal driving, the luxury-car cap is reduced to reflect your personal use. Say the business/personal split is 75%/25%. Your first-year depreciation deduction would be limited to $1,920, which is 75% of $2,560.

Leasing. Nothing should be simpler, right? You lease a business car and you can deduct the total of your monthly payments multiplied by the percent of business use. If the payments total $3,600 and you use the car 80% of the time for business, you deduct $2,880 (80% of $3,600). You still have to maintain careful records of your associated expenses, such as gas, oil, maintenance and repairs, but you escape the hassle of figuring depreciation allowances.

Indeed, that's how the tax rules work. But there's a significant *but*. To prevent you from sneaking around the luxury-car rules, you may have to report as income an amount to offset part of the tax savings generated by writing off your lease payments. This extra income is assigned to you if the value of the car when it is leased is more than $12,800. Just how much you must include depends on the value of the car at the beginning of the lease, when during the year the car is leased and the percentage of business use of the car. The amount also increases each year of the lease.

The IRS publishes a table of income-inclusion amounts for vehicles ranging in value fron $12,800 to $200,000. You'll find the full table in IRS Publication 917, *Business Use of a Car.* (The table was revised in August of 1988, so be sure you use an up-to-date version.) Here are a few examples:

Amount to Be Included in Taxable Income
for Each Year of Lease

Value of Car	1st Year	2nd Year	3rd Year	4th Year	5th Year & Beyond
$ 15,000	$ 31	$ 68	$ 101	$ 122	$ 140
20,000	97	211	313	375	433
25,000	163	356	527	632	729
30,000	232	507	752	902	1,041
50,000	510	1,115	1,653	1,982	2,288
100,000	1,177	2,574	3,816	4,575	5,281

The taxable amount for the first and last years of a lease depends on how much of the year you had the car. Also, note that for the year the lease expires, you use the income amount for the preceeding year. Consider this example:

Assume that on April 1, 1988, you leased a car worth $25,000 for three years. For 1988 and 1989, you use the car exclusively for business, but business use falls to 45% in 1990 and for the months in 1991 before the lease expires.

For 1988, you may deduct 100% of your lease payments. To know how much offsetting income to include, find the line in the table for a $25,000 car. The first-year income amount is $163. However, since you had the car for only part of the year—75% in this example—you report only part of that amount. The first-year amount is $122 (75% of $163).

In 1989, your exclusive business use again earns you the right to deduct all of your lease payments and you report the full second-year income amount: $356.

In 1990, when business use falls to 45%, you deduct just 45% of the lease payments, and the offsetting amount to include in income is 45% of the third-year amount: $237 (45% of $527).

In 1991, the last year of the lease, you again base the income amount on the third-year figure: $527. But you report only $59: $527 times 45% business use times the 25% of the year you had the car.

Getting too personal. Whether you own or lease the car, if business use falls to 50% or less there are extra restrictions on your write-offs.

The special rules for mostly personal autos had more bite in the past, not because the restrictions have been loosened but because Congress has put the skids on car write-offs in general. Prior to 1987, if your business use fell below the 51% threshold, you lost the right to the investment tax credit, could not use "expensing" to beef up your first-year write-off and had to depreciate the car over five years rather than three. But tax reform abolished the investment tax credit and stretched the depreciation period to five years for all business cars, and the luxury-car rules eliminate the use of expensing for cars.

Your tax benefits do drop if you fail the more-than-50% test, though. Instead of using the accelerated method of depreciation available for business cars, you must write off primarily personal vehicles over five years using the straight-line method.

Here's a side-by-side comparison of the depreciation allowed for business cars, depending on whether they pass the 50% test:

Year	Depreciation Allowed If Business Use Exceeds 50%	Is 50% or Less
1	20.00%	10%
2	32.00	20
3	19.20	20
4	11.52	20
5	11.52	20
6	5.76	10

What if you start out using the car more than 50% for business but later drop below the threshold? The law "recaptures" part of the depreciation write-offs you claimed in earlier years. You have to report as taxable income—for the year business use fails the 50% test—the amount by which your deductions using the accelerated write-off schedule exceeded what you would have claimed had you used the straight-line method in the earlier years.

In the past if a leased car failed the 50% test, the IRS demanded that you include an extra amount in your taxable income, beyond that required under the luxury-car rules. In August of 1988, however, the IRS revised the rules to eliminate that requirement. There is now no penalty if business use drops to 50% or less. (The change was retroactive to cover cars leased after December 31, 1986. If you leased a car in 1987 and reported extra income on your 1987 return because you failed the 50% test, you can file an amended return for a refund.)

Record keeping. It has always made sense to keep an up-to-date log of business trips, including notes about who you visited, where and why and the mileage involved, as well as saving receipts for gas, oil, maintenance and all other costs if you use the actual-cost method for figuring your car write-offs. But until a few years ago, the IRS could accept less, such as your word and some corroborating evidence. You even had the "Cohan rule" working for you. That dates back to a 1930 court case that pitted entertainer George M. "I'm a Yankee Doodle Dandy" Cohan against the IRS. Cohan won deductions the IRS wanted to deny when the court ruled that the lack of evidence didn't automatically obliterate the right to a tax deduction. If it was clear you incurred deductible expenses but you couldn't prove the exact amount, the court might allow an estimated write-off rather than none at all.

But Congress decided that that rule was too lenient and ordered that it no longer apply to auto deductions. The IRS has also been directed by the lawmakers to be extremely skeptical of any deductions that aren't supported by written records. New questions have appeared on the tax forms to help the IRS decide whose word to accept and whose to challenge with an audit. Those questions are said to add a "fear of the Lord" factor to the returns with the aim of unnerving taxpayers who might be tempted to claim higher deductions than they're due. The IRS wants to know:

• Total miles driven during the year, broken down by business mileage, commuting mileage and other personal mileage.

• If the car was employer-provided, was it available for personal use in off-duty hours?

• Is another vehicle available for personal use?

• Do you have evidence to back up your deduction and, if yes, is it written evidence?

Although Congress clearly hopes those questions will help put the brakes on creative tax-return preparation, the lawmakers have also called on the IRS and the courts to stop being pussycats about slapping negligence and fraud penalties on taxpayers caught claiming auto write-offs they don't deserve. The message is clear: Get in the habit of keeping the records and saving all the receipts that can successfully withstand any IRS assault on your deductions. In addition, keep a logbook in the glove compartment. Record the distance driven on business each day, with notes on the business purpose of each trip and any expenses incurred for which you did not get a receipt, such as parking fees or tolls.

If your business use of the car is fairly standard throughout the year, the IRS will permit you to use a "sampling method" to substantiate your business mileage. You may need only to keep a detailed log of business trips for the first week of each month, for example, if you can show that you followed the same routine throughout the month.

Remember that you need solid evidence of your business mileage even if you base your deduction on the IRS standard rate. With a good record of the business use of your car, it's easy at year-end to figure the business/personal breakdown by comparing the business mileage with the total number of miles racked up on the odometer.

Claiming your deductions. If you are self-employed, you claim your automobile-expense deductions along with other business expenses on Schedule C. If you use the actual-cost method, you also have to file Form 4562, where you figure the allowable depreciation.

Employees claim their car deductions along with other employee business expenses on Form 2106. Remember, though, that these unreimbursed business costs are now miscellaneous expenses, deductible only as itemized deductions and only to the extent that the total exceeds 2% of your adjusted gross income.

However, if your employer reimburses you for your car expenses and includes the reimbursement in your taxable income, your write-off can still qualify as an adjustment to income, available whether or not you itemize and not subject to the 2% rule. If the employer withholds income tax from the reimbursement, however, the IRS may challenge this write-off. When there is withholding, the tax agency assumes the money is really extra pay, rather than reimbursement. In that case, you're stuck with a miscellaneous itemized deduction subject to the 2% rule. You can still claim the write-off as an adjustment to income if you have evidence to convince the IRS that the extra money is reimbursement for your expenses. If you are required to provide an accounting of your business driving to your employer to be reimbursed, for example, you could dodge the 2% rule even if there was withholding on the reimbursement. The tax treatment of company-provided cars is discussed in Chapter 2.

COMPUTERS AND OTHER BUSINESS EQUIPMENT

Tax reform diluted the subsidy for the purchase of computers, furniture and other equipment used in your business. The investment tax credit, which afforded rebates of up to 10% of the cost of qualifying business equipment, was abolished completely, and the value of deductions you can claim has been diminished as a result of falling tax rates. There are also changes in the depreciation schedules for business property put into service after 1986. In some instances, though, the new timetables are actually beneficial.

Office furniture, such as chairs, desks and file cabinets, now have a seven-year tax life. And it takes eight years to deduct your full business costs, thanks to an accounting procedure that basically gives you half a year's worth of depreciation the first year, regardless of when during the year you put the property into use. Since you get only half a year's depreciation the first year, you need to tack an extra year on at the end to recover your full cost. (There's an exception to this "midyear convention" that comes into play if you put more than 40% of new business property into use during the last quarter of the year. In that case, the first year write-off for each piece of property is figured as though it was put into use in the middle of the quarter in which it was purchased.) Assuming the midyear convention applies, here's the depreciation schedule for office furniture put in service after 1986:

Year	Percent of Business Cost Deductible
1	14.29%
2	24.49
3	17.49
4	12.49
5	8.93
6	8.93
7	8.93
8	4.46

Computers, typewriters and copying machines earn faster write-offs. The tax law assigns such equipment a five-year life and the following depreciation schedule:

Year	Percent of Business Cost Deductible
1	20.00%
2	32.00
3	19.20
4	11.52
5	11.52
6	5.76

Special rules apply to computers, apparently growing out of congressional concern that the tax law was too heavily subsidizing the purchase of many home computers. If you use your home computer in connection with your job, it's almost impossible to write off its cost. To qualify for an employee-business-expense deduction, the computer must be required by your employer. If you're simply encouraged to take work home from the office, that's not enough.

Assuming you have your own business, too much personal use of your computer will retard your depreciation write-offs. If business use does not exceed 50%, you relinquish the accelerated schedule shown above and are stuck with this straight-line timetable.

Year	Percent of Business Use Deductible
1	10%
2	20
3	20
4	20
5	20
6	10

By slipping below the 50% threshold, your depreciation deductions during the first two years drop from 52% of the business cost to 30%. Whether or not you pass the 50% test, of course, your depreciation is based on the business proportion of the computer's cost.

Assume you buy a $3,000 computer and, once you've calculated all the kids' time on the machine for homework and games, business use is just 40%. Your first-year depreciation deduction would be just $120 (40% business use times $3,000 times 10% depreciation). Although the straight-line timetable is slower, the new law is actually more generous than the old on this point. In the past, computers that didn't pass the 50% test had to be depreciated over 12 years.

When figuring whether you meet the 50% requirement, you may not count any time spent using your computer to keep track of your personal investments, whether stocks and bonds, mutual funds or real estate. Only time spent on your business counts. If business use surpasses 50%, though, you can then add in investment time for purposes of determining what percentage of your cost is deductible.

If business use exceeds 50% when you first buy the computer but later falls below the threshold, the tax law "recaptures" some of your earlier depreciation. In the year personal use predominates, you have to report as income the difference between the depreciation you claimed for the computer in earlier years and what you would have been due using the slower straight-line schedule designed for mostly personal machines.

More important than sluggish depreciation, though, is that failure to use your computer mostly for business means forfeiting the chance to "expense" part or all of the business cost.

Expensing. This provision of the tax law offers the chance for superaccelerated depreciation. Expensing permits you to write off in one year up to $10,000 of business costs that would otherwise be depreciated over five or more years. You basically treat those costs as current expenses—fully deductible in the year incurred—as are what you pay out for salaries, office supplies or utilities.

Consider a $3,000 computer used 75% of the time for business. By passing the 50% threshold, you qualify for expensing and can deduct the entire business cost of $2,250 (75% of $3,000) on the tax return for the year you bought the computer, rather than in bits and pieces over six years.

When you consider expensing, remember that it gives you the greatest tax-saving boost when applied to property that would otherwise have the longest depreciable life. If you have your choice between applying expensing to seven-year property, such as furniture, or five-year property, such as a computer, choosing the furniture will maximize your write-offs.

There is a limit on expensing. If you put more than $200,000 of equipment into service in any one year, you gradually lose the right to use expensing. The $10,000 expensing limit is reduced dollar for dollar by every dollar your annual expenditure exceeds $200,000. If you buy more than $210,000 of new equipment in a year, you can say goodbye to expensing.

Record keeping. You need to keep records establishing the cost of the property you depreciate and, if there is a split between business and personal use, evidence supporting the business percentage you claim. When figuring the depreciable business cost—or basis—include any sales tax paid.

Because the IRS has a special eye on computers, your records of business and personal use must be particularly good. Keep a log book and have every user sign in, noting the date, the time use begins and ends, and the reason for using the computer. If the reason is not personal, cite the specific business or investment project. When you file your return, you will be asked flat out, on form 4562, whether you have written evidence to back up your business use of the computer.

HOME-OFFICE EXPENSES

If you qualify to deduct home-office expenses, you get IRS help to pay bills that are normally considered personal. These include part of what you pay to light and heat your home, a share of the rent if you are a tenant or depreciation on your house if you own it, a portion of your homeowners insurance and part of your maintenance and repair expenses. Not surprisingly, the rules are strict, and this is another area where tax reform eliminated some of the potential savings.

Although home-office deductions are open to both employees and self-employed taxpayers, as a practical matter it's almost impossible for employees to qualify. In addition to meeting all the other tests discussed below, for an employee to claim these tax-savers, the office has to be maintained for the convenience of the employer. Basically, that means you have to be required to work at home, not just elect to do so. Furthermore, employees who do qualify for home-office deductions must claim them as miscellaneous deductions, which subjects them to the 2%-of-AGI floor.

If you have a sideline business in addition to your job and run your business out of your home, you aren't tripped up by the convenience-of-your-employer test. This type of moonlighting is, in fact, the basis of many home-office deductions.

Exclusive use. The biggest roadblock to qualifying for these deductions is that you must use a portion of your home *exclusively* and *regularly* for your business. The office is generally in a separate room or group of rooms, but it can be a section of a room if the division is clear—thanks to a partition, perhaps—and you can show that personal activities are excluded from the business section.

The law is clear and the IRS is serious about the exclusive-use requirement. Say you set aside a room in your home for a full-time business and you work in it at least ten hours a day, seven days a week. Let your children use the office to do their homework, though, and you violate the exclusive-use requirement and forfeit the chance for home-office deductions.

The rule doesn't mean you're forbidden to make a personal phone call from the office or that you have to rush outside whenever a family member needs a moment of your time. Although individual IRS auditors may be more or less strict on this point, some advisors say you meet the spirit of the exclusive-use test as long as personal activities invade the home office no more than they would be permitted at an office building or factory. (Two exceptions to the exclusive-use test are discussed later in this section.)

There's no arbitrary definition of what constitutes regular use. Clearly, if you use an otherwise empty room only occasionally and its use is incidental to your business, you'd fail this test. But if you work in the home office a few hours or so each day, you'd probably pass. This test is applied to the facts and circumstances of each case that is challenged by the IRS.

Principal place of business. In addition to passing the exclusive- and regular-use tests, your home office must be either the principal location of that business or a place where you regularly meet with customers or clients. If you are an employee and have a part-time business based in your home, the home office is the principal location of your part-time business. The fact that you may spend much more time at the office where you work as an employee doesn't matter.

There is, though, the question of what constitutes a business. Making money from your efforts is a prerequisite, but for purposes of this tax break, profit alone isn't necessarily enough. If you use your den solely to take care of your personal investment portfolio, you can't claim home-office deductions because your activities as an investor don't qualify as a business.

Taxpayers who use a home office exclusively to actively manage several rental properties they own, though, may qualify for home-office tax status—as property managers rather than investors. As with the regular-use test, whether your endeavors qualify as a business depends on the circumstances involved. The more substantial the activities, in terms of time and effort invested and income generated, the more likely you'll pass this test.

Even if your business has more than one office and the away-from-home location is where you spend the most time, you can qualify for home-office write-offs if you meet or deal with customers, patients or clients in the business part of your house. That provision can prove helpful, for example, to doctors,

"We're disallowing some of the mileage you've declared...your entry for March 10 indicates you took a SCENIC route, not the most direct."

accountants and salespeople who have a business location elsewhere but maintain a home office for meeting with clients in the evenings or on weekends. Such at-home dealings must be an important, rather than an incidental, part of the business.

If your home office is in a separate, unattached structure—a loft over a detached garage, for example—you don't have to meet the principal-place-of-business or the deal-with-customers test. As long as you pass the exclusive- and regular-use tests, you can qualify for home-business write-offs.

Day-care facilities and storage. The exclusive-use test does not apply if you use part of your house to provide day-care services for children, the elderly or handicapped individuals. If you care for children in your home between 7 A.M. and 6 P.M. each day, for example, you can use that part of the house for personal activities the rest of the time and still claim business deductions. To qualify for the tax break, your day-care business must meet any applicable state and local licensing requirements.

Another exception to the exclusive-use test applies to a portion of your home used to store inventory you sell in your business. Assume your home-based business is the retail sale of mechanics' tools or home-cleaning products and that you regularly use half of your basement to store inventory. Occasionally using that part of the basement to store personal items would not cancel your home-office deduction. To qualify for this exception, your home must be the only location of your business.

Business percentage of house. Your business deductions are based on the percentage of your home used for the business. The most exact way to figure this proportion is to measure the square footage devoted to your home office and find what percentage it is of the total area of your home. If the office measures 150 square feet, for example, and the total area of the house is 1,200 square feet, your business percentage would be 12.5% (150 ÷ 1,200).

An easier way is acceptable if the rooms in your home are all about the same size. In that case, you can figure the business percentage by dividing the number of rooms used in your business by the total number of rooms in the house.

Special rules apply if you qualify for home-office deductions under the day-care exception to the exclusive-use test. In that case, your business-use percentage must be discounted because part of the time the space is available for personal use. To do that, you compare the number of hours the space is used for day care to the total number of hours the space is available.

Assume you use 20% of your house for a day-care business that operates 12 hours a day, five days a week, or 3,000 hours out of the total of 8,760 hours in the year. Because you use the space only 34% of the available hours for your business, your business write-off percentage is 34% of 20%, or 6.8%.

The payoff. Although this is a complicated area, the tax savings can be well worth the hassles involved. Here's what you can write off.

- *Direct expenses.* Money spent to repair or maintain the business space is deductible. If you paint the room that is your home office, for example, the entire cost can be deducted.

- *Indirect expenses.* These will probably be your most fruitful home-office deductions. Because part of your home qualifies as business property, part of the costs of running it can be converted from nondeductible personal expenses to business write-offs. If your office space takes up 20% of the house, you can deduct 20% of your utility bills, house insurance bills and overall home repairs and maintenance costs.

- *Interest and property taxes.* Mortgage interest and property taxes are deductible expenses whether or not you qualify for home-office deductions. But with a home office you convert part of those expenses from personal itemized deductions to business write-offs. Because business expenses reduce self-employment income, they can also trim what you owe in social security (FICA) taxes. For 1988, FICA taxes claim 13.02% of your first $45,000 of self-employment and wage income. For every $1,000 of mortgage interest and property-tax expense you shift to the category of business deductions, you can save $130.20 in FICA tax. (Social security taxes owed by self-employed individuals are discussed in Chapter 15.)

- *Rent or depreciation.* If you rent the home where your office is located, this computation is easy: You deduct the same percentage of your rent as the percentage of your home devoted to your business.

If you own your home, you must depreciate the business part of the house. Commercial real estate—which is how that part of your home is categorized—put in service after 1986 must be depreciated over 31.5 years, so a full year's depreciation would be just 3% of the business area. Under the law in effect in 1986, a 19-year accelerated-depreciation schedule permitted 8.8% of the business value to be written off the first year. If you established your home office before January 1, 1987, you continue to base your write-offs on the speedier schedule. (Depreciation of real estate is discussed in detail in Chapter 6.)

The first step in determining your depreciation deduction is to know the tax basis of your house. That's basically what you paid for the place, plus the cost of any improvements. You depreciate only the cost of the house, not the land, so you must make allowances for the value of your lot.

Assume your tax basis is $100,000 and you used 20% of the house all year for your home business. Your depreciation would be 20% of 3.04% of $100,000, or $608. (After the first year, the deduction would be slightly larger, based on 3.17% of the basis.)

Although that may seem like a lot of work to go through for a rather piddling deduction, remember that you exert most of the effort only once, when you set up your depreciation schedule, but get to claim the depreciation write-off year after year as long as you have the home office. Also, as with other home-office deductions, depreciation trims not only your income tax bill but may also limit the amount of social security tax owed on your self-employment income.

You can also claim depreciation deductions on furniture and equipment used in your business, as discussed later. You earn those write-offs whether or not you pass the home-office tests.

Limit on deductions. The law puts a cap on how much you can deduct for the business use of the home, and tax reform added new restrictions. Your home-office deductions can't exceed your home-based business income and produce a tax loss to shelter other income. The new restrictions come in the guise of a simple change in the order in which various expenses are to be deducted.

Before 1987, you started with your gross income and reduced it by the amount of mortgage interest and property taxes allocated to business use. From that adjusted income, you subtracted home-office expenses—except for depreciation. If net income remained after those deductions, you could write off your depreciation, too. Then you could deduct business expenses that qualify whether or not you meet the home-office tests, such as the cost of secretarial help and office equipment and supplies, even if those write-offs pushed you into the red.

Now the law demands that expenses that had been deductible without regard to the income limit—such as the cost of office help and supplies—be deducted from gross income first. That immediately lowers the ceiling and can knock you out of some home-office write-offs.

Here's an example of how the cap on deductions works. Let's say that in addition to your job, you moonlight running a consulting business. You set aside a large room at home as the only office of your business, and you meet the regular- and exclusive-use tests. Your home office takes up 20% of the house.

During the year, your business generates $10,000 of gross income. To find the limit on home-office deductions, you first subtract expenses that are deductible whether or not you qualify to write off home-office expenses.

Gross Income.....................................**$10,000**
   Less:
   Secretarial help $1,200
   Business phone 600
   Office supplies 300
   Postage.. 150

   Total   **$2,250**

Limit for home-office deductions: **$ 7,750**

Home-office expenses are then subtracted in the specified order, with each category reducing the income level against which later expenses may be deducted.

	Total	**20% Office Portion**
Mortgage interest	$10,000	$2,000
Property taxes	2,500	500
Total		**$2,500**

Limit on further deductions ($7,750 – $2,500):   **$5,250**

You next subtract operating expenses.

	Total	**Office Portion**
Lights	$600	$120
Heat	600	120
Insurance	500	100
Roof repair	300	60
Painting of office	300	300
Total		**$700**

Note that for each of the first four operating expenses, the office portion is 20% of the total cost, reflecting that 20% of the house is used as an office. The cost of painting the business portion of the house is deductible in full though, because it is a direct expense of the business.

Limit on further deductions ($5,250–$700):   **$4,550**

Next, you deduct depreciation.

Assume that your home (excluding the land) is worth $100,000. If you had the office in your house for the entire year, your depreciation would be $635, which is 20% of $3,175 ($100,000 ÷ 31.5 years).

	Total	**Office Portion**
Depreciation	$3,175	$635

In this example, the full amount is deductible because it is less than the amount left over after all the other write-offs. Had your gross income for the year been just $5,000 and all your expenses the same, you would not have been allowed the depreciation deduction. Furthermore, only $250 of your $700 of operating expenses could be written off. Here's why:

Gross Income		**$5,000**
Less:		
Secretarial help		$1,200
Business phone		600
Office supplies		300
Postage		150
Total		**$2,250**

Limit for home-office deductions:	**$2,750**

You would then deduct:

	Total	20% Office Portion
Mortgage interest	$10,000	$2,000
Property taxes	2,500	500
Total		**$2,500**

Limit for home-office deductions:	**$250**

Because your home-office deductions can't produce a tax loss, only $250 of your $700 operating expenses can be deducted. However, the law permits you to bank the remaining $450 and the $636 of depreciation. You can carry the losses over to use in future years when you have adequate income to permit their deduction.

Dodging a bullet. One problem with taking advantage of home-office tax benefits is that doing so can trip up some of the benefits written into the law for homeowners. By converting part of your house from a residence to a business property, you can forfeit the right to defer tax on part of the profit when you sell or lose the right to exclude a portion of the gain from tax altogether under the special provision for homeowners age 55 and older.

As discussed in Chapter 4, when you move from one home to another, the tax on the profit is generally put off. But the part of the house that is designated as business property may not enjoy that benefit, so a portion of your profit—the percentage you've been claiming as a home office—may be taxed in the year of the sale.

There's an easy way around this trap, though: Don't qualify to claim the home office in the year that you sell your house. By reconverting the space to personal use, you can defer tax on all the profit.

If you plan to take advantage of the special break that lets older taxpayers exclude from tax up to $125,000 of profit on the sale of a home, you should eliminate the home office at least three years before you plan to sell. To qualify for the exclusion, you must have owned and lived in the house for at least three of the five years prior to the sale. If part of the house was business property during that three-year period, that part doesn't qualify as part of your residence.

Record keeping. Employees claim home-office expenses as miscellaneous itemized deductions on Schedule A. Self-employed taxpayers use Schedule C. That form can be somewhat ominous. A question asks flat out whether you are claiming deductions for a home office. Answering yes might seem like volunteering for an audit and, although IRS scrutiny isn't automatic, you have to be prepared to back up your deductions if challenged.

That demands careful records to prove your write-offs are legitimate. Photographs of the office area will be helpful. Take pictures showing the desk, file cabinets, typewriter and other business equipment. Keep a sketch of your home to back up your calculations of the business percentage of total space. Have your home address and the number of your home-office phone printed on business cards and stationery. Keep a running log that shows when you use the office, what you work on and with whom you meet. This doesn't have to be fancy; notes on a desk calendar will do.

TRAVEL AND ENTERTAINMENT

Ah, the expense-account life! The chance to pile up tax subsidies to help pay for your meals, your nights on the town, your travel to wondrous and exotic places. That's the image often associated with tax write-offs for business travel and entertainment expenses. And it's accurate, as long as you can show that the costs involved are necessary to conduct your business. Again, tax reform puts a bit of a crimp in the expense account, though.

Only 80% of the cost of your business meals and entertainment can now be written off. In theory, you get at least some personal benefit from those business meals and good times. So, the argument goes, you should bear at least part of the cost. If you are an employee who is reimbursed for such business expenses, the 80% rule will probably have no effect. Your employer may still reimburse you for 100% of what you spend on business meals and entertainment, and you don't have to count the 20% portion as extra income. The 80% restriction falls on your employer, who can write off only 80% of the reimbursement.

Self-employed taxpayers, however, do feel the brunt of the 80% rule. When you tote up what you spent during the year on qualifying meals and entertainment, you must reduce the total by 20% to arrive at your business deduction.

Employees who are *not* reimbursed for their business meals and entertainment expenses are hit with a double whammy. Not only is 20% of the cost nondeductible under the new rules, but even the deductible portion is treated as a miscellaneous itemized deduction subject to the 2% threshold rule. Such expenses are deductible only to the extent that the combined total of miscellaneous expenses exceeds 2% of your adjusted gross income. An exception to this rule applies if you are reimbursed for your expenses *and* the reimbursement is reported as additional taxable income. In that case, you are still subject to the 80% rule, but the deductible part of your expenses can be written off whether or not you itemize deductions and without regard to the 2%-of-AGI rule. (If your employer withholds income tax from the reimbursement, however, the IRS considers it to be extra pay—not reimbursement for purposes of this exception.)

Tax reform also called a halt to the so-called quiet business meal. In the past, the cost of taking a customer or other business contact out to eat could be deducted even if not a word of business was discussed. Say you took a client out to dinner to maintain a relationship that might pay off in business down the road but didn't have any specific deal in mind at the time. The cost could still qualify as a deduction as long as it was associated with your business. Now to earn a deduction, business must be discussed during or immediately before or after the meal.

This is the same rule that used to—and still does—apply to business entertainment expenses, such as a night at the theater or a sports event. Although you don't have to try to close a specific business deal in the midst of a sudden-death overtime, the law requires you to talk turkey before or after the game to establish that the entertainment was associated with the conduct of your business.

What about annual dues you pay to belong to a country club or athletic club, for example, where you entertain business contacts? The new 80% restriction applies, along with a slew of other rules. As long as the primary use of the club is for qualifying business meals and entertainment, at least part of your annual dues are deductible. To qualify, you must show that more than half the days the club was used during the year were business rather than personal days.

To figure out what percentage you can deduct, you have to break down business use of the club into days it was used for purposes directly related to business—to discuss a specific business deal, for example—and days when club use was only associated with business, such as "goodwill" entertainment of business contacts. Both types of use count toward the 50% threshold, but only directly related business days matter when figuring what part of the club dues you may write off.

Assume annual club dues are $1,800 and you use the club 60% for business—20% for business meals, 25% for directly related entertainment (which means specific business was discussed before, during or after the entertainment) and 15% for associated entertainment. Passing the 50% test earns you the right to a business deduction, and in this case your write-off would be based on 45% of $1,800, or $810. Under the new 80% rule, $648 would be deductible. The key to this deduction, of course, is to make sure you talk business with clients when you take them to your club. Also, even if business use falls below 50%, you may still deduct 80% of the cost of qualifying business meals and entertainment at the club.

If your club membership permits family members to use the facilities, their use will count as personal days for purposes of determining the breakdown between business and personal use. What if you hold an important business meeting at the club the same day your kids use the pool and your spouse takes to the links? Your business use overrides the personal use and the day counts as a business day.

More crackdowns. With a trio of new restrictions, tax reform cracked down on taxpayer subsidies of certain business expenses.

Congress decided that taxpayers should not support ticket scalpers. The law now limits the deduction for tickets to entertainment events, including plays, sports events and concerts, to 80% of the *face value* of the tickets. If you have to pay extra for the choice seats needed to impress a client, for example, the added cost is a nondeductible personal expense.

To put more teeth in the general requirement that only "ordinary and necessary" business expenses be deducted, the law lowers the boom on taxpayers who lease skyboxes or other luxury seats at sports arenas. If you use a skybox for business entertainment, you can deduct only 80% of the cost of the highest-priced nonluxury seats available. To ease the pain, this restriction is being phased in. In 1988, one-third of the amount that would otherwise be disallowed by this rule may be deducted as a business expense. Also note that this crackdown applies only if you lease the skybox for more than one event. The full cost—subject to the 80% rule—can survive as a business write-off if you rent the box only once a year.

Another restriction applies if you prefer to do your business traveling aboard ship, rather than by car, train or plane. The new law applies a cap of twice the highest federal *per diem* rate for travel within the United States, multiplied by the number of days of the trip. In mid 1988, that rate was $136 per day, capping the travel-by-water write-off at $272 per day. Here's how the limit works. Say you hate to fly but need to get to London on business. You decide to travel via the Queen Elizabeth II liner. If the trip takes six days, the most you can deduct is $1,632 (2 × $136 × 6).

Travel away from home. Special tax benefits are available if your job or business takes you away from home. Suddenly, expenses that would be nondeductible if you were home— including the cost of your breakfast, lunch and dinner, commuting costs from your temporary residence (a motel or hotel) to your temporary work site, and laundry and dry-cleaning costs— become tax write-offs.

To qualify for this alchemy, you must be away from home on business at least overnight but not so long that the IRS figures you've really moved to the new location. The IRS assumes your away-from-home assignment is temporary if it lasts less than a year. If the assignment stretches between one and two years, the IRS presumes it's not temporary, which means no travel deductions unless you can show you expect the assignment to end by the end of the second year and that you will then return home. If the "temporary" assignment lasts more than two years, you're out of luck when it comes to these deductions.

Whether you're on a business trip that keeps you away from home for just one night or on assignment for several months, the major deductible travel expenses can include:

• The cost of getting to the new location, whether in your own car or via plane, bus or train;

• The cost of getting around on business while there, via your own car, a rental car or public transportation (including the cost of what would be nondeductible commuting at home: the trip from your hotel or other temporary quarters to the job and back); and

• The cost of meals and lodging while away from home, whether or not there is any specific business purpose for the

meal. Only 80% of the cost of your meals is deductible, though.
Mixing business with pleasure. What if you tack a personal
vacation on to the end of your business trip? The tax consequences turn mainly on whether business or pleasure was the
primary reason for the trip. That can be a tough call, but an
important factor is the amount of time spent on business
compared to the amount spent on pleasure. If more than half
your time is spent pursuing good times instead of business,
you're going to have a difficult time showing the primary
purpose was business.

Assuming the business trip takes you someplace within the
United States, you can deduct the full cost of your transportation to and from the business site, including the cost of any
meals and lodging en route. What you spend while vacationing
in the area would be nondeductible. Say you fly to Honolulu for
a five-day business meeting, then extend your stay for four days
of swimming, sight-seeing and luaus. The cost of the flight to
Hawaii would be deductible, as would your expenses for food
(80% only) and lodging during the business part of your trip.
The cost of food, lodging and other expenses on the personal
days could not be written off.

What if your spouse goes along? That does not obliterate
your right to business write-offs, but you can't deduct his or her
expenses unless you can prove a significant business reason for
your spouse's presence. The IRS says typing your business
notes or helping you entertain customers isn't enough to
transform a spouse's expenses into deductions.

Although you normally can't write off the extra costs incurred
because your spouse is along, your husband or wife may still
enjoy a tax-subsidized holiday. The reason: When your spouse
accompanies you, your costs are likely to be less—perhaps
significantly less—than twice what it would have cost you to go
alone. The cost of a double room in a hotel may be $150, for
example, compared to $135 for a single room. You get to deduct
the full single-room rate, not half the double-room cost. Also, if
you drive to the business meeting, the cost of operating your
car or a rental are the same whether you go alone or have
company—and so is your deduction.

When you mix in too much pleasure with your business, you risk losing the write-off for transportation costs. If the primary purpose of the trip is personal, you cannot write off any of the cost of getting to and from the site of the business meeting, although you may still deduct business-related expenses at the destination. Clearly, this is an area where careful planning can pay off in handsome tax savings and some personal pleasure to boot.

The rules are different if your business takes you out of the country—in some ways more strict, in others more lenient.

As with domestic travel, your costs, including transportation, food and lodging en route, are deductible if the primary purpose of the trip is business. But unlike the all-or-nothing rule for domestic travel, it's possible to qualify to deduct part of your foreign travel expenses.

You can pass the primarily business threshold—and write off all your travel expenses—if the foreign trip takes you out of the United States for a week or less. If the primary purpose of a trip to Paris was an important one-day business meeting, for example, you could spend six extra days sight-seeing without forfeiting your travel-expense write-offs. Your sight-seeing expenses would be nondeductible, of course, but the full cost of getting to and from France could be written off. For trips longer than a week, more stringent rules apply. At least 75% of the time you are out of the country must be devoted to business. If so, travel expenses are fully deductible. If you fail the 75% test, you have to split travel costs between business and personal purposes according to the number of days spent on each. If your breakdown shows a 60% business/40% personal split, for example, you would deduct just $1,200 of a $2,000 airfare. If the trip is primarily a vacation, though, none of the travel costs are deductible.

When counting up business days, include:

• Any day or part of a day when your presence is required at a particular place for a specific business purpose;

• Any day when you spend more than four hours on business;

• Any weekend or holiday days that fall between business days; and

• Days spent traveling to and from the business location.

Conventions. Because sponsors expend loads of time, energy and money to insure that business convention programs offer plenty of appealing diversions, it's no surprise that the IRS applies special rules to convention-cost write-offs.

When the convention is held within the "North American area" (the United States; Canada; Mexico; Puerto Rico; U.S. Virgin Islands; Guam; Jamaica; the Trust Territory of the Pacific Islands, including American Samoa; and Barbados), your expenses of attending are deductible as long as you can show that the convention agenda is connected with your business or job. For your traveling expenses to be deductible, of course, the primary purpose of the trip must be business-related.

Foreign conventions are a different matter. In fact, it's difficult for any convention outside the North American area to qualify for tax deductions. For expenses to be deductible, the convention must be directly related to your business; domestic meetings must be of only general benefit to your job or business. The tougher hurdle for a foreign convention is that it must be as reasonable to choose the foreign site as it would be to hold the convention within the favored North American area. Why hold the Sunbelt Widgetmaker's Annual Convention in Budapest rather than Phoenix? That is the question that must be answered to the satisfaction of a skeptical IRS.

What if the ingenious convention planners choose a cruise ship as the site of the seminar? The cost can still be written off if you can show the meeting is directly related to your business. But there is a $2,000 limit on how much you can write off for cruise conventions each year. Also, to qualify, the ship must be registered in the U.S., and all ports of call during the convention must be located in the United States or its possessions.

There's another special requirement for cruise conventions: To claim the deduction, you must include with your tax return a signed note from the convention sponsors listing the business meetings scheduled each day aboard the ship and certifying just how many hours you spent attending those activities.

There are also crackdowns on a couple of types of conventions. Before 1987, the cost of attending investment conventions and seminars could be deducted—not as business expenses but as investment-related expenses. No more. The law specifically outlaws write-offs for conventions focusing on personal investments or financial planning. It also puts the kibosh on conventions where the primary activity is the distribution of videotapes for participants to watch at their convenience. No matter how vital the videotape to your business, you can't deduct the cost of going to the convention to pick it up.

Record keeping. Be prepared for serious IRS scrutiny if you deduct business travel, entertainment or convention expenses. That's not to say you should steer away from any legitimate write-offs, only that careful record keeping is demanded if you want to preserve the deductions in the face of an IRS audit.

As with any deduction, it's up to you to maintain adequate records to justify the write-off. But in this area, Congress keeps reminding the IRS that it expects the revenuers to be rigorous and meticulous when enforcing the substantiation rules. In the report on the Tax Reform Act of 1986, for example, Congress "reemphasized" that neither the IRS nor the courts are to

© 1988 CARLSON—MILWAUKEE SENTINEL

permit approximations of these expenses. The message: Either have proof or don't take a deduction.

For business meals and entertainment, you must have a receipt for any expense of $25 or more. You also need a record—perhaps in a daily diary or business log—of:

• All expenses under the $25 threshold, including taxi fares, telephone calls and other incidental expenses;

• The date of the business meal or entertainment;

• The name and address of the restaurant or entertainment facility and the type of entertainment—a play, baseball game, etc.;

• The business relationship of the people entertained and the specific business reason for the meal or entertainment.

To deduct the costs of traveling away from home overnight on business, you must have a receipt for all lodging expenses— even in the unlikely event the charge is under the $25 threshold. Your records must also show the day you left home, the date of your return and the business purpose of the trip.

For those who don't want to bother keeping track of daily meal expenses, the IRS offers a standard allowance that can be claimed in lieu of actual expenses. It's a skimpy $14 a day if you're away from home fewer than 30 days and $9 a day if your job or business keeps you away 30 days or more. Unless you are an exceptionally light eater, you're sure to do better keeping track of what you actually spend on meals. Just jot down the amounts in a business log and keep receipts for any meals costing $25 or more.

When you're combining a vacation with a business trip, keep careful records of how much you spend each day so you can show that you pass the primarily business test necessary to convert your travel expenses into tax deductions. If a convention is involved, keep the program, with notations on which sessions you attended. When a cruise-ship convention is involved, you'll also need the signed statement mentioned earlier.

Thanks to the new 80% deductibility rule on meals and entertainment, you must segregate such costs from travel expenses—transportation and lodging, for example—which remain fully deductible. When you take a client out to lunch, for instance, the cost of the meal is only 80% deductible, but the cab fare retains its 100% deductibility.

JOB-HUNTING EXPENSES

When you look for a new job, the IRS might pick up some of your costs—via tax savings. The key to tax deductions is to seek a new position in the same line of work, rather than try to switch careers. Perhaps our lawmakers worry that someone changing occupations might be willing to take a pay cut to make the change, while a job hunter looking for a different job in the same field is likely to do better financially, and in the process produce more income for the government to tax. Whatever the reason, job-hunting expenses are deductible when you confine your search to the same line of work you're in—whether or not you wind up changing jobs. The cost of seeking a job in a different occupation is not deductible, nor are expenses connected with landing your first job—or of reentering the work force after a lengthy absence.

If you qualify for job-hunting deductions, your write-offs can include travel expenses, including the cost of food, lodging and transportation. Your meal expenses are covered by the new rule that limits the deduction to 80% of the cost of business meals and entertainment. In addition, deductible job-hunting costs encompass what you spend for employment-agency fees, want ads, telephone calls connected with the job hunt, and the cost of printing and mailing résumés.

There's a catch, though. Job-hunting expenses are miscellaneous itemized deductions, which means they are subject to the new 2% rule: You may claim a deduction only for the amount by which the total of your miscellaneous expenses exceeds 2% of your adjusted gross income. If your AGI is $30,000, for example, only miscellaneous expenses in excess of $600 would be deductible. Keep careful records of all your job-hunting expenses to determine whether you have a tax deduction.

EDUCATION EXPENSES

The tax law will subsidize your pursuit of knowledge—if the schooling passes several tests.

Just as the cost of hunting for your first job or a career switch is nondeductible, so are write-offs for the cost of education that prepares you for your first job or for a position in a different business or profession. To qualify for education deductions, you must already be working—either as an employee or self-employed—and the training must either be designed to maintain or improve the skills required by your present job or be required by your employer or the law to keep your present job.

You can't deduct the cost of courses taken to meet the minimum requirements of a job, and even if you could argue that a class improves the skills used on your present job, you can flunk the deductibility test if the education is also a step toward entering a new trade or profession.

What constitutes a new occupation? Clearly, if you sour on ditch-digging and sign on for night law-school classes, you're preparing for a new profession, and the costs would not be deductible. But if you're an attorney, the cost of continuing-education courses could be written off. What if you're a real estate agent who takes courses necessary to get a real estate broker's license? The Tax Court rejected such a deduction on the grounds that the broker's job was significantly different than the agent's. The IRS also says "no" to deductions for bar-review courses, even if you're already an attorney preparing for admission to the bar in an additional state.

Teachers required to take summer courses to keep their jobs can deduct the cost, and as far as the IRS is concerned, all teaching and related duties are considered the same general kind of work. Deductions are permitted for the cost of courses needed to switch from elementary education to secondary teaching, for example, as are those connected with a move from a job as a classroom teacher to a principal.

In general, to qualify to write off education expenses you need to mix work with schooling. But if you go to school during your vacation or during a temporary absence from your work, you can still qualify. The IRS will consider up to one year off the job temporary for these purposes, and in some cases the courts have permitted even longer absences. You don't have to go back to the same job to qualify to deduct educational expenses, either, just to the same line of work.

If you qualify, your write-offs include the cost of tuition, books, supplies, tutoring and any travel and transportation related to your studies. Whether you're temporarily a full-time student at a major university, attending a week-long continuing-education seminar or taking a correspondence course, keep careful records of your expenses.

If you have to go out of town for the course and you're away overnight, you can deduct travel expenses as long as the primary purpose of the trip is the educational activity. Basically, that means you write off the cost of getting to and from the site of the course or seminar, including what you pay for meals (subject to the 80% rule) and lodging en route and while there.

Say you're a tax practitioner who travels 1,000 miles for a five-day course on the ramifications of yet another new tax law. After the seminar you stick around for a couple of days of sight-seeing. Your travel costs as well as tuition and any other fees connected with the course are deductible as job-related educational expenses. If you spend three weeks on vacation instead of just a couple of days, though, the primary purpose of the trip would be considered personal, and you would get no deduction for travel expenses.

What you deduct for transportation to and from your classes depends in part on where the courses are held vis-a-vis where you work. If you have to travel beyond the general area where you work, you can deduct the full cost. When the schooling is within that general work area—the IRS offers no specific distance—you write off only the cost of going from your workplace to the school and back to the workplace. If you stop by home after work and before the class, the deduction is limited to what it would have cost to go straight from work. If you drive your own car, you can deduct either 22.5 cents a mile or your actual expenses. The cost of getting to and from classes on a nonwork day—such as on a weekend—is not deductible.

Travel as education. The Tax Reform Act of 1986 brought an end to an education write-off that had the aura of an awfully sweet deal. The law now bars the deduction for the cost of travel when the travel itself is the educational activity. Although the rules were strict under the old law, it was still possible for a French teacher to deduct the cost of a trip to France to maintain general familiarity with the language and culture, for example, or for a social studies teacher to write off the cost of a trip to another state to learn about and photograph its people and geography for use in the classroom. No more.

Self-employed taxpayers deduct qualifying educational expenses in full on Schedule C. Employees have to struggle past the 2% threshold to win their deductions. These costs are miscellaneous expenses deductible only if you itemize and only to the extent that your total in this category exceeds 2% of your adjusted gross income.

HOBBY-LOSS RULES

You've heard plenty about it: Play your cards right and you can convert your hobby into a sideline business and transform the cost of your avocation into tax deductions. An inviting idea, to be sure, and it *can* work. But the IRS isn't in the business of subsidizing your fun, which is why the hobby-loss rules are lurking in the tax law.

The best way to understand these rules is to think of the government as your partner in any business venture—willing to share the costs via tax-saving write-offs in exchange for the share of the profits it takes by taxing your earnings. Just as you wouldn't want to go into business with a ne'er-do-well nephew with a cavalier attitude toward the business, neither does Uncle Sam. You have to show that you're really out to make money, and at least occasionally show a profit, or the IRS will have nothing to do with the cost-sharing end of the arrangement.

Recognizing that profits are not automatic in any business venture, regardless of how hard you're trying to make money, the law does not demand that you show a profit every year for your endeavor to be classified as a business rather than a hobby. But you do have to make money in three out of five years to get the benefit of the doubt and deduct losses in the two profitless years. (If your enterprise consists primarily of breeding, training, showing or racing horses, you don't have to be as successful. Turn a profit two years out of seven to dodge the hobby-loss rules and qualify for business deductions.)

If you pass the test, the IRS can still audit your return and try to deny deductions, but it has to prove that you're not in business for a profit. When you fail, the burden of proof is on you to show that you really are trying to make money, and the cards are stacked in the government's favor. Profit from a hobby is always taxed; loss is never deductible. That does not mean none of your hobby expenses can be written off; just that the deductions are limited to the amount of income your hobby generates.

Staying away from the hobby-loss trap is more important than in the past because, here again, the 2% rule limiting miscellaneous itemized deductions rears its head. If your activity qualifies as a business, you deduct your expenses in full on Schedule C, even if your costs exceed income. If it is classified as a hobby, though, not only are write-offs limited to the amount of income earned, but those allowed are deductible as miscellaneous expenses on Schedule A. You get deductions only if you itemize and then only to the extent that all your miscellaneous deductions exceed 2% of your adjusted gross income.

Don't let the new rules discourage you from trying to blend money-making efforts into your avocation. The types of activities that often draw scrutiny from the IRS can be viewed as a list of opportunities as well as risks: free-lance writing; photography; painting; dog and cat breeding; stamp and coin collecting; raising flowers; boat chartering; and raising, showing or racing horses. If you are involved in those or any other activities that produce goods or services you could sell, consider mixing pleasure with profit, with the help of tax-saving deductions.

Say you're an amateur photographer, and you decide to try to capitalize on your skills by hiring yourself out to photograph weddings, birthday parties, award ceremonies, etc. You have business cards printed and buy ads in the local paper. You show your landscape photos at a gallery and sell several prints.

Your hobby as been transformed into a business. You have to report the income you earn, but you also earn deductions: for the cost of your film and processing, frames and mats, ads and business cards; the cost of getting to and from assignments, including food and lodging if you're away from home overnight;

the cost of attending a photography seminar; and depreciation on your cameras and equipment.

But what if, despite your best efforts, your costs exceed your income? Assuming you expect to turn a profit in the future and are running your activity in a businesslike manner, you can deduct the expenses even if you show a loss. If the IRS challenges your write-offs during the first five years—before you've had a chance to meet the three-of-five-year profit test— you can ask the government to postpone its hobby/business decision until the end of the five-year period. If at that time the decision still goes against you, you'd owe back taxes and interest.

Even if you lose on the three-of-five-year test, you can still win the right to deduct losses if you can convince the IRS that you're really trying to make money. Among the factors that will be considered:

• Whether you're managing the activity in a businesslike way (Are you keeping good books, trying to drum up business, holding down costs where possible, charging reasonable prices?);

• How much time and effort you devote to the activity;

• Whether you or your advisors have the expertise needed for the type of business you've chosen;

• Whether following a loss one year you make changes in an effort to make a profit in the future; and

• Whether your profit expectation is based in part on expected appreciation of assets used in the business.

Thorough records are essential, perhaps even more so with a sideline business that could be classified as a hobby than with a full-time business venture. If you are challenged, it's up to you to prove that your endeavor is a profit-motivated enterprise worthy of the tax deductions you have claimed rather than a hobby masquerading as a business.

CHILD-CARE CREDIT

Often, one of the biggest expenses associated with working is paying someone to care for your children while you're on the job. And here, too, the law is willing to lend a hand to help you earn money for the IRS to tax. The child- and dependent-care tax credit can serve as an annual rebate of as much as $1,440 of what you pay for child care. The details are in Chapter 11.

HEALTH INSURANCE FOR SELF-EMPLOYEDS

Tax reform brought a new write-off for self-employed taxpayers. If you have your own business, you can deduct 25% of the cost of health insurance for yourself and your family as an adjustment to income. That's an important change because otherwise the cost would be considered a medical expense, deductible only to the extent that total medical costs exceed 7.5% of adjusted gross income.

With the new rule, if you pay $3,000 for a family health policy, for example, you can write off $750 without worrying about the 7.5% floor. The remaining $2,250 would count toward that threshold.

There are some restrictions, of course. If you have employees, you generally must also provide insurance for them, too, in order to write off a quarter of your own cost. And your medical-insurance deduction can't exceed the net income of your business. Also, you can't claim this deduction if you are eligible for health coverage offered by your employer—if you have a job as well as your own business—or by your spouse's employer.

MISCELLANEOUS EXPENSES

There are plenty of other ways you spend money in connection with your job, whether you're an employee or self-employed. And many of those costs can translate into tax deductions. The often-repeated bad news in this chapter—about the 2% threshold for deducting employee business expenses—applies to the expenses discussed in this section, too. One reason Congress built the 2% obstacle was ostensibly to simplify your life: If it's unlikely you will surpass the threshold, the argument goes, you'll no longer have to keep track of these expenses. There's a serious catch-22 here, though. You'll never know if you will make it to the threshold unless you keep track of your expenses. The key difference is that in the past, you knew your record keeping would pay off in tax savings; now you can't be sure until you tote up all your expenses at year-end. If you are self-employed and write off business expenses on Schedule C, of course, you don't have to worry about the 2% barrier.

In addition to the types of expenses discussed earlier in this chapter, here are some of the others that can mean tax-saving deductions for you:

Special work clothes. You might be able to deduct the cost of your work wardrobe. To qualify, the clothes must be required by your job *and* not suitable for everyday use. Hard hats, work gloves and safety glasses qualify, for example, as do uniforms you must wear if you're a nurse, letter carrier, jockey, ballplayer, etc. Entertainers can deduct the cost of their theatrical wardrobe, assuming it's not fitting garb off the stage. What if you have to wear a suit to work but wouldn't be caught dead in such formal attire away from the office? No deduction because, regardless of your personal opinion, the IRS says the suit is suitable for everyday use.

If you can deduct the cost of your work clothes, you can also write off the cost of keeping them clean, including laundry and dry-cleaning bills. In one case an airline pilot was permitted to claim the cost of his shoeshines. The shoes were part of the uniform and not worn off the job.

Small tools. You don't have to spend thousands on cars, computers or office furniture to get Uncle Sam to help with the cost via a tax deduction. The cost of tools and equipment required in your work—a carpenter's saws, a lawyer's brief-case, a nurse's medical equipment, for example—all can qualify as tax-deductible business expenses. If the item is likely to last for more than a year, you have to depreciate it or use the expensing deduction discussed earlier in this chapter.

A physical exam required by your employer. By claiming this expense as an employee business expense rather than a medical expense, it becomes a miscellaneous itemized deduction subject to the 2% threshold instead of the tougher 7.5%-of-AGI threshold for medical expenses.

Professional expenses. The IRS permits deduction of such professional expenses as dues to professional societies, union dues and initiation fees, and subscriptions to professional journals and trade magazines.

Gifts. The cost of gifts you give in connection with your business is deductible, but Uncle Sam is something of a Scrooge here. You can't deduct more than $25 for the items you give to any one person during the year, regardless of how generous you actually are.

Job-security insurance. If you buy insurance to protect yourself against being ousted from your job for reasons other than poor performance—in the aftermath of a hostile takeover, say—the cost of the policy is a deductible employee business expense.

A BREAK FOR STRUGGLING ACTORS

Perhaps in recognition of President Reagan's early career as an actor, Congress opened a loophole through the 2% rule to help certain actors, actresses, musicians and other "qualified performing artists." If you fill the bill, you get to deduct employee business expenses—including travel expenses, job-hunting costs and agent's fees—as adjustments to income. That means they are fully deductible whether or not you itemize and without regard to the 2% test.

Congress didn't go overboard, though. To qualify:

• You must work for at least two employers during the year, earning at least $200 on each job;

• Your business expenses attributable to those jobs must exceed 10% of what you received for your services; and

• Your adjusted gross income for the year—before subtracting these business expenses—must be less than $16,000. If you're married, the $16,000 cap applies to you and your spouse's combined income.

10
ITEMIZED DEDUCTIONS

This is the *fun* part of taxes, if you'll forgive the use of that word in this context. Think of it as a treasure hunt. The more booty you discover, the lower your tax bill will be.

Over the years Congress has packed the tax law with goodies. Deductions are the lawmakers' invitations to you to let Uncle Sam pick up part of your expenses by reducing your tax bill. If you spend money for specifically sanctioned expenses, the IRS will ignore that part of your income. Every $1,000 of deductions knocks $1,000 off your taxable income, shaving $280 off your tax bill if you're in the 28% bracket. That effectively reduces your $1,000 out-of-pocket cost to $720.

To be sure, tax reform put the squeeze on itemized deductions and, by lowering tax rates, cut the value of those that remain. Rather than fretting about what used to be, however, your time is much better spent squeezing as much tax savings as possible out of the remaining deductions.

THE GROWING STANDARD DEDUCTION

Of course, deductions are worth absolutely nothing to you if you don't itemize. And for a growing army of taxpayers, itemizing doesn't make sense. In fact, millions who found itemizing profitable in the past will reject it now that the new beefed-up standard deductions are in place.

All taxpayers are permitted to reduce their taxable income by the standard deduction for their filing status. This is a no-questions-asked write-off. You don't need any records to prove to the IRS that you deserve the deduction. Even if you somehow made it through a year without incurring any of the deductible expenses detailed in this chapter, you still may claim the full standard deduction on your return.

The standard deduction is such a given that before 1987 it was built into the tax tables. It was known as the "zero-bracket amount" because a certain amount of income—depending on the taxpayer's filing status—was taxed at 0%. Now the 15% tax rate kicks in with your first dollar of taxable income, but to arrive at taxable income everyone gets to subtract the standard deduction or, if larger, the total of his or her itemized deductions.

One thing tax reform did not change: You itemize deductions only if the total of your allowable expenses exceeds your standard deduction. Here are the standard deduction amounts for 1988:

Filing Status	1988 Standard Deduction
Single	$3,000
Married filing jointly	5,000
Married filing separately	2,500
Head of household	4,400
Qualifying widow or widower	5,000

More for some. The standard deduction amounts are higher for taxpayers who are age 65 and over or legally blind. (As far as the IRS is concerned, a taxpayer is considered blind if he or she cannot see better than 20/200 in the better eye with glasses, or the field of vision is not more than 20 degrees.) This boost in the standard deduction makes up, in part, for Congress' decision to take away the extra personal exemption that used to be granted to these taxpayers.

Here's how much you can add to your standard deduction if you meet either the age or blindness test. A taxpayer who is both 65 or older *and* blind doubles the bonus amount and adds the combined total to his or her standard deduction.

Filing Status	Add for Age/Blindness
Single	$750
Married filing jointly	600
Married filing separately	600
Head of household	750
Qualifying widow or widower	600

For example, assume you and your spouse are both 65 and one of you is legally blind. To the regular standard deduction on a joint return of $5,000, you would add $1,800—three times the $600 joint-return amount for age or blindness. Your standard deduction would be $6,800.

Less for others. Taxpayers who can be claimed as a dependent on someone else's return—a scenario that applies primarily to children claimed on their parents' return—are often stuck with a stunted standard deduction. For dependents, the standard deduction is $500 or the total of his or her earned income, up to the regular standard deduction amount. (Earned income is basically earnings from a job rather than investment income. See the discussion of the kiddie tax in Chapter 3.) This rule basically prevents a dependent from using the standard deduction to shelter more than $500 of unearned income, such as interest and dividends. The $500 minimum is increased for taxpayers who qualify for the age or blindness addition. Thus, for example, a single taxpayer age 65 or older who is claimed as a dependent by a son or daughter would have a minimum standard deduction of $1,250—$500 plus the extra $750 allotted because of age.

Starting in 1989, the standard deduction amounts for all taxpayers will be indexed for inflation. If the inflation rate is measured at 5%, say, the deductions would rise by 5%—from $5,000 to $5,250 on a joint return, for example, and from $3,000 to $3,150 on a single return.

The hike in the standard deduction will undoubtedly bring renewed interest in "bunching" write-offs. This is the practice of alternating between claiming the standard deduction one year and itemizing the next. It can pay off if your deductible expenses routinely fall close to the standard deduction amount. Bunching is accomplished by accelerating the payment of deductible expenses in the year you'll itemize, effectively depleting the following year's supply, and deferring such payments in the year you'll use the standard deduction, thus pushing otherwise worthless deductions into the following year when they will have value because you'll itemize. See Chapter 12 for details.

MEDICAL EXPENSES

The list of medical costs that can be deducted stretches to the Mayo Clinic and back, but few taxpayers get any tax benefit. The reason for the seeming contradiction is that Congress keeps raising the ante for getting into the game. To deduct any medical expenses, your total outlay for qualifying costs during the year must exceed 7.5% of your adjusted gross income. (AGI is basically all your taxable income minus certain items, the most common of which are IRA and Keogh contributions and alimony you paid.) Before 1983, the threshold was 3% of AGI. Congress raised the hurdle to 5% for a few years, then boosted it to 7.5% for 1987 and later years.

To see the impact of this rule, consider a taxpayer with AGI of $50,000. The 7.5% test blocks the deduction of the first $3,750 of unreimbursed medical expenses. If qualifying costs totaled $4,000, for example, the deductible amount would be a skimpy $250.

The tougher Congress makes it to get any medical deductions, the more important it is to know what can qualify for this tax-saver. The basic definition of medical care is extremely broad. Qualifying expenses include what you pay for the diagnosis, treatment or prevention of disease or for treatment affecting any structure or function of the body. You also count the cost of transportation to where you received the qualified care and the premiums you pay for medical insurance.

Clearly, what you pay in doctors' and dentists' bills qualifies, as do hospital bills and what you pay for prescription drugs. (The cost of over-the-counter medicines can't be included.) Plenty of other expenses are accepted by the IRS, too, including many that may be less likely to be covered by insurance, such as some nursing home fees and what you pay for medically necessary improvements to your home. Before looking in detail at what you can claim, consider whose expenses you are permitted to deduct on your return.

In addition to what you pay for your own medical care, include what you pay for your spouse and anyone you claim as a dependent (see Chapter 3). If you were divorced during the year but paid medical bills incurred by your spouse while you were married, you can deduct those costs even though you file a separate return. Also count medical expenses you pay for someone who would qualify as your dependent (either individually or under a multiple-support agreement) except that he or she earned more than $1,950 ($2,000 in 1989) or filed a joint return.

If you are divorced, you can include in your deductible medical expenses any qualifying bills you pay for your child, even if he or she is claimed as a dependent by your ex-spouse.

Now, what's deductible?

Insurance. Qualifying costs include premiums you pay for policies that either pay directly or reimburse you for:
• Doctor, hospital and surgical fees and other medical and dental expenses, including the cost of membership in an HMO or similar plan;
• Prescription drugs; and
• Replacement of lost or damaged contact lenses.

You may also deduct what you pay for Medicare B supplemental insurance and, if you're not covered by social security but choose to enroll in the program, your Medicare A premiums as well.

You can't deduct premiums you pay for any policy that promises to pay you a set amount—$100 a day, say—for time you're in the hospital, insurance that pays you for lost earnings, or a policy that pays a flat amount for the loss of a limb, for example, or sight. To be deductible, the insurance benefits must be tied to the actual cost of medical care. (On the bright side, benefits you receive under a nondeductible policy are tax-free.)

Special break for self-employed. If you are self-employed, you may be able to deduct 25% of what you pay for medical insurance for yourself and your family without worrying about the 7.5% test. If you qualify, you can deduct a quarter of your premiums whether you itemize deductions or not. This write-off was first available in 1987 and is scheduled to disappear after 1989. Note this, too: If you have employees, you must pay for their

health insurance, too, in order to qualify for this deduction of 25% of the cost of your own coverage.

You can lose this deduction if, in addition to your self-employment, you or your spouse has a job as an employee. If you could be covered by insurance offered through that job, forget this deduction even if you choose not to participate in the employer-provided plan.

If you do qualify for the write-off, the 75% of your insurance premiums not deductible as an adjustment to income should be included with other expenses to which the 7.5% test is applied.

Swimming pools and other home improvements. You've probably heard stories about taxpayers writing off the cost of swimming pools as medical expenses. What quicker way to meet the 7.5% of AGI test than spend $20,000 or so on a backyard pool?

There's a catch, of course. First of all, the pool—or whatever improvement—must be primarily for medical care. The improvement should be recommended by a doctor to treat a specific ailment. Putting in a pool for regular exercise to improve your general health doesn't cut it even if your doctor suggests it. For example, in the cases in which courts have okayed medical deductions for the cost of pool construction, the pools were recommended for therapy for patients with such diseases as polio and severe osteoarthritis. To qualify for a tax deduction, the capital improvement must also pass the "reasonableness" test the IRS applies to most expenditures. It could be tough for a private pool to pass that test, for example, if you had ready access to another pool.

Still, medical deductions for pools have been approved. So have write-offs for the cost of installing home elevators for heart patients unable to walk up and down stairs, central air-conditioning systems for people with breathing problems, and special plumbing fixtures for the handicapped. If an improvement qualifies as a medical expense, so does what you pay for its operation and maintenance.

You don't necessarily get to deduct the full cost of medically required improvements. Your write-off is limited to the difference between what you pay and any increase in the value of your home. If you spend $20,000 on a pool, for example, and it boosts the value of your property by $15,000, the qualifying medical expense would be $5,000.

To claim a capital improvement as a medical expense, you should have a written statement from a doctor recommending that you make the improvement and evidence, such as before-and-after appraisals, showing how much, if any, the value of your property increased due to the improvement.

The cost of certain improvements made for handicapped individuals is fully deductible, even if the improvements increase the value of your home. These include:

• Constructing entrance and exit ramps;
• Widening doorways and hallways to accommodate wheelchairs;
• Installing railings, support bars and other modifications in bathrooms;
• Lowering or otherwise modifying kitchen cabinets and equipment; and
• Adjusting electrical outlets and fixtures.

Although capital improvements usually increase the basis of your home for tax purposes (see Chapter 4), the portion of the cost you claim as a medical deduction is not an addition to basis.
Travel. The cost of getting where you have to go for medical care is deductible, too. Count what you pay for cab, bus or subway fare, or ambulance hire. If you drive your own car to the doctor's office or hospital, tote up the deduction at 9 cents a mile, plus parking and tolls. (You can use the actual cost of gas and oil in the unlikely event that that gives you a bigger deduction than the cents-per-mile rate.)

Trips to a local doctor are nickel-and-dime expenses that won't help much toward the 7.5% threshold. But out-of-town travel counts, too, and those costs can mount up quickly. Say, for example, that your local doctor recommends you go to the Mayo Clinic to see a specialist because the needed treatment is not available locally. The cost of travel to Minnesota would be deductible. What if you need care that is available locally but instead you choose to travel to a nicer clime—such as going to Hawaii for cataract surgery? No surprise here: The cost of the travel would not be deductible (but the cost of the surgery still would be.)

In addition to the cost of trips to a distant hospital or clinic, you may be able to deduct the cost of travel that's recommended by a doctor as part of the treatment for a specific ailment. Taxpayers have won deductions for the cost of traveling to spend the winter in Florida, for example, when their doctors recommended that they avoid cold weather as part of their treatment. If you make such a trip for general health purposes, however, the cost is not deductible.

What about food and lodging costs connected with your medical care? The basic rule is that such expenses are not deductible unless they are part of the cost of a stay in a hospital or similar institution.

However, you may deduct the cost of lodging (but still not food) associated with deductible medical care. If you stay in a hotel while you are receiving treatment in an outpatient clinic, the cost can be included in your deductible medical expenses— up to $50 a day. The daily dollar limit is per person. If you travel with a sick child to get medical care, for example, you could deduct up to $100 a day for your lodging expenses. And if you have to stay in a nearby hotel while a child is hospitalized, you may deduct up to $50 a day of your costs.

Here's a handful of less-than-obvious situations in which travel expenses have been permitted as medical deductions:

• Plane fare to and from the hospital paid by a prospective kidney donor.

• Cost of transportation to and from Alcoholics Anonymous meetings recommended by a doctor.

• Fare for parent or nurse who accompanies a patient on medically required trip.

• Cost of a trip to Florida, on the recommendation of a physician, to aid recuperation from a stroke.

• Cost of parents' transportation to visit mentally ill child, when doctor recommended visits as part of the child's treatment.

Nursing homes and special schools. Include in your medical expenses wages and other amounts you pay for nursing services, including social security taxes you pay on the caregiver's wages. The person providing care does not have to be a registered or licensed nurse for the cost to be deductible, but you must be able to show that the services provided were for the medical care or treatment of a patient. If the person also performed nonmedical chores, such as housekeeping, only the part of the expense attributable to medical care is deductible. The rest is a nondeductible personal expense. To back up your deduction, you or the attendant should keep a log showing the breakdown of time spent on personal versus medical duties.

Nursing home fees can quickly mount up to 7.5% of almost anyone's income. Such costs may be fully deductible, partially deductible or not deductible at all, depending on why someone is in the institution. If the availability of medical care is the primary reason, the full cost can be deductible, even though much of the cost is actually for otherwise nondeductible expenses such as food and lodging. When someone chooses to live in a rest home or retirement center primarily for personal, rather than medical, reasons, the cost is generally nondeductible. If part of the monthly fee is specifically for medical facilities available at the institution, however, that segment of the charge can qualify as a medical expense.

The key to deductibility is the level of medical services provided at the institution and the condition of the resident.

What about advance payments, such as life-care or founder's fees, required by some institutions? The portion of such charges allocated to medical care is deductible in the year paid as long as the fee is required as a condition of the institution's promise to provide future medical care.

Your medical deduction can also include costs for a special school or training for a physically or mentally handicapped person if the main reason for the expense is the school's resources for relieving the handicap. The IRS has approved deductions for the cost of a school that teaches Braille to a blind child or lip reading to a deaf child or that gives remedial language training to correct a condition caused by a birth defect. If the primary reason the person is at the school is for medically related treatment, the cost of food and lodging can also be included in the deduction. Sometimes, colleges and private schools include in their tuition charges a fee for student medical care. If you can get a breakdown of the bill showing what part of the total goes to those fees, you can include that amount in your deductible medical expenses.

Other possible medical deductions. Here's a rundown of some of the other expenses you may be able to include when figuring your medical-expense deduction:

- *Abortion.* You can include the expenses of a legal abortion.
- *Acupuncture.* The cost for such treatment is deductible.
- *Alcoholism.* Payments to a treatment center qualify, including the part of the fee that pays for room and board.
- *Artificial limb.* The cost of the prosthesis and associated expenses are deductible.
- *Birth control pills.* As with other prescribed medicines, the cost qualifies for the deduction.
- *Braille books and magazines.* The amount by which the cost exceeds that of regular reading material may be written off.
- *Car.* The cost of outfitting an auto with special controls needed by a handicapped person may be included with your medical expenses.
- *Chiropractors.* Their fees qualify.
- *Christian Science practitioners.* Their fees also qualify.
- *Contact lenses.* Their cost qualifies, as does the cost of insurance against their loss.
- *Cosmetic surgery.* The cost of a face-lift or any other cosmetic surgery qualifies as a medical expense. It doesn't matter whether the operation is done to correct a physical defect or simply to serve your vanity.
- *Crutches.* What you pay to buy or rent crutches or other medically necessary equipment is deductible.
- *Dental treatment.* The cost of everything from diagnostic x-rays to orthodontic treatment to dentures qualifies as a medical expense.
- *Doctor's fees.* When adding them up, count payments to anesthesiologists, dermatologists, gynecologists, neurologists, obstetricians, ophthalmologists, osteopaths, pediatricians, podiatrists, psychiatrists, surgeons and any other recognized medical practitioners.

- *Drug addiction.* As with treatment for alcoholism, treatment for drug addition is deductible.
- *Electrolysis or hair removal.* Yes, it's deductible when performed by a licensed technician.
- *Eyeglasses.* Include in the deductible amount the fees for eye exams as well as the cost of the glasses.
- *Guide dog.* Your medical expenses can include the cost of a guide dog for the blind or deaf, including the cost of the dog's care.
- *Hair transplant.* As with hair removal, it's deductible.
- *Health club dues.* As efforts to improve your general health aren't deductible, it's highly unlikely that you could persuade the IRS to let you write off these costs. However, if your doctor recommended that you join a health club as part of necessary therapy for a specific medical condition, the cost may be deductible.
- *Hearing aid.* The cost of the device itself and associated fees are deductible.
- *Lead-based paint removal.* This is one of the stranger examples of the way the IRS views qualifying medical expenses. You can count as a deductible expense the cost of removing lead-based paint if the paint is within the reach of a child who has suffered from lead poisoning. The cost of removing paint out of the reach of the child doesn't count toward the medical deduction, nor does the cost of repainting the scraped area.
- *Medicine.* Include in your deductible medical expenses what you pay for any prescription medicines and insulin. The cost of over-the-counter medicines is not deductible.
- *Oxygen.* The costs of oxygen equipment and oxygen to relieve breathing problems that are caused by a medical condition are deductible.
- *Psychoanalysis.* Include in your medical expenses fees paid for psychoanalysis.
- *Psychologist.* Also count what you pay a psychologist for care.
- *Stop-smoking program.* Despite the Surgeon General's long-standing campaign against smoking, the IRS says the cost of a program designed to help a taxpayer kick the habit does not qualify as a medical expense. However, if you take such a course

on your doctor's orders to relieve the symptoms of an existing disease—say, emphysema—the cost would be deductible.

• *Sterilization.* The cost of such an operation, including a vasectomy, is deductible.

• *Telephone.* What you pay for special equipment to permit the deaf to communicate over the phone is deductible.

• *Television.* The cost of a decoder so that a TV picks up closed-caption signals for the hearing-impaired can be included with your medical expenses.

• *Weight-loss program.* As with stop-smoking courses, what you pay for a weight-loss program to improve your general health is not deductible. However, you may write off the cost of such a program recommended by your doctor as part of the treatment for a specific medical problem, such as hypertension.

• *Wheelchair.* The cost of a wheelchair, whether manual or motorized, is deductible.

Timing deductions. Medical bills are deductible in the year you pay them. If you pay by check, the day you mail or deliver the check is the date of payment, even if the check isn't cashed until the following year. If you charge a medical expense to a credit card, payment is considered made the day you make the charge regardless of when you actually pay the credit card bill.

The 7.5% threshold for medical deductions gives added importance to the issue of timing. If you incur heavy expenses one year and it's clear that you will pass the 7.5% test, you may want to try to cram in other medical expenses before year-end. Buy that new pair of contact lenses, for example, or give extra thought to scheduling that elective surgery before December 31. By paying the bills before the end of the year, you can guarantee their deductibility. Pushed into the following year, such expenses might not tip the 7.5%-of-AGI scale.

On the other hand, if you will fall short of the 7.5% threshold one year, try to hold off paying medical bills until after New Year's Eve. By pushing payment into a new year, you have at least a chance that the expense will be deductible.

Reimbursement. When figuring your medical-expense deduction, you must, of course, subtract any reimbursement you received from your medical insurance. What if you pay a doctor's bill or other qualifying expense one year and get the check from your insurance company the next? The answer depends on whether you received any tax benefit from the expense in the year you paid the bill. If not—because your total costs fell below the 7.5% threshold so you didn't get to claim medical expenses—you can just pocket the reimbursement. If the reimbursement is for an expense that was deducted in an earlier year, however, all or part of the reimbursement is considered income. The taxable amount is either the full reimbursement or the amount of your medical deduction write-off for the year in question (total expenses minus 7.5% AGI)—whichever is less.

What if insurance pays you more than your medical expenses? Whether the excess reimbursement is considered taxable income depends on who paid for the insurance. If you did, the extra cash is nontaxable. But if your employer paid for the medical insurance, the "profit" is considered taxable income to you. And if you and your employer shared the cost of the insurance, the tax status of the excess reimbursement turns on the portion of the premiums each of you paid. If the premiums were split 50/50, for example, half the excess reimbursement would be taxable and half tax-free.

Damages. If you receive a settlement in a damage suit that includes money for medical expenses you deducted in an earlier year, that amount is considered taxable in the year you receive it, but only to the extent that the deduction actually reduced your taxable income for the year you wrote off the expenses. If a settlement includes funds for future medical expenses, the amount is not taxable, but neither are those future medical expenses deductible until they exceed the amount of the award allocated to future medical care.

TAXES

One way tax reform *did* simplify things was by abolishing the deduction for state and local sales taxes. No longer do you need to worry about keeping all your receipts to be certain you get all of the sales-tax deduction you've got coming. Congress now automatically assigns the same write-off to everyone: $0.

Before looking at the taxes you can still deduct, remember that what probably amounts to your biggest tax bill—what you pay Uncle Sam in income taxes—cannot be written off on your federal return. Nor can you deduct what you pay in social security (FICA) tax, which amounts to 7.51% of your first $45,000 of wage income in 1988.

State and local income taxes. If you don't own a home and don't deduct mortgage interest, your state income-tax bill is likely to be your largest single itemized deduction. It's fairly easy to keep track of this deduction. Amounts withheld from your paychecks by your employer will show up on your W-2 form; any income tax you pay via estimated payments will be recorded on your copies of estimated tax forms; and if you pay an extra amount when you file your state return, that amount will be on the return.

As with other expenses, you deduct state and local income taxes on the return for the year in which you made the payment, which may be a different year than that for which you owe the tax. Say for example, that when you complete your 1988 state return in the spring of 1989, you discover that you owe an extra $500, which you pay when you file the return. Although the tax was assessed against your 1988 income, the fact that you paid it in 1989 means it should be deducted on your 1989 federal return. That's the one you'll file in 1990.

If you owe estimated taxes on self-employment or investment income, the state tax bill offers some planning opportunities. In most states, the final estimated tax payment is due in January of the following year. If you make your final 1988 payment in January 1989, it would be deductible on your 1989 federal return. Make that payment by December 31, 1988, however, and you can include the amount in your 1988 deductions. (The payment is considered to have been made in 1988 as long as your check is in the mail by the end of the year, even if it's not cashed until the following year.) For the deduction of such a payment to withstand IRS scrutiny, it must be a reasonable estimate of the tax you owe for the year involved. You may not, for example, make a huge fourth-quarter estimated payment to beef up your federal deductions if the outlay is actually a deliberate overpayment of your state taxes that you'll soon get back in the form of a state tax refund.

In some cases, it's better not to accelerate the tax payment. If you are not itemizing deductions—because your total expenses won't pass the standard deduction amount—holding off the fourth quarter payment until January has a double benefit. It lets you hold on to your money a little longer and preserves the possibility that you'll get to write off the payment the next year. Also, if you expect to be in a higher tax bracket the following year, the value of the deduction would escalate. Finally, if you are subject to the alternative minimum tax (AMT, which is discussed in Chapter 15) don't prepay your taxes. State income taxes aren't deductible at all under the AMT.

State tax refunds. This is a confusing issue for many people, particularly now that state governments send out 1099-G forms reporting the refunds to taxpayers and the IRS. But don't let that form persuade you that the refund is automatically taxable. The tax status depends on whether you received a federal tax benefit from deducting the state overpayment.

If you did not itemize on your federal return for the previous year, you received no benefit and the refund is tax-free. If you did itemize, part or all of the state refund is taxable on your federal return. You should include in income the lesser of the entire refund or the difference between your itemized deductions the previous year and the standard deduction amount for your filing status.

Consider an example: You filed a joint return in 1987 and claimed itemized deductions of $5,100, including $2,000 of state income taxes paid. In 1988, you receive a $500 state income-tax refund based on your 1987 state return.

Is it taxable? Yes, the entire $500 should be reported as taxable income on your 1988 federal return. The standard deduction on 1987 joint returns—for filers under 65—was $3,760. By itemizing $5,100 worth of deductions you knocked an extra $1,340 off your taxable income. Even if you had paid your state taxes on the button and claimed $500 less in that category, you still would have itemized rather than claiming the standard deduction. In this example, every dollar of the $500 state-tax overpayment pushed down your federal taxable income in 1987. Uncle Sam evens things up by demanding that you report the $500 refund as taxable income in 1988.

If the identical situation occurred in 1988, however, only $100 of the state refund would be taxable. That's because in 1988, the standard deduction on a joint return is $5,000. Because that's just $100 less than the itemized deductions in this example, the $2,000 state tax deduction actually trimmed only $100 more from your taxable income than the standard deduction would have. Therefore, you would report only $100 of the refund as taxable income to even the score.

State disability insurance. Residents of four states—California, New Jersey, New York and Rhode Island—can include in their state tax deduction required contributions to state disability-benefit funds.

Real estate taxes. State and local real estate taxes you pay on your home or other property are deductible.

© 1986 STEVE KELLY—THE SAN DIEGO UNION

If you pay your property taxes through an escrow account funded by part of your monthly mortgage payments, you don't actually earn the deduction until funds are transferred out of the account to pay the tax bill. Your lender will probably send you a statement showing how much real estate tax was paid for you during the year—an amount that may differ from the total of the installments you paid into the escrow account during the calendar year. If you don't receive such a statement from the lender, ask for one.

If you are a renter, you may not claim a deduction for the part of your rent you figure goes to cover the landlord's property taxes. Even if you're hit with a rent increase specifically tied to a property-tax increase, you don't get a deduction. The law allows a write-off only for the person on whom the tax is directly imposed.

What about special municipal assessments imposed on homeowners for widening roads or adding sidewalks or street lights? As discussed in Chapter 4, such levies generally are not deductible but rather are added to the tax basis of their homes. The distinction between deductible real estate taxes and nondeductible assessments is that the tax-favored levies are for the general public welfare and assessments primarily benefit and add to the value of the specific properties involved.

When general revenues pay for such services as trash and garbage pickup, the cost is part of your deductible real estate taxes. However, if your community imposes a separate fee for such services, that charge is nondeductible.

Property sold during the year. If you buy or sell property during the year, your real estate tax deduction may be more or less than you actually paid the taxing authority. The deduction is allocated between buyer and seller, based on the part of the property-tax year (which may not be the same as the calendar year) each owned the property. The settlement sheet should show the allocation. If you can deduct more or less property tax than you actually paid, the selling price of the house is adjusted—in the eyes of the IRS—to reflect the difference, as discussed in Chapter 4.

Personal property taxes and auto license tags. State and local personal property taxes are deductible if the tax is imposed annually and based on the value of the property being taxed. Although only a few states and municipalities have a levy that's specifically called a personal property tax, in many states at least part of what you pay annually to register or license your car fits the definition and can be deducted.

The key to deductibility is that the annual license fee be based—at least in part—on the value of your car. Any part of the charge based on the auto's age or weight, for example, isn't deductible. To know whether you can deduct any part of the tag fees you pay, check with local officials.

INTEREST

Simplification is a word that simply cannot be applied to the rules that now cover the deduction of interest. Before tax reform, matters were relatively simple. Interest was pretty much interest, and when you paid it on a debt for which you were legally responsible, you could almost always write it off. Uncle Sam stood by to subsidize your borrowing. When the cost of carrying debt came up, the pertinent issue was the after-tax cost. If you were in the 50% tax bracket—back when there was one—you knew the IRS would effectively pay half of the interest. On a 15% loan, that pulled the real, after-tax cost down to 7.5%. If inflation was running higher than that, the effective cost to you was less than zero.

Congress worried that such a system—when combined with the taxation of earnings on savings and investments—was cockeyed, encouraging debt and discouraging savings. As a partial remedy, and to raise needed revenues, the lawmakers concocted a complicated set of new rules that crack down on interest deductions. The restrictions demand that you separate interest expenses into five categories, each with its own tax status:

• *Qualified mortgage interest.* As every homeowner knows, mortgage interest dodged the new restrictions and remains deductible, as long as the debt doesn't exceed the limits detailed in Chapter 4.

● *Personal interest.* This category probably encompasses most of the interest you pay beyond that due on a mortgage. It includes interest on car loans, vacation loans, student loans, debt-consolidation loans and, of course, the ubiquitous credit card. And it is hit hardest by the new rules. The deduction for personal interest is being wiped out completely according to this schedule:

Year	Amount Deductible
1988	40%
1989	20
1990	10
1991 and future years	0

● *Business interest.* This remains fully deductible. Although interest on a loan to buy a personal automobile, for example, is subject to the phaseout, interest on a loan to buy a car for your business can be written off on your business tax return. You have to have your own business to write off business interest, however. An employee toting up employee-business expenses, for instance, has to count interest paid on a loan for a car used on the job as personal interest.

● *Investment interest.* As in the past, the deduction of this kind of interest—on a margin account, for example—is restricted by the amount of investment income you report. New limits apply, however, as discussed in Chapter 5.

● *Passive-activity interest.* If you borrow to invest in a passive activity, discussed in Chapter 6, the interest has a special tax status rather than being added to other investment interest. It is deductible only against passive-activity income.

Tracing. Before looking at your interest deductions in detail, consider this zinger: It's up to you to trace the use of debt to prove which type of interest you pay during the year. The IRS has made it clear that it is how borrowed money is used—not the source of the loan or how it is secured—that determines the tax status of the interest paid.

The tracing rules are best illustrated with an example. Assume you borrow $100,000 on January 1 and put the proceeds in a checking account. On April 1, you withdraw $20,000 to invest in a limited partnership—a passive activity. On September 1, you use $40,000 from the account for a trip to Europe that includes the purchase of a new car—two major personal expenses.

Assuming no other expenditures from the account and no repayment of the debt, here's how the IRS sees things:

All the interest charges that accrued between January 1 and March 31 are considered investment interest (whether or not you earned interest on the checking-account balance). From April 1 through August 31, 20% of the interest is considered passive-activity interest and 80% investment interest. From September 1 to year-end, 40% is investment interest, 20% is assigned to the passive activity and 40% is personal interest.

There is a major exception to the IRS commandment that how borrowed money is used determines the tax status of the interest. When home-equity debt is involved (see Chapter 4), the fact that the loan is secured by your home generally makes the interest deductible regardless of how the money is used.

Now, consider the issue of commingling. Mixing borrowed funds with unborrowed money begs trouble. Consider another example:

You borrow $10,000 and put it temporarily in an account with $10,000 of unborrowed funds. A month later, you withdraw $10,000 to pay for a vacation, and when you return from your trip two weeks later, you use the $10,000 left in the account to buy mutual fund shares.

Don't assume it's up to you to say which funds went where. The IRS applies a handy-dandy "first-out" rule: The first money out of the account is considered to be the borrowed money. In the example, the vacation was paid for before the investment was made, so it's assumed you used the borrowed money for the vacation and your own money for the investment. Thus, the interest on the loan is subject to the personal interest phaseout.

There is an exception that short-circuits the first-out rule if funds are withdrawn from the commingled account within 15 days of the time the borrowed money was deposited. During this "window," you get to decide whether the funds coming out of the account are the proceeds of the loan or the unborrowed money.

These are rules only an accountant could love, but you have to play by them to maximize your interest deductions. In fact, the new restrictions open new opportunities. And the IRS worries that they are open to manipulation and abuse.

Consider this scenario: A taxpayer who owns an apartment building needs a new car. If he borrows to buy the auto, the interest is personal interest subject to the phaseout. Instead, he takes a month's worth of rent—money that normally would go to pay the mortgage on the building—and uses the cash to buy the car. He then borrows to pay the mortgage. Since the IRS says the use of the loan proceeds controls the tax status of the interest, the interest isn't tainted with the "personal" label.

Short of such finagling, timing your purchases takes on new significance. In the example of commingled funds presented above, if you made the $10,000 mutual fund investment before paying for the vacation, the interest on the loan would be deductible investment interest.

Better yet, however, is to avoid mixing borrowed and unborrowed funds. Commingling means forfeiting flexibility. One thing the confusing rules make absolutely clear is the need for precise records so you can trace the source and use of borrowed funds.

The basics. In addition to meeting the new tests, to deduct interest you must be legally liable for the debt involved. Although it's doubtful that you go out of your way to pay someone else's debts, it can happen. Perhaps a down-on-his-luck relative asks that you make a mortgage payment or two while he's looking for a new job. If you do, don't expect Uncle Sam to join in your generosity. You can't deduct the interest part of the mortgage payment and neither can your relative. The better move would be to give him the money and let him make the house payment himself. By doing so, at least he preserves the deduction.

The question of who is liable to repay a debt sometimes comes up with student loans. If a parent repays a loan for which a child is liable, for example, no one gets a deduction. If you co-signed the loan note with your son or daughter, you are jointly liable, so the interest paid by either parent or student is deductible—subject to the phaseout rules.

You write off interest on the return for the year you pay it. If you make an interest payment by check, it is considered paid on the day you mail or deliver the check. Drop your December mortgage payment in the mail December 31, 1988, for example, and you include the interest in the deduction claimed on your 1988 return, even though the check won't be cashed until 1989. (Note that the mortgage lender might not include such a year-end payment in the statement sent to you—and the IRS—listing the amount of interest paid during the year. You may still include it with your deduction, however. If you are uncertain exactly what part of the payment was interest, ask the lender. Claiming a deduction larger than the amount shown on the report to the IRS is perfectly legal, but will probably prompt an inquiry from the IRS. You should attach a statement to your tax return explaining the discrepancy or, better yet, make the payment early enough so it is included on your year-end statement.)

Prepaid interest. This is generally not deductible when paid but rather written off over the life of loan. Assume, for example, that you borrow $10,000 on December 1 and agree to pay $100 interest a month for 12 months, at which time the principal will be repaid. To beef up your interest deduction and beat the next step in the phaseout, you decide to prepay the full $1,200 of interest the same month you get the loan. Forget it. On the tax return for the year you got the loan, you are considered to have paid just the one month's worth of interest, $100, which accrued during the year. The other $1,100 would be considered paid in the following year.

Sometimes you are effectively required to prepay the interest, as in the case of discount loans. Say you give a lender a note for $1,500 payable in 15 monthly $100 installments, but you actually receive only $1,300. The $200 discount is prepaid interest, and one-fifteenth of it ($13.33) is the interest portion of each payment. If you make six payments during the first calendar year, $80 in interest would be considered paid on the loan. Your deduction would be based on that amount.

When a discount loan requires no payments until the end of term, the interest is considered paid when you repay the loan. Assume in the example above that rather than monthly payments, the full $1,500 was due in a lump sum at the end of the 15-month term. In that case, the $200 interest would be deductible—subject to the phaseout rules—in the year the loan was paid off.

An important exception to the prepaid interest rule applies to points paid to get a mortgage to buy your principal residence. As explained in Chapter 4, such points may be fully deducted in the year paid. Points paid on other mortgages, such as a loan to buy a vacation home, are treated as other prepaid interest. Those charges must be written off over the life of the loan.

Unstated interest. It's possible, though unlikely, that the IRS will let you deduct interest you *don't* pay. This topsy-turvy result can occur thanks to the unstated-interest rules.

Basically, the tax rules demand that a reasonable rate of interest be charged on loans. If little or no interest is charged, the IRS thinks something's fishy and requires the lender to report as interest income the amount the tax agency figures is the minimum that should be charged on such a loan. As the borrower, you get to count as interest paid the same amount of unstated interest that the lender has to report as income.

Actually, though, it's doubtful you'll find yourself in this situation. For one thing, exceptions to the unstated-interest rules protect most intrafamily loans, which are the most likely to carry bargain interest rates. See Chapter 3 for details.

Until a few years ago, it was possible for the unstated-interest rules to benefit taxpayers who got great financing deals—such as a super-low interest rate on a new automobile. If you bought a new car with a 2% factory-subsidized loan, for example, you might have been permitted to calculate your interest deduction as though you were paying 10%. To save you from the mind-boggling computations required to figure an unstated-interest deduction, however, Congress decided in 1984 to deny unstated-interest deductions to buyers of personal use property, such as a car.

Nondeductible interest. Just as it's possible for interest you don't pay to be deductible, some interest that you do pay—on a debt you're legally liable to repay—can be nondeductible.

Interest on funds borrowed so you can buy or carry tax-exempt investments, such as municipal bonds, isn't deductible. No wonder. If you're not going to be taxed on the fruits of your investment, the government doesn't want to be subsidizing your purchase.

The word "carry" is used above because the IRS can deny an interest deduction even if you don't directly invest borrowed funds in tax-exempts. If you buy tax-free securities with unborrowed money and then pledge the bonds as security for a loan, the IRS says "no" to the deduction of interest on that loan. The connection doesn't have to be so blatant, either. If you have substantial investments in tax-free municipals and are claiming big interest deductions, the IRS may contend that only because of the debt are you able to afford to keep, or carry, the tax-free investment. That could lead to the denial of a deduction. (There may be increasing numbers of questions raised on this issue now that taxpayers must report on their returns the amount of tax-exempt interest earned.)

That doesn't mean all of your interest deductions are at risk if you own tax-exempt securities. Borrowing for personal purposes—such as a home or a car—is safe. But if you have a substantial position in tax-exempts and take out a large loan to invest in a real estate deal, for example, don't be surprised if the IRS comes knocking.

Also nondeductible is interest on a loan used to buy single-premium life insurance. As discussed in Chapter 5, single-premium life is a tax-advantaged investment. Denying the deduction for interest on loans to buy it is a way to prevent double-dipping for tax benefits.

If you buy life insurance under a plan that relies on systematic borrowing against the policy's cash value to pay the premiums, the interest on the loans is not deductible. There's an important exception to this rule, however, which insurance companies have used to design policies promoted on the basis of the deductibility of the interest. If during the first seven years the policy is in force at least four annual premiums are paid with unborrowed money, the interest on borrowing to pay any other premiums can be written off. If you have such a policy, note that this interest is subject to the deduction phaseout. After 1990, even the interest on these carefully designed plans will be nondeductible.

Another threat to interest deductibility can nix the deduction of interest on life insurance loans. Remember that a key to any deduction is that you actually pay the expense. On life insurance loans, the policyholder may choose to have the amount of interest due added to the balance of the loan rather than paying the bill directly. That choice means no interest deduction, however, until you ultimately pay off the loan.

This same rule applies to other kinds of borrowing, too. Basically, if you borrow more money from the original lender to pay the interest due, you're not really paying the interest as far as the IRS is concerned. If you must borrow to cover interest due on a loan, getting the loan from a different lender will preserve your right to a deduction.

A closer look at personal interest. With Congress squeezing the life out of the write-off for personal interest, you need to redouble your efforts to keep track of every dime of partially deductible interest you pay and, where practical, rejigger your borrowing to preserve full deductibility.

The jeopardized personal interest category includes all interest you pay that's not secured by your home or a second house or not connected with your investments or a business. Remember that it is generally how you use borrowed money, not the source of the loan, that determines the tax status of the interest. If you borrow against a life insurance policy to pay your premiums or buy a car, for example, the interest on the loan would be personal interest. If you used that same loan to invest in stock, however, the interest would be investment interest not threatened by the deduction phaseout.

Most types of personal interest are obvious, and it's likely the lender will send you a year-end notice showing the total interest paid during the year. Include what you pay on auto loans, student loans, personal notes to pay any expenses not tied to your investments or business, credit cards and revolving charge plans. Count one-time charges to your bank credit card account for each cash or overdraft advance you receive. Also include any late-payment charges by a public utility or any other fee for being tardy with a loan payment, as long as the charge isn't simply a service charge. (A late-payment charge on your mortgage, however, would go into the more-privileged mortgage-interest basket.) If you pay off a personal loan early and are hit with a prepayment penalty, the amount can be included when you figure your interest deduction.

Home-equity loans. The evaporation of personal interest deductions puts the borrower's spotlight on home-equity loans. As discussed in detail in Chapter 4, Congress gave homeowners an invitation to avoid the loss of the personal interest deductions. To the extent that you can convert soon-to-be-nondeductible personal interest to fully deductible home-equity interest, you can reduce the real cost of borrowing. Keep a close eye on the price tag on making the change, though. Home-equity loans can carry heavy up-front charges, and you must never forget that your home is at risk if you fail to repay the debt. Weigh such costs against the potential tax savings. If you have substantial credit card bills racking up personal interest at a rate of 18% or higher, using a home-equity loan to pay off the debt could let you trade in high-cost interest that's only partially deductible for lower-rate interest that's fully deductible.

CHARITABLE CONTRIBUTIONS

Give and you shall receive—a tax deduction that is.

Uncle Sam encourages generosity by subsidizing it. Your gifts to qualified organizations reduce your taxable income dollar for dollar via an itemized deduction. That, in turn, reduces the true cost of your gift. Every $1,000 someone in the 28% bracket gives away to a qualified cause saves the donor $280 in federal taxes. The bottom line: Giving away $1,000 really costs just $720.

Yes, the cost of gift-giving has increased in recent years as tax rates—and therefore the government's subsidy—have declined. But this deduction survived tax-reform suggestions to set a threshold—akin to the 7.5% hurdle you must pass in order to deduct medical expenses—for charitable gifts. If you itemize, your write-off begins with the first dollar you give.

Qualified organization. To be deductible, your gift has to go to a nonprofit religious, educational or charitable group that meets IRS standards. There's no shortage of qualified groups, ranging from the U.S. government itself to a volunteer nonprofit fire company. Almost all churches and other religious organizations qualify, of course, as do schools and hospitals, government agencies, veteran's groups, the Salvation Army, the United Way, the U.S. Olympic Committee, the Boy Scouts, the Girl Scouts and on and on.

If you're not certain whether the object of your generosity is approved by the IRS, ask an official of the group. If you're still uneasy, check with the IRS. The tax agency has a master list of qualified tax-exempt organizations: *Publication 78*.

Note that the gift has to go to an organization. If you give money to needy individuals, no one will question your generosity, but neither will the government subsidize it. Such gifts don't count as charitable contributions.

It's possible, too, that donations to a qualified group can lose deductible status. There's no charitable write-off for contributions used by an organization in an attempt to influence legislation. If a group you support is involved in lobbying Congress, for example, contributions you make that are earmarked for that effort are not deductible. The organization should tell you if part of your contribution is not deductible.

Too much of a good thing? There is a limit to how much you can deduct in any single year, but few taxpayers have to worry about reaching the ceiling. The rules are complicated, but basically your deductions for gifts to public charities, colleges and religious organizations can't exceed 50% of your adjusted gross income (AGI). Within that overall limit, gifts of appreciated property—discussed starting on page 286—can't total more than 30% of your AGI. Stricter limits apply to gifts to certain types of organizations. Contributions to veterans' groups, for example, come under an overall 30%-of-AGI limit, with a 20%-of-AGI cap on gifts of certain appreciated property.

The key to remember is that you can claim charitable-contribution deductions against up to 20% of your AGI without worrying about the twists and turns of the IRS limits. If your generosity exceeds that level, you may need professional advice to structure the gift for the best tax outcome. If you give more than you can deduct on a single year's return, the excess can be written off in future years. Any leftover deduction not used within five years, however, is lost for good.

When figuring your deduction, you can include what you contributed in cash, property and out-of-pocket costs incurred in your volunteer work.

Cash is the easiest to keep track of and the easiest to value. Keep your canceled checks and a receipt from the organization or some other written record of your gift, including how much was given to whom and when. When a receipt is impractical—say your regularly put a $5 bill in the collection plate at church or make it a habit never to pass a Salvation Army bell-ringer without dropping a buck or two in the bucket—make notes of the contributions for your tax records. The better your records, the less likely an IRS agent will deny your write-off for such cash contributions if you're audited.

As with other itemized deductions, you write off your gifts for the year you make them. A check delivered or mailed by December 31, 1988, for example, is deducted on your 1988 return. If you charge a contribution to your bank credit card—yes, fund-raisers are ingenious at finding ways to simplify your gift giving—you get the deduction for the year of the charge regardless of when you pay the bill. You have to make the contribution to earn the deduction, however. A pledge to make gifts in the future has no tax value; you get the deduction only when you fulfill the pledge by making the donation.

Something in return. If you get something in return for your gift, you can't write off the full amount. Say, for example, that a local charity sponsors a special showing of a new motion picture. Tickets go for $50 each, with the proceeds going to the charity. If tickets to such a movie would normally cost $5, your deduction is reduced by that amount, to $45 per ticket.

What if, after buying the ticket, you decide not to go to the show? Still, the IRS says your deduction is limited to $45. If you turned the ticket in to the charity before the performance, however, you could deduct the full $50. Your best bet if you don't plan to attend such benefit performances but want to support the cause is to make a direct contribution rather than buying tickets you don't intend to use.

Charities often raise money through raffles or lotteries. Who hasn't been asked to buy chances on a new car, television or basket of cheer? Regardless of how generous the motives behind your purchase, however, you get the chance to win something. That mean's you're gambling, not giving, as far as the IRS is concerned. You can deduct what you pay for raffle and lottery tickets only against winnings you report as income. (Yes, if you win a raffle, you're supposed to report the fair market value of the prize as taxable income.)

Doing good work. In addition to funds you give directly to charity, you can deduct money you spend doing volunteer work for a qualified organization. If you drive your car—to volunteer

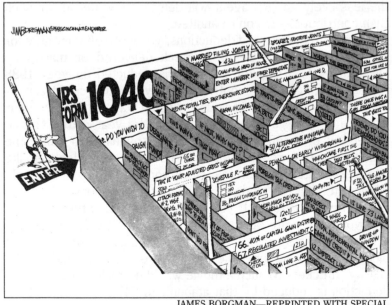

JAMES BORGMAN—REPRINTED WITH SPECIAL
PERMISSION OF KING FEATURES SYNDICATE, INC.

at your church, a hospital or a school, for example—you can include in your charitable deductions an amount based on 12 cents a mile, plus parking and tolls. If you use taxicabs or public transportation, you can count the fares as charitable donations.

Other deductible out-of-pocket expenses may include the cost and care of any special uniform you're required to wear while performing services for the charity and any materials and supplies you pay for—such as stationery and stamps—that are used in your volunteer efforts. If you pay a baby-sitter to take care of your children while you perform volunteer services, however, you can't deduct the cost. The IRS sees that as a personal expense regardless of what takes you away from home.

You can't write off the cost of your meals while you're doing volunteer work unless your duties take you out of town overnight. Nor can you write off the value of services you donate. Assume, for example, that a carpenter who usually charges $25 an hour spends 20 hours helping build a wing on his church. He can't deduct $500—or any other amount—for his time (although his transportation to and from the work site and the cost of any supplies he paid for can be deducted).

Forbidding the deduction may appear unfair, but consider this: If the carpenter had charged for his time and then donated the $500 to the church, he would have earned a $500 deduction. But the tax-saving value would have been wiped out by the extra $500 of taxable income he would have had to report. The tax result is identical to blocking the deduction for the value of donated services.

This rationale also works to prevent a deduction if you give a qualified organization reduced-rent or rent-free use of property you own. The same thinking is also behind the IRS's position that you may not claim a deduction for the value of blood you donate. If you sold your blood, you'd have taxable income to report. By donating it, this argument goes, you dodge that tax bill so there's no need for a deduction.

If you are a foster parent, you may deduct as a charitable contribution the cost of providing for your foster children that exceeds reimbursement you receive.

You can also earn a charitable deduction if a student lives in your home under a program sponsored by a qualified organization. To qualify for this deduction, the student may be American or foreign and must be a full-time elementary or high school student. You can deduct up to $50 a month of what you spend for the student, including the cost of books, tuition, food, clothing and entertainment. When toting up the deduction, you can't include anything for the value of the housing you provide. For purposes of figuring how many $50 allotments you can claim, count any month that the student lives with you 15 or more days. (You lose the right to this write-off if the student is staying in your home as part of program that will involve your child living with a family in a foreign country.)

Travel expenses. Beyond local transportation expenses—and potentially far more valuable in terms of tax savings—you can write off the cost of travel when your charitable services take you away from home. That includes the full cost of transportation and lodging but, under a tax-reform crackdown, only 80% of the cost of your meals while you're away from home.

If you are chosen as an official delegate to your church's national convention, for example, the costs of attending can be deducted as a charitable contribution. If you attend such a convention on your own, however, your costs are considered nondeductible personal expenses.

Tax reform brought new restrictions on the charitable-travel deductions, in response primarily to a proliferation of highly publicized trips—sometimes called tax-deductible vacations. The idea was that taxpayers would travel to appealing locations and write off their costs on the grounds that they were performing services to assist the charities. Congress worried, though, that the amount of time spent benefiting the charitable organizations was relatively small compared to the time reserved for recreation. The solution the lawmakers came up with was to forbid a charitable deduction if the travel involves a "significant element" of personal pleasure, recreation or vacation.

That doesn't mean you have to have a miserable time doing

your volunteer work to qualify for a tax deduction. Consider these examples:

• As a troop leader, you take your Girl Scout troop on a camping trip. You can deduct your travel expenses, assuming you are on duty in a substantial sense during the trip, even if you have a great time. If you have only nominal duties or for much of the trip aren't required to render services, you don't get a charitable deduction for your expenses.

• You work for several hours each morning on an archaeological excavation sponsored by a charitable organization. The rest of the day is free for recreation and sight-seeing. The IRS says no charitable deduction is allowed for your travel expenses, regardless of how hard you work during the morning hours.

• You spend an entire day attending a charitable organization's regional meeting. In the evening you go to the theater. Going to the show doesn't cost you the right to deduct your travel expenses as a charitable contribution.

Donating property. Whether it's old clothes or Old Masters' paintings, donating property can earn you a tax deduction just like donating cash. Admittedly, giving anything but greenbacks makes it tougher to know just how big a deduction to claim and is more likely to raise eyebrows at the IRS. The law adds to the confusion, too, because the type of property donated, how long you've owned it, who you give it to and how they will use it all can come into play in setting the amount you can deduct.

Begin with what are probably the most typical property donations: used clothing and household goods. Your write-off for such gifts is the fair market value of the property at the time you give it. That's usually far less than you paid for it.

To set a reasonable value—that is, one the IRS will accept—you have to consider anything that can affect the item's worth. Factors include its original cost, current condition, cost of comparable items, replacement cost and opinions of experts. For relatively inexpensive items, this is a do-it-yourself job.

If you give away an old car, for instance, you can start with used-car value guides available at banks and used-car dealerships. Don't assume prices listed in such guides pinpoint the value of your car, however. You've probably heard stories about owners of old clunkers who decided the tax deduction for giving them away would be worth more than they could get by selling them. As you undoubtedly suspect, the IRS frowns on that approach. If the vehicle you plan to bestow on a qualified organization—a high school shop class, for example—is a pile of junk, the allowable deduction is probably closer to salvage value than the average retail price shown in used-car guides. On the other hand, if you plan to give away a cream puff, you may deserve a larger deduction. You may need to visit used-car lots and talk with dealers or mechanics to arrive at a fair figure.

You don't need an expert's opinion to set the value of used, everyday clothes you donated to Goodwill Industries, the Salvation Army or similar organizations. For that, a trip to a secondhand clothing shop will tell you what people are paying for similar items. The same kind of research is sufficient for household goods you donate, such as furniture and appliances.

The IRS has a helpful booklet—Publication 561, *Determining the Value of Donated Property*—that can be a valuable aid in setting the deductible amount for your gifts.

When the deduction you claim for donated property exceeds $500—in total, not per item—you need to file an extra form with your tax return: Form 8283, *Noncash Charitable Contributions*. The information required on the form is basically the same as you need to substantiate any charitable gift—what you gave, when and to whom and, for items valued at over $500 each, when and how you acquired the property and your cost or adjusted basis. (Your basis is the property's value for tax purposes. It's usually what you paid for the property—the cost of stock, including brokerage commissions, for example—but if real estate or other depreciable property is involved, the basis is the cost minus any depreciation claimed.) Rather than just keeping the information with your records in case you're audited, the IRS demands that you send it in with your return when your write-off for gifts of property exceeds $500.

Appreciated property. When your philanthropic urge prompts you to give away appreciated property—such as stocks, real estate, art or antiques—the tax-saving potential can be much greater. And the rules are much more complicated.

First of all, your deduction depends in part on whether the property donated is considered capital-gain or ordinary-income property. Basically, capital-gain property is any that, if sold, would produce a long-term capital gain. Although the law no longer distinguishes between short-term and long-term gains for setting the tax rate that applies to your profit, the distinction still comes into play here. To qualify as capital-gain property, you must have owned it for more than one year before giving it away. (For property purchased before 1988, the holding period was six months.)

When you donate capital-gain property, your deduction is the fair market value of the property. This can be a major advantage because you get to write off the current value of the property without having to pay tax on the appreciation that built up while you owned it.

Say you own stock now worth $10,000 that you purchased more than a year ago for just $2,000. If you give the stock to your alma mater, church or other qualified organization, you earn a $10,000 deduction. In the 33% tax bracket, that would save you $3,300 in taxes. But your tax benefit is actually bigger than that. If you sold the stock rather than giving it away, you'd owe tax on the $8,000 profit on the deal. That would cost you $2,640, a bill you avoid by giving the stock away.

A potential catch is that the untaxed appreciation of charitable gifts—the $8,000 in the example—is now considered a "preference" item for the alternative minimum tax (AMT). If you are subject to the AMT—which is explained in Chapter 15 and generally applies only to high-income taxpayers with exceptionally large deductions—the appreciation is taxed at the 21% AMT rate.

If your gift is tangible personal property—such as antique furniture, jewelry or a painting—how the organization uses the donation can affect your write-off. If your gift is sold for cash, for example, or used for a purpose unrelated to the organization's charitable function, your deduction is limited to your cost. You don't get to write off the appreciation. For example, say you give your alma mater a valuable painting that you've owned more than one year. If it is put on display for study by art students—a related use—you may deduct the full market value of the painting. However, if the painting is sold and the proceeds used by the school, your deduction is limited to what you paid for the painting.

Ordinary-income property includes assets owned one year or less and any business inventory, works of art or manuscripts donated by the creator. The deduction for such gifts generally is limited to the donor's cost.

An artist who gives away a painting, for example, is limited to deducting the cost of the canvas, paint and frame, regardless of how much the painting would sell for.

The distinction between capital-gain and ordinary-income property is probably most important when it comes to stocks and other assets for which the deduction is controlled by the holding period. In the earlier example of stock purchased for $2,000 and worth $10,000 at the time of the gift, if the donor had owned the property for one year or less, the deduction would have been limited to $2,000. Watch the calendar if you consider such gifts.

Bargain sales. What if rather than giving property away outright, you decide to sell it—100 shares of stock, 2 acres of prime land, or whatever—at a bargain-basement price? Can you deduct as a contribution the difference between what you charge the charity and what you could have made on the open market? As logical as that might seem, it's not necessarily so.

First of all, if ordinary-income property is involved, you get no charitable contribution if the bargain price is as much or more than your cost or other basis in the property—regardless of how big a discount is involved. Say, for example, that you own stock worth $10,000 that you purchased less than one year ago for $5,000. If you sell the stock to a charity for your original cost of $5,000, you get no deduction even though you are effectively giving the charity $5,000. Since the short-term gain would not be deductible if you simply gave the stock to the charity, you earn a deduction only if you sell it to the charity for less than your cost. In this example, if you sold the stock for $6,000—still $4,000 under its value—you not only are denied a charitable deduction, but also have to report $1,000 as a taxable gain.

What if you sell it for $4,000? Can you at least deduct the $1,000 discount below your cost? You get the tax benefit of a $1,000 deduction, but you must travel a twisted road to get it.

In the eyes of the IRS, this kind of transaction combines a sale with a charitable contribution. The first thing you have to do is allocate your basis ($5,000 in this example) between the sale and the donation. Since the $4,000 selling price is 40% of the $10,000 fair market value in this illustration, 40% of the basis would be allocated to the sale. Subtracting your $2,000 basis (40% of $5,000) from the $4,000 proceeds of the sale leaves you with a $2,000 taxable gain. Yes, the gain when you sell for $4,000 in this illustration is *more* than when you sell at $6,000. But, the gain is more than offset because you get to claim a charitable deduction for the other 60% of your basis—or $3,000.

Remember that the discussion so far applies to bargain sales of ordinary-income property. Different, more beneficial rules apply to capital-gain property. You still must allocate your basis between the sale and the contribution, but your deductible amount is based on the fair market value of the property sold rather than your basis.

Again, consider stock now worth $10,000 that you purchased for $5,000—and that you've owned for more than a year so it qualifies as capital-gain property. If you gave the stock away outright, your deduction would be the full $10,000 fair market value. Here's how things work if you sell it to charity at the bargain price of $4,000.

Forty percent of the basis (the ratio of sales price to fair market value) is applied to the sales price; the other 60% to the contribution. Your taxable gain would be 40% of the $4,000 sales price, or $1,600. Your charitable contribution would be 60% of the $10,000 fair market value, or $6,000. It's no coincidence that that's the same as the difference between the bargain price and the fair market value.

Appraisals. When the property you give is publicly traded stocks or other securities, it's easy to pinpoint the fair market value. It's what the securities were trading for on the day of your gift. For other types of gifts, however, you may well need an outside appraisal. When your generosity passes a certain dollar threshold, in fact, the IRS demands that you get a written appraisal from a "qualified appraiser." Such appraisals are required when any single item of property, or a group of similar items, has a claimed value greater than $5,000. For stock that is not traded publicly, the triggering point is $10,000. The appraisal must be made by someone skilled in evaluating the specific kind of property you are giving away.

Beware that the IRS, worried that it has been burned often by charitable deductions based on inflated appraisals, casts a particularly skeptical eye on such write-offs. The agency has its own panel of experts to review the appraised value of art and other high-ticket property donations. (Starting in 1988, the IRS began demanding illustrated tax returns from taxpayers claiming large deductions based on the donation of works of art. When such art is valued at $20,000 or more, an 8- by 10-inch color photo or a 4- by 5-inch color transparency showing the gift must accompany the tax return.)

The importance of an accurate appraisal is emphasized by the penalty the IRS imposes if the value of the donated property is significantly overstated. If the value on which your deduction is based is determined to be more than 150% of the property's actual worth and the inflated deduction resulted in your understating your tax bill by $1,000 or more, the penalty is 30% of the underpayment.

The cost of the required appraisal can't be folded into your charitable contribution. Instead, it can be deducted only as a miscellaneous itemized expense, which—as discussed beginning on page 300—makes it impossible for most taxpayers to get any tax benefit.

Life insurance. Here's a way to get a tax deduction now for a gift the charity won't benefit from until after your death: Give the charity a life insurance policy on your life. The organization must be named both owner and beneficiary of the policy and you must irrevocably give up the right to change your mind. Folks often give paid-up whole life policies they no longer need or universal life policies that can be paid up in just a few years. Such gifts are frequently promoted by charities as an affordable way to make a substantial contribution.

Your tax deduction is the value of the policy when you give it away, which is generally a little more than the cash-surrender value, or the replacement value. Your insurance agent should be able to help set the value of your gift. If you make contributions to cover future premiums, you can deduct those gifts, too.

Giving away the house. You can give away your home, claim an immediate tax deduction for your generosity and still get to live in the house for the rest of your life. This type of gift is often most attractive to single people with no close relatives to whom to leave the property.

The provision of the law that allows an immediate deduction for the delayed gift of your home applies to vacation homes and farms, too. Here's how it works: The property is deeded over to the charitable organization, but you retain the right to live on or work on the property for the rest of your life (and, if you wish, the lifetime of one survivor) or for a specific number of years. Your deduction is based on the current value of the property and your life expectancy. The older you are when you make the gift—and therefore the shorter the anticipated length and consequentially lower value of your retained interest—the less you have to reduce the current value to arrive at your deduction. The charity to which you consider giving your property should be able—and quite willing—to help you get the necessary assistance to set the size of your deduction.

CASUALTY AND THEFT LOSSES

This is another category of itemized deductions that, for most taxpayers, is more illusory than real. It's held out as Uncle Sam's helping hand to ease the financial pain when you suffer economically due to such misfortunes as accidents, storms or theft. But Congress has erected a grueling gauntlet between you and the write-off. For all intents and purposes, casualty- and theft-loss deductions are available only to those of modest income—who may not benefit anyway because they may not be itemizing deductions—or those who are hit by catastrophic losses. Here's why:

The amount of any uninsured loss must be reduced by $100. If you suffer more than one loss during the year, the first $100 of each is ignored by the tax law.

Much tougher is a restriction that permits a deduction only when your remaining losses exceed 10% of your adjusted gross income (AGI). You get a deduction only for the amount above the threshold. Unlike the $100 rule, the 10% threshold does not apply to each separate casualty or theft. It applies to the total of your losses, after each one has been trimmed by $100.

Assume you are mugged and the thief gets away with $200 in cash and $3,500 worth of jewelry, and this is the only casualty or theft you suffer during the year. For tax purposes, you first reduce your loss by $100 and then subtract 10% of your AGI from the remaining $3,600. If your AGI is $30,000, the $3,000 reduction would leave you with a $600 loss deduction. If AGI is $36,000 or more, the 10% rule would bar the deduction altogether.

Although it's unlikely that you'll ever benefit from a casualty- or theft-loss deduction, it's important to be briefed on the rules in case you are unfortunate enough to qualify for this write-off. **What's a casualty?** According to the law, it is damage to or destruction of property caused by an identifiable event that is sudden, unexpected or unusual. As you may assume, taxpayers and the IRS often disagree over what fits the bill.

Clearly, damage from these "identifiable events" count: earthquakes, lightning, hurricanes, tornados, floods, storms, volcanic eruptions, sonic booms, vandalism, riots, fires, car accidents and, oh yes, shipwrecks. What if you accidentally knock a vase off its pedestal and into a million pieces? The IRS says that's not a casualty. How about when Rover romps through the house, knocking down the cabinet that holds your television, VCR and stereo? Again, the IRS says there's no tax deduction to help pay for the damage. What if you're driving along and your car's engine suddenly freezes up, resulting in thousands of dollars worth of damage? You guessed it: no deduction. The IRS figures the damage was due to normal wear and tear on the engine over a lengthy period of time.

What if you lose something valuable, like a diamond ring? That's not a casualty in the eyes of the tax law. However, in a case where a ring falls into a garbage disposal, the damage would qualify for a casualty-loss deduction. So would the loss of a diamond when the taxpayer shows that it happened because the setting was damaged when the owner's hand was slammed in a car door.

Damage caused by termites or moths doesn't qualify as a casualty. It lacks the suddenness requirement. Even when the cause of damage can be laid to progressive deterioration, however, you may have a deductible loss. If your hot-water heater bursts, for example, any resulting water damage qualifies even though the cost of repairing or replacing the heater does not.

Even if the damage is your fault, you can earn a casualty-loss deduction—unless willful negligence is involved. If you're responsible for a car crash, for example, or accidentally apply a chemical that kills your lawn and shrubs, the damage can qualify as a casualty loss.

You also qualify for a deduction if you lose money because a bank or other financial institution goes under and your deposits aren't insured. You actually have a choice of how to deduct such a loss: either as a casualty loss or as a nonbusiness bad debt, which is treated as a short-term capital loss. There are restrictions either way.

The casualty loss is subject to both the $100 reduction and the 10% test. The nonbusiness bad debt, as other short-term losses, is deductible first against capital gains and then against up to $3,000 of other income. (Any leftover bad-debt loss would be deductible in future years.) Although you may claim a casualty loss in the year you can reasonably estimate your loss—probably the year the bank goes under—you can't claim a bad-debt deduction until the actual amount of the loss is determined, which may well be in a later year.

What is a theft? The answer here is much easier than when determining what qualifies as a casualty. You have a theft loss when property you own is taken illegally. The key here is to show that the property was stolen rather than lost or mislaid. Be certain the theft is reported to authorities. If you are the victim of an investment scam or other swindle, whether or not your loss qualifies for a deduction turns on whether the venture that separated you from your money was illegal under federal, state or local law.

Pinpointing your loss. The amount of your loss is generally the decrease in fair market value of the property or your adjusted basis in the property, whichever is less. The decrease in market value is the difference between what the property was worth before and after a casualty or the full market value in the case of a theft. The question of value turns on what a disinterested person would pay for the property. You don't get any credit for sentimental value. The adjusted basis is usually your original cost plus the cost of any improvements you've made. You may need appraisals to set the before- and after-market values, although what you have to pay for repairs—after an automobile accident, for example—can serve as evidence of your loss. If you are restoring landscaping after a storm, you can base your casualty loss on what you pay to remove or prune damaged trees and shrubs and for the replanting necessary to restore your property to its value before the storm.

Note that your loss doesn't depend on the replacement value of the damaged or stolen property. Say that you bought a chair for $400 and that four years later it is destroyed by fire. At the time, you could have sold the used chair for $100, but to replace it with a comparable new chair would cost you $700. What's your casualty loss? The decline in fair market value—$100— caused by the fire.

When your loss involves several separate items, as would be the case if your home burns or thieves clean out your apart-ment, you are expected to calculate the loss on each item rather than come up with an overall estimate. The IRS offers a free booklet—Publication 584, *Nonbusiness Disaster, Casualty, and Theft Loss Workbook*—to help you inventory lost, damaged or stolen items and determine your deductible loss. (Even if you don't suffer a loss, the booklet is helpful as a handy tool for keeping a household inventory.)

As with any deduction, if you are audited you'll need evidence to back up your write-off. For starters, keep any newspaper articles reporting on the calamity that caused your loss, whether it was a fire, major storm, auto accident or robbery. Also make copies for your tax file of any pertinent police or fire reports. You'll also need to show that you owned the property at issue. You can't claim a casualty-loss deduction for damage to an auto registered in your daughter's name, for example, even if you pay for the repairs.

Proving the size of your loss is tougher. In addition to receipts for repairs, you may need appraisals of the property's value before and after the loss. Before-and-after photographs can also serve to back up your deduction. Although it may be impossible to take such pictures after the casualty or theft, it's still a good idea to maintain a regularly updated photo file of your belongings. Such pictures may also serve to jog your memory after a fire or theft when you're putting together a list of your losses. The cost of photos and what you pay for appraisals

TAX REFORM

BEFORE

AFTER

Distributed by King Features Syndicate
JIM MORIN—REPRINTED WITH SPECIAL
PERMISSION OF KING FEATURES SYNDICATE, INC.

cannot be added to your casualty loss but may be deducted as miscellaneous expenses if you pass the 2%-of-AGI threshold discussed later in this chapter.

The role of insurance. The amount of your casualty or theft loss is reduced, of course, by any reimbursement you receive from insurance. If you have insurance, in fact, you must file a claim or forfeit your right to a tax deduction for the insured part of the loss. Before 1987, that rule didn't apply, and some taxpayers chose to go for the tax write-off rather than file a claim and risk cancellation of their policy or an increase in premiums. You no longer have that option.

If you can reasonably expect to be reimbursed for part or all of your loss—through insurance or a damage suit—you must trim your deduction by the amount you expect to get, even if you won't get it until a future year. If you wind up getting less than you expect, the difference is considered a casualty loss in the year of the final settlement. At that time, the amount would again be subject to both the $100 and 10%-of-AGI rules. Since that could easily wipe out any tax benefit, be particularly careful when estimating future reimbursements.

When insurance pays for your living expenses after you lose the use of your home, the payments are not counted as reimbursement for your loss and therefore do not reduce your deduction. In some cases, however, the IRS views such payments as taxable income to you if the money covers your normal living expenses rather than extra expenses resulting from the casualty.

Say, for example, that the apartment you rent for $700 a month is damaged by fire and you are forced to live in a motel for two months while your place is repaired. The motel bill is $900 a month, of which your insurance policy pays $850. Because $200 a month pays the extra expense, that part of the insurance payment is tax-free. The other $650 is considered payment of normal expenses and should be reported as income. In a similar situation, a homeowner who had to continue mortgage payments on the damaged house while living in the motel would not report any of the insurance reimbursement as income because the entire motel bill is an added expense.

Gaining from losses. Regardless of how much you suffer from a casualty or theft, the tax law may view you as a winner and demand that you report insurance reimbursement as taxable income. This seemingly hard-hearted result occurs when the reimbursement is more than your adjusted basis in the lost or damaged property.

Say, for example, that an item of antique furniture is stolen from your home. Assume you paid $800 for the antique but it was worth much more when it was stolen. Thanks to a rider on your insurance policy, you are reimbursed $3,000. As far as the IRS is concerned, the $2,200 difference between your $800 basis and the $3,000 is taxable income.

Or assume that you have a replacement-value clause in your household insurance policy. After a fire, you determine that your basis in destroyed furniture and appliances is $10,000, but the replacement value paid by your insurance company is $15,000. Taxable gain: $5,000.

There is an important exception to this rule. If you use all the insurance proceeds to buy replacement property—that is, items similar to or having a related use as the lost or damaged property—you don't have to report any of the money as income. To dodge the tax bill on what the IRS sees as excess reimbursement, the replacement property must be purchased within two years of the end of the year in which you are reimbursed.

The basis of the replacement property is its cost minus the amount of "gain" from the insurance. This rule doesn't matter much when you're dealing with things like furniture or appliances, but it's vitally important when your house is involved.

Assume that your home is destroyed by fire. Your basis in the house is $50,000 (see Chapter 4). Because it's worth far more at the time of the fire, you receive a $150,000 insurance settlement on the house itself. That's a $100,000 gain—just as if you had sold the house for $150,000. You avoid the tax bill, however, by spending $200,000 on a new home within the replacement period. What's the basis of the new place? It's $100,000: the $200,000 cost minus the $100,000 gain from the casualty. Another way to look at it is that you carry over your original $50,000 basis and add to it the extra $50,000 you put into the new place—over and above the "excess" insurance settlement.

Disaster areas. Generally, you deduct a casualty loss in the year the damage occurs. However, if you suffer a loss as a result of an event that prompts the President to declare your area a federal disaster area, you can write off your loss on the return for the *previous* year. This unusual option is designed to put a tax refund in your hands to help pay for the damage. You can use this provision even if you've already filed your return for the preceding year. You can order your tax-refund check via an amended return (see Chapter 14).

Assume, for example, that a tornado rips through your town in May 1989, causing $20,000 of uninsured damage to your home. Usually, you would wait until you file your 1989 return in the spring of 1990 to claim a casualty loss. But if the President declares your town a disaster area, you could claim the loss by amending your 1988 return.

If your 1988 adjusted gross income was $40,000, the casualty-loss deduction for the $20,000 loss would be $15,900—$20,000 minus $100 minus $4,000 (10% of AGI). If you were in the 28% bracket in 1988, the amended return would bring a refund of $4,452.

An important consideration in deciding which year to claim the write-off is how your adjusted gross income will compare. Because of the 10% rule, your tax savings will be greater in the year your AGI is smaller.

Business property. The $100 and 10% restrictions on casualty and theft losses apply only to personal-use property, such as your own home, car or personal possessions. If you suffer a loss to business property, such as a business auto or a rental house, you do not reduce the damage by $100 or 10% of your AGI when figuring your casualty or theft loss.

MOVING EXPENSES

Tax reformers decided to make moving expenses an itemized deduction. But that's bad news. Before 1987, job-related moving costs could be written off as an adjustment to income. That meant the tax savings were available whether or not you itemized deductions.

Even if you normally don't itemize deductions, it may pay off to do so in a year you make a job-related move. The moving-expense deduction, when combined with other qualifying costs, could add up to more than your standard deduction. Deductible expenses include not only the cost of moving your family and your household goods but also some of the costs of selling your old place and buying a new house.

To qualify for these deductions, the move must be connected with taking a new job that is at least 35 miles farther from your old home than your old job was. If your former job was 10 miles away from your old home, for example, the new job has to be at least 45 miles away from that old home. The point of the mileage test is not to shorten your commute: Note that it does not matter how far the new home is away from your new job. If you are moving to take your first job, the 35-mile test applies to the distance from your old home to your new job location.

In addition to the mileage test, to be eligible to deduct moving expenses you must work full time for at least 39 weeks during the 12 months after the move, or at least 78 weeks out of the first 24 months if you are self-employed. You can claim the deductions on your tax return for the year of the move even if you haven't yet met the 39- or 78-week test by the time you file. If it turns out you are not eligible, you should either file an amended return for the year or report as income on your next tax return the amount previously deducted as moving expenses.

When you qualify, your deductions can include:

• The cost of trips to the area of the new job to look for a new house. There's no requirement that the house-hunting expeditions be successful for the costs to be deductible.

• The cost of having your furniture and other household goods shipped, including the cost of packing, insurance and storage for up to 30 days.

• The cost of getting yourself and your family to the new home, including the cost of food and lodging on the trip.

• The cost of food and lodging for up to 30 days in the new hometown if these temporary living expenses are necessary because you have not yet found a new home or it is not ready when you arrive.

• Certain costs associated with the sale of your old house and purchase of the new one. These expenses—including real estate commissions, legal fees, state transfer taxes and appraisal and title fees—could alternatively be used either to reduce the gain on the sale of the previous residence or boost the basis of the new one, as discussed in Chapter 4. It's usually beneficial to count them as moving expenses, up to the dollar limits discussed later, since that gives you an immediate tax benefit.

• You don't have to be a homeowner to deduct moving expenses. Although a renter won't have the buying and selling expenses, you can write off the other expenses of the move, including any penalty you had to pay to break a lease or legal fees or commissions involved in renting a new apartment or house.

There is a dollar limit on the amount you can write off for certain expenses. The cap for house-hunting trips and temporary living expenses is $1,500, and those costs plus buying and selling expenses can't exceed $3,000. There is no limit on how much you can deduct for the cost of shipping household goods or travel expenses for yourself and your family. Any reasonable amount you pay can be deducted. You report your expenses on Form 3903.

If your employer reimburses you for moving expenses, the amount should show up on your W-2 form for the year. You must report that amount as income on your tax return, but get to offset it by claiming your moving-expense deductions.

MISCELLANEOUS DEDUCTIONS

This is the flea market of the tax code, but don't let the all-encompassing sound of this category raise your hopes too high. Although the range of acceptable expenses is broad, this is another write-off that has been ravaged by tax reform. Most miscellaneous expenses are now deductible only to the extent their combined cost exceeds 2% of your adjusted gross income. Although that's not as high as the thresholds for medical and casualty-loss deductions, the 2% test will block enough write-offs that Congress expects it to cost taxpayers about $5 billion a year.

Expenses that count toward the threshold fall in three basic categories.

Employee business expenses. These are the costs you incur in connection with your job, including the following:

• Automobile expenses.
• Home-office expenses.
• Job-hunting expenses.
• Travel, entertainment and gift expenses.
• Educational expenses.
• The cost of special work clothes.
• The cost of small tools used in your work.
• The cost of a physical examination required by your employer.
• Dues to professional societies.
• Union dues.
• The cost of subscriptions to professional journals and trade publications.
• Job-security insurance.
• Hobby expenses to the extent of your hobby income.

These expenses are discussed in detail in Chapter 9. If you are reimbursed by your employer for job-related costs, your deduction generally is not affected by the 2% threshold. Instead, since the reimbursement is reported to you as taxable income, you usually may deduct the expenses as adjustments to income whether or not you itemize.

Investment-related expenses. Money you spend in the pursuit of taxable investment income can qualify for deduction. Your write-off of miscellaneous expenses can include the following costs:

• Custodial fees for your individual retirement account.
• Safe-deposit-box rental.

• Investment management fees, including those charged by mutual funds.

• The cost of subscriptions to investment-advisory newsletters.

• The cost of books and magazines you buy for investment advice.

• The cost of travel to see your broker to check on your portfolio or to buy or sell investments.

These expenses are discussed in Chapter 5.

If you use a computer to analyze or track your investments, you may include in your miscellaneous expenses an amount for depreciation if you keep careful records that break down the amount of time you use the machine for investment versus personal purposes. The depreciation deduction is sure to be modest.

If you have a $3,000 computer that you use 20% of the time on your investments, for example, the first-year depreciation deduction would be just $60. The first-year write-off for a computer not used more than half the time for business is 10% of the qualifying cost. In this example, the qualifying cost is $600 (20% of $3,000). That's not much, but every dollar counts when you're trying to scale the 2% cliff between you and any miscellaneous deductions. (For more on deducting a computer, see Chapter 9.)

Tax-related expenses. One of the low blows of tax reform was that as Congress sowed new seeds of confusion, it made it difficult for most folks to deduct the cost of coping with the new rules. What you pay for tax advice and return preparation is still deductible. But as a miscellaneous expense it's subject to the 2% rule.

Make sure you count every dime you can. If you hire someone to prepare your return, include the cost. If you consult with an accountant about the tax consequences of investments, include the fee. If you wind up in court fighting the IRS over a tax bill, include what you pay your lawyer, as well as all filing fees. Count what you pay for a return-preparation manual or other tax-planning books (including this one), the cost of long-distance calls to the IRS to answer your tax questions and even the cost of postage to mail in your return. If you use a home computer to plan your taxes or prepare your return, you can deduct depreciation under the same rules that apply to the investment write-off discussed above. Remember that expenses you incur in 1989 in connection with your 1988 return are not deductible until you file your 1989 return.

Write-offs not subject to the 2% rule. Schedule A, the form on which you list itemized deductions, includes a section for miscellaneous expenses *not* subject to the 2% threshold. You can be certain that qualifying expenses are few and far between. These two are most likely to be of any benefit:

• *Amortizable bond premium.* The premium is the amount over face value that you pay for certain bonds. This issue is discussed in Chapter TK.

• *Gambling losses.* This write-off comes with its own restriction. You can't deduct more than the amount of gambling winnings you report as taxable income.

11
TAX CREDITS

If itemized deductions are the cake, tax credits are the frosting. How sweet it is! Rather than reduce the amount of income on which you have to pay tax, a credit reduces your tax bill straight away. For someone in the 28% tax bracket, every dollar of deductible expenses saves 28 cents. Regardless of your tax bracket, however, every tax-credit dollar trims the bill by a full dollar.

There aren't as many credits as there once were. The investment tax credit is gone. So is the credit that refunded part of your contributions to the folks who make the tax law: politicians. During the height of the energy crisis, Congress allowed a credit for part of what homeowners spent to save energy. For awhile, there was even a credit for people who bought diesel-powered cars. No more.

Still, the law includes several credits that can save you money. Here's the rundown on those most likely to have a place on your tax return.

CHILD- AND DEPENDENT-CARE CREDIT

With the growth of single-parent and two-earner couples, Congress created this credit to help cover the costs you incur so you can leave home to go to a paying job. The credit is based on what you pay for the care of qualifying individuals—including dependent children under age 15 or disabled dependents or a disabled spouse of any age—to enable you to work. The basic rules are the same whether care is provided for children or disabled dependents or spouses, but this discussion will focus on child care since it is the most common.

If you pay for the care of one child, the maximum amount for computing the credit is $2,400; if you pay for the care of two or more, that amount doubles to $4,800. The size of the credit turns on your adjusted gross income. If your AGI is under $10,000, for example, your credit is 30% of your expenses, up to the $2,400 or $4,800 cap. Taxpayers with AGI of more than $28,000 get a 20% credit. Those with incomes in between figure their credit based on this sliding scale:

AGI	Credit Percent	Top Credit One Individual	Two or More
Under $10,000	30%	$720	$1,440
$10,001–$12,000	29	696	1,392
$12,001–$14,000	28	672	1,344
$14,001–$16,000	27	648	1,296
$16,001–$18,000	26	624	1,248
$18,001–$20,000	25	600	1,200
$20,001–$22,000	24	576	1,152
$22,001–$24,000	23	552	1,104
$24,001–$26,000	22	528	1,056
$26,001–$28,000	21	504	1,008
Over $28,000	20	480	960

In addition to the $2,400/$4,800 caps on qualifying costs, the credit is limited by the amount of earned income you make during the year. (Earned income is basically income from a job or self-employment rather than from investments.) If you earn just $2,000 during the year, for example, that's the highest amount of child-care expenses you can count toward the credit. The IRS doesn't want to be subsidizing your getaway from the kids if you're not earning taxable income.

If you're married, you and your spouse must both work to qualify for the credit, and the earned income limit is the salary of whoever earns less. There's a special rule if your husband or wife is a full-time student or disabled. He or she is assumed to have earned income of $200 a month if you're paying for the care of one individual, $400 if you're paying for care for two or more. If your husband is a full-time student all year, for example, his fictitious income for purposes of this test would be either $2,400 or $4,800—the same levels as the regular caps on qualifying costs. If he or she was a student only nine months of the year, though, the assumed amounts drop to either $1,800 or $3,600. Any earnings during the months your spouse is not in school can be included when figuring your credit.

Qualifying payments. You have almost unlimited latitude in choosing the type of care provided for your children. Until 1988, in fact, you could even count the cost of summer sleep-away camp when figuring the credit. Congress put an end to that, but you still have lots of leeway.

When you send a child to a nursery school or a day-care center while you work, you can include the entire amount paid

"Sir, we've come to the conclusion that it's absolutely impossible to assemble a tax plan that doesn't benefit the rich."

when figuring your credit—including the cost of meals provided as part of the care. The full cost of attending kindergarten counts, too, but when your child-care choice includes school for first grade on up, the part of the cost allocated to education is not a qualifying expense. If your fees to a private school include an amount for before- or after-school care, though, that cost can be included when computing your credit. Be sure to get an itemized bill.

What you pay for in-home child care counts, too. Even if your care-provider spends a good deal of his or her time on housekeeping chores and cooking, the entire salary is considered to be a qualifying cost as long as those services benefit the child being cared for so that you can work. The IRS draws the line at gardeners and chauffeurs, though. Also not counted toward the credit are amounts you pay to your child under age 19 or any dependent. (See Chapter 3 for the rules on who qualifies as a dependent.)

When you hire someone to come into your home to provide care, you'll become an employer in the eyes of the tax law. That means you will probably have to pay the employer's share of the social security tax—which is currently 7.51%—and possibly the federal unemployment tax as well. (See Chapter 15 for the details.) The tax you pay can be included in the amount on which you base your credit.

A couple of final points. Remember that the person for whom care is provided must be your dependent. Thus, if your disabled father moves in with you and you hire someone to care for him while you work, the cost would qualify only if he is your dependent. When your child is involved, he or she must be under age 15. If the child reaches that age during the year, only amounts spent on care before the birthday count. Regardless of when the child reaches age 15, though, the full $2,400 or $4,800 expense cap applies.

There is also an exception to the general rule that you must be able to claim the child as a dependent on your return in order to qualify for the credit. This doesn't apply if you are divorced and have custody of the child but the noncustodial parent gets to claim the dependency exemptions. Finally, if you are married, you must file a joint return to claim the credit, unless you otherwise qualify and your spouse did not live with you during the last six months of the year.

You claim the child-care credit on Form 2441, and because it is a credit rather than a deduction, you can get the tax benefit whether or not you itemize.

CREDIT FOR OVERPAYING
SOCIAL SECURITY TAX

This credit is for well-paid individuals who have more than one job or who change jobs during the year. It's designed to protect you from paying too much social security tax.

For 1988, that tax is 7.51% of your first $45,000 of salary for a maximum levy of $3,380. Your employer is supposed to stop withholding the tax once you've paid in that amount. However, if you change jobs during the year, your new employer can't take into account the social security tax withheld by your previous employer. As a result, if you earn more than $45,000 from the two jobs, you'll wind up paying more than $3,380. (The social security wage base—the amount of earnings to which the tax applies—increases each year, so the maximum tax goes up annually, too.)

Say, for example, that you have a job that pays you $5,000 a month between January and August. On eight month's pay totalling $40,000, your employer withholds $3,000 of social security tax. You start a new job September 1 that pays you $6,000 a month for the final four months of the year. On that $24,000, your employer will withhold $1,800 for social security. The total social security tax withheld, $4,800, is $1,420 over the 1988 maximum.

You get a credit for that amount when you file your 1988 return. You don't even have to file a special form. Just claim the credit in the section of the Form 1040 for payments.

If a single employer goofs and withholds more than the maximum amount of social security from your pay, you can't recoup the difference with this credit. Instead, you'll have to get your employer to refund the overpayment to you.

CREDIT FOR TAX PAID BY A MUTUAL FUND

On rare occasions, mutual funds declare capital gains but retain the profits and pay tax on them rather than distributing the gains to shareholders (see Chapter 5). If this happens, you have to report and pay tax on the income you didn't get. To even the score, you get to claim a tax credit for the amount of tax paid by the fund on your portion of the undistributed profits.

The fund will tell you how much tax was paid on Form 2439, *Notice to Shareholder of Undistributed Long-Term Capital Gains.* You claim the credit on Form 1040 and attach a copy of the Form 2439 to your return.

FOREIGN TAX CREDIT

If you paid foreign income taxes—on earnings from overseas employment, for example, or on investments in foreign securities—you may be in line for this credit. It's designed to prevent you from paying tax twice on the same income.

You actually have a choice of either claiming foreign taxes paid as a credit that will reduce your federal tax bill dollar for dollar or including the amount with the state and local taxes you write off as itemized deductions. Although the credit will almost always produce the bigger savings, restrictions on the credit can sometimes make the deduction the better deal. This is most likely to occur only if the foreign tax rate is higher than your U.S. tax bracket and the ratio of foreign income to U.S. income is low.

A certain advantage of taking the deduction route is that you get to avoid the two-page morass of the Form 1116, which is necessary if you claim the foreign tax credit.

If you own shares in a mutual fund with substantial foreign holdings, you may be due a credit or deduction for foreign taxes paid by the fund on your behalf (see Chapter 5).

CREDIT FOR THE ELDERLY OR DISABLED

Despite the sound of it, this credit doesn't suddenly become available when you turn 65. It's available only to low-income

taxpayers. The first qualification is that you must be at least 65
or, if younger, must be retired on total and permanent disability
and must have received taxable disability benefits during the
year. If you pass either test, your income comes into play.
Before you get your hopes up, consider who can't claim this
credit.

• You don't qualify if you are single, a head of household or a
qualifying widow or widower with adjusted gross income (AGI)
of $17,500 or more, or if you receive nontaxable social security
or other nontaxable pension or disability benefits of $5,000 or
more. (For an idea of how stingy the $5,000 limit is, it limits
your nontaxable benefits to just $417 a month).

• If you file a joint return, the rules differ depending on whether
one spouse or both meet the age or disability requirements. If
only one qualifies, the credit is out of reach if your AGI is
$20,000 or more or your nontaxable benefits total $5,000 or
more. If both spouses qualify, you can't take the credit if your
AGI is $25,000 or more or your nontaxable benefits are $7,500
or more.

• If you are married filing separately (which is permissable for
this credit only if you and your spouse did not live together
during the year), you can't qualify if your AGI is $12,500 or
more or your nontaxable benefits are $3,750 or more.

If you're still in the game after those restrictions, your credit
can be as high as $1,125 on a joint return or up to $750 on a
single return. To figure the credit, begin with the base amount
for your filing status.

Filing Status	Base Amount
Single, head of household or qualifying widow or widower	$5,000
Married filing jointly and only one spouse qualifies	5,000
Married filing jointly and both spouses qualify	7,500
Married filing separately	3,750

If you are under 65 and qualify for the credit based on disability, your base amount is the applicable figure above or the amount of your disability income, whichever is less.

From your base, you must subtract any nontaxable social security or other nontaxable pension or disability payments (such as Veterans Administration disability benefits) you received. Then, you must subtract half of the amount by which your AGI exceeds: $10,000 if you are married filing jointly; $7,500 if your are single, a head of household or qualifying widow or widower; or $5,000 if you are married filing separately.

If there's anything left of your base amount, you get a tax credit! It's 15% of the leftover amount. (In the very unlikely event that both you and your spouse qualify for this credit and are subject to the alternative minimum tax, however, the credit is further limited.)

EARNED INCOME CREDIT

This credit is designed primarily for low-income taxpayers with children. In fact, if your earned income (basically income from a job or self-employment) or adjusted gross income (which can include investment earnings) exceeds $18,576, you make too much to claim this credit.

If both earned income and AGI are below that level, you may qualify for a very worthwhile tax-saver: The top earned income credit in 1988 is $874. (The credit and the income figures used to determine it are adjusted each year for inflation.)

In addition to meeting the income tests, to qualify for this credit you must have a child living with you for more than half the year (the full year if the child is a foster child or if you file as a qualifying widower or widower) and your filing status must be married filing jointly, qualifying widow or widower or head of household.

There is a complicated formula for figuring the credit, but you don't have to do it yourself. The IRS provides tables showing the size of the credit to claim based on your earned income or AGI. There's no special form to fill out to claim the earned income credit, but the tax instructions include a work sheet for determining your eligibility.

Note that if you claim this credit on the Form 1040 (you can also claim it if you file the shorter 1040A), it doesn't go in the section for credits. Rather, it's listed among your tax payments. The result is the same.

Unlike most tax credits, which can't reduce your tax bill below $0, if an earned income credit exceeds the amount you owe, the excess will still be refunded to you. Also, you don't have to wait until you file your return to take advantage of this credit. If you expect to be eligible for it, you can get your employer to include a portion regularly in your paychecks. To get advance payment of the credit, ask your employer for a copy of Form W-5, *Earned Income Credit Advance Payment Certificate.* That form is filed with your employer, not the IRS.

12
YEAR-END TAX TIPS

What part of the year, more than any other, is tax time? If April 15 leaps to your mind, you flunk this test, and the consequences can be painful. Mistaking the return-filing deadline for tax time probably means you're paying more income tax than you have to—year after year. The lifetime cost can be enormous.

Taxes are a year-round sport. The borrowing, spending and investment decisions you make from January 1 through December 31 shape the tax bill that's due April 15. Still, one part of the year is especially important: the days between Halloween and New Year's Eve. Think of the final weeks of the year as a cornucopia overflowing with opportunities to trim your tax bill. To cash in, you must invest some time, an ingredient often in short supply around the year-end holidays. But as you draw up your "to do" list for this busy time, keep in mind that you can be richly rewarded for carving out time to plan and implement tax strategies. Don't wait until after Christmas to begin. By that time, the doors to many money-saving moves will be closed.

The harvest of savings begins with a survey of where you stand in early November. Tote up your earnings for the year to date from salary, interest, dividends, investment profits, self-employment, rental income and any other sources. Estimate how much more income you expect in each category before the old year gives way to the new.

Now figure how much you can shrink that income before the IRS gets a crack at it. Draw up a list of your adjustments to income: write-offs for such expenditures as alimony and individual-retirement-account contributions that reduce taxable income whether or not you itemize deductions. Next, estimate your itemized deductions. The numbers don't have to be precise. Guesses based on your previous year's return and any significant differences you know will apply this year are okay.

With a fix on your taxable income, check the tax rates that apply (page 437). That will tell you exactly how well you'll be paid for maneuvers that reduce taxable income. If you're in the 28% bracket, for example, every $1,000 you shave off that income figure cuts your tax bill by $280.

Although it's usually best to do what you can to push income down and deductions up, in some circumstances that's a prescription for disaster. If you are likely to be subject to the alternative minimum tax (AMT), which is discussed in Chapter 15, it may pay to accelerate the receipt of taxable income and delay paying deductible expenses. The same goes if you will be in a higher tax bracket the following year, a point to watch carefully if Congress decides to start pushing tax rates toward their prereform levels. Savvy year-end tax planning involves looking to the year ahead as well as the one that's winding down. If spending an extra dollar on taxes this year will save you two dollars next year, for example, the standard recommendations stand on their head.

With that caveat in mind, consider the following year-end strategies.

DEFER INCOME

The theory here is simple: Income you don't receive until after midnight on New Year's Eve isn't taxed until the following year. Even if you'll be in the same tax bracket, you win by putting off the tax bill by an entire year.

It's tough for employees to postpone wage and salary income. You can't ask your employer to hang on to your December paycheck until January; nor do you push income into the next year by not cashing your check until then. Income is taxable in the year it is "constructively received." Basically, that means the year you could have had the money if you wanted it. Assume, for example, that in December of 1988 your boss offers you a choice of receiving a Christmas bonus in December or the following January. Regardless of which you choose, the IRS expects you to report and pay tax on the income in 1988. If standard practice in your company is to pay year-end bonuses the following year, however, the income would be taxed in the year you get the check.

If you are self-employed or do free-lance or consulting work in addition to a job, you have more leeway, assuming you use the cash basis of accounting. Delaying billings until late December, for example, can assure you won't receive payment until the following year. If you are pressing for payment on an overdue account, it might make sense to give your tardy client a bit of a breather. Business considerations certainly come first. But if it's unlikely you have anything to lose by holding off on collections, doing so can push some taxable income into the following year.

ACCELERATE DEDUCTIONS

This is the opposite side of the defer-income coin. It can be just as effective in trimming taxable income—and your tax bill—for the current year.

Medical expenses. Since medical bills are deductible only to the extent that they total more than 7.5% of your adjusted gross income, timing your payments may be the only way to garner a tax benefit from these costs. Chapter 10 spells out which expenses are deductible. By early December, you should have a good idea whether you'll pass the 7.5% test. If it's doubtful, try to hold off paying any medical bills until the following year, when they might have some tax-saving power. On the other hand, if you are close to or already over the threshold, see what you can do to pump up the deduction.

One sure way, of course, is to pay any outstanding medical bills—including health insurance premiums—by December 31. If you charge expenses to a bank credit card or borrow money to pay the bills, you get the deduction for the current year when you pay the bill, regardless of when you repay the debt.

Taxpayers who know they'll get to deduct medical expenses should also consider scheduling, being billed for and paying for elective medical and dental work before the end of the year to lock in Uncle Sam's subsidy. The same goes if you need new glasses, contact lenses, dentures, a hearing aid, or modifications to a car to enable a handicapped person to drive.

State and local taxes. If you make estimated income-tax payments, mailing the fourth-quarter installment by December 31 earns you the deduction in the current year—even if part of the payment is returned to you via a state tax refund the following spring. As discussed in Chapter 10, however, the payment has to be based on a reasonable estimate of your actual state-tax bill. You can't inflate your fourth-quarter payment just to hike the write-off on your federal return.

You may have similar flexibility with state and local property-tax bills. In some areas of the country, these bills are mailed out in the fall, for example, but they don't have to be paid until January of the following year. Beating the deadline by paying

© 1985 GORRELL—RICHMOND NEWS LEADER

before year-end lets you claim the tax savings a year earlier.

Interest. Be sure you're up to date with your payments on credit cards and other loans. There's a double benefit when it comes to personal interest. In addition to getting to write off the interest a year earlier, you'll get to deduct more of it. As detailed in Chapter 10, 40% of such interest is deductible in 1988, but only 20% in 1989 and 10% in 1990. As of 1991, you get no write-off for personal interest.

The phaseout may persuade you to pay off a loan early to avoid the dwindling tax subsidy—perhaps with funds obtained through a home-equity loan, the interest on which can remain fully deductible. If paying off a loan ahead of schedule triggers a prepayment penalty, the charge is considered interest and should be included when figuring your deduction.

You may be able to beef up your home-mortgage deduction by making your December payment before year-end, even if it's not due until the following January. If you make a payment on your mortgage or home-equity loan late in the year, the interest portion might not be included on the Form 1098 your lender sends you and the IRS to show how much interest was paid during the year. Watch this point carefully. If you mailed the check by December 31, you get the deduction in the current year even if the lender didn't register the payment until the following year. But you'll need to attach a note to your tax return explaining the discrepancy between the Form 1098 and the amount you're deducting.

Points paid on a mortgage to buy your principal residence remain fully deductible in the year paid, assuming the points amount to prepaid interest. If you plan to settle on a home around the end of the year, closing the deal and paying the points by New Year's Eve can give you a big deduction on the tax return you file the following spring.

Charitable contributions. Your gifts to charitable organizations probably give you the most flexibility for timing deductions. If you're thinking of making a substantial gift to your alma mater, for example, doing so before the end of the year locks in the deduction for the current year. If you normally give $100 a month to your church, making the January contribution by

December 31 boosts your write-off by that amount. If you make a pledge to make future contributions, however, you don't get the deduction until you actually make the gifts.

As discussed in Chapter 10, there's a special advantage to giving away appreciated property—such as stock—rather than cash. You can earn a write-off for the current value of the stock rather than what you originally paid for it, and you avoid having to pay tax on the profit that built up while you owned it.

If you routinely go through your closets for used clothing to give away, find time for a year-end sweep. Making the donation by New Year's Eve earns you a tax deduction for the current year.

Miscellaneous expenses. As with medical costs, you get a deduction in this catchall category only if your expenses exceed a threshold—2% of your adjusted gross income in this case. The list of qualifying expenses is long (see Chapter 10) but you get no tax savings unless you pass the 2% test. As you get your bearings in November, see how close you are to the threshold. If it is certain that you'll fall short, hold off paying qualifying expenses, such as professional dues and the cost of subscriptions to tax or investment publications, or postpone buying small tools for use in your job. If it's likely your expenses will surpass 2% of AGI, speed up such spending to exploit the tax subsidy.

BUNCHING

Before going on a spending spree to hike your deductible expenses, be absolutely certain that you'll be itemizing. Thanks to higher standard deductions—$3,000 for singles and $5,000 for joint returns in 1988 and progressively higher in the future to keep up with inflation—fewer taxpayers than in the past get any benefit from itemizing. (The standard deductions are even higher for taxpayers age 65 and older and those who are legally blind, as explained in Chapter 10.) It pays off only if your qualifying expenses total more than the standard deduction for your filing status.

If you are on the itemize-or-not borderline, your year-end

strategy should focus on bunching. This is the practice of timing expenses to produce "lean" and "fat" years. In one year, you cram in as many deductible expenses as possible, using the tactics outlined above. The goal is to surpass the standard-deduction amount and claim a larger write-off. In alternating years, you skimp on deductible expenses to hold them below the standard deduction amount—because you get credit for the full standard deduction regardless of how much you actually spend. In the "lean" years, year-end plans stress pushing as many deductible expenses as possible into the following "fat" year when they'll have some value.

INVESTMENTS

Your portfolio cries out for special attention as the year draws to an end. Because it's up to you when to sell securities—and convert paper gains and losses to real ones—you can mix and match your trades to deliver the tax outcome you desire.

Begin with an outline of exactly where you stand. Draw up a list of your trades so far during the year and the gains or losses on each. Make another list showing your current holdings and the paper gain or loss to date. In other words, if you sold the securities today what would your profit or loss be? If you have purchased shares of the same stock mutual fund at different times, track the holding period and paper gain and loss on each block of shares. As discussed in Chapter 5, by selecting which shares to sell you can affect the taxable gain or loss.

Although both long- and short-term gains are now fully taxed, it's still important to distinguish between long- and short-term transactions. For one thing, there's always a chance that Congress will reestablish some sort of tax break for long-term profits. If the law is changed, you'll want to be prepared to take full advantage of it. Also, as discussed in Chapter 10, special rules apply to charitable gifts of long-term capital-gain property.

Property you own more than a year before selling it produces a long-term gain or loss. Property owned one year or less generates short-term results. (For property purchased before January 1, 1988, the holding period was six months).

Once you have a clear picture of your position, see what you can do to make it brighter.

If your trades to date have resulted in a net gain, take a hard look at the securities still in your portfolio that show paper losses. Maybe now is the time to unload some of those stocks, using the loss to offset the gain on other deals and pull down your tax bill.

On the other hand, if your sales so far this year have produced a net loss, perhaps you should go in for some year-end profit-taking. Remember that only $3,000 of net losses a year can be used to offset income other than capital gains, with the tax value of extra capital losses postponed to future years. However, you can benefit from such losses this year by taking gains for the losses to absorb. That lets you take profits, up to the amount of your losses, without increasing your tax bill.

Don't let the search for tax savings lead you into bad investment decisions. Your investment goals must be your primary concern. But if a particular investment is on the sell-or-hold borderline, perhaps the tax consequences can be decisive.

What if your tax sense collides with your investment sense? Say you want to sell a stock, but the tax angles make doing so before year-end a costly mistake. Never fear. There are ways to lock in your gain without having to pay tax with your current year's return.

Selling short against the box. This is a classic year-end technique designed to defer recognizing a taxable gain until the following year without having to worry that by January a falling stock price could make the issue moot.

It works this way: You borrow from your broker stock identical to that which you already own, and then sell the borrowed stock at today's price. That locks in your gain, but as far as the IRS is concerned the deal isn't closed for tax purposes until you deliver your shares to the broker to repay the loan. If that's after December 31, you push the taxable gain into the following year. (Note that there has been some talk of the IRS trying to short-circuit this maneuver.)

Put options. Buying a put—an option giving you the right to sell stock at a set price until a certain date—can also defer recognition of gain while insuring against market loss. A put has a potential advantage over a short sale, too. Rather than lock in today's price, using a put protects you on the downside but lets you claim future appreciation. If the stock price falls, you can exercise the put and sell the stock at the set price. If the price rises, you let the put expire and sell the shares on the open market for the bigger gain. In either case, the profit is not recognized until you sell.

If you exercise the option, the cost of the put is subtracted from your taxable gain; if you let it expire, the cost is considered a capital loss.

Last-minute sales. Since it takes several days to settle a securities trade—between the time you order the sale to the time you get your money—sales during the last few days of the year often straddle year-end. Before 1987, that gave the seller the option of reporting the profit in the year of the trade or the year of settlement. But that choice is no longer available. The IRS now demands that gains or losses be reported on the tax return for the year the trade occurs, regardless of when settlement takes place. That means profits and losses taken as late as the closing bell on New Year's Eve go on the current year's return.

Installment sales. As Mark Twain once said about reports of his death, reports of the demise of the installment method have been greatly exaggerated. This method lets you hold off reporting taxable income from a sale until you actually receive the proceeds.

You can't use the installment method to defer recognition of income from the sale of publicly traded stocks and bonds. But it is available to individuals who sell a vacation home, for example, or rental property on an installment note. If the buyer will pay you over a number of years, you can report the income as you get it rather than all at once in the year of the sale. See Chapter 5 for details.

Bond swaps. This is another classic year-end maneuver. The point of the swap is to lock in a tax loss by selling bonds that have fallen in value and reinvesting the proceeds in other bonds. Done right, you can maintain the income stream from your bonds. Consider this example:

Assume you own $100,000 worth of New York Power Authority AA-rated bonds with a 7% coupon and a maturity date in 2016. In November, as you begin your year-end planning, the market price of your bonds has slipped to $84,750. If you sell at that price, you'll have a $15,250 loss.

At the same time, assume you can buy $100,000 face value Intermountain Power Agency AAA-rated bonds, with a 7% coupon and a 2015 maturity, for $83,612.

If you sell one set of bonds and buy the other, look what happens: Since they have the same par value and coupon rate, your annual income remains the same: $7,000. Your bond rating increases from AA to AAA. You pull $1,138 out of the investment—the difference between what you got for the old bonds and what you paid for the new ones. And you can claim a $15,250 tax loss. If it offsets gains that otherwise would have been taxed at 28%, you save $4,270.

As with much year-end tax planning, the earlier you begin scouting for promising candidates for swapping, the better. The supply dwindles and competition from other investors heats up as the year draws to an end.

Beware the wash-sale rule. What if you'd like to lock in a loss for tax purposes but really want to hold on to the securities you own? Why not just sell to transform the paper loss to a real one and then buy back the same stock or bonds? The wash-sale rule, that's why. A tax loss is disallowed if within 30 days before or after the sale you buy the same or substantially identical securities. Despite all the similarities in the bonds used in the bond-swapping example above, the wash-sale rule does not come into play because different issuers are involved.

You may be able to accomplish your goal of claiming a loss while maintaining your market position without running afoul of the wash-sale rule. Perhaps, for example, you could trade your stock for that of another company in the same industry that's likely to perform similarly. Your broker may be able to offer recommendations.

INTEREST INCOME

You have a bit of leeway on when you report interest income, but to capitalize you need to begin long before year-end. Interest earned on a savings account or money-market fund is taxable in the year it is made available to you, regardless of whether you withdraw the cash.

But if you buy a Treasury bill—with a maturity of three, six or 12 months—interest earned isn't taxed until the bill matures. Buy a new six-month bill on July 1 or later, for example, and you put off the tax bill on the interest earned until the following year when the bill matures. The same goes for bank certificates of deposit with a maturity of a year or less. If the interest isn't available to you without penalty until the end of the term, you don't report or pay tax on the interest until the CD matures.

BUSINESS MOVES

If you have your own business, whether full- or part-time, you have significant control over the timing of deductible expenses. Bills for qualifying expenses you pay before year-end are deductible on the current year's return; those you hold off on until the new year are deductible the following year. If you qualify to write off 25% of your health insurance costs (see Chapter 9), for example, paying the premiums by December 31 lets you claim the deduction this year.

Buying business property at year-end can prove either an advantage or disadvantage. First, the plus side. Although tax reform slowed down the depreciation timetable for most business property, the law generally still lets you claim six months' worth of the depreciation in the year you put the property into service, regardless of how late in the year you make the purchase. Even if you buy on the last day of the year, you can earn a substantial depreciation write-off. This "half-year" convention works against you, of course, if you buy your business property early in the year. Even if you buy in January, for example, you still get only half a year's worth of depreciation for the first year of ownership.

Now, the potential problem. You can trip yourself up if you

buy too much business property at year-end. If the cost of assets put into service during the final three months of the year exceeds 40% of the total cost of business property put into service during the year, the half-year convention is replaced by a "midquarter" convention. That means depreciation is calculated as though each asset was put into service in the middle of the calendar quarter during which it was first used.

A year-end purchase would earn just six weeks' worth of depreciation, then, instead of six months. However, triggering the midquarter convention rule would also boost write-offs for property put in service early in the year: Assets placed in service during the first quarter would earn 10½ months' worth of depreciation rather than six months'. (For more on depreciation of business property, see Chapter 9.)

Expensing. This is the provision of the tax law that lets you write off immediately up to $10,000 of otherwise depreciable property. If you choose expensing, you don't have to bother with the midyear or the midquarter convention. Regardless of how late in the year you put the property into service, you can deduct the full cost of up to $10,000 of qualifying items.

Consider how that can boost your deduction. Say you buy $10,000 of business property with a five-year tax life. Under the midyear convention, your first-year depreciation deduction would be a healthy $2,000. Choose expensing, though, and you can write off the entire purchase price on the current year's return. Expensing won't let you deduct $10,000 of the business cost of a car all at once, however, regardless of how much the car costs. Under the "luxury car" rules, the biggest first-year auto write-off is $2,560 (see Chapter 9).

Social security. Successful efforts to trim your taxable business income can produce double savings. In addition to cutting your income tax bill for the year, you may also save on social security taxes. As discussed in Chapter 15, self-employment income is subject to a 13.02% social security tax in 1988. The tax applies to the first $45,000 of earnings from salary, wages and net self-employment income. If your self-employment income is subject to this levy, every $1,000 of extra business deductions would save $130 in social security taxes.

Hobby expenses. If you have to worry about the hobby-loss rules, your strategy may be the opposite of that outlined above. As discussed in Chapter 9, to qualify to deduct your expenses, you must be able to show that you're in business for profit. Basically, the IRS doesn't want to subsidize your hobby. If your endeavor shows a profit in at least three years out of every five, the law assumes you're trying to make money. Fail the three-of-five-year test, however, and it is assumed the activity is a hobby. Unless you can prove otherwise, your deductions are limited to the amount of income you report. You can't claim a loss.

Your year-end planning needs to consider both where you stand on the profit-or-loss front and how you're doing on the three-out-of-five-year test. If you need to show a profit this year to avoid having your activity branded a hobby, you may want to press for collection of any income you're due and put off paying expenses or buying new equipment until the new year.

Rental property. Owners of rental property can pull down their taxable income by scheduling and paying for repairs on their units before year-end. Be sure, too, that you're up to date on paying other deductible expenses, such as property taxes, mortgage interest and insurance premiums. These costs will trim taxable rental income or increase your loss.

As long as you actively manage the property and your adjusted gross income is under $100,000, you can deduct up to $25,000 of rental losses against other income. That $25,000 allowance is phased out as AGI moves between $100,000 and $150,000. Any excess losses fall in the category of "passive losses," which can't be deducted unless you have passive income to offset. (See Chapter 6.)

If your rental losses can't be written off because of the passive-loss rules, forget about speeding up rental expenses. The extra loss will have no current tax benefit.

Passive investments. As year-end draws near, the pain of the passive-loss rules becomes acute. These are losses from rental activities (except for the $25,000 allowance mentioned above), limited partnerships and any business in which you do not materially participate. Such losses can no longer be used to shelter other income. Losses generated by passive activities can be used only to offset income produced by passive activities. Any excess loss is suspended for use in future years when you have passive income. (It's possible they'll be worth more to you then than they would be currently—if tax rates head back up, for example.)

There is an exception that permits taxpayers who invested in their passive activity before October 23, 1986, to write off a portion of their losses against other types of income. For 1988, 40% of otherwise suspended losses can be deducted. That percentage falls to 20% in 1989 and to 10% in 1990.

As the limited exception fades away, year-end planning demands that you focus on losses you can't use. Promoters may try to interest you in a PIG—passive-income generator. These are investments, such as limited partnerships, designed to produce passive income to soak up passive losses. Be careful not to let your pursuit of tax savings lead you into a bad

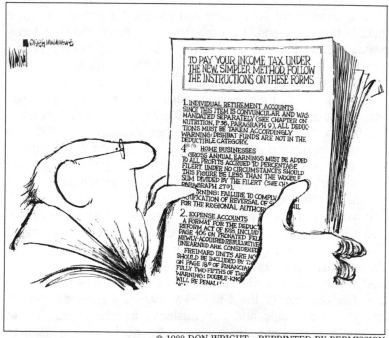

investment. Any investment touted as "tax-favored" around year-end—when many taxpayers are desperate for tax savings—begs for especially careful scrutiny.

A potential year-end tax-saver would be to unload the activity that's producing the passive losses. When you sell a passive investment, any losses produced during the year—and any losses suspended from previous years—are free to be deducted against any kind of income.

Christmas at the beach? Owners of vacation property may have an extra incentive to use their getaways around year-end. If you own property that you rent out part-time, you probably are well versed in the vacation-home rules: Use the place for more than 14 days or 10% of the number of days it is rented and the house is considered a personal residence. That limits your rental-expense deductions to the amount of rental income. In other words: no tax loss to shelter other income. Limit personal use to pass the 14-day test, though, and the house is considered a rental property. Qualifying it as such lets you deduct losses under the $25,000 rule—if you actively manage the place and your AGI is below $150,000 so you're not tripped up by the passive-loss rules.

In the past, the tax subsidy from writing off losses was a key part of financing many vacation homes, so owners were careful not to let personal use tip the scales against them. Now, however, passing the rental-property test can cost you mortgage-interest deductions. The law permits you to deduct all mortgage interest on your principal residence and a second home. If you keep your personal use of the vacation place under 15 days, however, it doesn't qualify as a second home. That means mortgage interest attributed to your use of the house is personal interest, the deduction for which is being phased out.

If your rental losses are threatened by the passive-loss rules, you may find it advantageous to squeeze in enough extra days of personal use at year-end to qualify the vacation house as a second home. At least that would preserve your mortgage-interest write-off. (See Chapter 4.)

Retirement plans. Taxpayers who are considering opening a Keogh retirement plan have to decide by New Year's Eve. If you want to write off a contribution to a Keogh on this year's return, the plan must be established by December 31, although contributions can be made anytime up to the due date of your return. (See Chapter 8.)

There's no year-end pressure if you're thinking about an individual retirement account. Contributions opened anytime up to April 15 can be deducted on the previous year's return.

When you take money out of an IRA, much—if not all—of it is taxable. As you consider a withdrawal around year-end, weigh the potential advantage of holding off until the new year arrives. If you can wait to put your hands on the money, you can make Uncle Sam wait an extra year before he gets his share. But if you'll find yourself in a higher tax bracket in the future— due to higher income or increases in the tax rates—you may want to speed up IRA withdrawals to avoid the stiffer tax bite.

In the year you reach age 70½, the law demands that you begin withdrawals from your IRA, as discussed in Chapter 7. But the first mandatory distribution—the one for the year you turn 70½—can be put off until as late as the following April 1. Holding off trims your taxable income and your tax bill in the current year. But you must double up in the second year. In addition to the withdrawal made by April 1, another has to be made by December 31. If the resulting boost in taxable income shoves you into a higher tax bracket, your income-deferral strategy could backfire.

PROTECT YOUR EXEMPTIONS

Now that Congress has greatly increased the value of exemptions—to $1,950 each in 1988, $2,000 each in 1989 and more each year after that to keep up with inflation—it's more important than ever to protect your right to claim exemptions for your dependents. If you're in the 28% bracket, a $1,950 exemption knocks $546 off your tax bill.

Chapter 3 outlines the various tests you must pass to claim someone as your dependent. The two most likely to trip you up—that you can do anything about at year-end—are the support test and the gross-income test.

The support test demands that you provide more than half of a person's support in order to claim him or her as your dependent. That's usually no problem when your children are involved, but it can be dicey if you are supporting an elderly parent. By November at the latest, you should get a fix on what percentage of your parent's support you've supplied during the year. If it appears that things are going to be close, you may want to beef up your support and have your parent cut back a bit on spending his or her own money.

Money a dependent puts into savings doesn't count as support, but cash that's pulled out and spent on support does. Say, for example, that your father—who you intend to claim as a dependent—wants to tap his savings account to buy a new car. If what he takes out for the car pushes his own contribution to his support over the 50% mark, you lose the tax-saving exemption. Suggesting that your father delay the car purchase until the new year could preserve your right to the exemption.

The gross-income test blocks you from claiming as your dependent someone with gross income that exceeds the exemption amount. This test does not apply, however, to your children who are either under age 19 or who were full-time students for at least five months during the year.

The exception for children means that here, too, the most likely threat is to dependency exemptions for parents. Social security benefits or other tax-exempt income don't count for purposes of the gross income test.

You need to keep an eye on the earnings of potential dependents from savings, investments or jobs. It may pay off to recommend that a dependent parent move money out of a taxable savings account and into a tax-free money-market mutual fund, for example, if doing so would preserve the dependency exemption. Your tax savings could outweigh the slightly lower yield your parent would earn in the tax-free investment.

As with year-end investment decisions, factors other than taxes come into play here. You have to weigh the potential tax savings against other considerations. And remember this: If you can arrange things so that you claim someone as a dependent, that person may not claim a personal exemption on his or her own tax return.

GIVE MONEY AWAY

As discussed in Chapter 16, you can give away as much as $10,000 a year to any number of people without triggering the federal gift tax. The tax-free amount doubles to $20,000 if your spouse joins you in making the gift. You don't get a tax deduction for such gifts unless the object of your generosity is a qualified charitable organization. But there's an important advantage: Assets given away during your life—and any future appreciation—won't be in your estate to be taxed after you die. And income generated by the gift is taxed to the new owner, not to you. (If you give assets to your own children, however, the income can be taxed in your tax bracket until the children reach age 14. That's explained in Chapter 3.)

This issue is raised here, among possible year-end maneuvers, because if you're planning to make substantial gifts, you face a December 31 deadline. If you don't use your $10,000 annual exclusion by that date, you lose it. Each new year presents you with a new exclusion, but you can't reach back to benefit from a previous year's unused allowance.

Assume, for example, that a couple plans to give $40,000 to their son. If they give it all during one year, $20,000 of the gift would be sheltered from the gift tax, the other $20,000 subject to it. However, if half the gift was given in December and the other half in January, the full $40,000 would be protected.

GET MARRIED, OR NOT

If you're planning to tie the knot around the end of the year, you may want to check with Uncle Sam before setting the date. Whether you marry in December or January could have a major impact on your tax bill. No, it's not romantic. But playing the tax angle could save enough to pay for a nice honeymoon.

Whether you and your intended are better off married or single at year-end depends mostly on how your incomes compare. (See Chapter 3.)

If you think weighing the tax consequences of the wedding date is somewhat less than sentimental, how about the folks who consider a year-end divorce as a tax strategy? As far as the IRS is concerned, your marital status on the last day of the year generally determines your filing status. With that in mind, some "shrewd" taxpayers thought they had discovered a way around the marriage tax penalty: Divorce in December and remarry in January. If the tax savings happened to be enough to finance a wintertime trip to the Caribbean for the quickie divorce, all the better.

Alas, it doesn't work. The IRS and the courts consider the divorce a sham and it is ignored for tax purposes.

WATCH YOUR WITHHOLDING

The federal income tax is on a pay-as-you-go basis. Although the final accounting isn't due until April 15 of the following year, the tax is supposed to be paid as you earn the money. That's why employers withhold tax from your paychecks and why you're expected to make estimated tax payments on self-employment or investment income. If you don't pay enough as you go along, you can be hit by a penalty.

As part of your year-end planning, compare your tax payments—through withholding or estimated payments—with what you expect to owe. If your payments will be at least as much as the tax you owed for the previous year or at least 90% of what you'll owe this year, you're safe from the penalty. If you will fall short, however, some year-end maneuvering can save you some money.

Estimated tax payments are considered made when you send the money to the IRS, which means you can't make up for an underpayment early in the year by beefing up your final estimated payment, which is due the following January 15. Withholding, however, is treated as though it is paid evenly over the year, even if a big chunk is taken out of your paycheck late in December. That means overwithholding in November and December can make up for underpayments earlier in the year.

If you have a job, then, you have a last-minute opportunity to dodge, or at least mitigate, an underpayment penalty: Arrange with your employer to withhold extra amounts from the final paychecks of the year. (See Chapter 13.)

13
PAY AS YOU GO

Despite all the worrying, grousing and remonstrating we do about high taxes and all the planning and conniving we do to minimize what we owe Uncle Sam, the vast majority of us let the government dip deeper into our pockets during the year than we have to. The evidence is incontrovertible: The millions of tax-refund checks the Treasury mails out each spring are proof positive that employees had too much withheld from their payroll checks.

This chapter will show you how to keep your withholding down to the legal minimum. Ditto if investment or self-employment income requires you to pay estimated taxes during the year. The point is for you to get the use and enjoyment of more of your money when you earn it rather than making an unintentional—albeit generous—interest-free loan to the government.

The extent of overwithholding is as massive as it is ironic. In the spring of 1988, the government churned out close to 80 million tax-refund checks. The total amount sprinkled on appreciative taxpayers was around $80 *billion*. The average size of the checks fell between $900 and $1,000. (The interest you could earn on the average overpayment in a 5¼% savings account would pay for this book many times over.)

On the flip side of the coin, a growing number of taxpayers are tripped up each year by having too little withheld or failing to pay enough estimated tax. This is a particular problem for two-earner married couples. If underwithholding is your problem, you'll find here the formula for dodging the expensive penalty the IRS slaps on those who fail to meet its pay-as-you-go expectations.

Undoubtedly some taxpayers who are hit with underpayment penalties really don't have to pay. The law includes exceptions, but since the IRS computers don't know who might have a valid excuse, penalty notices go to those who appear to be guilty. Filing the right form can deflect the fine and turn the IRS away empty-handed, as discussed later.

Giving Uncle Sam a crack at your paycheck before you get it is likely the linchpin of the federal income-tax system. Although ours is widely hailed as a "voluntary" tax system, it works best when there is the least opportunity not to volunteer.

Most taxpayers have lived with withholding since their first jobs, but it is a relatively recent development. Congress put us on the pay-as-you-go system in 1943. Before then, the tax bill for one year was due in installments during the following year. During World War II, however, the tax was expanded to cover more Americans, and withholding was introduced as a method of speeding up the collection of needed revenues and in recognition of the fact that many of the new taxpayers were probably spending most if not all of their income as they earned it. Expecting them to come up with cash for the IRS the following year could cause problems.

Although we all think of April 15 as tax day, taxes are actually due as income is earned, and employers have become the country's primary tax collectors. The government also expects its share of income not covered by withholding—including income from self-employment, investments and alimony—in installments during the year. In both cases, social security taxes as well as income taxes are due on a pay-as-you-go basis.

THE FORM W-4

The amount withheld from your pay is determined by two things: how much you are paid and the information you provide your employer on the Form W-4, *Employee's Withholding Allowance Certificate*. Your employer knows how much you're being paid; the form shows whether you are married or single and how many withholding allowances you want to claim. The more allowances, the less tax is withheld.

You get a W-4 when you start a new job and often never see one again. In 1987, however, every employee had to file a revised W-4. That demand grew out of the worry that mixing old W-4's with all the new rules brought by the Tax Reform Act of 1986 was asking for disaster. Congress feared that withholding could wind up so far out of whack with actual tax bills that taxpayers would be furious.

The IRS's first version of the modified W-4 was itself a disaster. Not only was it convoluted—even by IRS standards—but many taxpayers found that using the new form would result in *more* tax being withheld from checks. A firestorm of taxpayer protest sent the IRS back to the drawing board, and the current version of the W-4 is much more manageable.

Although you are not required to file a new form, doing so may be a smart move. To see the financial power of the W-4, consider the case of a married employee with a nonworking wife and two children and a $50,000 salary. Assume his current W-4 claims four allowances, the same number of exemptions he claims on his tax return. Each month, his employer withholds $595 for the IRS. A new W-4 claiming ten allowances would drive withholding down to $345—putting an extra $250 a month in his pocket. That's $3,000 a year.

It's not found money, though. The number of withholding allowances does not affect your tax bill for the year, only how much you shell out in installments each payday. Assuming the $3,000 in our example would otherwise have found its way into a springtime tax refund, adjusting withholding effectively lets the taxpayer claim the refund in installments—by not overpaying in the first place.

Each allowance you claim exempts from withholding the same amount of income that exemptions knock off your taxable income—$1,950 in 1988, $2,000 in 1989 and more in the future as the exemption amount is adjusted for inflation. The table on the following page shows approximately how much each extra allowance you claim will trim withholding and add to your take-home pay each month.

	Salary	**Monthly Value of Each Withholding Allowance**
Single:	Up to $18,000	
Married:	Up to $30,000	$24
Single:	$18,000 to $45,000	
Married:	$30,000 to $72,000	$45
Single:	$45,000 to $90,000	
Married:	$72,000 to $150,000	$54
Single:	Over $90,000	
Married:	Over $150,000	$45

Alas, you can't just make up a number for your W-4. IRS regulations control how many you can claim, and you can be slapped with a $500 fine if you deliberately claim more than you deserve. It's clear from all the refunds, however, that most taxpayers claim too few allowances rather than too many. If you're in that group, consider taking the time to closely match withholding to your actual tax bill.

Yes, doing so would mean giving up that luscious tax refund check in the spring. There are plenty of willing victims of overwithholding, including taxpayers who see it as a convenient means of forced savings. In 1988, in fact, the national tax-preparation firm of H&R Block began offering—for an extra fee—to help taxpayers file a W-4 designed to produce a refund.

If you have the discipline, however, there are plenty of better ways to save. Uncle Sam doesn't pay interest, and inflation gnaws away at the value of your money while it's hibernating. When inflation was running at an annual clip of 12% in the late 1970s, a dollar of excess withholding in January was worth just 85 cents when it was released in May of the following year.

Perhaps more costly, overwithholding can play games with your psyche. We've all heard this joyous springtime comment: "Oh, I didn't owe any tax this year. I'm getting money back."

Of course, the gratified taxpayer undoubtedly paid hundreds—perhaps thousands—of dollars in tax and was simply recouping funds that had been overpaid. This delusion can inflict financial pain if it leads you to lower your guard when you're preparing your tax return. It is likely you'll work harder at tax time if you're trying to shave the amount due instead of trying to pump up a refund.

How to do it. You can get a Form W-4 from the IRS or your employer. If you're not certain how many allowances you are now claiming, check with your company's personnel office. Now figure out whether you can legitimately claim more.

Start by shaking off the notion that all you need to do is count the number of bodies around the house. It's true that you get an allowance for each exemption you will claim on your tax return, but that's just the beginning. You can add an extra allowance if:

• You are single and have only one job;

• You are married, have one job and your spouse isn't employed; or

• Your wages from a second job or your spouse's wages are $2,500 or less.

You also get an extra allowance if you have at least $1,500 of child- or dependent-care expenses and will claim a tax credit for these costs.

And you're permitted an additional allowance if you file your return as a head of household.

Next, you determine whether you should claim extra allowances for the itemized deductions and adjustments to income that will cut your taxable income. The W-4 comes with a work sheet for that figuring, but it might shortchange you.

Basically, the work sheet asks for an estimate of your itemized deductions and adjustments to income, then has you reduce that amount by nonwage income—such as dividends and interest not covered by withholding—before determining how many allowances you should claim to reflect your tax-saving write-offs. What the work sheet does not indicate is that you are also permitted to take anticipated losses into account. If you expect a deductible loss from a business or rental activity or investment, for example, you can adjust your withholding to account for the resulting reduction in your tax bill. Every $2,000 of net loss can buy an extra withholding allowance. Such losses are first used to reduce any estimated tax payments you must make, but if a loss will more than wipe out your estimated tax liability, you can use the excess to curtail withholding.

Making all those estimates might sound like more trouble than it could possibly be worth, but IRS restrictions can simplify the job. Begin with your tax return for the previous year. If you can reasonably expect your write-offs to be at least as high for the current year, you can use last year's figures for the W-4. You can use higher figures only if you can point to something that justifies the increase, such as in the following examples:

• You buy a new home for which mortgage interest and property-tax payments will be higher than your previous write-offs in those categories.

• You are divorced this year and have to pay alimony, a tax-deductible expense you didn't pay in earlier years.

• You suffer a substantial loss in the stock market—so bad that you'll be in the red even after accounting for profits you expect to take before the end of the year. You may use your estimated net loss to raise the number of allowances claimed on your W-4.

The rules don't permit adjusting withholding in anticipation of a tax-saving event. If you are simply worrying about a stock loss

THE WRITING OF FORM W-4 XXVII

or are considering making a big charitable contribution, for example, you can't use your fears or intentions for the future to reduce withholding. If the IRS challenges the number of allowances you claim, you'll have to show that you used a reasonable method to arrive at the number.

Working couples. If both you and your spouse have jobs, you figure the number of allowances you are entitled to together, then split the allowances however you choose. They are usually worth more—in terms of reduced withholding—when claimed by the higher-paid spouse.

Unfortunately, however, many married couples are plagued by underwithholding rather than overwithholding. The new W-4 takes this notorious reality into account with a second work sheet for working couples. Based on the income of each spouse, this work sheet walks you through the process of eliminating allowances the other rules say you deserve.

Although these negative allowances may seem like a penalty, the IRS says they are necessary to accurately match withholding to a couple's tax bill. It's possible that claiming zero allowances might still leave you underwithheld. Don't worry, the IRS has a solution. The W-4 work sheet is designed to show how much extra tax to ask your boss to withhold each payday.

Whether you decide you need more or less money withheld from your pay, filing a new W-4 with your employer—not the IRS—will trigger the change, usually within a month. That guarantees a quick payoff if your efforts cut withholding.

Although the IRS usually never sees the W-4 forms filed by employees, an exception requires employers to send the government copies of any form that claims more than ten allowances. If a review of previous tax returns doesn't convince the tax collectors you deserve the number of allowances claimed, you'll be asked for an explanation. Failure to provide convincing support for you claim can trigger an IRS order to your employer to ignore the W-4 and withhold from your salary at a much higher rate.

Don't be intimidated by the possibility of IRS scrutiny. If your calculations show you should claim more than ten allowances, do so.

Part-year withholding. This special brand of withholding is tailor-made for spring and summer college graduates who sign on for their first full-time job. The part-year method sets withholding according to what you'll actually earn during the part of the year you work, rather than on 12 times your monthly salary. That can make a significant difference in how much is held back from your checks.

The part-year method can be used by anyone who expects to work no more than 245 days—approximately eight months—in continuous employment during the year. It could pay off handsomely, for example, if you land a high-paying summer job.

You must give your employer a written request asking that the part-year method be used. Employers don't have to comply, but if yours does, you'll get more of your pay as you earn it.

Exemption from withholding. Before tax reform, students could often avoid withholding altogether on earnings from summer jobs. New rules, however, greatly restrict the opportunity to dodge withholding if your income for the year exceeds $500. You must pass two tests to be exempted:

• You didn't owe any income tax in the previous year.
• You don't expect to owe any tax this year.

As discussed in Chapter 3, taxpayers who can be claimed as dependents on someone else's return, such as children claimed on their parents', can't claim their own personal exemption and therefore owe tax on smaller amounts of income than in the past. Generally, in fact, if you can be claimed on someone else's return and have any nonwage income (such as interest on a savings account), you can't claim the exemption from withholding if total income for the year exceeds $500.

If you make $200 a week or more and claim the exemption from withholding on your W-4, your employer has to send the form to the IRS. As with taxpayers who claim more than ten allowances, the IRS will ask you to justify your claim.

Withholding on tips. If you receive more than $20 a month from tips, that income is subject to withholding, too. You are supposed to report the tip income to your employer, who takes it into account when figuring how much to withhold from your wages.

Because Congress is concerned that a lot of tip income goes unreported, in 1982 the lawmakers enacted new rules to encourage voluntary compliance with the law. Basically, the law now assumes that customers tip at an average rate of 8%. If restaurant and bar employees don't report to their employer tips totalling at least 8% of the establishment's gross receipts, the employer has to do it for them.

The shortfall between what's reported to the employer and the 8% level is allocated among the employees—but only for the purpose of a report to the IRS. No money will change hands, and waiters and waitresses are still expected to report their actual tip income, whether it's more or less than their share of the 8% kitty. Those who report less, however, should be more prepared than ever for questions from the IRS. (The tip-allocation rule applies only to establishments with ten or more employees where tipping is customary.)

Retirement income. Unless you choose otherwise, tax will be withheld from your retirement payments. That includes what you receive from a company pension or profit-sharing plan, an annuity, an individual retirement account or a Keogh plan. (Social security benefits are safe from withholding, even though social security is sometimes taxable, as discussed in Chapter 8.)

Note that you don't have to submit to this withholding unless you want to. You can forbid Uncle Sam to dip into your retirement checks simply by filing a form with the payer. The company that pays your pension, annuity or IRA distributions should periodically remind you of your option to block withholding and tell you how to exercise it.

Withholding on these payments isn't necessarily a bad thing, since it stretches the tax bill over the entire year rather than requiring you to pay all at once at tax-return time. Withholding might make life easier if the alternative is to make quarterly estimated tax payments, which are discussed later.

The amount that will be withheld depends on whether you receive "periodic" payments (such as monthly checks for a set period of time or indefinitely) or "nonperiodic" payments (such as a single payment). On periodic payments, the amount held back for the IRS is based on information you provide on a form

W-4P, just as withholding on wages is controlled by your W-4. Payers shave off a flat 10% for Uncle Sam if you get a nonperiodic payment, unless the payment is considered a "qualified total distribution" eligible for the special averaging method of taxation discussed in Chapter 8. In either case, your employer or whoever is in charge of making the payment can tell you how much will be withheld if you don't opt to block withholding.

You don't have to retire to be affected by these rules. If you quit a job and get a payout of your vested share of a pension or profit-sharing plan, for example, part of your money will be diverted to the IRS unless you direct the payer not to withhold. If you plan to roll your money into an IRA—and thereby postpone the tax bill—be sure to tell the payer not to withhold.

Gambling winnings. If you score big at the track or hit the winning number in the state lottery, you're not the only one who's lucky: so is the IRS. The winnings are taxable and, if high enough, subject to withholding at a flat 20% rate.

Withholding is required if you win more than $5,000 from a state lottery or more than $1,000 from other wagering, such as a church raffle or drawing, dog and horse racing, jai alai or a sweepstakes. Winnings from bingo or slot machines are exempt from withholding.

The 20% withheld isn't necessarily all the tax you owe on the winnings. The total amount is added to your other taxable income and taxed in your top bracket—meaning Uncle Sam can claim as much as 33%.

You should get a copy of form W-2G showing the amount you won and how much was withheld. The IRS gets a copy, too.

Backup withholding. The IRS would love to get a crack at your dividends and interest income before you do. In the early 1980s, in fact, Congress actually approved a plan to automatically divert 10% of such earnings to the IRS as a prepayment of the tax due. A taxpayer protest—fueled by banks and other institutions that didn't want to become tax collectors—convinced Congress to reverse itself before the first dime was withheld.

Still, it is possible for a bank or business to claim a chunk of your interest or dividend payments as "backup withholding." The rate is a flat 20%.

Backup withholding applies when the bank or other payer doesn't have, or doesn't think it has, your social security number—the taxpayer identification number used to report the income to the IRS. If you forget or refuse to give the bank or business your social security number, or the IRS tells the payer that you provided an incorrect number, 20% of your dividends or income will be diverted to the IRS. Backup withholding can also be ordered by the IRS if it concludes you failed to report on your tax return interest or dividends you received during the previous year.

Backup withholding shouldn't cause you any trouble if you've been reporting all your interest and dividend income properly. But it does mean more forms to fill out and sign when you open an account, to certify that you've provided the right social security number and that you're not subject to IRS-ordered backup withholding.

ESTIMATED TAX PAYMENTS

There are plenty of sources of income not nipped by withholding: income from self-employment, investments, rents, alimony, prizes, etc. But avoiding withholding doesn't mean escaping the government's pay-as-you-go demands.

If you expect to owe $500 or more in tax when you file your return—beyond the amount of tax withheld from wages—you are expected to make quarterly installment tax payments. The $500 triggering point is a general rule and can often be ignored, as discussed later in this section.

You use form 1040ES, *Estimated Tax for Individuals,* to calculate whether and how much estimated tax you owe at various times during the year. This involves time-consuming estimates of your projected taxable income for the year, the amount of income and social security tax you'll owe and how much, if any, of it will be paid via withholding. The easiest way to make your estimate is to use your previous year's return as a guide. Take a stab at how income and deductions are likely to differ in the current year and apply the latest tax rates to the best guess of your taxable income. If self-employment income is involved, be sure to take into account what you'll owe in social security taxes, as discussed in Chapter 15.

If the gap between what you expect to owe and the amount you expect to be withheld is $500 or more, you may have to make estimated payments.

Those payments are due only if failing to make them would subject you to the penalty for paying too little during the year. That means shaving estimated payments to a minimum—a worthy goal that lets you keep more of your money working for you during the year—demands that you understand the underpayment penalty and the exceptions to it.

The penalty is the IRS's not-so-subtle reminder that taxes are due as income is earned, not just on April 15 of the following year. Basically, it works like interest on a loan with the penalty rate applied to the amount of estimated tax due but unpaid by each of four payment dates during the year. The penalty rate is set by the IRS and can change each quarter. In mid 1988 the rate was 10%.

The IRS generally expects you to pay your entire estimated tax bill in four installments during the year. If any payment is short or late, the penalty rate is applied on a daily basis until you pay up. If you ignore the first payment and double up on the second, for example, you would still owe a penalty based on the skipped payment and the number of days between the time it was due and when you paid.

Your estimates don't have to be precise to avoid the penalty; as long as your payments cover 90% of your actual tax liability, the penalty doesn't apply. (Before 1988, you had to pay only 80% to earn this reprieve.) Say, for example, that your figuring on the 1040 ES work sheets suggests you'll owe $4,000 more in tax than will be withheld from your paychecks. The minimum quarterly installment amounts would be $900 ($4,000 ÷ 4 × 90%).

In several situations, even the 90% rule is thrown out.

● If you owed no tax in the previous year and were a U.S. citizen or resident for the whole year, you don't have to make estimated payments regardless of how much you make or how much tax you'll owe. This applies only if you had no tax liability in the previous year, not if you just didn't have to pay extra tax with your return.

• There is no underpayment penalty if your payments for the year—via withholding and quarterly payments—equal your tax bill for the previous year. This is an important exception. Even if your income jumps, thanks to a big profit on an investment, say, this exception lets you ignore estimated taxes if the amount withheld on your salary will be at least equal to your tax bill for the previous year.

Even if none of your income is subject to withholding, this exception to the underpayment penalty can greatly simplify estimating how much you must pay each quarter. You can simply divide the previous year's bill by four. If you expect your tax bill to be lower this year, however, this streamlined method would result in paying more than the required minimum.

• Although the general rule calls for your minimum tax payments to be made in equal, quarterly installments, the law does recognize that in some cases that would make no sense. Say, for example, that the only reason you need to make an estimated payment is a $50,000 profit on a stock sale in mid November. Why should you make an estimated tax payment on that income the previous spring? You shouldn't and you don't have to.

Under the "annualized income" exception to the underpayment penalty, the amount due on each payment date can be based on the actual amount of taxable income you have received at that point during the year. Although it involves some extra number crunching, taking the annualized income approach can save you from a penalty due to a bulge in income during the latter part of the year.

Employees have an extra, and particularly potent, way to avoid the penalty. Say you discover late in the year that you should have been making estimated payments all along on your investment income. Even if you make up for the oversight with a big estimated payment for the final quarter, the IRS will stick you with the penalty for missing earlier installments.

However, if your employer will increase withholding from your salary for the year so that the total withheld will cover 90% of your tax bill (or 100% of the previous year's liability), you can retroactively eliminate the underpayment penalty. Unlike estimated payments, which are considered paid when they are paid, withholding is treated as though it is taken out of your checks evenly throughout the year. To initiate that penalty-saving overwithholding, you need to file a new W-4 form with your employer.

Farmers and fishermen. Taxpayers who earn at least two-thirds of their gross income from farming or fishing—professions for which projecting income is notoriously difficult—are covered by special rules. Rather than being required to make estimated payments during the year, farmers and fisherman can pay their estimated taxes in a single payment, due January 15 of the following year. To avoid the underpayment penalty, that payment must be just two-thirds of the actual tax liability for the year, or 100% of the tax owed on the previous year's return. Farmers and fishermen can even skip the January 15 payment

© 1986 DON WRIGHT—REPRINTED BY PERMISSION
TRIBUNE MEDIA SERVICES

without penalty if they file their returns and pay the full tax due by March 1.

When and how to pay. Never accused of oversimplifying things, the IRS doesn't break the tax year into four three-month quarters. No. The first quarter is three months (January 1 to March 31), the second "quarter" is two months long (April 1 to May 31), the third is three months (June 1 to August 31) and the fourth covers the final four months of the year. The installment payments are due on April 15, June 15, September 15 and January 15 of the following year. You can skip the final payment if you will file your return and pay all the tax due by February 1. If a due date falls on a weekend or legal holiday, it is pushed to the next business day.

As mentioned earlier, you don't have to make any payment until you have income on which estimated taxes are due. If you know early in the year that you must make estimated payments, each of the four payments should be 25% of the amount due.

But what if you receive income during the third quarter that, for the first time, makes you liable for estimated tax payments? Your first payment would be due on the third installment date— September 15—and you are expected to pay 75% of the tax that is due.

To hold your payments to a minimum, base each installment on what you have to pay to avoid the penalty, using any exceptions that benefit you.

If you have a tax refund coming from the IRS, you can elect on your return to have part or all of the money applied to your estimated tax bill. Although the IRS doesn't pay any interest on such advance payments, it may make sense to use the refund to pay the first installment (due April 15) and perhaps even the second (due June 15) just to save yourself the hassle of writing and sending in the checks.

The first time you pay estimated tax you have to get a copy of the Form 1040-ES from a local IRS office and complete and send in a payment voucher. After that, the tax agency will send you a package of preprinted vouchers showing your name, address and social security number. The payments are made to the IRS service center for your area.

PENALTIES: REAL AND MISTAKEN

When you file a tax return showing that you owe $500 or more in additional tax, and that amount is more than 10% of your tax bill for the year, the IRS assumes you are guilty of underpayment. If you are, you can figure the penalty on Form 2210, *Underpayment of Estimated Tax by Individuals,* which should accompany your return.

But that same form has a more benevolent purpose: It can exonerate you by showing which of the exceptions shelters you from the penalty.

If you are safe but don't file the Form 2210, you'll probably get a bill from the IRS. The official notice demanding prompt payment can be intimidating. It can also be mistaken. The IRS computers don't know whether you can squeeze into one of the safety zones and, therefore, assume you can't.

Before responding to a penalty notice with a check, take the time to work through Form 2210, searching for an exception that might reduce or eliminate the penalty. IRS Publication 505, *Tax Withholding and Estimated Tax,* includes work sheets and hypothetical cases that can help. If you qualify for one of the exceptions to the penalty, send the IRS the completed Form 2210.

14

SETTLING WITH UNCLE SAM

C lever people, those folks at
the IRS. Each year in early December they send out millions of
sets of tax forms; then they ask the Postal Service to sit on the
forms until the last week of the year. After all, Uncle Sam
doesn't want to get blamed for flooding the mails at Christmastime and delaying your cards and gifts. But the government
does want you to receive its package right after the holidays—
perhaps as much to beat the Christmas bills' claim on your
income as to give you a head start on completing your return.

When the forms arrive, they bring something of an official
reminder that yes, Virginia, there is another April 15 in your
future.

DO YOU HAVE TO FILE?

Whether you're one week or 101 years old, you're never too
young or too old to fall into the grasp of the IRS. The table on
the following page presents the gross income levels that trigger
a demand that you file a return. The various filing statuses are
discussed in Chapter 3. These figures are for 1988 returns.
They will be adjusted upward for inflation in subsequent years.

If you can be claimed as a dependent on someone else's
return—a situation most likely for children claimed by their
parents or for elderly parents claimed by their adult children—
you must file a tax return even if you have less income.
Dependent taxpayers under age 65 must file when earned
income—from a job or self-employment—exceeds $3,000 in
1988. If you're 65 or older, the threshold is $3,750.

Who Must File?

Status and Age	Gross Income*
Single	
Under 65	$ 4,950
Age 65 or older	5,700
Married filing jointly	
Both under 65	8,900
One age 65 or older	9,500
Both age 65 or older	10,100
Married filing separately	
Under 65	1,950
Age 65 or older	1,950
Surviving spouse	
Under 65	6,950
Age 65 or older	7,550
Head of household	
Under 65	6,350
Age 65 or older	7,100

Gross income does not include tax-exempt income from social security, for example, or interest from tax-free bonds.

However, if you have any unearned income—from investments, say—still lower limits apply. You have to file if your combined earned and unearned income exceeds $500 if you're under 65, $1,250 if you've reached that age.

Even if your income is so low that you don't have to file, you may want to do so; it's the only way to get a refund of taxes withheld from your pay.

The tax forms are usually the first of the flood of tax-related mail to arrive. Soon after you'll begin to receive the forms that will remind you of income to report to the IRS: the W-2 form from your employer showing what you were paid; the 1099-DIV forms listing stock dividends; the 1099-INT forms showing interest earned; the 1099-B form from your broker showing the proceeds of your sales; the 1099-Gs, showing a state tax refund, perhaps, or unemployment compensation; the 1099-

MISC for various other types of income; and on and on.

Unfortunately, the IRS isn't nearly as concerned that you remember your deductible expenses. You should get a 1098 form from your mortgage lender, showing how much mortgage interest you paid. Other lenders will usually send an accounting, too. Sometimes the report of interest paid shows up on a regular year-end statement. Watch for it. Beyond that, you're pretty much on your own. The success of all your tax-planning efforts during the year rests on your records.

Pulling together all the necessary paperwork isn't an appealing prospect. But it makes sense to answer the call of the tax return as early as possible in the year. There is no point in dallying. Procrastination can cost you money. If you deserve a refund—along with the vast majority of taxpayers—inflation is gnawing away at its value while you're making what amounts to an interest-free loan to Uncle Sam. The earlier you file, the sooner you can put that money back to work for you. Get your return in the mail by the end of February and you'll probably be banking—or spending—your refund while your neighbors are burning the midnight oil to meet the April 15 deadline.

If you're among the unhappy minority who owe more tax, getting started promptly still makes sense. Why risk missing a trick that could trim your tax bill because you run out of time to explore an option or to search for mislaid records? Tackling your return early in the filing season is insurance against a bleary-eyed, last-minute rush into a costly shortcut.

Remember that preparing your return doesn't mean you have to mail it right away. If you owe extra tax, you can hold on to your return—and your check—until April 15. And if your bottom line shows that you owe so much that you face a penalty, as discussed later in this chapter, the earlier you file the less you'll owe.

GETTING STARTED

A good way to gear up for your return is to review all the forms and schedules you used to settle up with Uncle Sam for the previous year. Seeing what you did then serves as a quick reminder of what's ahead. Sort through the papers used to back up your deductions, exemptions, adjustments and credits. The idea is to reacclimate yourself to the subject of taxes, to get your mind on the right track.

Of course, you can't follow your old tax return exactly. Your circumstances may have changed significantly. Or, perhaps more likely, the tax law may have changed significantly. Congress just can't seem to leave the Internal Revenue Code alone. This is another reason an early start is important. You may simply need more time to grapple with this year's forms that you needed last year. In the spring of 1988, for example, accountants often found themselves spending between 30% and 100% more time on clients' returns than had been necessary the previous year—all because of new tax rules.

Your first decision is which tax form to use. There are three basic choices: the baby blue 1040 long form, the pastel pink 1040A short form or the even shorter, light green 1040EZ. You don't necessarily have to file the one you get in the mail. In some cases you're not permitted to, in other circumstances choosing a different form will save you money. What you get from the IRS is the agency's best guess of what you need, based on your previous year's return.

The 1040EZ (as in *easy*, get it?) was introduced for 1982 returns and has already won an army of followers. More than 17 million taxpayers—almost one in five—use this simplest-of-all returns. If you can join them, filing is a breeze. The EZ has just 11 numbered lines, compared with nearly seven times as many on the standard 1040. There are no supplementary forms to file with the EZ, either, and all the instructions fit on the back of the single-page form.

Before you become too enamored of all that simplicity, consider the restrictions that put the EZ out of reach of most taxpayers. It can be filed only by single people who don't itemize deductions, have no dependents and have income under $50,000. You can't use the form if you have any income from dividends or capital gains, self-employment income or more than $400 in interest income to report. Nor can you use the 1040EZ if you want to claim a deduction for a contribution to an individual retirement account or have a taxable pension, social security benefits or alimony to report.

Between the EZ and the standard 1040 long form stands the 1040A—the form of choice for about 20 million taxpayers. This return can be used if you file as married, single, head of household or as a qualified widow or widower. Income is limited to $50,000, but unlike the 1040EZ, in addition to wages it can include any amount of interest, dividends and unemployment compensation. You can write off an IRA contribution and claim the child-care tax credit, but you can't use the short form if you have any taxable pension, social security benefits, alimony or capital gains to report.

If you have income that doesn't fit on the 1040EZ or the 1040A—income from self-employment, capital gains, rent or pensions, for example—you must use the 1040 long form. It's also required if you itemize deductions or claim adjustments to income, such as the write-off for alimony paid or the penalty paid for early withdrawal of savings from a certificate of deposit.

Never pass up a tax break simply because taking advantage of it will force you to use the long form. You can skip any lines that don't apply to you. Using the 1040 usually involves completing extra forms and schedules, too. The IRS paperwork collection—and what each form is for—is detailed in the appendix.

DRAWING BY STUART LEEDS
© 1984 THE NEW YORKER MAGAZINE, INC.

Another reason to get an early start on your return is that there's a good chance you'll need forms that don't come in the mail. The 1040 package mailed out routinely by the IRS contains the most commonly used forms, but you may well require others. For example, the basic package you receive may not include the forms you need to report self-employment income (Schedule C) or rental income (Schedule E), or the ones for figuring the "kiddie tax" (8615), calculating your investment interest write-off (4952) or determining your deduction for passive losses (8582).

You may be able to find the forms you need at a bank, post office or public library. The easiest way—if you have time—is to call the IRS and have the agency mail them to you. Find the number for a local IRS office in the phone book under U.S. Government. You may be referred to a nationwide toll-free number for ordering forms. Or you can order forms by mail using the order form that comes with the tax package. In either case, allow a couple of weeks for the forms to arrive. If you plan to drop by a local IRS office, call first to make sure it has the forms you need.

Don't be intimidated. Before you begin gathering the records you need to fill out the forms, check your attitude. Are you afraid of the IRS?

Sure, we're all supposed to have a healthy respect for the tax agency. The ever-present threat that the IRS can use part of its multi-billion-dollar budget to scrutinize anybody's financial affairs is supposed to keep us all in line and on our toes. There has to be a method to force the unscrupulous to comply with the law. Otherwise, as a former IRS commissioner concedes, the tax system would let the taxpayer "with the least conscience get the best result."

Nobody wants that, of course. But neither should taxpayers be scared into making costly mistakes on their tax return. Excessive worry makes some taxpayers reluctant to claim legitimate deductions. They pass up tax savings rather than risk arousing what they see as a sinister Big Brother. In effect, they try to buy peace of mind by overpaying their taxes. Don't fall into that trap. Don't be frightened into paying more tax than you owe. If you are like the vast majority of Americans, you have nothing to fear from the IRS.

Before you begin pulling together your records, give yourself a pep talk. Attack this annual chore aggressively. Know your tax bracket—it's listed on page 437—so you can put a price tag on each tax write-off you find.

Throughout the record-gathering phase, collect any document that might help reduce your tax bill. It's better to discard later a paper that doesn't translate to tax savings than to overlook one that could shave your bill. At least at this stage, make all close calls in your favor. Be sure to make a note about any missing receipt, canceled check or other item. That way a temporarily misplaced paper won't become a permanently lost deduction.

GETTING HELP:
WRITTEN, COMPUTERIZED OR HUMAN

Considering that federal income taxes take one of the largest bites out of the family budget, it's no wonder that we have an insatiable appetite for help with this annual chore. Such assistance comes in all shapes and at all prices.

Written help. For do-it-yourselfers there's a library of written material. Most visible is the garden of hardy perennial paperback tax-return guides that blooms in the bookstores from around Christmas until April 15. These road maps of the federal forms offer professional guidance at bargain-basement prices.

At ten bucks or so, any of the guides can easily pay for itself. Even if you don't find a money-saving tip, the books will save you time and stave off anxieties about missing tax breaks you deserve.

If you consider buying one of these guides, choose among the field by testing books on a specific tax question. This isn't bedtime reading. The key to a book's value is how easily you can find what you're looking for, how much information is provided and how clearly the book presents it. Check the index for its thoroughness and ease of use.

Before you spend a dime, though, get a copy of the IRS's own entry in this field: *Your Federal Income Tax,* also known as "Publication 17." You might be somewhat skeptical about the publisher's motives, but you can't complain about the price: It's free. You can get a copy by contacting your local IRS office.

Publication 17 is thorough and well organized, has a good index and should answer most of your questions about filling out the forms. Especially helpful is a filled-in, hypothetical tax return. Nearly every line of each form and schedule is keyed to the page in the guide that offers information on the issue at hand.

One drawback is the tone. The commercial tax guides generally come with the exciting promise to steer you to tax breaks and save you money. *Your Federal Income Tax* makes no such pretense. The information is there, but don't expect flashing neon lights to grab your attention. You also have to keep in mind that what you're getting is the official IRS view of the tax law. In most cases, that's all that counts, but on some matters courts have taken a position that is more favorable to taxpayers. If the IRS is sticking with a position despite having been whipped in court by a taxpayer, you won't find any reference to the case in Publication 17, whereas a commercial guide might at least alert you to the conflict.

In addition to Publication 17, the IRS offers a library of booklets focusing on specific tax issues. They are listed in the appendix and are free.

Letting software do the hard part. As your tax return becomes more complex—whether because of changes in the law or new complications in your financial life—you may be drawn more and more to the idea of forsaking do-it-yourself status and turning your return over to a professional preparer. First, though, you may want to consider a middle ground that a growing number of taxpayers find appealing: putting their home computers to work on the IRS forms.

Several tax-preparation programs have been around long enough to have had the bugs worked out. They have kept up with the changing tax law, and most have become both better and cheaper, too. Some fans of this genre of software actually claim it makes doing a tax return fun. That's going too far. But if you enjoy working on your computer, a tax program lets you blend that pleasure with the unpleasant task of tackling your return.

Before you rush out to buy software, recognize what it *can't* do. There's no magic involved. You still have to gather all the information about your income, deductions, credits and so forth. That's the scut work, and it is inescapable whether you do your return with a pencil, use a computer or turn the whole mess over to a professional preparer. GIGO—garbage in, garbage out—applies as much to tax-return programs as anything else.

Nor is computer technology a substitute for thinking or for keeping up with changing tax rules. As the guide for one popular program notes, this software is a labor-saving tool, not a brain substitute. And, when you're imagining the time you'll save, remember that it will take a while to get the hang of the program itself.

Still, the computer can be an amazing accessory for this tedious job. The more you know about the tax law, the better you can imagine how a program can help. The less you know, perhaps the more you stand to benefit from a computer's help.

Did your children reap more than $500 of investment income, for example? If so, returns must be filed for them, and investment income over $1,000 is nipped by the kiddie tax, discussed in Chapter 3. That means an extra form. Most tax software not only reminds you of what's required but also handles the calculations with aplomb.

Do you own rental property? If so, you not only have to report the income or loss on your Form 1040 but also need a Schedule E, plus a Form 4562 to figure your depreciation and a Form 8582 if you show a loss. Some of the programs on the market handle all the necessary calculations based on your input.

Tax programs don't stop at doing your arithmetic and transferring data among related forms—although their facility in those realms removes much of the drudgery from return preparation. If you report self-employment income on Schedule C, for example, the software not only carries it over to the proper line on the Form 1040 but also generates a Schedule SE showing whether you owe any self-employment tax. If so, the program will figure the amount and transfer it to the proper line on the 1040.

In addition to written documentation—which ranges from brief booklets to thick, almost intimidating manuals—different programs offer various levels of on-line assistance to help speed you through your return. At the touch of a key, some programs fill the computer screen with an explanation of the issue at hand.

One of the great virtues of these programs is the ease with which they let you correct mistakes. Almost everyone has had this experience: Just as you're ready to mail your completed return, you discover a receipt that earns you an extra deduction. If you do your return by hand, you may decide to punt—forgo the tax savings rather than redo the arithmetic and start from scratch on all the affected forms. But with a tax program you enter the new deduction and almost instantly your computer does all the recalculations.

By the same token, you can test different strategies easily. You can quickly see how a contribution to an individual retirement account will affect your bottom line, for example, or use the computer to analyze whether you and your spouse would be better off filing separately or using a joint return.

There are different methods for getting your tax information out of the computer and onto paper for the IRS. Except for the Form 1040—for which the IRS is particularly picky—the software will print IRS-acceptable versions of the various forms and schedules. A few programs will even print a 1040 that the IRS will accept. Others have you print directly on a 1040 form, although lining up the paper so the right numbers appear in the proper spaces can be frustrating and time-consuming. Another option is to print the numbers on a blank sheet and photocopy it with a transparent overlay of the Form 1040. Many taxpayers find it easier to simply copy numbers by hand from the computer screen to an IRS-provided form.

As home computers have become more common and the tax law more complex, a growing number of tax-preparation programs has appeared. Prices of popular software range from around $40 to $300 or so. As with all software, choosing the right program is a subjective matter. The program one person swears by may be the one another taxpayer only swears at.

The best way to choose would be to try out several packages. That's not only impractical, but who would want to mess with the tax forms more than once? If you have friends who have used tax programs in the past, ask for advice. Also, watch around year-end for reviews of various programs in newspapers and magazines.

Although it flies in the face of the get-started-early advice, you probably should not buy a tax-preparation program until mid to late January at the earliest. Although some publishers get new versions of their programs into stores by December, those copies are sometimes incomplete—awaiting final IRS revisions of forms required by last-minute tax-law changes. The publisher may offer you an updated disk free, but you might as well wait until you can get the final version for the current tax year.

The cost of tax software can be deductible. It's considered a miscellaneous expense, deductible to the extent that your total write-offs in this category exceed 2% of your adjusted gross income.

Human help. Sometimes books and computers just can't cut it. If you have a question, you want to talk to someone about it. Or perhaps you suffer from that common tax-time malady: form phobia. Or maybe you just don't trust yourself to capture all the tax breaks you deserve. After all, it was Albert Einstein who, after jousting with his tax return, commented: "This is too difficult for a mathematician. It takes a philosopher." Many modern-day taxpayers unabashedly declare that one of their best investments is what they pay someone else to do their tax returns.

There is no doubt that as a nation of taxpayers we are willing to spend a bundle for help figuring how little we can send to the IRS. A study a few years ago estimated the annual bill for tax help at between $3 and $3.4 billion. That's cash out of pocket. Add an estimated value for the two billion or so hours that taxpayers spend doing returns or gathering the records necessary for someone else to do the job and the estimated yearly cost zoomed to the $17 billion to $27 billion range.

And that study was done before the latest round of tax reform introduced so many changes in the name of "tax simplification" that millions of taxpayers gave up trying to do their own returns. If you're looking for help, you have plenty of choices— so many, in fact, that picking the right kind of help can be a major problem in itself.

Before you begin your search, face this inescapable fact: No matter how much you are willing to pay, a lot of the work just can't be done by an outsider. It's up to you to pull together the information that translates into tax savings. Even if you hire someone to ask all the right questions, you have to supply the records that provide the answers. There's no guaranteed correlation between price and perfection, nor does paid help guarantee a lower tax bill. Also, no matter who does your return, the IRS will hold you responsible for its accuracy.

How about the IRS? To some folks, going to the IRS for tax help is akin to donning a cement overcoat for a swim. Although such cynicism is unwarranted, it is true that on close calls the government's employees are likely to rule in the government's favor. (The same goes for some paid preparers, though.) Still, a call to the IRS might produce the answer you need to do your own return. The IRS has offices around the country and operates a toll-free telephone service to respond to taxpayer inquiries.

Although such assistance is free, unfortunately it's far from foolproof. During the 1988 filing season, for example, government investigators posing as taxpayers put the IRS phone service to the test. About 36% of the time, the IRS employees dished out erroneous answers.

If you decide to call the IRS, the earlier in the January-through-April crunch, the better your chances for getting through rather than getting a busy signal. The best days to call are Wednesday, Thursday and Friday. Mondays are worst, apparently because taxpayers who run into trouble over the weekend are on the phone. Also, try to avoid calling around lunchtime, when the lines are particularly busy.

Commercial preparers. Anyone can hang out a shingle declaring himself or herself to be a tax preparer. If that sounds like a warning, it is. There are no federal standards for commercial preparers. In fact, the IRS staunchly opposes any kind of testing or licensing program. However, all paid preparers are covered by rules aimed at rooting out the unscrupulous or incompetent. A preparer can be fined for deliberately or negligently understating a taxpayer's liability. Notice, though, that there is no penalty if the preparer's goof causes you to *overpay* your taxes.

Commercial preparers generally fall in two categories: the independents and those associated with a national firm, such as H&R Block. Block is the nation's single largest tax preparer, with about 8,000 offices opened around the country during the January-through-April filing season. The company handles about ten million individual returns each year. The cost is relatively modest, averaging around $50 for a Form 1040 with itemized deductions and an accompanying state return. Simpler returns cost less, more complicated ones more. Price can range all over the lot with independent preparers.

An advantage of a national firm is that employees—who often work only temporarily during the filing season—are given substantial training in the tax law to keep them up to date with changes. With an independent preparer, training and experience can range from nonexistent to exquisite. Be wary of tax-preparation operations that pop up in the spring and disappear just as quickly in mid April. Some local services offer first-rate help, but others fall in the category dubbed "drugstore cowboys." It's up to you to evaluate the preparer's qualifications.

Can you trust a commercial preparer? You've probably read stories about tests in which someone posing as a taxpayer visits several preparers, provides the same data to all of them and is presented with tax returns with widely disparate bottom lines. The results probably say as much about the complexity of the tax law as the competence of the preparers. Also, preparers have argued that in such tests the "taxpayers" are deliberately reticent—unwilling to volunteer any information that might reduce their tax bill. In the real world, they say, it's the taxpayer's job to help.

Certainly, some commercial preparers are better than others. If you go this route, these tips should help you get the most for your money.

• Go early. One criticism of commercial firms is that they rush taxpayers in and out to build a high-volume operation. If you're part of the last-minute rush, you might be shortchanged.

• Find out how much you'll be charged at the outset for federal and state forms. You don't want any surprises.

• Ask the preparer about qualifications and experience. If you get the feeling you know as much about taxes as the preparer, go elsewhere.

• Be suspicious of a preparer who doesn't ask you a lot of questions. His or her job is to probe into your financial affairs, mixing your answers with knowledge of the tax law to get you all the breaks you have coming.

• When you get your completed return, check it carefully. Be certain all the forms and schedules the preparer discussed with you are included.

Beyond tax-return preparation. If all you want is for someone to figure out what you owe and fill out your forms correctly, a commercial preparer may be just the ticket. Paying higher fees to an accountant or other tax professional might buy you nothing extra except, perhaps, status. Face it: Once you sit down to do your return, it's too late for nearly all of the tax-saving maneuvers a certified public accountant or other tax pro might steer you to.

The real question is whether you need more than tax-return preparation. Depending on your income and the complexity of your financial life, you might benefit handsomely from year-round tax help, with the mechanics of filling out the forms coming as frosting on the cake. That kind of broader assistance is what accountants, enrolled agents and CPAs can offer. (Although some attorneys specialize in federal taxes, few handle actual preparation of tax returns—except as a courtesy to valued clients.)

Even if your tax life has been simple, a tax adviser might come up with some valuable suggestions to complicate things with tax-saving maneuvers. As income increases, so does the importance of the tax angles of financial planning. Many taxpayers prize their tax men and women for knowing how to exploit the gray areas of the tax law. One CPA told *Changing Times* that he sees his mission as steering clients through the "fairyland of confusion" that is the tax law. The destination, of course, is the utopia of a lower tax bill.

Although tax-return time is a lousy time to try to initiate a tax-saving strategy for the previous year, it can be the perfect time to begin a relationship with a tax pro. Doing your return will give him or her a detailed look at where you stand, and once the April 15 rush is past you and your accountant can map out a strategy for the year ahead.

If you decide you want more than simple tax preparation, you'll pay more—perhaps a lot more—than the fees at H&R Block. CPA charges vary widely, with hourly fees ranging from $25 to $250 or more. Accountants with national firms are likely to charge more than smaller, local firms, but it is not at all unusual for a tax return and related services to cost several hundred dollars.

Clearly, you'll be cheating yourself if you pay that kind of

freight for fill-in-the-blanks return preparation. There are choices between commercial preparers and high-powered CPAs: public accountants. Public accountants are likely to be full-time, year-round tax advisers, but they haven't passed the exams or met the experience requirements demanded of CPAs. In most states, public accountants must be licensed, but in some anyone can claim the title.

Also bidding for your tax business are enrolled agents, the only tax practitioners who have to meet IRS standards. The 15,000 or so enrolled agents earned their status by passing a tough IRS exam or by virtue of having experience as an IRS auditor. Public accountants and enrolled agents usually charge less than CPAs, but count on a minimum of $100 and perhaps far more depending on the complexity of your return.

Regardless of what level of help you choose, you have to bare your financial soul to your tax preparer. What's to prevent him or her from blabbing it all over town or—perhaps more threatening—turning over the details to some folks who might try to sell you investments? Preparers are required by law to keep the information confidential. It's against the law to divulge it, except under court order.

Shopping for help. If you decide to seek a tax pro's help, start your search early. By early in the filing season, many firms have all the work they can handle. Since you're after more than return preparation, you should count on investing some time in making the right choice.

Hiring a CPA is a lot like choosing a doctor. You want someone who is smart and with whom you feel comfortable. Start by asking your friends and business associates for recommendations. The most useful references are likely to come from people who are in financial and business situations similar to your own.

Before you sign on with an accountant, take the time to interview him or her. Ask about professional education, including how the accountant keeps up with tax-law changes. Is the firm computerized? Will your financial data go into a computer for quick retrieval to answer a question about the tax ramifications of a potential investment? Ask for a few examples of ideas the accountant has come up with to save other clients money.

Some CPAs wonder whether colleagues who work alone or in small firms can possibly keep up with the growing complexity of the tax law and financial universe. Others dismiss such concerns, saying that because taxpayers so seldom need a true specialist, what's important is to have a CPA who is astute enough to know when other kinds of help are needed and who has access to assistance. Ask the accountant you are considering where he or she turns when stumped.

Because tax planning is probably a key element of what you'll be buying, ask what your accountant offers. Is the firm among those branching out more and more into financial planning? You may also want to ask for copies of transmittal letters that accompanied other clients' completed tax returns last year, so you can review the suggestions that were made. What you're after, of course, is how aggressive the accountant is in offering advice and encouraging you to ask for it.

Be sure to talk fees. Ask for an estimate of what a full year's service is likely to cost, from return preparation through year-end planning.

Shopping for either a public accountant or an enrolled agent is similar to the search for a CPA. Rely on recommendations and interviews. If you consider a public accountant, ask why he or she has not become an enrolled agent with the privilege of representing clients before the IRS. The National Society of Public Accountants encourages all of its members to take the IRS test. You can get a list of enrolled agents in your area by contacting the National Association of Enrolled Agents at 800-424-4339.

If you haven't been referred to the tax pro by a client, ask for the name of one you can call and chat with about the accountant's services. Ask that person about the availability of the accountant, whether work is delivered on time, and for a general impression of the adviser's creativity and financial-planning skills.

If that sounds like a lot of work, remember that the stakes are high. Picking the right kind of help for your taxes is a major financial decision.

THE CONSEQUENCES OF BEING LATE

Everyone knows the deadline for filing tax returns is midnight, April 15—unless that date happens to fall on a Saturday, Sunday or legal holiday, which pushes the deadline to the next business day. If for whatever reason you can't get your tax forms completed, signed and in the mail by the deadline, you can buy extra time. Each year, millions of taxpayers do so, and the number of tardy returns seems to increase with the growing complexity of the tax law.

You can put off the filing deadline by four months—to August 15—by filing Form 4868, *Application for Automatic Extension of Time To File U.S. Individual Income Tax Return.* Note that glorious word "automatic" in that mouthful of IRSese. This is a no-questions-asked deal. You don't have to offer any explanation of why your return will be overdue.

There is, alas, a catch. Although the extension gives your more time to file your return, it doesn't put off the deadline for paying the tax you owe. When you file the form, you must send along a check for any difference between your tax liability for the year and what you've already paid via withholding or estimated tax payments.

Estimating what you owe is what complicates the otherwise simple single-page Form 4868. There's a line for your estimated tax liability—a figure that's tough to come up with unless you've already done most of the work necessary to complete your return. It's important that you estimate accurately, too. Even with the extra time to file your forms, you will be charged interest on any unpaid tax from April 15 on. The IRS interest rate is adjusted each quarter in line with what it costs the government to borrow money. In mid 1988, for example, the rate was 10%. (Any interest you are charged for late payment of your taxes is considered personal interest, the deduction for which is being phased out, as discussed in Chapter 10.)

If you underpay your tax by 10% or more, you'll probably also be hit with a failure-to-pay penalty. It builds up at a monthly rate of ½ of 1% of the amount due. If you owe an extra $1,000 with your return, for example, the penalty would be $5 for each month (or part of a month) you fail to pay up. If you procrasti-

SETTLING WITH UNCLE SAM

nate too long and ignore IRS notices to pay, the penalty can double to 1% of the balance due each month. In no event can this penalty exceed 25% of the tax due, however.

Although that penalty may seem modest, getting an extension lets you avoid a much stiffer one, too: the failure-to-file penalty. If you file neither your return nor a Form 4868 by April 15, this penalty is 5% of the tax due for each month your return is late. A $1,000 balance due on a return three months late, for example, would trigger a $150 penalty.

If your return is more than 60 days late, the failure-to-pay penalty is a minimum of $100 or 100% of the tax due. By accurately estimating and paying your tax with your Form 4868, you avoid interest and both penalties during the extra four months you get to complete your return.

File the request for an extension by April 15 with the IRS service center to which you send your return. When you file your completed return, attach a copy of the Form 4868 and be sure to give yourself credit—in the payments section of the Form 1040—for the amount of tax paid with the Form 4868.

Pushing the filing deadline beyond August 15 is possible, but you need a good reason. You can apply for an extra two months by filing Form 2688, *Application for Additional Extension of Time to File U.S. Individual Income Tax Return.* If it appears you'll need to push the deadline back to October 15, try to file Form 2688 well before August 15. That way, if the IRS turns down your request, you'll have a chance to file on time. If the IRS okays the extra time, you'll get a notice approving the extension. Attach that notice to your return when you finally file.

Or, ignore this advice. It may come as a surprise—and the IRS would just as soon this not become common knowledge—but the vast majority of taxpayers do not really have to file by April 15. Notice in the discussion above that the penalties for failing to meet that deadline are based on the amount of tax you owe with your return. But the vast majority of taxpayers don't owe a dime with their returns. Instead, they get refunds. Hmmmmm. If there is no tax due on which to levy a penalty for late filing, then . . .

That's right: Even without an extension, there is no penalty for missing the April 15 deadline *if* you are due a refund. That piece of knowledge might come in mighty handy if you find yourself scrambling to finish things up in mid April. If you are certain you have a refund coming, you may be able to skip that late-night rush to the post office.

Of course, if you have a refund coming you should be making every possible effort to file early—so you can get your money back—rather than putting things off. Generally, the IRS has to pay interest on refunds that aren't paid to taxpayers by June 1. That rule doesn't apply if you file your return late, though. If the IRS pays the refund within 45 days of the time you file, you get no interest.

(Most states also have provisions for extending their income-tax-filing deadlines. If you're going to be late, be sure to check with state tax officials for specific requirements.)

IF YOU GOOF ON YOUR RETURN

Confession, so they say, is good for the soul. It can also pay off for the pocketbook if you're admitting to the IRS that you made a mistake on your tax return. Although blowing the whistle on yourself might sound like unsound tax strategy, tens of thousands of taxpayers who do it each year are rewarded with refunds. Why? Because they correct errors that caused them to overpay their tax with the original return.

The amended tax return, filed on Form 1040X, can be a handy weapon in your tax arsenal. With it you can apply newly discovered tax-saving knowledge to returns filed in previous years. That means a once neglected tax advantage isn't irretrievably lost.

You might need to file a 1040X, for example, if you discover you failed to claim a dependency exemption you deserved, overlooked an itemized deduction or credit, or reported too much income due to an erroneous K-1 income report from a partnership.

Of course, the 1040X wasn't designed as a one-way street. You're supposed to use it to correct any errors or oversights that resulted in paying less than you really owed in an earlier tax year.

You generally have three years from the due date of a return to file an amended version, although the period can stretch to seven years if the revision involves a bad debt or worthless security. The three-year limit means, for example, that 1988 returns, due April 15, 1989, are usually open for amendment until April 15, 1992.

But is it risky to file a 1040X? If you use one to ask for an extra refund, are you begging for an audit, too? The IRS says the answer is no. Although that's what you might expect to hear from the tax agency, there's no reason to believe a 1040X marks your original return for audit. An accountant who has filed several hundred amended returns for clients told *Changing Times* that not a single one has ever triggered an audit.

If your amended return shows that you owe more tax for the year involved, send a check along with the form. The IRS will bill you for the interest due. If the mistake you correct results in the government owing you money, you can expect a refund check in two to three months.

You can get a copy of the 1040X and the instructions for filing it from your local IRS office. Send the completed form to the IRS Service Center for the area where you now live, even if the return you are correcting was filed to a different center. Be sure to note on the 1040X the year of the return you are amending. And remember that any change on your federal return might require revisions on your state income tax forms, too.

WHEN THE IRS SAYS "PROVE IT!"

The odds are reassuring. Of more than 100 million individual tax returns filed each year, the IRS audits just over 1 million. That's a one-hundred-to-one shot against the IRS demanding that you back up what you put down on your forms. Still, more than 1 million Americans each year win (or should we say lose) the audit lottery.

If you are part of that unfortunate band, why were you

singled out and what's in store?

Most of the returns selected for audit are chosen as the result of computer analysis. The IRS plugs the data from your return into a computer that scrutinizes the numbers every which way and ponders how the picture you paint of your financial life jibes with what it knows about other taxpayers. The computer tries to spot the returns that are most likely to produce extra income if put through the audit wringer. The computer's choices are reviewed by a human being who can overrule them if, for example, an attachment to your return satisfactorily explains the entry that set the computer all atwitter. Short of such a veto, your name will go on the list.

Even if your return survives the computer's scrutiny, you're not necessarily safe. You may have listed an investment in a tax shelter the IRS is particularly interested in, for example, or the agency might decide to take a closer look at your return because it is auditing the forms sent in by a business associate. And there's always the chance that someone has fingered you as a tax cheat. The IRS encourages such tips and even pays a bounty on those that pay off in extra tax. Or you could be the prey of the random Taxpayer Compliance Measurement Program (TCMP). That's how the IRS gets the data on the overall taxpayer universe that serves as the computer's frame of reference for selecting returns that are the best audit targets. If you are chosen for a TCMP audit, you'll be asked to verify *everything* on your return.

Don't panic. Whatever the reason, it's chilling to get the word that the IRS wants to examine your return. After all, everyone remembers that the IRS was able to do what J. Edgar Hoover and all the G-men of the FBI couldn't do: put Al Capone behind bars. Even if you have no reason to think you did anything wrong, you can't escape the anxiety that accompanies an audit notice. For one thing, the return being audited is likely to be the one you filed at least six months and perhaps 1½ years earlier. Where are the records?

Still, it's important not to panic. On the bright side, the odds of walking out of the audit with an extra tax *refund* are actually far better than the odds of your being picked for the audit in the first place. Compared to the 1% chance of an audit, the latest IRS statistics show that about 5% of all exams end with the conclusion that the taxpayer paid too much tax rather than too little. There's even a better chance—around 15%—that the government will concede that your return was accurate.

Despite such encouraging statistics, the bottom line is that most folks called in for an audit come out poorer. And even if you escape without owing an extra dime in tax, the time, hassle and stress involved are indisputably costly.

You'll get a letter announcing your fate. The simplest audit— a correspondence audit—requires only that you mail in the records needed to verify a specified claim on your return. In a field audit, an IRS agent comes to your home or place of business to go over your records. Most common, though, are office audits, which involve getting yourself and your papers to a local IRS office.

The written notice will identify the items on your return that are being questioned—usually such broad categories as employee business expenses or casualty losses—and outline the types of records you'll need to clear up the matter. Office audits are usually limited to two or three issues, so you won't be expected to haul in all your records.

You'll probably have at least a couple of weeks to prepare. If the appointment is set for an inconvenient time or you find that you'll need extra time to get your records together, call the IRS promptly to request that the audit be rescheduled.

First, audit yourself. The best way to begin preparing for your meeting is to pull out your copy of the return being audited. (If, as luck would have it, you can't find the return, call the IRS office that contacted you and ask for details on how to get a copy.) Before the IRS puts your forms through the wringer, do the job yourself. Pore over the items being questioned and pull together the documents that support your entries.

Of course there will be gaps, but don't automatically concede defeat. Try to reconstruct missing records. Get copies of canceled checks from the bank or duplicates of receipts or written statements from individuals who can back up your claims. Where you can't come up with written evidence, prepare your oral explanation.

Your records don't have to be perfect. If you have a reasonable explanation for how you came up with a figure that's not fully corroborated by the evidence, the IRS may well accept it. The IRS likes to stress how *reasonable* audit personnel are. The agency's official manual for auditors notes, for example, that on some issues oral statements may be acceptable. "Adequate evidence," the manual says, "does not require complete documentation." However, when you're pulling together your records, remember this: The more thorough your documentation is in general, the more likely an auditor will cut you some slack on an occasional point.

Do you need help? You don't have to go to the audit at all. You can avoid it by hiring someone to go in your place. Such a representative must have written authorization to act for you, and the IRS provides a power-of-attorney form—Form 2848—for this purpose. Whether you go alone or hire a representative to go with you or in your place depends primarily on the issues involved. If they are relatively simple, cut-and-dried matters, you may be able to settle things without help. When matters are more technical or require interpretation of the law, however, it's more likely you'll need assistance. You have to make this judgment, and it will turn in part on how you feel about going head to head with the IRS. If you are scared, by all means get someone to go with your or in your place.

If someone else prepared your return, let him or her know about the audit and ask for tips on how to get ready for it. Whether or not you want this person to go along may depend on how much it will cost you. Although the IRS prefers to wrap up cases with a single meeting, if you don't agree with the auditor's conclusions or need time to round up extra evidence, a follow-up meeting can be scheduled. Unless you fear you might capitulate if you go to the audit alone, your best bet is probably to settle as many issues as you can by yourself.

If disagreements remain and the amount of money at stake justifies the expense, you can take an adviser along to the next session. That way you'll have help when you really need it but won't have to pay for hand-holding while you clear up routine matters. Remember that if you pay your pro by the hour, the meter will be running while he or she travels to and from the audit and while you're cooling your heels waiting your turn, as well as during the time spent with the IRS agent.

The big day. The key to success is being well prepared. Forget the old slapstick routine of dumping a box of canceled checks and ratty receipts on the auditor's desk. That suggests your records are sloppy, and that's the last impression you want to give. Remember it's up to you to back up the information on your return.

The better organized your records, the more smoothly things will go. Try to develop credibility right from the start. Say, for example, that the audit notice announces that your interest deductions, charitable contributions and travel and entertainment write-offs will be reviewed. If you are solid on interest and contributions but a little shaky on T&E, try to steer the audit to your strongest suits first. If you establish credibility early on, there's a better chance a gap later may be overlooked.

"Oh, by the way, the IRS called . . . they're running an audit on you!"

Don't go into the session looking for a fight. Being cooperative doesn't mean giving in whenever the auditor raises an eyebrow, though. If the agent tells you your records don't substantiate a deduction, for example, ask what might suffice. Perhaps you can mail it in later.

Be on your guard against chatting your way into a problem. Keep in mind that the agent is trained to zero in on tax issues. A comment you consider totally unrelated to your return might lead you into a thicket. Defending a deduction by saying you've taken it in the past, for example, could prompt a review of previously filed returns; discussing the family's cross-country driving vacation might lead the agent to recalculate the business/personal ratio of your car's use; or bemoaning the problems that led a child to drop out of college could cost you a dependency exception.

Above all, keep your wits about you. Don't be pressured into settling an issue just to bring the audit to an end. Although the IRS argues strenuously that agents aren't judged on how much extra money their audits produce, the fact is that one of the best guides to an agent's efficiency is the amount of additional tax he or she generates without going through all the formal assessment procedures or litigation.

There may be room for compromise on the issue at hand. It may save time and money all around to agree on some in-between point or even for one side to give up on one disputed item in order to win on another.

The audit will last from 20 minutes or so to two hours or longer. You'll spend a lot of that time watching the agent crunch numbers. When it's over, you'll get the auditor's decision—which in most cases is that you owe more tax. Each proposed change to your return and the reason for it should be explained.

If you agree, fine. But remember that the auditor doesn't have the final say. Often, in fact, auditors make mistakes that cost taxpayers money. If you disagree with a finding, tell the auditor so and restate your position. He or she may be willing to compromise to close the case promptly.

Battling the IRS. If you and the auditor come to an agreement, you'll be asked to sign a form saying so. Within a few weeks you'll get a bill for the extra tax, plus interest and any penalty. Most audits end this way.

But if you can't come to a meeting of the minds, tell the agent so and go home. You'll receive a report explaining the proposed adjustments to your return. At this point, in the less-heated environment of your own home, you might decide it's not worth the time or trouble to carry on your dispute. If so, you can simply agree to pay the bill.

You have several options if you decide to fight on, and at this point you may want to seek professional help. You can ask for another meeting with the auditor to present additional evidence, for example, or you can make an informal appeal to the auditor's boss. If you're still unhappy, you can go to the IRS regional appeal level. At any point, you can take your case to court.

If you want to appeal within the IRS, you have 30 days after you receive the audit report to request a conference. After that, you'll probably have at least a couple of months to prepare. Regional appeals are handled informally, and IRS statistics indicate that taxpayers who appeal do very well. Don't assume that means an appeal guarantees a better deal. One important factor behind the favorable statistics is that generally only taxpayers with strong cases take their cases to this level.

If you are still dissatisfied after an appeal, your only choice is to go to court. Most tax disputes are settled in the U.S. Tax Court, although you can also take your case to the U.S. District Court for your area or the U.S. Claims Court in Washington, D.C. One important difference is that you can go to the Tax Court before paying the disputed amount of tax; otherwise you must pay the tax and go to court for a refund of what you think you were overcharged.

The Tax Court, which hears cases at sites around the country, has a special procedure for cases in which the disputed amount is $10,000 or less. With relatively informal procedures, you can represent yourself in a small tax case. However, unlike regular Tax Court cases and those heard by other courts, decisions by the small-claims division can't be appealed.

If you wind up going to court and winning, there's a chance that the government will pay your legal fees. To be reimbursed for your costs, you must "substantially prevail" in court and be able to show that the rejected IRS position was unreasonable. You must also have tried to settle the matter within the IRS before resorting to court. When toting up the costs to be reimbursed, attorney's fees are usually limited to $75 an hour.

Repetitive audits. What if the IRS computer decides to pick on you year after year, its suspicions aroused by the same item? Believe it or not, the IRS has a procedure to short-circuit repetitive audits of same taxpayer on the same issues. If you receive an audit notice that targets the same items that were examined in either of the two previous years—and that audit resulted in little or no change in your tax liability—call the IRS office that sent you the notice. There's no guarantee that you'll escape the new audit. But it will be suspended while the IRS considers whether there's any reason to believe the audit results are likely to be different this time around. If not, you may be spared.

RECORD KEEPING

Nothing can convince you of the importance of good records quicker, or more unequivocally, than an audit notice. Unfortunately, at that point, the revelation is of little help. When you are called before an auditor, a missing receipt—something you may have tossed away as a meaningless scrap of paper—can cost you dearly.

What do you need to keep, and for how long, to avoid that unhappy fate?

It's simple: Keep whatever you need to persuade the IRS that everything on your return is accurate. And hang on to the evidence for as long as the IRS has the right to question your return.

Your record-keeping system doesn't have to be elaborate or sophisticated. What is important is to have a system and the discipline to keep your files up to date. The better organized you are, the easier it will be to put your hands on the information you need to complete your return. Your tax forms themselves can serve as an outline for what you need.

Set up files for your itemized deductions: medical, taxes, interest, etc. Save any bills, receipts and canceled checks that correspond to those deductions. If you write off the cost of a business car, you'll need a logbook recording your trips as well as evidence of the costs you incur. If you have rental property, you need another folder for all income and expenses. Do you claim someone as a dependent who is not your child? If so, keep a separate file for the evidence that you provide more than half of the person's support. Homeowners need a file for the house to keep track of additions to the basis that will affect the profit when they ultimately sell the place. Thanks to the new rules on the deductibility of interest (see Chapter 10) you also need to keep careful records of your loans and how the borrowed money was spent.

Investors face special demands. You need to hang on to the documents that show what you paid for every investment—whether it's mutual fund shares, stock purchased from a broker, a dividend-reinvestment plan, real estate or whatever. It's easy to show on your return how much you got when you sold an asset. You'll need good records to establish your basis and, from it, your taxable gain or loss.

You get the idea.

But how long do you have to save all this stuff? That depends on what's involved.

The general rule is to keep your tax records until the statute of limitations on your tax return has expired. In most cases, that's three years after the due date of a return. Your return for 1988 is due April 17, 1989, so the basic period for auditing it ends April 17, 1992. If you haven't been alerted to an audit by then, you're probably safe to toss most of the records.

In some cases, though, the IRS gets six years to come after you. The extended jeopardy applies if you fail to report income that is 25% or more of the amount of gross income you do report. And if you fail to file a return or the IRS can prove that you committed fraud, there's no limit on when the IRS can audit you.

The basic three-year rule is somewhat misleading, though, because items on one return often carry over to future years. If one of those subsequent returns is questioned, you may need records substantiating your claim on the original one.

• A return reporting the sale of one home and the purchase of another—where the profit from the first home is rolled over into the second, as discussed in Chapter 4—should be kept indefinitely, along with the pertinent documents.

• If you make nondeductible contributions to an individual retirement account and file Form 8606, as discussed in Chapter 7, you need to keep that form and related information from your IRA sponsor until all funds are withdrawn from that IRA.

• If one year's return includes losses you can't deduct because of the passive-loss rules—discussed in Chapter 5—hang on to the return and associated records until after you dispose of the passive activity and get to use the loss. Then you should keep the records for another three years, until the statute of limitations on the return reporting the loss has expired.

• Unused losses from home-office expenses can also be carried forward, so you need to keep the records substantiating them until after the loss has been used.

When you're cleaning out your tax files, err on the side of caution—particularly when it comes to your investments.

What about your tax forms themselves? Six years is probably long enough to hang on to them—except those that have a bearing on future returns. That's as long as the IRS keeps its copies of your returns.

15

OTHER TAXES TO CONSIDER

Self-Employment Tax, Employment Taxes for Household Workers, Medicare Tax and Alternative Minimum Tax

For millions of Americans, the income tax isn't the only federal tax that demands attention. The next chapter discusses estate and gift taxes. Here we focus on several other levies, including one that applies for the first time in 1989.

SELF-EMPLOYMENT TAX

How would you like to send an extra 13.02% of your income off to Uncle Sam?

That's what you could owe in social security tax if you earned self-employment income. It doesn't matter whether the earnings come from a full-time business, say, or occasional moonlighting. If that net income is $400 or more, say hello to the self-employment tax.

Employees don't have to worry about this levy because their employers are required to withhold social security tax from their wages. When you are your own employer, however, you have to figure and pay this tax yourself.

Unlike the income tax, there is a limit on how much income is vulnerable to the self-employment tax. For 1988, the cap is

$45,000. That figure includes self-employment income and wages you earn on a job on which social security taxes are withheld. An employee who earns $40,000 from which the tax is withheld, for example, would owe the 13.02% tax on no more than $5,000 of self-employment income. If you earn more than $45,000 of wages subject to withholding, you don't owe any extra social security tax—regardless of how much self-employment income you might have. (Both the $45,000 cap and the 13.02% rate will increase in the future.)

What income is subject to this tax? Basically it applies to the net income you report on Schedule C, *Profit (or Loss) From Business or Profession.* If you are a member of a partnership that carries on a trade or business, your share of partnership income counts as self-employment income, too, and any losses reduce the income subject to the tax. But if you're an investor in a limited partnership, your share of income and losses don't come into play for purposes of the self-employment tax.

This tax does *not* apply to investment income, such as interest, dividends or capital gains, or to rental income (unless you are a real estate dealer or you provide hotel-like services in connection with the rental).

When you owe the tax, figuring your bill is easy. Just multiply the amount of income subject to the tax by the tax rate. If you have $20,000 of self-employment income in 1988, for example, the tax would be $2,604 ($20,000 × 13.02%). You use Schedule SE, *Computation of Social Security Self-Employment Tax,* and attach the form to and pay the tax with your income tax return. As discussed in Chapter 13, this tax must be taken into account when figuring quarterly estimated tax payments.

When you work on the Schedule SE, you'll notice a discussion of optional methods for figuring the tax due. It's doubtful that you'll want to spend any time trying to see if an alternative technique can save you money. The options are available only to those with minimal net self-employment income—less than $1,600 in one case—and are designed to permit individuals to pay *extra* self-employment tax. The point is that by doing so a taxpayer may be able to increase the income base used to set his or her social security benefits.

EMPLOYMENT TAXES FOR
HOUSEHOLD WORKERS

If you hire someone to work in your home—as a housekeeper, for example, or to provide child care—chances are you are an employer in the eyes of the IRS. That means more work and more cost is involved in settling with Uncle Sam.

You are caught up in these rules if you pay a household employee $50 or more during any calendar quarter. Anyone who works regularly in your home is probably considered your employee, too, unless he or she is assigned by an agency that is considered the legal employer. Your domestic help doesn't have to be full-time to trigger a employer/employee relationship. A maid who works in your home once a month, for example, could easily qualify as your employee under these rules. (An exception lets you ignore employment taxes if the employee is your parent, except in rare circumstances involving a mentally or physically handicapped child in the home.)

What are your responsibilities as an employer?

Social security. First, if you pay cash wages of more than $50 in a quarter, you are liable for social security taxes. You don't put off the bill until April 15, either. The tax must be paid quarterly.

You and the employee share this burden. The 1988 tax rate of 15.02% is split evenly between you and your employee. You each owe 7.51%. As with the self-employment tax discussed in the previous section, the social security tax applies to the first $45,000 of wages.

The tax applies only to cash wages. The value of food, lodging or other noncash benefits—which may count as income to the employee for income tax purposes—is not clipped by the social security tax.

Although the tax is divided between you and your employee, it's up to you to see that the government gets the money. You can either withhold 7.51% of your employee's wages for this tax or pay the full 15.02% yourself. If you do pay the employee's share, that amount is considered extra taxable income to the employee.

For example, assume that you pay a child-care provider

$5,000 during the year, and rather than withhold social security taxes you pay the full tax yourself. The 7.51% employee share would be $375.50, so as far as the IRS is concerned your employee earned $5,375.50.

However you decide to handle this point, you report and pay the social security taxes quarterly with Form 942, *Employer's Quarterly Tax Return for Household Employees*. Call the IRS to get a copy. The first time you file, you may not have the employer identification number that's requested. Don't worry. Just write "none" in the space provided for the number and the IRS will assign one to you. Once you file, the IRS will send you a Form 942 preprinted with your name, address and employer ID number for each subsequent quarter.

The due date for filing is the end of the month following the end of the calendar quarter for which social security taxes are being paid. The Form 942 for wages paid in January, February and March, for example, is due by April 30.

Income tax withholding. You don't have to withhold income

"I THINK THAT'S GOOD... IT MEANS TWO-THIRDS OF OUR GUESSES ABOUT THE NEW TAX FORMS ARE RIGHT!"

© 1988 STAYSKAL—TAMPA TRIBUNE

tax from your employee's wages, but you can if the employee requests it. Although that might sound like a hassle to be avoided, it's not that much trouble considering that you're already required to file Form 942. Income tax withholding is reported and paid with the same form.

If you decide to withhold, you'll need to get a completed W-4 form, *Employee's Withholding Allowance Certificate,* from your employee. You'll also need a copy of IRS Publication 15, *Circular E, Employer's Tax Guide,* which explains how to figure the amount withheld based on the employee's income and the information on the W-4.

Note that the amount on which you withhold income tax may be different than the amount subject to the social security tax. For income tax purposes, you generally must count the value of food, lodging, clothing or other noncash items provided to an employee, as well as cash wages paid. However, the value of food and lodging provided in your home and for your convenience is not considered income. This exception generally exempts from the income tax the value of food and lodging provided to a household employee who lives in your home.

W-2 forms. As an employer, you also have the responsibility to give your employee a W-2 form showing compensation paid during the year and how much tax was withheld. Since you have filed Form 942, the IRS knows you are an employer and will send you the forms you need. By February 1, you are required to give a completed W-2 to your employee for the previous year. Copies of the form must be filed with the Social Security Administration by the end of February.

Federal unemployment tax (FUTA). This is yet another tax you may face if you hire household help. FUTA pays for your employee's unemployment insurance. As the employer, you are subject to the tax if you paid wages of $1,000 or more in any calendar quarter during the current or preceding year. Note that paying less than $1,000 during a quarter does not necessarily exempt you from FUTA on those wages. It still applies if you paid wages of $1,000 or more during a different quarter of the current or previous year.

The FUTA tax is 6.2% of the first $7,000 of cash wages paid

during the calendar year. (It does not apply, however, to wages paid to your spouse, parents or children under age 21.) Unlike the social security tax, this levy must be paid entirely by the employer. You can't withhold part of it from your employee.

The federal tax is reduced by the amount of state unemployment tax you are required to pay on your employee's wages. When you hire a household employee, contact your state's employment-tax office for information on paying the state's tax and getting the reporting number you need to get credit for the state tax paid.

You report and pay FUTA tax on Form 940, *Employer's Annual Federal Unemployment (FUTA) Tax Return.* The IRS should send you a copy of the form sometime in December. It's due by the following January 31. If you owe more than $100 in FUTA tax for any one quarter, however, you must make quarterly payments.

MEDICARE TAX

This is the new tax that applies for the first time in 1989. It's basically a surtax on anyone eligible for Part A (hospital benefits) of medicare. Generally, that means taxpayers age 65 and older who qualify for social security benefits. You'll be clipped by this tax for the first time in the first year you qualify for medicare for more than six months. If your 65th birthday falls after June 30, for example, you will not fall subject to this tax until the following year.

Euphemistically known as a "supplemental premium," the tax is designed to help pay for the expansion of medicare to provide protection against catastrophic medical expenses. Here's how it works:

The surtax does not apply at all if your federal income-tax bill for the year is under $150. (However, to owe so little to escape the surtax, your taxable income would have to be under $1,000.) Once you arrive at the $150 threshold, a 15% surtax applies to claim an extra $22.50 for every $150 in tax. If your income tax bill for the year is $600, for example, the medicare tax would be $90.

Although Congress concocted the $22.50-per-$150 formula, it's doubtful that the surtax will jump in $22.50 increments. When this book went to press, the IRS had not decided exactly how to handle things. However, tables will be published showing the applicable medicare tax based on the income tax you owe—similar to the tables that now show the income tax due for taxable income in $50 increments.

The 15% surtax applies only for 1989. After that it goes up according to this schedule:

Year	Medicare Tax Per $150 of Income Tax	Medicare Tax as % of Income Tax
1989	$22.50	15%
1990	37.50	25
1991	39.00	26
1992	40.50	27
1993	42.00	28

There is a annual limit on this tax. For 1989, the medicare tax will claim no more than $800 from a single taxpayer or $1,600 from a couple filing a joint return—assuming each spouse is age 65 or older and eligible for medicare. For 1989, the maximum will be paid by singles with taxable income of $27,500 or more and by couples with taxable income of $52,000 or more. The top tax will rise in the future, too.

Year	Maximum Medicare Tax	
	Single	Couples
1989	$ 800	$1,600
1990	850	1,700
1991	900	1,800
1992	950	1,900
1993	1,050	2,100

If you file a joint return and only one spouse is subject to this tax—because your husband or wife does not qualify for medicare—the surtax is based on one-half of the tax liability shown on the return. (Special rules apply to make it disadvantageous for couples to try to skirt the surtax by choosing married-filing-separately status.)

If you are subject to this tax, it effectively hikes your tax bracket until you hit the surtax ceiling. The higher rate must be taken into account when figuring the after-tax return of investments, say, or the tax-saving power of deductible expenses. If you are in the 28% tax bracket (see the tax tables on page 437) your tax rate for 1989 is really 32.2% if you are hit by the 15% surtax. In 1993, when the surtax is 28%, a taxpayer in the 28% bracket will be hit by an effective tax rate of 35.8%.

THE ALTERNATIVE MINIMUM TAX

It is sometimes said that AMT stands for *A Magic Tax* because taxpayers who think they have done a great job whittling down their tax bill are sometimes astonished to see their savings disappear when the IRS pulls a new set of rules out of a hat. Really, AMT is the acronym for the alternative minimum tax, a levy that grew out of congressional embarrassment over reports that numerous millionaires were playing the tax game so shrewdly that they could pull their tax bills down to $0.

The point of the AMT is to insure that taxpayers with substantial income pay at least a reasonable amount of income tax. To accomplish that, Congress created what amounts to a separate tax system, lurking in the shadows and ready to spring into action if you benefit too much from tax breaks offered by the regular tax rules.

Unfortunately, there's no easy answer to the question of who needs to be concerned about the AMT. Clearly, though, it is not reserved solely for millionaires. Although folks with high incomes generally are most vulnerable, taxpayers with relatively modest incomes can be tripped up by the AMT.

A couple of things are certain. First, if you are subject to the AMT, you are almost sure to need professional help with your tax return. The rules here are so complex that they make other parts of the tax law seem crystal clear. Second, the AMT throws a major-league curve at traditional year-end tax planning.

To know whether you have anything to worry about, you have to do your tax return twice: first applying the regular rules, then recalculating everything for the AMT. Things are rigged against you, too: You're stuck with whichever method produces the *bigger* bill.

The AMT tax rate is a flat 21%, well below the top 33% rate of the regular tax. How can a lower rate produce a higher tax bill? That's the key to the AMT: It applies to more income than the regular tax. Many of the deductions and other tax breaks that are perfectly proper for holding down regular taxable income aren't permitted by the AMT.

Figuring AMT income. The first step toward determining whether you fall victim to the AMT is to pinpoint your AMT income (AMTI). The starting point is your regular taxable income. Not surprisingly, almost all the adjustments demanded by the AMT increase that amount. The most likely to affect you:

Personal exemptions. They aren't permitted to reduce AMT income. Since they pulled down your regular taxable income, you must add back the amount of those reductions.

Itemized deductions. Many of the write-offs that reduce regular taxable income don't count for AMT purposes. Add back deductions claimed for the following:

• State or local taxes.

• Miscellaneous itemized deductions subject to the 2% floor.

• Medical expenses not in excess of 10% of adjusted gross income. (The threshold for regular tax purposes is 7.5%).

• Personal interest deducted under the phaseout rules of the regular tax. (Although 40% of such interest is deductible in 1988 under the regular tax, for example, 0% is deductible for AMT purposes).

• Investment interest in excess of investment income. (Again, although the regular tax is phasing out the allowance for excess investment interest, the AMT permits no excess interest to be written off).

• Certain mortgage interest. Under the regular tax, you can use a home-equity loan to skirt the law's crackdown on the deduction of personal interest—as discussed in Chapter 4. For the

AMT, however, only interest on loans used to buy, build or substantially improve your first or second home can be deducted. If you deducted any interest on home-equity loans used for nonhome purposes—such as to buy a car or pay college tuition—you must add that amount to your AMTI. Also, if your regular mortgage deduction included an amount on a loan used to buy a boat, that amount doesn't count for AMT purposes. A boat can't qualify as a first or second home under the AMT.

Charitable contributions. As discussed in Chapter 10, gifts of appreciated property can earn you a deduction for the full market value of the property while letting you avoid the tax on the gain that would be due if you sold the property. That's how the regular tax works. For AMT purposes, that untaxed appreciation is a "preference" item to be included in AMTI.

Depreciation. The AMT has its own set of depreciation rules, which generally result in smaller write-offs than the deductions you get under the regular tax. To the extent that regular depreciation exceeds what you are allowed under the AMT, you have another add-on to your AMT income. It's possible, however, that the special depreciation rules will reduce AMTI. That happens if you deserve a bigger write-off using the AMT approach than you do by following the regular tax rules.

For example, residential real estate put in service after 1986 is depreciated over 27.5 years for the regular tax but over 40 years for the AMT. If you are depreciating a $500,000 building, annual write-offs for the regular tax would be $18,182 ($500,000 ÷ 27.5) but just $12,500 ($500,000 ÷ 40) under the AMT. You'd have to add the $5,682 difference to your regular taxable income when toting up your AMTI. If you still own the building after 28 years, it would be fully depreciated for regular tax purposes, but you'd still have a dozen years' worth of $12,500 annual depreciation write-offs under the AMT. In those years, you'd get to subtract that $12,500 from regular taxable income when calculating your AMTI.

These rules promise to greatly complicate your record keeping. The different depreciation schedules mean your adjusted basis in the property (basically, that's cost minus depreciation) will be different for AMT versus regular tax purposes. That, in turn, will affect your gain or loss when you sell. If you are subject to the AMT, you'll have to keep separate sets of books tracing the tax basis of the property under each system.

Incentive stock options. Here's an AMT preference item that doesn't show up at all on the regular tax return. When you exercise an incentive stock option, you get to buy shares for less than current market value. The bargain element is ignored by the regular tax, but it is considered part of your AMT income. Include in AMTI the difference between what you paid for the shares and their market value when you exercised the option to buy.

In the year you sell the stock, however, you'll get to reduce AMTI by the same amount. That's because your shares have a different basis for regular and AMT purposes. Since you don't report the bargain element as income under the regular tax, your basis in the shares is what you pay for them. Under the AMT, however, your basis is what you paid plus the amount you had to report as an AMT preference item. The higher basis means you have a smaller taxable profit—for AMT purposes—when you sell. The larger profit is included in regular taxable income, so you subtract the difference when calculating AMT income.

Passive losses. This item may push a lot of taxpayers into the AMT. As discussed in Chapter 5, for regular tax purposes you can deduct losses from a passive activity, such as a limited partnership, only if you have income from passive activities to offset. Under a transition rule, however, a portion of otherwise nondeductible losses can be deducted until 1991. For 1988, for example, 40% of those losses can be deducted against other types of income, such as your salary or investment income. It's 20% in 1989 and 10% in 1990. But there's no such break under the AMT. Taxpayers who reduce regular taxable income with passive-loss deductions during the transition years may find themselves hit by the AMT because those deductions have to be added back when figuring AMTI.

Tax-exempt interest. Thanks to the AMT, there's such a thing as taxable tax-free interest. Tax-exempt interest on certain "private activity bonds" issued after August 7, 1986, is a preference item to be added to AMTI. Interest on such bonds—basically those issued by states or municipalities for nongovernmental purposes—is still tax-free under the regular tax. The issuer, or the broker trying to sell you the bonds, should be able to tell you whether interest is threatened by the AMT.

Excess depletion and intangible drilling costs. These can also be considered AMT preference items for investors in oil and gas operations.

The AMT exemption. Once you arrive at your bloated AMT income figure, you get to subtract an exemption amount based on your filing status: $40,000 if you are married filing jointly or a surviving spouse; $30,000 if you are single or a head of household; $20,000 if you're married filing a separate return.

The exemption is phased out, however, for taxpayers whose AMTI exceeds certain levels. It begins to disappear when AMTI hits $150,000 for taxpayers filing joint returns, $112,500 on individual returns, and $75,000 if you're married filing separately. For every $100 of excess income, the exemption shrinks by $25 until it is completely phased out at the income levels shown in this table:

Filing Status	Exemption Amount	Phaseout Begins	Exemption Wiped Out
Married/joint	$40,000	$150,000	$310,000
Single	30,000	112,500	232,500
Married/separate	20,000	75,000	155,000

The phaseout has the effect of creating a second—and higher—AMT rate, similar to the "phantom" 33% bracket for the regular income tax, discussed in Chapter 1. AMT income that falls in the phaseout range is effectively hit by a 26.25% tax rate. Here's why: Each dollar within the range wipes out 25 cents of the exemption, so you wind up being taxed on an extra $1.25. The 26.25% rate is 125% of the stated 21% AMT levy.

After you subtract your exemption amount from your AMTI, multiply the result by 21%.

The only tax credit available for AMT purposes is the foreign tax credit. If you claimed that credit on your regular tax return, you can use it here, too (although it can't offset more than 90% of your AMT bill). The result is your *tentative* minimum tax.

Compare that amount to your regular tax bill. If the minimum tax is higher, the difference between the two is actually your alternative minimum tax. You pay it in addition to your regular tax.

The AMT credit. Ready for more confusion? Part, if not all, of the extra tax you are forced to pay by the AMT may be refunded to you in the future via an AMT credit to offset your regular tax liability.

This surprising generosity stems from the fact that the AMT attacks two different kinds of tax benefits: those that defer your tax liability, such as accelerated depreciation and the bargain element of incentive stock options, and those that wipe out part of your tax bill completely, such as itemized deductions and the untaxed appreciation of charitable gifts.

The AMT credit is Congress's way of refunding to you in a later year the amount attributable to the "timing preferences," that is, the tax the AMT forces you to pay sooner rather than later.

Figuring the credit requires yet another set of calculations. After you know how much alternative minimum tax you owe, find what the bill would be if the only add-ons to regular taxable income were from these four preferences: disallowed itemized deductions, untaxed appreciation of charitable gifts, depletion allowances and tax-exempt income from private-purpose bonds. These are the breaks that permit the permanent avoidance of the regular tax and therefore don't count toward the credit.

The difference between the AMT figured this way and the amount you actually have to pay is your minimum tax credit.

Say, for example, that your regular tax is $10,000 and the AMT calculation delivers a $14,000 bill. Assume the entire difference is attributable to your inclusion in AMT income of the bargain element of incentive stock options you exercised—a timing preference. In this case, the full $4,000 alternative minimum tax becomes an AMT credit for the future.

There is a catch, however. The AMT credit can be used only in a year you are subject to the regular tax. If you find yourself facing the AMT year after year, the credit will be of no use. Also, no part of the credit can be used to pull your regular tax liability below the AMT liability in a future year. Remember that reducing the regular tax bill below the AMT obligation would toss you back into the AMT quagmire. Any unused part of the AMT credit can be carried forward to future years, however, when you have regular tax to offset.

Alternate strategies. Before the introduction of the AMT credit—first available in 1988—year-end planning for the alternative minimum tax was relatively straightforward. Conventional wisdom called for standing the standard year-end strategy on its head. Rather than accelerating deductible expenses, for example, you would have wanted to push them into the future. Not only would that have preserved the tax-saving power of

© 1988 CARLSON—MILWAUKEE SENTINEL

itemized deductions ignored by the AMT—such as state and local taxes—but even write-offs that counted for AMT would have been worth more when you were subject to a 28% or 33% regular tax rate than in a year you were hit by the 21% AMT.

On the other side of the coin, the AMT encouraged accelerating income rather than putting it off. After all, a $100,000 capital gain realized in a year you were subject to the 21% AMT would have cost $7,000 less in tax than if the profit were hit by the 28% regular tax. When boosting taxable income, you had to be careful, though, not to push the regular tax bill above the AMT levy. Doing so would have backfired by pulling you out of the AMT and subjecting income to regular tax rates.

The AMT credit does not alter that strategy for the four preference items that do not give rise to the credit. If you are subject to the AMT, for example, hold off on a gift of appreciated property. Otherwise, you lose forever the regular tax benefit of writing off untaxed appreciation. Ditto with itemized deductions that are disallowed by the AMT.

But things are trickier when it comes to other items. Accelerating income may not save you money at all, despite the advantage of the 21% rate over your regular tax bracket, but only accelerate your payment of taxes. Why? Because taking extra income in an AMT year can result in reducing the AMT credit available in future years.

Assume, for example, that your AMT is $5,000 more than your regular tax and the full amount produces an AMT credit. If you realize a $10,000 capital gain at year-end, your AMT would increase by $2,100, but your AMT credit would actually fall by $700. It's no coincidence that the $2,800 combination equals what you'd owe on the gain in the 28% regular tax bracket. The credit shrinks because the spread between your AMT and regular tax has narrowed. The $10,000 of extra income would boost your regular tax by $2,800, compared to the $2,100 hike in AMT.

The same interaction means it's not necessarily advantageous to hold off on deductions (other than those ignored by the AMT) in hopes of getting the write-off against a higher regular tax rate.

In the example above, assume that rather than an extra $10,000 of income, you make a $10,000 charitable contribution in cash. The deduction would knock just $2,100 off your AMT bill for the current year. But it would also hike the AMT credit by $700, by widening the spread between the regular tax (which is reduced $2,800 by the donation) and the AMT.

When blending the AMT credit into your tax planning, remember that it is available only in years you are subject to the regular tax.

16
ESTATE AND GIFT TAXES

Which came first, the chicken or the egg? That question has confounded generations. Here's an easier one: Which comes last, death or taxes?

You guessed it. Taxes.

After you die, Uncle Sam gets one last crack at the assets you've accumulated during your life. Because federal estate-tax rates soar as high as 60%, the U.S. Treasury can become the primary beneficiary of your legacy.

You've probably heard that relatively few taxpayers really have to pay this tax. That's true. It kicks in only if your taxable estate exceeds $600,000. Ironically, though, you probably hope you'll have enough to leave to your heirs that you have to worry about this tax. If so, strategies abound for limiting or eliminating the tax on estates well above the $600,000 level.

First, the basics.

The estate tax applies to the transfer of property at death. The tax is paid by the estate, not by the person who inherits the property.

To avoid a loophole that would let people dodge the estate tax by giving away their property before death, there is a unified system for taxing gifts you make during your lifetime and property you leave in your estate. The same tax rates apply, and almost everyone gets a credit that permits the tax-free transfer of up to $600,000 worth of assets through gifts made during your lifetime, through your estate or by a combination of the two. (As explained later, you can make gifts of up to $10,000 a year to recipients without using up any of the credit.)

DON'T UNDERESTIMATE YOUR ESTATE

Don't let the $600,000 amount lull you into thinking you'll never have to worry about the estate tax. One of the greatest threats is to underestimate the size of your estate and blissfully ignore planning opportunities.

The fact is, your estate—as the law defines it for tax purposes—may already be much larger than you imagine. It includes the value of your home and other real estate holdings, of course, as well as your savings and the value of your investments, cars, boats, jewelry and other personal property. Also included are benefits from retirement plans, whether an IRA, Keogh or company plan. Another asset that can go into

continued on page 400

ADDING UP YOUR ESTATE

Use this work sheet to size up your estate to see whether your legacy is threatened by the federal estate tax. The *ownership* column is included because how you own property is pivotal to how much of its value at the time of your death will be included in your estate. In the *value* column, list the following:
- The full value of property of which you are the sole owner.
- One-half of the value of property that you own jointly with your spouse with right of survivorship.
- Your proportionate share of property owned in conjunction with others. (If you and two brothers are equal co-owners of a piece of property, for example, you would include one-third of the value.)
- One-half of the value of community property, which basically includes assets acquired during marriage in one of the community-property states: Arizona, California, Idaho, Louisiana, Nevada, New Mexico, Texas, Washington and Wisconsin. (Gifts or inheritances received during marriage are not considered community property, however, so their full value is included in your estate.)

Also include the full value of the proceeds of an insurance policy on your life if you retain "incidents of ownership" in the policy, such as the right to change the beneficiary or borrow against the policy; your interest in pension and profit-sharing plans; and the value of property you have placed in a revocable trust.

Once you know the approximate size of your net estate use the work sheet on pages 402 and 403 to see how it would be affected by the federal estate tax.

ASSETS   OWNERSHIP   VALUE

ASSETS	OWNERSHIP	VALUE
Cash in checking, savings, money-market accounts		
Stocks		
Bonds		
Mutual funds		
Other investments		
Home		
Other real estate		
Personal property including furniture, cars, clothing, etc.		
Art, antiques, collectibles		
Proceeds of life insurance policies you own on your life		
Pension and profit-sharing benefits, IRAs, Keogh plans, etc.		
Business interests: sole proprietorships, partnerships, closely-held corporations		
Money owed to you, such as mortgages, rents, professional fees		
Other assets		
Gross estate		

LIABILITIES

LIABILITIES	
Mortgages	
Loans and notes	
Taxes	
Consumer debt	
Other liabilities	
Total liabilities	

NET ESTATE
(assets minus liabilities)

your taxable estate, but which you might not think about because it doesn't exist until after your death, is the proceeds of a life insurance policy. If you own the policy—which you do if you can change the beneficiary or borrow against cash value—the proceeds are considered part of your estate.

Use the work sheet on pages 398 and 399 to get a snapshot of your estate. When you get to the bottom line, keep two things in mind as you consider whether the estate tax poses a threat. First, project how your net worth is likely to grow as you grow older. Second, there is a possibility that Congress will reduce the $600,000 tax-free level—perhaps to $400,000 or so—so that more estates are nicked by this levy.

MARITAL DEDUCTION

On the other hand, your taxable estate can be much less than your net worth. If you are married, in fact, you can avoid the estate tax altogether—regardless of how much you're worth. Every dime you leave your spouse is excluded from your taxable estate. This unlimited marital deduction covers bequests made in your will and assets that aren't controlled by it, such as life insurance or retirement benefits of which your spouse is the beneficiary.

The unlimited marital deduction is evidence of the government's patience as much as its generosity. Although the deduction can shield estates of any size from the tax when the first spouse dies, the IRS will be waiting when the survivor dies—unless he or she has remarried. Although leaving everything to your spouse may at first appear to solve your estate-planning worries, that can be a costly mistake, as discussed later in this chapter.

THE UNIFIED CREDIT

Whether or not you can take advantage of the marital deduction, nearly everyone gets a $192,800 estate- and gift-tax credit—enough to offset the tax bill on a $600,000 taxable estate. (The credit is available to "nearly" everyone because in 1987 Congress decided the benefit of the credit should be phased out for estates that exceed $10 million.)

Even if you're well below the $10 million mark, if your taxable estate exceeds the $600,000 sheltered by the credit, the tax bill mounts quickly, as shown in this table.

Taxable Estate	Tax After Credit
Up to $ 600,000	$ 0
700,000	37,000
800,000	75,000
900,000	114,000
1,000,000	153,000
1,500,000	555,800
2,000,000	780,900
5,000,000	2,198,000

Those staggering sums leave no question about the importance of tax planning as your net worth moves into the vulnerable range. Use the work sheet on pages 402 and 403 to estimate the tax due on your estate.

GIVING IT AWAY AND THE GIFT TAX

Before looking at other basic estate-tax planning strategies, consider the role of gifts and the workings of the gift side of the estate and gift tax. This is perhaps the most misunderstood of all taxes. When it comes into play, the gift tax is owed by the giver, not the recipient. You probably have never paid it and probably will never have to.

The law completely ignores gifts of up to $10,000 each year that you give to any number of individuals. (You and your spouse together can give up to $20,000 a year.) If you have 1,000 friends on whom you wish to bestow $10,000 each, you can give away $10 million a year without even having to fill out a federal gift-tax form. That $10 million would be out of your estate for good. But if you made the $10 million in gifts via your will, the money would be part of your taxable estate and would trigger an enormous tax bill.

Consider a more practical example than the multimillion-dollar giveaway outlined above: Assume that the work sheet on pages 398 and 399 shows a net estate far above the $600,000 taxable level. To hold down the ultimate estate-tax bill, you initiate a series of annual gifts to your three married children. If both you and your spouse give the full $10,000 to the three children and their spouses, you can distribute $120,000 ($20,000 to each of the six children and in-laws) each year tax-free. Imagine how your tax-free gift total could grow if you also included grandchildren in your beneficence.

In addition to removing the gift property itself from your taxable estate, any future appreciation is also spared from any tax in your estate.

The rules get complicated if your generosity passes the

FEDERAL ESTATE-TAX WORK SHEET

Depending on how much you leave behind, Uncle Sam might squeeze into line as an unintended beneficiary. With the work sheet on pages 398 and 399 you can estimate the projected size of your estate. This work sheet and the tax rates provided on page 404 can show you the potential estate tax.

Begin with the size of your net estate, as estimated on the work sheet on page 399. Subtract the value of all property left to your spouse and sheltered from tax by the unlimited marital deduction.

Next, subtract the value of assets bequeathed to charity.

Then add the value of gifts made after 1976 that exceeded the $10,000 annual exclusion ($20,000 if your spouse joined in the gift).

The total is your estate-tax computation base. Find the tentative tax on that amount using the rates in the table on page 404.

From that amount, subtract any gift tax you actually paid during your life—that is, any gift tax beyond that covered by the $192,800 unified credit.

The results is the tax on your estate.

Before you write a check to the IRS, though, you get to subtract your unified credit and perhaps other credits, such as those for death taxes paid to a state.

(States differ in the way they tax estates. A few impose an estate tax similar to the federal levy. Others impose an inheritance tax

$10,000 threshold. For one thing, larger gifts require you to file a gift tax return. If the gift falls in the $10,000 to $20,000 range and is not taxable because you and your spouse join in making it, you can use the short gift tax form, Form 709A. If it's not such a gift, however, you must use Form 709, *United States Gift Tax Return,* and to figure the tax due on the amount over $10,000. And to calculate the tax, you must take into account all taxable gifts made in previous years. Here's an example of how it works.

You decide to give your son $50,000 each year for three consecutive years. (For simplicity's sake, assume your spouse does not join you in the gift.) The first $10,000 gift each year is protected by the annual exclusion. You would report the $40,000 taxable portions and figure the tax as follows.

---

directly on those who inherit property, with the lowest rates and highest exemptions often reserved for your spouse and children. More than half the states levy a "pickup" tax, which applies only to estates with a federal tax liability. This tax doesn't really increase the total amount of tax due on your estate because it equals the amount of the credit you're allowed on the federal estate tax return for death taxes paid to a state.)

	SAMPLE ESTATE	YOUR ESTATE
Net Estate	$1,070,000	
Less marital deduction	300,000	
Less charitable bequests	20,000	
Plus taxable gifts made after 1976	12,000	
Estate-Tax Computation Base	$762,000	
Tentative tax from table on page 404	252,980	
Less gift tax paid after 1976	0	
Tax on Taxable Estate	$252,900	
Less unified credit*	192,800	$192,800
Estate Tax Due	$60,180	

Other credits may be available to reduce the tax, such as the credit for death taxes paid to a state.

Using the rate schedule below, the tax on the first $40,000 gift is $8,200.

In the second year, you add the new $40,000 taxable gift to the previous year's $40,000 and find the tax on $80,000. That's $18,200. From that amount you subtract the $8,200 due on the first gift. That makes the tax on the second gift $10,000.

In the third year, you again add the new $40,000 to the $80,000 of taxable gifts given in previous years. Find the tax on $120,000, which is $29,800, and subtract the combined $18,200

GIFT- AND ESTATE-TAX RATE SCHEDULE

Taxable Amount	Tentative Tax*
Up to $10,000	18%
$10,001 to $20,000	$1,800 + 20% of amount over $10,000
$20,001 to $40,000	$3,800 + 22% of amount over $20,000
$40,001 to $60,000	$8,200 + 24% of amount over $40,000
$60,001 to $80,000	$13,000 + 26% of amount over $60,000
$80,001 to $100,000	$18,200 + 28% of amount over $80,000
$100,001 to $150,000	$23,800 + 30% of amount over $100,000
$150,001 to $250,000	$38,800 + 32% of amount over $150,000
$250,001 to $500,000	$70,800 + 34% of amount over $250,000
$500,001 to $750,000	$155,800 + 37% of amount over $500,000
$750,001 to $1,000,000	$248,300 + 39% of amount over $750,000
$1,000,001 to $1,250,000	$345,800 + 41% of amount over $1,000,000
$1,250,001 to $1,500,000	$448,300 + 43% of amount over $1,250,000
$1,500,001 to $2,000,000	$555,800 + 45% of amount over $1,500,000
$2,000,001 to $2,500,000	$780,800 + 49% of amount over $2,000,000
$2,500,001 to $3,000,000	$1,025,800 + 53% of amount over $2,500,000†
Over $3,000,000	$1,290,800 + 55% of amount over $3,000,000†

* *This is referred to as a tentative tax because every taxpayer gets a $192,800 credit to offset the tax on the first $600,000 of taxable transfers.*
† *The law calls for the abolition of the 53% and 55% brackets after 1992. Starting in 1993, amounts over $2,500,000 will be taxed at 50%. Also, as noted on page 411, a "phantom" 60% rate applies to taxable estates ranging from $10 million to just over $21 million.*

tax on the previous gifts. The tax on your third gift is $11,600.

The point of adding in the previous gifts is to force you to march up the graduated rate schedule. Note that although the same size gift was given in each of the three years in the example, the gift tax rose from $8,200 on the first gift to $10,000 on the second and $11,600 on the third.

Our example assumes that these gifts are the only ones made by you so far, so no tax would actually have to be paid. Rather, your $192,800 unified estate-and-gift-tax credit would be reduced by $29,800 (the bill on the $120,000 of taxable gifts). The remaining $163,000 of the credit would be enough to shelter another $480,000 of taxable transfers, either as gifts made during your lifetime or through your estate.

Taxable gifts made during your life also come into play when figuring the tax due on your estate. As you see on the work sheet on pages 402 and 403, the taxable portion of gifts made after 1976 is included in the amount on which the estate tax is based. That may seem like double taxation, but it's not that sinister. Instead, as with the requirement that previous gifts be taken into account when calculating the gift tax, the point is to prevent you from using the lower estate-tax brackets more than once. Although you have to bring gifts back into the estate, you also get to use the full credit to offset the estate-tax bill—even though part of it was used during your life to shield you from the gift tax.

Assume that during your life you made $600,000 of taxable gifts, using up your entire credit. When you die, your taxable estate is also $600,000. Without the requirement to "gross up" the estate for taxable gifts, the tax on $600,000 would be $192,800. To prevent you from using the 18% through 34% brackets a second time, however, the law requires you to find the tax on $1.2 million (the total of the taxable gifts plus the taxable estate). Stacked on top of the gifts, the estate is taxed in the 37% through 41% brackets. The bill on $1.2 million is $427,800. Subtracting the $192,800 credit amount leaves your estate with a $235,000 liability.

Although pulling taxable gifts back into the estate may seem to defeat the tax-saving aim, it does not. The assets are counted in your estate at their value at the time of the gift. Any appreciation between that time and your death avoids being taxed in your estate. That can be extremely important, particularly when rapidly appreciating assets are involved.

There may also be income tax advantages to making gifts, as discussed in Chapter 3. But you should be aware of a potential income tax drawback, too. The IRS forgives the tax on any profit that has built up on assets that you own at the time of your death. Assume that stock you bought for $50,000 is worth $100,000 when you die. That $50,000 profit escapes the income tax. If you were to give away the stock before death, however, the recipient would be responsible for the income tax on the appreciation that accrued while you owned the stock.

MIXING THE MARRIAGE DEDUCTION AND THE UNIFIED CREDIT

As mentioned earlier, if you are married you can leave everything you own to your spouse free of estate tax. Relying too much on the marital deduction to protect the estate of the first spouse to die could, however, set up the survivor for unnecessary taxes.

To illustrate the potential problem, and a solution for it, consider an example. Assume you have a taxable estate of $1 million and your spouse owns property worth $200,000. If you leave everything outright to your spouse, the unlimited marital deduction will permit it to pass free of estate tax.

But if the $1 million plus the $200,000 remains intact, when your spouse dies the taxable estate will be $1.2 million. The unified credit will protect just half that amount, letting the IRS claim $235,000 in tax on the extra $600,000. That's money that, with a little planning, could have been passed on to the next generation. One of the most common estate plans for a couple with more than $600,000 in assets is to make sure the first spouse to die takes advantage of the unified credit as well as the marital deduction. Note that in our example, by relying fully on the marital deduction, the first spouse effectively threw away the $192,800 credit.

To avoid forfeiting that tax break, you can use what's variously known as a bypass or exemption-equivalent trust. Basically, in our example you would split your estate, putting $600,000 in a trust and leaving the other $400,000 outright to your surviving spouse. (You can split your estate however you choose, of course, but the goal is often to make maximum use of the unified credit.)

Although the money put in this type of trust would not qualify for the marital deduction, it would be protected from tax by the credit. The $400,000 left outright to your spouse would be shielded from tax by the marital deduction. As in the first example, then, no tax is due on the death of the first spouse.

A key feature of the bypass trust is that income from the trust can go to your survivor—just as if he or she inherited the assets outright—but at his or her death the principal would be distributed to other heirs, such as your children, without being included in your spouse's estate.

In our example, that estate would include the $400,000 left under the marital deduction plus the $200,000 of personal assets. The unified credit would shelter the full amount from the estate tax. The bottom line is that the family comes out $235,000 ahead.

QTIP trusts. Until recently, to qualify for the estate-tax marital deduction, assets had to be left to the survivor in a way that permitted him or her to control their ultimate distribution. In other words, if you left $1 million to your wife, she'd get to decide who would inherit what remained at her death.

Now, however, you can use a qualified terminable interest property (QTIP) trust that qualifies for the marital deduction without giving away ultimate control of the property. A QTIP trust gives your surviving spouse income for life and possibly some principal, but after his or her death the distribution of the assets is controlled by your wishes in the trust document rather than by your spouse's will.

Although the QTIP trust is similar to the bypass trust in that the survivor receives income for life and assets are then passed on according to the trust, there are two key differences. One is that the QTIP protects property from the estate tax with the marital deduction rather than the unified credit used by the bypass trust. And, unlike a bypass trust, assets in a QTIP trust are included in your survivor's taxable estate.

QTIP trusts may be especially appropriate for those who have children from a former marriage. A husband, for example, can use such a trust to provide for his second wife while insuring that when she dies, the assets will pass on to the children from his first marriage. Childless couples can also use QTIP trusts so that either spouse can be sure that, after providing for the survivor, his or her blood relatives will ultimately inherit specified assets.

JOINT OWNERSHIP OF PROPERTY

Married couples often own a significant part of their estate together, either by joint tenancy with the right of survivorship or tenancy by the entirety. The key is that when one owner dies, the other automatically becomes sole owner of the property. That promise and the concept of owning things together rather than individually is understandably appealing to married couples. Beyond the harmony and peace of mind such economic unity can promote, property owned jointly bypasses probate when the first spouse dies, saving time, hassle, publicity and expenses.

Many people also think that because jointly owned property dodges probate, its value also escapes the estate tax. That's only half right. When the first spouse dies, half the value of jointly owned property is included in his or her estate. The unlimited marital deduction will protect that amount from the estate tax. So, what's the problem?

Owning too much property jointly can foul up planning efforts to hold down the tax on the estate of the second spouse. Only property you own individually can go into a bypass trust; jointly owned assets go automatically to the survivor. Estate planners generally like to see at least enough separately owned property to take full advantage of the unified credit. If joint ownership makes that impossible, you are considered to be turning down part of Uncle Sam's $192,000 generosity.

If your projections of future net worth suggest that you may benefit from a bypass trust, pay particular attention to how you take title to property. As with all estate planning, you are almost certain to need professional advice to insure that your efforts produce the outcome you desire. Seek the help of an experienced professional, such as an attorney or certified public accountant, who specializes in this area.

LIFE INSURANCE

Proceeds of a policy on your life could be the asset that pushes your estate into the taxable range. It doesn't matter who the beneficiary of the policy is, if you own the policy when you die, the money is considered part of your taxable estate. If your spouse is the beneficiary, the proceeds would be shielded from the estate tax by the marital deduction.

But there's a simple way to avoid having the money poured into your estate at all: Don't own the policy yourself. If you give the policy to your spouse or adult children, for example, the proceeds bypass your estate.

Don't overlook the cost of this move though: Giving up ownership means giving up control of the policy. If you retain any "incidents of ownership" of the policy, the proceeds go into your taxable estate. To avoid that, you have to give up the right to change the beneficiary and forsake your right to borrow against the policy. If the arrangement permits you to change your mind and regain control of the policy, you are not considered to have ever given up ownership.

Giving the policy away doesn't always work, either. If you die within three years of the gift, the proceeds of the policy are brought back into the taxable estate.

Rather than give a life insurance policy to an individual, another option is to put the policy into an irrevocable life insurance trust. Again, that would mean giving up control of the policy. Proceeds of the policy would go into the trust and be controlled by its provisions. Income could go to your surviving spouse, for example, with the principal going to your children after the survivor's death. This arrangement would prevent the proceeds from being taxed in the estate of either spouse.

IF YOU OWN A BUSINESS

The best-laid plans for passing a business from one generation to the next can collapse if you fail to consider the demands of your invisible partner: Uncle Sam. The value of your business could be the bulk of your estate. If you fail to plan for the potential estate-tax liability, your family could be forced to give up control. Even if your heirs planned to sell out, they could be forced to accept a fire-sale price in the scramble to pay the tax.

The first step in preserving options for the next generation is to have a realistic estimate of the value of the business and the potential estate-tax bill. The IRS has stunned some families with a tax bill based on a value far higher than they dreamed the business was worth. Once you have a handle on what your business is worth, you have a basis for estate planning. One option is to buy enough life insurance to cover the potential estate-tax bill. Another is to leave the business to your spouse to take advantage of the marital deduction. Keep in mind, though, that there will be no similar protection when it comes time to pass the business on to the next generation.

"Have a seat. Taxes is in with him now."

DRAWING BY ED FISHER
© 1986 THE NEW YORKER MAGAZINE, INC.

You could also begin giving away interest in the business, taking advantage of the annual $10,000 gift-tax exclusion for each recipient and preventing future appreciation from winding up in your taxable estate.

Another alternative is to build a buy/sell agreement into your estate plan. That would obligate someone, perhaps your partners or key employees, to buy your share of the business and obligate your estate to sell it at a price set under methods spelled out in the agreement. To make certain the survivor has the funds to cover the price, parties to the agreement often buy insurance policies on each other's lives.

There is also a special estate-tax break for the part of your interest you leave to an employee stock-ownership plan (ESOP). Also, you may be able to take advantage of rules designed to prevent families from being forced to sell closely held businesses in order to satisfy the estate-tax law. If you qualify and your interest in the business represents 35% or more of your taxable estate, the tax bill can be paid over 14 years, with only interest due during the first four years. And the estate gets a break on the interest charged on the postponed tax bill—it's just 4% of the tax due on the first $1 million of the taxable estate attributable to the business. As with the other estate-planning strategies outlined in this chapter, this abbreviated discussion is designed to alert you to the options that may be available for limiting your estate-tax liability. Deciding which will work best for you demands expert professional help. The earlier you begin planning, the more choices you have.

ANOTHER PHANTOM BRACKET

The top estate-tax rate was supposed to drop to 50% in 1988, but late in 1987 Congress decided to retain the rate schedule shown on page 404—with rates rising to 55%—until 1993. The lawmakers also created a 60% bracket for certain estates, although they don't call it that.

It works similarly to the "phantom" 33% income tax bracket discussed in Chapter 1. Here, a 5% surcharge applies to taxable estates between $10 million and $21,040,000. The point is to deny those estates the use of the graduated tax rates and the benefit of the $192,800 credit. By applying a 60% rate in the phaseout range, the effect is to hit estates valued at $21,040,000 and above at a flat 55%.

QUESTIONS AND ANSWERS

Over the years, one of the most popular tax-time features in *Changing Times* magazine has been tax questions from readers—with the answers conveniently attached. The format seems particularly well suited to this subject matter. Areas of the law that are too often shrouded in fog can come into sharp focus when defined by a specific, real-life question.

This chapter is a collection of such questions. Most of the issues addressed here are also covered elsewhere in the book, often in greater detail. If you need more information, check the index for references. If a term used in an answer is unfamiliar, see the glossary.

DEDUCT THIS BOOK?

Q. *Is the cost of this book deductible?*

A. Maybe. Before 1987, the cost of tax-planning books was fully deductible by itemizers, as were fees paid to professional tax advisers and return preparers. Now such costs can be written off only to the extent that they and all your other miscellaneous itemized deductions exceed 2% of your adjusted gross income. If your qualifying expenses exceed the threshold, you can deduct what you paid for *Successful Tax Planning*.

TOO MUCH SOCIAL SECURITY

Q. *I changed jobs and now discover that doing so will cost me more than $2,000 in extra social security tax. My salary from the two jobs will be $74,000, from which a total of about $5,300 FICA tax will be withheld. I thought the maximum social security tax was about $3,000. Is that limit per job instead of per taxpayer? Am I being overtaxed?*

A. The same limit applies regardless of how many jobs you hold during the year, so you are being overtaxed. The good news is that it's relatively easy to get your money back. The social security wage base for 1988 is $45,000, and the tax rate for employees is 7.51%. That means the maximum FICA tax anyone owes on wages is $3,379.50. Employers are supposed to stop withholding the tax once earnings exceed the wage base. Your problem is that your second employer can't take into account wages paid by your first, so as far as either employer knows, your wages never passed $45,000.

You can reclaim your money by claiming a credit on your tax return. You won't even have to file an extra form. Show the excess social security tax paid on your tax return. That will either reduce the amount you owe with your return or boost your refund.

POINTERS ON POINTS

Q. *When we refinanced our home mortgage to get a lower rate, our lawyer told us that, thanks to an IRS crackdown, we can't deduct the points all at once. Somehow, we're supposed to write off part of the points each year as we pay off the mortgage. Is the proper amount included in the interest the bank says we paid on our loan, or is there a special method for figuring it out?*

A. It's an extra deduction and you have to figure it out yourself.

The IRS says points paid on refinancing a home mortgage are prepaid interest and should be deducted proportionately over the life of the loan. If you paid $3,000 in points on a 15-year mortgage, for example, $200 would be deductible each year. The deduction for the first year would depend on when you refinanced, though. If you did so at midyear and made just six monthly payments during the year, your deduction would be limited to half of the full year's amount.

Although mortgage interest paid should be reported to you by the lender, you'll get no reminder to deduct each year's share of the points. Once you determine how much to claim each year, note it on the special line for deducting points on Schedule A. Don't include the amount with your mortgage interest write-off; that would just confuse the IRS.

AUTO-LOAN INTEREST

Q. *I use my car a great deal for my job and have found it profitable to apply the actual-cost method rather than the standard mileage rate when determining my car-expense deduction. I base my deduction on the fact that I use the car 80% of the time for business. I bought a new car last year and am not sure how to handle the interest on the auto loan. Does the fact that I use the car mostly for business protect the interest from the rules that make interest on other loans nondeductible?*

A. No. If you had your own business, the portion of the interest treated as a business expense—80% in your case—would be fully deductible as a business expense. However, employees who use their cars on the job don't get that break. All the interest is considered personal interest, the deduction for which is being phased out. For 1988, only 40% can be deducted. The percentage falls to 20% in 1989 and 10% in 1990. After that, personal interest can't be deducted at all. The loss of this write-off may make it profitable for you to switch to the standard mileage rate.

JURY FEES

Q. *When I was called to jury duty for two weeks last year, my employer continued my salary but required that I turn over the $250 in jury fees I received. The IRS instructions say I have to report jury fees as taxable income, but that doesn't seem fair because I really didn't get the money. What am I supposed to do?*

A. This is a sticky issue because the IRS clearly considers jury fees taxable income and says they should be reported as "other income" on your Form 1040. Unfortunately, the agency has no clear answer to your question.

In the past, taxpayers who had to assign jury fees to their employers often claimed that amount as a miscellaneous itemized deduction. That offset the amount reported as income and avoided a higher tax. Now, however, miscellaneous expenses are deductible only to the extent that they exceed 2% of your adjusted gross income, a rule that puts such write-offs out of reach of most taxpayers.

As you struggle with your dilemma, you may want to consider this comment from a candid IRS insider: "In real life, if I get a check for $120 and have to turn it over to my employer, I'm not going to report the $120 on my tax return, so there's no need to deduct it anywhere."

THE FIRST TIME

Q. *Our 2-year-old son's investments will earn just over $600, including about $100 in capital gains from the sale of mutual-fund shares I traded as custodian of his account. Since it's so little, can we just report his income on our return, or will we have to file a special return for him?*

A. A separate return will be necessary. A return is required if a dependent child has any investment income at all and total income exceeds $500. Because your son's income includes capital gains, you will have to use the long Form 1040 instead of the simpler 1040A or 1040EZ. And you will have to attach a copy of Schedule D showing the capital gain. If the income includes more than $400 of either interest or dividends, you will also need to file Schedule B to report the specifics.

Even though he is under 5—the age at which children claimed as dependents on their parents' returns must have social security numbers—your son will need one for his own return. If he doesn't have one, apply at a local social security office.

On the bright side, because your son's investment income will be less than $1,000, you won't have to mess with Form 8615. That's the "kiddie tax" form that can result in having part of the investment income of a child under age 14 taxed at the parents' tax rate.

When it comes time to sign the child's return, don't give your son a crayon. You can sign his name, followed by a note that you signed it as his parent.

SOCIAL SECURITY TAX ON SPOUSE

Q. *I run a small, unincorporated business and employ my wife as my bookkeeper. Last year, as usual, I didn't pay any social security tax on the wages I paid her. My accountant tells me that the law has been changed so that I must now pay FICA on those wages. Is that so?*

A. Your accountant is correct. Beginning in 1988, wages paid to a spouse lost their exemption from social security. For 1988, the social security tax rate is 7.51% for both employer and employee.

QUIT-SMOKING COURSE

Q. *I finally beat my smoking habit by taking an expensive stop-smoking course. Can I write off the cost?*

A. The IRS has taken a stand on this one: No. Despite the Surgeon General's warnings that smoking contributes to cancer and other diseases, the tax agency holds that courses aimed at kicking the habit generally don't meet the law's demand that, for the expense to be deductible, the medical care must treat or prevent disease.

KIDDIE CARDS

Q. *I understand that I have to get social security cards for my children so I can claim them as dependents on my tax return. How do I apply for the cards?*

A. Social security numbers are required for every dependent you claim who is at least 5 years old. To apply for cards for your children, contact your local social security office for a Form SS-5. (The forms may also be available at your local post office.) In addition to completing the SS-5, you'll have to provide evidence of the child's age, identity and U.S. citizenship. Check with the local office for specific demands. Once you apply for a card, you should receive the child's number within two weeks.

CAR-POOL PAYMENTS

Q. *I'm in a car pool and take two fellow workers to the office each day. Do I have to report what they pay me as income?*

A. No. Car-pool payments are considered a nontaxable reimbursement of your expenses.

LIFE INSURANCE PAYMENTS

Q. *After my elderly aunt died, I learned she had named me beneficiary of a $25,000 life insurance policy. Is that money taxed, and if so, where do I report it on my return?*

A. The proceeds of the policy are free of income tax.

SUMMER CAMP

Q. *At a PTA meeting, I overheard two parents talking about how they deducted what they paid to send their children to a two-week summer camp session. Is that legal?*

A. Until 1988, it was possible for payments for overnight summer camp to qualify for the child-care tax credit. Even the part of the fee that paid for food and lodging at the camp could qualify. Due to a change in the law, however, that is no longer permitted.

BUSINESS TRIP

Q. *I drove to a business convention in Chicago last spring. My wife went along, and while I attended meetings she went sight-seeing and visited relatives. Since there was no business purpose for her trip, are we limited to deducting only half of our expenses?*

A. There's no arbitrary 50% rule, and you can probably claim more. If you qualify to write off your costs as a business expense, you can deduct the full cost of driving your car to and from Chicago. After all, it costs the same whether you go alone or take a passenger. (If you and your wife had taken a plane, of course, only your fare would be deductible.) On the hotel bill, you can deduct the amount it would have cost you to stay in a single room, which is often close to or the same as the double-room rate. Thanks to a restriction that came into the law in 1987, only 80% of the cost of your business meals can be deducted. The cost of your wife's meals is a personal, nondeductible expense.

SUMMER JOB

Q. *I had a great summer job and earned almost $3,000. I'm going to file a return and claim my own personal exemption; does that mean my folks can't claim me as a dependent?*

A. That's right. If you claim your personal exemption, your parents can't claim an exemption for you as their dependent. However, it is possible that they—not you—deserve the tax-saving exemption. Basically, if you're a student and your parents provided more than half of your support for the year in question, you're a dependent. That means you can't claim a personal exemption for yourself.

LEGAL FEES FOR A DIVORCE

Q. *I was divorced last summer, and the lawyer's bill was staggering. My ex-husband says he's deducting part of his legal fees. Is that legal, and if so, can I deduct part of mine?*

A. Legal fees and court costs involved in a divorce are generally nondeductible, but any part of the lawyer's fees attributable to tax advice is deductible. If you receive alimony, you may also deduct the portion of the fee your attorney charged for setting the amount of taxable alimony. If you don't have an itemized statement from your lawyer, ask for one that breaks down the fee, so you can pinpoint the deductible amount. The tax benefit may still elude you, however, because these costs are among the miscellaneous expenses that can be written off only to the extent that the total exceeds 2% of your adjusted gross income.

CLOSED CAPTION DECODER

Q. *Our son has a severe hearing impairment, and we purchased a special adapter that lets our TV display subtitles for certain programs. The decoder was expensive, and I think we ought to be able to deduct it as a medical expense. Can we?*

A. The cost is a deductible medical expense, but such costs are deductible only to the extent that your total medical costs exceed 7.5% of your adjusted gross income.

KEEPING MY NAME

Q. *Rather than take my husband's surname, I decided to keep my own. Will that cause us problems with the IRS when we file a joint return?*

A. It shouldn't, despite the fact that the tax form doesn't provide space for two surnames. You should separate your names with an "and," such as John Brown and Mary Smith. Also, be sure your names appear in the same order as your social security numbers. If your husband's name is listed second, for instance, his social security number should go in box provided for "spouse." If the names and numbers don't match, processing of your returns will be delayed.

CHANGING MY NAME

Q. *I was married during the year and took my husband's last name. Do*

I have to report my name change to the IRS?
A. No, but you should advise the Social Security Administration. You use Form SSA-5 to change your name on your social security records. Since the IRS uses the social security number as your taxpayer identification number, confusion could result—and any refund you have coming could be delayed—if name and number don't match.

UNION DUES

Q. *When I itemize deductions, where do I write off my union dues?*
A. Union dues are considered a miscellaneous expense that you deduct on Schedule A, but only to the extent that your total expenses in this category exceed 2% of your adjusted gross income.

WHEN TO REPORT INCOME

Q. *I wrote a free-lance article for a newspaper in early December but didn't receive payment until January 8 when the check arrived in the mail. The check was dated December 31 and I received a 1099 form from the paper showing that the payment was made in the year I wrote the story. That doesn't seem right, since I didn't get the money until the following year. Do I have to report the income for the year I did the work or the year I actually got paid?*
A. The answer turns on the "constructive receipt" of the payment. If you could have gotten the money during December—by picking up the check at the newspaper office, say—you should report the income on the return for the year you wrote the story. If you had no choice but to wait for the company to cut the check and mail it—so you had no control over when you received it—you should report it on the return for the year you actually received the check.

The 1099 form you received does complicate things, as you probably guessed. Since the IRS got a copy too, you need to attach a statement to your return to deflect questions or a possible deficiency notice. Explain that you are not reporting the specific amount because you were paid by a check that did not arrive in the mail until January of the following year. Note, too, that you will report the income on the return you file for that year. Keep the check stub and the envelope it came in with your tax records.

COMPUTER WRITE-OFF

Q. *I bought a computer last summer and use it primarily to get information from investment data bases, analyze stock for possible purchase, track my portfolio and do my tax return. Can I deduct the cost of the computer?*
A. Such deductions are tough to come by. First of all, since you

apparently don't use the computer more than 50% of the time in a business, your deductions are automatically limited. You can't "expense" the computer—a special break that lets business users deduct up to $10,000 of the qualifying cost all at once rather than depreciating it over several years—and you can't use accelerated depreciation to beef up your write-offs in the early years. Instead, you're stuck with depreciating 10% of the qualifying cost in the first year, 20% for each of the next four, and the final 10% in the sixth year.

What's the qualifying cost? That depends on what you paid for the computer and what percentage of its use is devoted to investment and tax purposes. (Good records showing the time you spent for various purposes are essential to substantiating any deduction.) Say that you paid $3,800 for the computer and that 70% of its use was for investment and tax purposes and the other 30% was for personal use. The qualifying cost would be $2,660—70% of $3,800—and your first-year deduction would be 10% of that amount, or $266.

But there's another restriction that can wipe out even that paltry write-off. The cost of investment and tax advice and assistance is considered a miscellaneous expense. That means it is deductible only to the extent your total costs in this category exceed 2% of your adjusted gross income. When adding up these costs, include what you paid to use the investment data bases and for any tax-return-preparation software.

IRA CUSTODIAL FEE

Q. *Each year my broker takes $25 out of my IRA account to pay his custodial fee. Is that cost deductible?*
A. No. If you paid the fee separately, however, it might have a tax benefit. The cost would be included with your other miscellaneous expenses. You get a deduction for the amount by which the total exceeds 2% of your adjusted gross income. Even if you don't earn a deduction, you will be better off paying the fee separately rather than having your broker dip into your IRA, since money left in your IRA will continue to grow tax-deferred.

ERRONEOUS W-2

Q. *The W-2 income report I got from my employer has a whopping computer error. It shows that I earned $330,000 rather than $33,000. Can I just ignore the extra zero?*
A. Only if you want to hear from the IRS. You can bet that your employer sent the same incorrect W-2 to the government, so Uncle Sam is expecting tax on about $300,000 more than you made. Contact your employer and ask for a revised W-2. Your employer should also send the corrected version to the IRS.

NO ROLLOVER

Q. *When my wife and I were married, I sold my condo and moved into her house. Is there any way to put off paying tax on the profit I made on my apartment?*

A. Not unless you and your wife decide to buy a new home and you move into it within two years of the time you sold your condominium. To postpone the tax bill on the sale of a personal residence, you must buy a new home that costs at least as much as the one you sold. If you do so, the gain from the first home is rolled over into the new house, and the tax bill put off until you sell that place. Since you didn't buy a new home, however, you don't qualify for the rollover.

If you were at least 55 years old when you sold the condo and had owned and lived in it for at least three of the previous five years, however, you may qualify for the exclusion that lets qualifying taxpayers avoid the tax on up to $125,000 of home-sale profit.

EXTRA CASH

Q. *In addition to my job, I do a little carpentry work on the side. Last year, I made about $1,000 doing odd jobs for neighbors. I know it's taxable but am not sure where to report it. Do I count it as "other income" on the Form 1040?*

A. No. It is self-employment income and should be reported on a Schedule C. On the plus side, that will also permit you to deduct the cost of any materials you used, plus the cost of transportation to and from the jobs. Since your self-employment income was more than $400, you may also have to file a Schedule SE and pay social security taxes on the income.

STUDENT LOAN

Q. *Our daughter has a series of student loans but my husband and I are actually paying off the loans. Can we deduct the interest?*

A. Not unless you or your husband co-signed the note. Only the person legally responsible for repaying the debt can deduct the interest. If you gave the money to your daughter to make the loan payments, she would be able to deduct the interest—if she itemizes deductions. This issue will soon be moot, however, since interest on student loans is considered personal interest, the deduction for which is being phased out.

CREDIT CARD PAYMENT

Q. *My son had an emergency appendectomy in early December, and I charged the hospital bill to my bank credit card. I didn't get the bill until January, and I'm still paying it off. Can I include the hospital bill in my* *medical deductions for the year of the operation, or is it deductible only as it is paid?*

A. You get the write-off for the year you charged the bill to your credit card. The IRS figures paying with plastic is the same as paying with borrowed funds, so you get the deduction for the year you say "charge it" regardless of when you pay the credit card bill.

THE $125,000 EXCLUSION

Q. *I know there's a special break that lets you avoid taxes on up to $125,000 of profit on the sale of your home. If I die before I sell the house, does that tax break disappear with me and therefore mean my children will have to pay tax on the $125,000?*

A. You can exclude from taxable income up to $125,000 of profit from the sale of you home if, at the time of the sale, you are at least 55 years old and have owned and lived in the house for at least three of the five years leading up to the sale. But don't feel rushed into selling your home. If you still own it when you die, another section of the law forgives the tax on all the profit that built up while you owned the place—even if it's far more than $125,000.

REPORTING THE SALE OF A HOME

Q. *I sold a house and bought a new one last year. Since the new house cost more than the old one, I know no taxes are due. Do I have to file any forms with the IRS about the sale, anyway?*

A. Yes. File Form 2119, *Sale or Exchange of Personal Residence*, with your tax return. Among other things, it shows how much profit you made on the sale. Although you are permitted to defer the tax on that gain since you bought a new house, your basis in the new house is reduced by the amount of untaxed profit from the old one.

THE VALUE OF LABOR

Q. *My sons and I spent most of the summer building a garage. It cost us $8,000, but if I had hired people to do the work, I'm sure the price would have been at least twice as much. When figuring the addition to the basis of the property, how do I calculate the value of our labor?*

A. You don't. The addition to the basis is the actual cost of the improvement to you. If you hire workers, you include the wages you pay them, but you get no credit for your own time and skills.

TAKING A LOSS

Q. *The housing market here is the pits. When we sold our house, we actually got less than we had paid for it. Can we deduct the loss?*

A. No. A loss on the sale of a personal residence is not a deduction, nor does it affect the basis of the next house you buy.

FIGHTING AN ASSESSMENT

Q. *When I received the new property-tax assessment on my home, I was stunned by the increase and decided to appeal for a reduction. I wound up hiring a lawyer and paying several hundred dollars in legal fees but finally won a significant reduction. Can I deduct that cost?*

A. No, but you can add it to your basis in the property.

A BIG REFUND

Q. *I suppose I shouldn't complain, but once again I see that I'm getting a big tax refund. How can I get my employer to withhold less from my paychecks?*

A. Withholding is controlled by the number of allowances you claim on the W-4 form filed with your employer. Ask your personnel office for a W-4 and use the work sheets that come with it to determine how many withholding allowances you can claim. Giving your employer a new W-4 claiming more allowances should promptly result in less withholding and, consequently, more take-home pay.

MUTUAL FUNDS

Q. *I recently sold all my shares in a mutual fund that I began buying several years ago. I had added to it from time to time and also reinvested all the dividends. How do I figure how much tax I owed?*

A. Get out your records and begin by adding up your total investment in the fund: what you paid for shares purchased outright and those bought through the reinvestment program. That's your cost basis for tax purposes and your profit or loss is generally the difference between this amount and what you received when you sold the shares. In some cases, the profit or loss has to be adjusted to reflect returns of your investment received from the fund over the years or undistributed capital gains credited to you while you owned the shares.

SAVINGS-BOND INTEREST

Q. *When my father died last year, he owned several thousand dollars' worth of Series EE savings bonds that named me as his beneficiary. Do I have to pay tax on the interest that built up on the bonds while he was alive?*

A. Any interest that wasn't reported by your father must be reported as income by you when you cash the bonds. However, interest that had accrued up to the day of your father's death may be reported on his final income tax return. Depending on your father's other income for the year, doing so could significantly reduce the tax due.

ACCRUED INTEREST

Q. *Late in the year, I purchased a corporate bond and had to pay an extra $391 for the interest that had accrued but not been paid. A few weeks later I received the first of my semiannual interest payments— $418. The entire amount was reported to the IRS as interest received by me. Since most of the payment only reimbursed me for the accrued interest I had to pay, it doesn't seem fair that I should have to pay tax on the full $418. My interest from the bond was really only $27. Do I have to pay tax on the other $391?*

A. No. The accrued interest you paid is considered the seller's income, not yours. Here's how to handle it on your tax return. When you fill out Schedule B, list the full $418 as well as any other interest you received during the year. Skip down a few lines on the form and enter a subtotal of interest income. On the next line, write *accrued interest* and enter $391. Subtract that from the subtotal to arrive at your taxable interest.

INHERITED STOCK

Q. *I inherited some stock last year and sold it for several thousand dollars. Do I have to pay any tax on the amount I received from the sale?*

A. Perhaps, but the sale might actually result in cutting your tax bill. Your basis in the stock—that is, the amount from which you figure your gain or loss—is probably its value on the date the previous owner died. On rare occasions an alternative valuation date is used. In either case, the executor of the estate should be able to pinpoint the value. If you sold the stock for more than that amount, you must pay tax on the difference. If you sold for less, you have a deductible capital loss.

STATE TAX REFUND

Q. *I got a $600 state tax refund last year and see that I'm supposed to report it as income on my federal return. That doesn't seem fair, since the refund just made up for my overpayment of state taxes. Do I have to pay tax on it?*

A. All, part, or none of the state tax refund may be taxable. First of all, if you did not itemize on your federal return last year, none of the refund is taxable. If you itemized, however, the deduction you claimed for state taxes paid whittled down your federal taxable income and, therefore, the amount you paid Uncle Sam. In a sense, the refund from the state is evidence that you claimed too big of a deduction for state taxes.

NO MORE CHECKS

Q. *My bank no longer returns canceled checks and I'm worried that that might lead to problems if the IRS decides to audit my tax return. Would an auditor accept the copies the bank says it will give me in such a case, or throw out a deduction just because I can't produce the actual check used to pay a bill?*
A. Such copies would almost certainly be a satisfactory substitute. In the unlikely event that questions would be raised about the validity of the copy, the IRS might ask to see a transcript of the account showing all deposits and disbursements made around the time that the check was written.

FORGIVENESS OF DEBT

Q. *Last year we accepted our bank's offer to pay off our low-interest-rate mortgage for an amount substantially below the outstanding principal due. Is it true that we have to pay tax on the amount we saved?*
A. Yes. The amount of forgiven debt—the difference between the principal owed and what you paid—is considered taxable income and should be reported as "other income" on your tax return.

TEMPORARY RENTAL OF HOME

Q. *I put my home on the market last October when I bought a new house. The old place didn't sell, though, and after several months I had to rent it out. After several months, I found a buyer. Now I'm told that because I rented it out I forfeited the right to defer the tax on the sale by rolling the profit into my new home. Is that true?*
A. Not necessarily. The deferral of tax applies only when you sell your principal residence and buy another home that costs at least as much within two years. Although that break isn't available for profit from the sale of a rental property, temporarily renting your home doesn't automatically deny you the chance to roll over the profit. The IRS permits such a rental as a matter of convenience if you can show that you continued to try to sell the house and indeed did sell it within the two-year rollover period.

TAXING GOOD FORTUNE

Q. *Our church raffled off a $14,000 car as part of a fund-raising drive. I was the lucky winner. Am I right in assuming that prizes awarded by churches are tax-free?*
A. No. The fair market value of the car is considered taxable income to you. You can deduct what you paid for the raffle tickets, though. Remember, too, that the taxable income is the value of the car, which may be less than the sticker price—such as what the dealer who

provided the car to the church would have been willing to pay you for it immediately after you won the raffle.

MARRIAGE AND DEPENDENTS

Q. *Our daughter was married last fall, but she and her husband are still in college and we send them money each month. Can we still claim her as a dependent, or does the wedding mean we gained a son but lost a $1,950 deduction?*

A. The marriage doesn't automatically deny you the deduction, but it does add an extra hurdle. As usual, to claim your daughter as a dependent you must have provided more than half of her support. (You can include wedding costs you paid when toting up your support.) The possible catch added by matrimony is that you can't claim an exemption for your daughter if she files a joint return with her new husband, unless neither of them is required to file a return but do so only to get a refund of withheld wages. Remember that if you claim her as a dependent, your daughter can't claim a personal exemption on her own tax return.

AUTO REBATES

Q. *I got a $700 rebate when I bought my new car last year. Since I got a check rather than having the amount applied to the cost of the car, my neighbor says I have to count the money as income and report it on my return. Is that true?*

A. No. Regardless of how you took advantage of the rebate program, the $700 is considered a reduction of the car's price, not income to you.

FAIR RENT

Q. *I own a house that I rent to my parents, and my accountant says I have to charge them as much rent as I would charge anyone else. Otherwise, he says, I jeopardize my rental tax deductions. Is that right?*

A. Not necessarily, according to the outcome of a case that wound up in Tax Court a few years ago. The case involved a taxpayer who argued that the lower-than-market rent he was charging his parents was based on financial reasons, not kinship. He even got the IRS expert witness to concede that a 10% to 20% reduction was reasonable because the parents could be expected to take good care of the house, and another 5% to 10% could be knocked off the rent because renting to a relative freed the son from paying a management fee to a real estate agent. The court ruled that 20% off for relatives could still be fair rent for purposes of figuring whether the landlord qualified for rental-loss deductions.

SOCIAL SECURITY

Q. *I just started getting social security benefits. Can you explain how I determine whether I have to pay tax on the money?*

A. Up to half of the benefits can be taxable if your income exceeds a certain level. The income figure used for this purpose is the total of your adjusted gross income plus any tax-exempt interest you received during the year plus one-half of your social security benefits. If that amount is less than $25,000 (if you file an individual return) or $32,000 (if you file a joint return) none of your benefits will be taxed.

If the income figure exceeds the threshold for your filing status, however, you have to report as taxable income either that excess or half of your benefits, whichever is less.

GIVING ONE'S TIME

Q. *Last year my church had a major fund-raising drive. I was asked to donate my services as a photographer in lieu of cash. Billed at my standard rate, the time I spent would have brought me $2,000. An accountant tells me that all I can deduct is the cost of the film and other supplies I used. I think he's being too conservative. Can I claim the full $2,000 as a charitable contribution?*

A. Your accountant is correct that the law doesn't permit a deduction for the value of your services. Here's why: If you had charged $2,000 for your services, that would have been taxable income. Turning around and donating the cash to the church would have earned you a $2,000 write-off. The result would be no change in your taxable income. Similarly, donating your time means you don't have the extra income to report in the first place, so there's no need for a deduction to offset it.

INTEREST OR DIVIDENDS

Q. *We received $875 in interest from our money-market mutual fund last year. Several people have told me the IRS considers this income to be dividends. How should I report it?*

A. As dividends. Although most of the income earned by money-market funds is interest, the funds pay it out as dividends. In either case the tax bill is the same, but reporting it as interest rather than dividends would confuse the IRS and trigger an inquiry.

SAVINGS BOND BACKFIRE

Q. *Last fall our daughter cashed in her collection of savings bonds to pay college tuition. At the time, the bank gave her a 1099-INT form stating that she collected about $2,600 in interest. It's clear that the same information was sent to the IRS. We thought one of the main reasons for* *using savings bonds for a college fund was to get what amounted to tax-free interest. We followed the advice to file a tax return for the first year we purchased bonds in our daughter's name, to establish that she was reporting interest annually rather than letting it build up. Have we been doubled-crossed? Does our daughter have to pay taxes on all the interest?*

A. No. Although the IRS did receive a copy of the form your daughter received, you don't have to report the interest again. Your daughter should report the interest shown on the 1099-INT along with all other interest received during the year on Schedule B if she files a Form 1040 or Schedule 1 of the 1040A short form. A couple of lines below the subtotal, she should write "U.S. savings bond interest previously reported" and enter the total interest reported over the years under the election to report annually. Subtract that amount to arrive at the amount of taxable interest.

HOW MUCH INTEREST

Q. *We are reporting savings bond interest annually on the bonds we have purchased for our minor children. How do we know how much interest accrues each year?*

A. The amount of income to report each year is the increase in the redemption value. The 1988 income, for example, would be the difference between what the bond was worth at the end of 1987 and it's value at the end of 1988. Your bank should have copies of the redemption tables, or you can get one by writing the Saving Bond Division, U.S. Treasury, Washington, D.C. 20226.

LOTTERY

Q. *I won $10,000 in the state lottery, but when I picked up my winnings I got only $8,000. The other $2,000 was sent to the IRS for taxes. Do I have to report the remaining $8,000 as income, or am I considered to have already settled up with Uncle Sam?*

A. You should report the entire $10,000 as "other income" on your Form 1040. The $2,000 that was deducted from your winnings was a prepayment of your taxes, similar to withholding from paychecks. You get credit for the $2,000 by including it with the amount of taxes already paid. The $10,000 is gambling winnings, so if you itemize deductions you can deduct your gambling losses for the year, including what you spent to enter the state lottery. The write-off for such losses is limited to the amount of your winnings.

DEPRECIATE A GIFT

Q. *My kids got together and bought new furniture for my office as a*

Christmas gift. I don't want to play Scrooge, but if I had purchased the furniture myself I could have depreciated it as a business expense. Does the fact that I received it as a gift deny me the opportunity to write off the cost?

A. No. If you could depreciate the furniture if you bought it yourself, you can write it off even though you received it as a gift. Your basis—the amount to be depreciated—is either the fair market value of the furniture when you received it or what your children paid for it, whichever is less.

IRA ROLLOVER

Q. *Last summer I gave up on the mutual fund where I had my IRA, withdrew the $4,700 and rolled it over into a new IRA. I got a 1099-R form from the mutual fund that lists the $4,700 as a distribution. I assume the IRS got a copy of the form and expects me to include the payout in taxable income. I know that because I made the rollover the money is not taxable, but how do I let the IRS know the money is still in an IRA so they don't hassle me?*

A. The tax form makes provisions for your situation. There's a line to report the full distribution—that's the amount the IRS compares to the reports it receives from IRA trustees—and another line to report the taxable part. That's where you'll show $0. To qualify as a rollover, the funds must have been deposited in the new IRA within 60 days after you received the distribution.

MUTUAL FUND SWITCHING

Q. *I invest in a family of mutual funds, primarily so I can easily move my money around from stocks to bonds to money-market funds. Is it true that when I order the transfer of funds from one fund to another the switch can result in taxable income?*

A. Yes. When you tell the fund to transfer funds from a stock fund, for example, to a money-market fund, what occurs is the sale of your shares in the stock fund—for a taxable gain or deductible loss—and the reinvestment of the money in the money-market fund. Although telephone switching can be convenient, don't ignore the tax consequences.

FAMILY LOAN

Q. *I want to loan my daughter and her husband the money for the down payment on a house. It seems to me that I've heard that the IRS demands that I charge them interest. Is that right?*

A. It depends on the size of the loan you have in mind. First, consider why Uncle Sam thinks this is any of his business. Congress was worried that parents in a high tax bracket could make an interest-free "loan" to a child, and income generated by the funds would be taxed at the child's lower tax rate. To prevent that, the IRS now treats such loans as though the lender was charging a reasonable rate of interest and making a gift to the borrower of the amount necessary to pay it. The lender had to report that "phantom" interest as income.

There are exceptions to that rule, however, and one may exempt you from having to worry about it. First, if the amount of the loan is $10,000 or less, the IRS doesn't care about the interest rate. And, for loans up to $100,000, the government won't get involved as long as the borrower's investment income doesn't exceed $1,000. (For both the $10,000 loan limit and the $1,000 investment-income level, a husband and wife are treated as one person.)

HEAD OF HOUSEHOLD

Q. *I own my own home and live alone. Since I'm the only person in the household, can I use the head-of-household tax rates?*
A. No. To qualify as an unmarried head of household—and benefit from rates lower than those that apply to single people—you must pay more than half the cost of maintaining a home where you live with a "qualifying individual."

WHEN TO DEDUCT

Q. *I gave a check to my church at Christmastime, but it wasn't cashed until the following year. Can I deduct the amount for the year I gave the check, or do I have to wait?*
A. You can claim the deduction on the return for the year you gave the check.

PERSONAL CHARITY

Q. *There is a growing number of street people in our community, and over the course of the year I'm sure I gave well over $100 in handouts. Can I add that amount to my charitable contributions.*
A. No. The IRS says only donations to qualified *organizations* can be deducted.

MORE THAN CHILD CARE

Q. *The lady who takes care of our kids also cleans and cooks dinner for our family. Can we include her full salary when figuring the child-care credit, or do we need to break it down between child care and other services?*
A. Assuming that providing care for the children while you work is one of the reasons you hire the care giver and that the other services

performed benefit the children, you can include the full salary.

HAIR TRANSPLANT

Q. *I've given up waiting for a product to grow hair and have decided to have a hair transplant. Is the cost of that kind of operation deductible?*
A. Yes, you can include it with your other medical expenses.

SAFE-DEPOSIT BOX

Q. *Where do I write off the annual fee for my safe-deposit box?*
A. Assuming you keep investment or tax-related documents in the box, the cost is considered a miscellaneous expense. Include it with other expenses in this category and you can deduct the amount by which the total exceeds 2% of your adjusted gross income.

SCOUTMASTER'S UNIFORMS

Q. *I'm a scoutmaster and had to spend nearly $100 on the uniform and associated paraphernalia I need to wear to meetings. Is there any tax break for that kind of expense?*
A. You can deduct, as a charitable expense, the cost and upkeep of such special uniforms needed when you donate your services. The key to the deduction is that the clothes be necessary and not suitable for everyday use.

WASH-SALE RULE

Q. *I own stock that has taken a beating in the market. I'd like to sell to get the loss deduction but think the company has a lot of upside potential. Is it true that the tax rules say that if I sell I have to wait a certain amount of time before buying it back?*
A. You don't have to wait, but if you buy back too quickly you can be tripped up by the wash-sale rule. Basically, the loss on the sale is disallowed if within 30 days before or after you sell you buy back the same stock. The IRS figures you're really in the same position you were before the sale, so you don't deserve the tax break of a loss. To accomplish your purpose but get around the wash sale rule, you could buy additional shares of the stock at the current, depressed price and then wait 30 days before selling the older block of shares for a loss. Or, you could sell now and wait 30 days to buy the shares back.

HOBBY-LOSS WORRY

Q. *We own a vacation home that we rent out most of the year. Year after year we show a tax loss, and I'm worried about the hobby-loss rules. After a while will the IRS reject our loss deductions because we never make a profit on the place?*

A. Not necessarily. The hobby-loss rules presume you're in business to make a profit if you report a profit in at least three out of five years. If you fail that test, you may be called on to prove you're trying to make money. You'd need records showing that you charge a reasonable rent, for example, and make reasonable attempts to keep the place rented. Remember, too, that profit on real estate is often based significantly on the appreciation of the property, something that doesn't show up on annual tax returns.

CHILD'S 15TH BIRTHDAY

Q. *My daughter's 15th birthday was April 8, and I see the rules on the child-care credit say that you can only count expenses for the care of children under 15. Does that mean I lose the child-care credit?*
A. No. You can still claim the credit, based on the amount you paid for her care during the part of the year before her birthday. Despite the fact that your child qualified for only part of the year, you may base the credit on up to $2,400 of qualifying costs—the same limit that applies to expenses paid for a single child for the entire year.

PAYING MOM FOR WATCHING THE KIDS

Q. *My mother lives with us and I'd like to supplement her income by paying her to watch the kids while I work. Will what I pay her count toward the child-care credit?*
A. Yes, assuming you don't claim your mother as a dependent on your tax return.

PAPER-ROUTE INCOME

Q. *Our son has a paper route and earns about $200 a month. Does he have to file a tax return and pay tax on that money?*
A. If that's his only income, he doesn't have to file a return. But if he has any "unearned" income—interest on a savings account, say—he must file. His standard deduction would be large enough to cover the $2,400 paper-route earnings, but tax would be due on his unearned income.

LOST RETURN

Q. *I filed my return in mid February, and now, in mid July, I still haven't received my refund. I'm afraid the return is lost. Is there a special form to file when sending in a duplicate return?*
A. No. Your first step should be to check the status of your return. There's a number to call in the instruction packet that came with your return, or you can get it by contacting a local IRS office. If the IRS hasn't received your return by now, you can assume it's lost. Send a

copy of the return, marked "duplicate," to the service center where you originally filed, along with a letter explaining what has happened. Since you have a refund coming, you won't be penalized for filing late.

If you had owed money, however, you would want to include with your duplicate return evidence that you had filed earlier—a copy of the checkbook register showing the date on which you wrote the check for the taxes due, for example. There's a good chance that will deflect the late-payment penalty. If not and you are assessed a penalty, you should write to the service center again, explaining the situation and asking that the penalty be dropped.

NEGLIGENCE PENALTY

Q. *I got a notice from the IRS showing that I failed to report about $1,200 of interest on a bank account. I checked my records and, sure enough, I somehow failed to include that income with my other interest. I don't mind having to pay the tax, but I'm also being charged a penalty for negligence. Can the IRS impose that penalty just because I forgot to report the income?*

A. Yes. In fact, the negligence penalty is automatic whenever a taxpayer fails to report income that is separately reported to the IRS by the payer—such as interest and dividends.

SHORTED ON A REFUND

Q. *When I got my refund check, it was for $188 less than I had requested on my return. I don't know why the IRS shorted me. If I cash the check, does that mean I agree with them?*

A. No. Cashing the check wouldn't prevent you from disputing the IRS on whatever issue is involved. There's a good chance that the difference between what you expected and what you got is due to a mathematical error or other simple mistake—such as using the incorrect tax rates for your filing status—that was caught by the IRS. You should receive a notice from the agency explaining why the change was made. (The explanation is sent by a different office than the refund.)

BAD DEBT

Q. *I paid a $2,000 deposit to a builder who went bankrupt before even beginning work on our new house. I've been unable to recover any of the money and have been told I might be able to mitigate my loss by claiming a tax deduction. Is that possible?*

A. If you can show that you tried to recover the money and that there is no chance of doing so, the $2,000 could qualify as a nonbusiness bad debt. If so, it's deductible as a capital loss on Schedule D.

FINGERING A TAX CHEAT

Q. *I'm getting sick and tired of listening to a neighbor brag about all the ways he finagles to beat the IRS. Is it true the IRS offers rewards to people who turn in tax cheats?*

A. Yes. The law authorizes the IRS to pay rewards to informants whose tips lead to the detection and punishment of someone guilty of violating the tax law. Although the IRS says only a small percentage of the tips it receives actually pan out, informants have been paid millions of dollars over the years. The reward can be as much as 10% of the tax recovered. The exact amount is set by the IRS depending on how important the information you provided was to catching the tax cheat.

60 DAYS FROM WHEN

Q. *I asked my IRA sponsor to close my account and send me a check so I could open a new IRA. I know I have only 60 days after closing one account to put the funds in new one. But when does that 60-day period begin, the day the old account is closed or the day I get the check?*

A. The 60-day rollover period begins when you receive the distribution from the first IRA. In one case, for example, three weeks passed from the time the first IRA was closed and the time the taxpayer received the proceeds in the mail. The IRS reaffirmed that the 60-day clock didn't start ticking until the day the proceeds were received.

SOLVING TAX PROBLEMS

Q. *After an exchange of several letters with the IRS, I'm convinced I'm dealing with a computer that just won't listen. Is there any way to break out of the bureaucracy and get a real live person to consider my situation?*

A. Sounds like your case is the kind for which the IRS Problems Resolution Offices were set up. Basically, if it seems the system has failed you, you can ask a problems-resolution officer to intervene, review what's gone on to date and solve the problem. You can go to the problems-resolution office if you feel you're getting the runaround instead of an answer to a question, for example, or after your attempts to find a lost refund fail. A local IRS office can direct you to the problems-resolution office for the area. Problems-resolution officers step in to assist more than half a million taxpayers a year.

65 ON NEW YEAR'S DAY

Q. *I turned 65 on New Year's Day. Is it true I can claim the higher standard deduction on the return I file for the prior year?*

A. Yes. In this case the law considers you to be 65 on the day before your birthday.

HOUSEHOLD HELP

Q. *Do we have to pay social security tax for the woman who cares for our kids and, if so, can we deduct that amount with our other deductible taxes?*

A. Yes to the first question, no to the second. If you pay a household employee $50 or more during a calendar quarter, FICA (social security tax) is due. You can withhold half of the amount due from your employee's wages or pay the full amount yourself. In either case, what you pay can be included in the amount on which you base your child-care credit, but it's not deductible.

REINVESTED DIVIDENDS

Q. *In the past I always had my mutual fund pay me my dividends in cash. Last year, however, I started having the payments reinvested in additional shares. Are the dividends still taxable even though I never put my hands on the cash?*

A. Yes. Be sure to keep track of the reinvested dividends because they are part of your basis in the mutual fund and will reduce the amount of taxable profit when you sell the shares.

ANNUITY INCOME

Q. *When I retired, I bought a $25,000 single-premium annuity that pays me $185 a month for the rest of my life. Since I paid the premium myself, are the payments I receive tax-free?*

A. Not all of them. Only the part of each payment that represents a return of your investment isn't taxed. The rest is made up of earnings on your investment and is taxable.

DEPRECIATING A NEW ROOF

Q. *I own a commercial office building and recently paid $11,000 for a new roof. How do I depreciate that cost?*

A. Such improvements to property are treated the same as the property itself. Since a commercial building put into service after 1986 would be depreciated over 31.5 years, a roof added to such a building would be depreciated over that period. You would continue to depreciate the building itself according to the schedule in effect when you first put it into service. Basically, you treat the roof as a separate piece of property, depreciating the $11,000 over 31.5 years.

LOSING WITH TAX-FREES

Q. *I invested in a tax-free municipal bond fund for three years, and when I sold it the shares were worth less than what I paid. Can I deduct the loss even though this was a tax-free investment?*

A. Yes. If you sold for less than your basis in the shares, you have a capital loss. You can use it to offset any capital gains and up to $3,000 of other income.

DIPPING INTO AN IRA EARLY

Q. *Is it true there is a way to get money out of an IRA without penalty before age 59½?*
A. Yes. The 10% early-withdrawal penalty is waived if you arrange to take the money out evenly over your life expectancy, even if the first payment comes before you are 59½.

REFINANCING A MORTGAGE

Q. *Our mortgage is paid down to about $75,000 and we want to refinance for $125,000, using the extra money to add a swimming pool and to pay off some bills. Will all the interest on the new mortgage be deductible?*
A. It depends. The law permits the deduction of interest on up to $1 million of "acquisition indebtedness" plus up to $100,000 in home-equity loans secured by your principal residence or second home. When you refinance, acquisition indebtedness is the amount outstanding on the old mortgage—$75,000 in your case—plus any amount of the new loan used for substantial improvements—like your pool. If you spend $25,000 on your pool, then, interest on $100,000 of the new mortgage would be deductible for sure. Interest on the other $25,000 would be deductible if it doesn't push you over the $100,000 allowance for home-equity debt.

NO PENALTY FOR FILING LATE

Q. *Each year, my procrastination results in my staying up late on April 15 to complete my return and then rushing to the post office and hoping the envelope is postmarked before midnight. A friend told me that if I've got a refund coming—which I always do—there's no reason to kill myself to make the April 15 deadline. Is it true there's no penalty for being late?*
A. The point your friend is making is that the penalty for missing the filing deadline is based on the amount of tax you owe with your return. If you are absolutely certain you have a refund coming, you don't risk a penalty by filing late. Of course, if you have a refund coming you ought to be filing as early as possible so you can get your money back.

APPENDIX

TAX RATES FOR 1988

Taxable Income	Tax
Married Couples Filing Jointly and Surviving Spouses	
Up to $29,750	15% of taxable income
$29,751 to $71,900	$ 4,462 plus 28% of amount over $29,750
$71,901 to $149,250*	$16,264 plus 33% of amount over $71,900
Over $149,250	$41,790 plus 28% of amount over $149,250
Unmarried Individuals	
Up to $17,850	15% of taxable income
$17,851 to $43,150	$ 2,677 plus 28% of amount over $17,850
$43,151 to $89,560*	$ 9,761 plus 33% of amount over $43,150
Over $89,560	$25,076 plus 28% of amount over $89,560
Heads of Household	
Up to $23,900	15% of taxable income
$23,901 to $61,650	$ 3,585 plus 28% of amount over $23,900
$61,651 to $123,790*	$14,155 plus 33% of amount over $61,650
Over $123,790	$34,661 plus 28% of amount over $123,790
Married Individuals Filing Separately	
Up to $14,875	15% of taxable income
$14,876 to $35,950	$ 2,218 plus 28% of amount over $14,875
$35,951 to $113,300*	$ 8,119 plus 33% of amount over $35,950
Over $113,300	$33,644 plus 28% of amount over $113,300

For each filing status, the 33% bracket is extended by $10,920 for every exemption claimed on the return for yourself, your spouse and your dependents. For example, for a married couple filing jointly and claiming four exemptions—one each for the husband and wife and one each for two dependent children—the 33% bracket would cover income from $71,901 to $192,930. The 28% rate would be reinstated for taxable income above that level. This bulge bracket is discussed on pages 8 and 9.

TAX FORMS AND IRS PUBLICATIONS

The list of tax forms you're most likely to need to settle up with Uncle Sam appears on pages 439 and 440. Don't be intimidated. Millions of taxpayers get by with a single form; most of the rest need just a few. Following the list of forms is an inventory of IRS publications that address various tax issues. These booklets often include several hypothetical examples that can be particularly helpful to understanding the issue at hand.

You should receive from the IRS each year a tax package including the basic forms and instructions for filling them out. There's a good chance, however, that you'll need additional forms. You can get any of those listed here, as well as any of the informational publications, free. To order, contact your local IRS office (check the "U.S. Government" listings in your telephone book) or write to the IRS forms distribution center for your area at the address listed below:

If You Live In	Order From IRS Forms Distribution Center
Alabama, Arkansas, Illinois, Indiana, Iowa, Kansas, Kentucky, Louisiana, Michigan, Minnesota, Mississippi, Missouri, Nebraska, North Dakota, Ohio, Oklahoma, South Dakota, Tennessee, Texas, Wisconsin	P.O. Box 9903 Bloomington, Ill. 61799
Alaska, Arizona, California, Colorado, Hawaii, Idaho, Montana, Nevada, New Mexico, Oregon, Utah, Washington, Wyoming	P.O. Box 12626 Fresno, Cal. 93778
Connecticut, Delaware, District of Columbia, Florida, Georgia, Maine, Maryland, Massachusetts, New Hampshire, New Jersey, New York, North Carolina, Pennsylvania, Puerto Rico, Rhode Island, South Carolina, Vermont, Virginia, West Virginia	P.O. Box 25866 Richmond, Va. 23260

IRS FORMS

Form	Use
Form W-2	Report income you paid household employees
Form W-4	Control the amount your employer withholds from your pay
Form W-4P	Control the amount of withholding on pension or annuity payments
Form W-5	Request advance payment of earned-income credit
Form 1040	Basic tax return
Form 1040A	Simplified version of basic return
Form 1040EZ	Simplest version of basic return
Form 1040X	Amend previously filed return
Form 1040-ES	Make estimated tax payments on nonwage income in addition to or instead of withholding
Schedule A	Claim itemized deductions
Schedule B	Report interest and dividend income
Schedule C	Report income, deductions, and profit or loss from a sole-proprietorship business or profession
Schedule D	Report capital gains and losses from sale of securities or other assets
Schedule E	Report "supplemental" income, including rents, royalties and income or loss from partnerships, S corporations, estates and trusts for real estate mortgage investment conduits (REMICs)
Schedule F	Report farm income and expenses
Schedule K (Form 1045)	Shows partners' share of income, credits and deductions from partnership interest
Schedule R	Claim the credit for the elderly or permanently and totally disabled

Form	Use
Schedule SE	Compute the social security tax on self-employment income
Form 2106	Report deductible employee business expenses
Form 2119	Report the sale or exchange of a principal residence
Form 2120	Claim a dependent under a multiple-support agreement
Form 2441	Claim the credit for child- and dependent-care expenses
Form 3903	Claim moving expense deductions
Form 4506	Request copies of previously filed returns
Form 4684	Claim casualty- and theft-loss deductions
Form 4868	Automatic four-month extension of filing deadline
Form 4972	Figure tax on lump-sum distribution from retirement plan
Form 5500EZ	Report on Keogh plan covering only the self-employed individual who set up the plan
Form 6251	Compute the alternative minimum tax for individuals
Form 6252	Report installment sale of property
Form 8283	Report noncash charitable contributions exceeding $500
Form 8332	Permit noncustodial parent to claim child as dependent
Form 8582	Compute limits on passive-loss deductions
Form 8598	Compute limit on mortgage-interest deduction
Form 8606	Report nondeductible IRA contribution
Form 8615	Compute "kiddie tax" on unearned income of children under age 14
Form 706	Estate-tax return
Form 709	Gift-tax return
Form 709-A	Gift-tax return for couples to report nontaxable gifts of more than $10,000 but less than $20,000
Form 940	Unemployment taxes for household workers

IRS PUBLICATIONS

Title	Number
Accounting Periods and Methods	538
Alternative Minimum Tax for Individuals	909
Automobile, Business use of	917
Bad Debts, Deduction for	548
Bankruptcy	908
Basis of Assets	551
Business Expenses	535
Business Use of Your Home	587
Casualties, Nonbusiness Disasters and Thefts	547
Casualty Loss Workbook	584
Charitable Contributions	526
Child and Dependent Care Credit	503
Children and Dependents	929
Civil Service Retirement Benefits	721
Community Property	555
Condominiums, Cooperative Apartments and Owners of Homes, Tax Information for	530
Corporations	542
Credit for the Elderly or the Permanently and Totally Disabled	524
Depreciation	534
Direct Sellers	911
Divorced and Separated Individuals	504
Donated Property, Determining the Value of	561
Earned Income Credit	596
Educational Expenses	508
Employers Tax Guide (Circular E)	15
Employment Taxes	539
Entertainment, Travel and Gift Expenses	463
Estate and Gift Taxes	448
Estimated Tax	505
Examination of Returns, Appeal Rights, and Claims for Refund	556
Executors, Survivors and Administrators	559
Exempt Status for Your Organization	557
Exemptions and Standard Deduction	501
Farmer's Tax Guide	225
Foreign Tax Credit	514
Handicapped and Disabled Individuals	907
Home, Tax Information on Selling Your	523
Individual Retirement Accounts	590
Installment Sales	537
Interest Expense	545
Investment Income and Expenses	550
Medical and Dental Expenses	502
Miscellaneous Deductions	529
Moving Expenses	521

Title	Number
Mutual Fund Distributions	564
Net Operating Losses	536
Original Issue Discount Instruments	1212
Partnerships	541
Passive Activity and At-Risk Rules	925
Pension and Annuity Income	575
Recordkeeping, Information for Business Taxpayers	583
Rental Property	527
S Corporations	589
Sales and Other Distributions of Assets	544
Scholarships and Fellowships	520
Self-Employed Retirement Plans	560
Self-Employment Tax	533
Selling Your Home	523
Separated Individuals	504
Small Business (General Guide)	334
Social Security Benefits and Equivalent Railroad Retirement Benefits	915
Tax Services, Guide to Free	910
Tax-Sheltered Annuity Programs for Employees of Public Schools and Certain Tax-Exempt Organizations	571
Taxable and Nontaxable Income	525
Tips	531
Withholding	505
Your Federal Income Tax (General Guide)	17

GLOSSARY

The lexicon of the federal income tax can often seem like a foreign language. Here are translations of some of the key terms you'll encounter. For additional information on any subject, see the index for references to other parts of the book.

Accelerated depreciation. For most business property, except real estate, the law allows you to depreciate the cost at a rate faster than would be allowed under straight-line depreciation. For example, automobiles and computers are assumed to have a five-year life for tax purposes. With straight-line depreciation you would be permitted to write off 20% of the cost each year; the accelerated method generally lets you deduct 20% of the business cost the first year, 32% the second, 19.2% the third, 11.52% in years four and five, and the remaining 5.8% in the sixth year. It takes six years to fully depreciate the property, thanks to the "midyear convention."

Acquisition indebtedness. Mortgage debt on which the interest is deductible. To qualify as acquisition indebtedness, the debt must be used to buy, build or substantially improve your principal residence or a second home and must be secured by the property. There is an overall $1 million limit on the amount of acquisition indebtedness on which interest is deductible.

Active participation. The level of involvement that real estate owners must meet to qualify to deduct up to $25,000 of losses from rental real estate. Failure to pass the active-participation test could make such losses nondeductible under passive-loss rules.

Adjusted basis. Your basis in property is the stepping-off point for determining taxable gain or loss when you sell it. Adjusted basis generally starts out as what you pay for the property, although special rules apply to assets you inherit or receive as a gift. Your basis can be adjusted while you own property. When you buy a home, for example, the basis begins at what you pay for the place. It's adjusted upward to take certain buying expenses into account and is raised further by the cost of any permanent improvements. Basis is reduced by any casualty losses you claim while you own the property and also by the profit from any previous home you roll over into the new place. When rental property is involved, you reduce your basis by the amount of any depreciation you deduct while you own the property. You use your adjusted basis to figure the gain or loss on the sale. When stock or mutual fund shares are involved, your adjusted basis is the cost of the shares plus any brokerage commissions or load fees minus any return of capital payouts.

Adjusted gross income (AGI). This is your income from all taxable sources minus certain adjustments. These adjustments—sometimes called above-the-line deductions because you can claim them whether or not you itemize deductions—include deductible contributions to individual retirement accounts and Keogh plans, any penalty paid on early withdrawal of savings, and alimony payments.

Alternative minimum tax (AMT). A special tax designed primarily to prevent the wealthy from using so many tax breaks that their regular tax bill is reduced to little or nothing. The AMT applies a flat 21% tax rate to an income base larger than that hit by the regular tax.

Alimony. Qualifying payments to an ex-spouse that can be deducted as adjustments to income whether or not you itemize. The recipient of alimony must include the payments in taxable income.

Audit. As if you didn't know, this is a review of your tax return by the IRS, during which you are asked to prove that you have correctly reported your income and deductions.

Bargain sale to charity. Selling property to a charity for less than the property's actually worth. Depending on the circumstances, you will be able to claim a charitable-contribution deduction or have to report taxable income.

Basis See adjusted basis.

Below-market-rate loans. If you make an interest-free or bargain-rate loan to a friend or relative, you may be required to include in your taxable income some of the interest the IRS figures you should have, but didn't, receive.

Bond premium. The amount over face value that you pay to buy a bond paying higher than current market rates. With taxable bonds, a portion of the premium can be deducted each year that you own the securities.

Capital expenditure. The cost of a permanent improvement to property. Such expenses increase the property's adjusted basis.

Capital gain or loss. The profit or loss from the sale of such property as stocks, mutual-fund shares, real estate and collectibles.

Capital-loss carryover. Capital losses can be used to offset capital gains, and up to $3,000 of any excess loss can be deducted against other income, such as your salary. Losses not currently deductible because of the $3,000 limit can be carried over to future years.

Casualty loss. Damage that results from a sudden or unusual event.

Such losses are deductible to the extent that they exceed 10% of your adjusted gross income.

Child- and dependent-care credit. A tax credit available to offset part of the cost of providing care for a child or disabled dependent while you work. The credit can shave as much as $720 off your tax bill if you pay for the care of one individual or as much as $1,440 if you pay for the care of two or more.

Child support. Payments made under a divorce or separation agreement for the support of a child. The payments are neither deductible by the spouse who pays them nor considered taxable income to the spouse who receives the money.

Constructive receipt. A concept of tax law that taxes income at the time you could have received it, even if you don't actually have it. A paycheck you could pick up in December 1988 is considered constructively received and taxed in 1988, for example, even if you don't get and cash the check until 1989. Also, interest paid on a savings account is considered constructively received and taxable in the year paid, whether or not you withdraw the money.

Consumer interest. See personal interest.

Deductions. Expenses you are permitted to subtract from your taxable income. All taxpayers may claim a standard-deduction amount—$5,000 on joint returns and $3,000 on individual returns for 1988—which will increase in step with future inflation. If your qualifying expenses exceed your standard deduction, you may claim the higher amount by itemizing your deductions. Although no records are needed to substantiate your claim to the standard deduction, you must maintain records of qualifying expenditures if you itemize.

Dependent. Someone you support and for whom you can claim a dependency exemption on your tax return. For each dependent you claim, the exemption knocks $1,950 off your taxable income in 1988. Exemptions are worth $2,000 in 1989, then will increase each year with inflation.

Depreciation. A deduction to reflect the gradual loss of value of business property as it wears out. The law assigns a tax life to various types of property, and your basis in such property is deducted over that period of time. Rental residential real estate put in service after 1986 is depreciated over 27.5 years, so owners basically deduct 3.6% (100 ÷ 27.5) of the cost each year.

Direct transfer. A method to move individual-retirement-account funds from one sponsor to another. With a direct transfer, you order one sponsor to transfer the money directly to your new IRA; you do not take possession of the funds. The IRS imposes no limit to the number of times you can move your money via direct transfer.

However, if you take possession of the funds and personally deposit them in the new IRA, the switch is considered a rollover. You can use the rollover method only once each year.

Earned income. Compensation, such as salary, commissions and tips, you receive for your personal services. This is distinguished from "unearned" or investment income, such as interest, dividends and capital gains.

Enrolled agent. A tax preparer who, by virtue of passing a tough IRS test or experience as an IRS employee, can represent clients at IRS audits and appeals.

Estate tax. The federal estate tax applies to taxable estates larger than $600,000.

Estimated tax. If you have income not subject to withholding, such as investment or self-employment income, you may have to make quarterly payments of estimated tax to cover your expected tax liability for the year. You can be penalized if estimated payments, combined with any withholding from your wages, don't equal at least 90% of the tax owed.

Exemptions. You can claim a personal exemption for yourself, and if you file a joint return, one for your spouse. You can also get an exemption for each dependent you are eligible to claim on your return. See dependent.

Expensing. Also known as the Section 179 deduction, expensing lets you treat up to $10,000 of expenditures that normally would be depreciated over a number of years as current business expenses to be deducted immediately.

Filing status. Your status determines the size of your standard deduction and which tax-rate schedule applies to your income: single, married filing jointly, married filing separately, head of household, or qualifying widow or widower.

Five-year averaging. A special tax-computation method for lump-sum distributions from pension and profit-sharing plans. Among other requirements, to use averaging you must be at least 59½ years old when you receive the distribution. Taxpayers born on or before January 1, 1936, may qualify for ten-year averaging, a method that can produce even greater tax savings. If you qualify to use either averaging method, part of the distribution may be completely tax-free.

Fixing-up expenses. Costs incurred to spruce up your home prior to its sale. If certain requirements are met and you replace the home with a house that costs less than the one sold, fixing-up expenses can reduce the tax due on the sale. In no event are the costs deductible, however, and they have no impact if you buy a replacement home that costs more than the one you sold.

401(k) plan. An employer-sponsored retirement plan that permits employees to divert part of their pay into the account. The money invested in the plan is not included in the employee's income and therefore is not taxed until it is withdrawn, presumably in retirement. The maximum annual deferral increases each year in step with inflation. In 1988, the cap was $7,313.

Gift tax. To prevent people from avoiding the estate tax by giving their property away, the law includes a gift tax, too. You may give up to $10,000 yearly to as many people you want without worrying about taxes. (The annual tax-free amount is $20,000 per recipient if your spouse joins in making the gift.) Larger gifts are taxable, but a tax credit offsets the tax on the first $600,000 of taxable gifts. When the gift tax is owed, it is owed by the giver, not the recipient.

Gross income. All of your income from taxable sources, before subtracting any adjustments, deductions or exemptions.

Head of household. A filing status with lower tax rates than apply to single individuals, available to unmarried taxpayers who pay more than half the cost of maintaining a home for a dependent relative or unmarried child. Generally, the taxpayer and dependent must live in the same home.

Hobby-loss rule. One requirement for deducting business losses is that you show you are trying to make a profit. The law presumes you're in business for profit if you report a taxable profit for three years out of any five-year period. Otherwise, your activity is assumed to be a hobby, unless you can prove otherwise. The distinction is important because if the expenses of a hobby exceed the income, the difference is considered a personal expense, not a tax-deductible loss.

Holding period. The length of time you own an investment. It was extremely important before 1987, when the law treated long-term gains and losses much differently than short-term ones. The holding period is what distinguished between the two. In 1986, for example, the profit on property held more than six months qualified as a long-term capital gain, 60% of which was tax-free. Short-term gains on property owned six months or less, however, were fully taxable. Now the holding period that separates long- and short-term results is one year, but the distinction is of much less importance. The law now treats long- and short-term gains and losses the same.

Home-equity borrowing. Loans secured by your principal residence or second home. The interest on up to $100,000 of home-equity debt is deductible regardless of the purpose for which the money is used. The interest beyond the $100,000 limit is considered personal interest.

Imputed interest. Interest you may be assumed to have earned—

and therefore owe tax on—if you make a below-market-rate loan. The term is also used to refer to the interest income you must report on taxable zero-coupon bonds. Although the bonds pay no interest until maturity, you must report the interest as it accrues.

Indexing. To prevent inflation from eroding certain tax benefits, they are automatically adjusted for increases in the consumer price index. Starting in 1988, for example, the maximum amount that can be deferred into a 401(k) plan was boosted to keep up with inflation. The standard deductions will increase starting in 1989, and the value of exemptions will be indexed to inflation as of 1990.

Individual retirement account (IRA). A tax-favored account designed to encourage you to save for your retirement. If your income is below a certain level or you are not covered by a retirement plan at work, deposits into an IRA can be deducted. The maximum annual contribution—deductible or not—is $2,000 or 100% of the compensation you earned during the year, whichever is less. The tax on all earnings inside the IRA is postponed until you withdraw the funds. In most cases there is a penalty for withdrawing funds before you reach age 59½.

Installment sale. With an installment sale you agree to have the purchaser pay you over a number of years, and you report the profit on the sale as you receive the money instead of all at once in the year of the sale. Although this method can no longer be used for the sale of securities, it may be beneficial if you sell real estate, for example.

Investment interest. Interest on loans used for investment purposes, such as interest on a brokerage margin account. You can deduct this type of interest up to the amount of investment income you report.

Itemized deductions. See deductions.

Keogh plan. Also known as an H.R. 10 plan after the number of the bill that authorized them, Keogh plans are retirement plans for the self-employed. As much as 20% of self-employment income can be deposited in a Keogh, and contributions can be deducted. There is no tax on the earnings until the money is withdrawn, and there are restrictions on tapping the account before age 59½.

Kiddie cards. A reference to the social security cards needed by all children age 5 and older who are claimed as dependents on their parents' returns. The social security number of such children must be listed on the parents' return.

Kiddie tax. The tax—at the parents' tax rate—imposed on unearned income in excess of $1,000 of children who are under age 14 at the end of the year.

Limited partnerships. Investments—in real estate and oil and gas, for example—that pass both profits and losses on to investors. By definition, limited partnerships are passive investments, subject to the passive-loss rules.

Listed property. Certain kinds of property—including automobiles, cameras and computers—that come under special restrictions if they are not used more than half the time in business.

Long-term gain or loss. See holding period.

Lump-sum distribution. The payment within one year of the full amount of your interest in a pension or profit-sharing plan. To qualify as a lump-sum distribution—and for favorable five- or ten-year averaging—other requirements must be met.

Luxury-car rules. The restriction that limits annual depreciation deductions for business automobiles that cost more than $12,800.

Marginal tax rate. The rate that applies in the highest tax bracket in which your income falls. Knowing your marginal rate tells you how much of each additional dollar you make will go to the IRS and how much you'll save for every dollar of deductions you claim.

Market discount. The difference between what you pay for a bond and it's higher face value. The tax treatment varies depending on whether the bond is taxable or tax-free and whether you redeem it at maturity or sell it before that time.

Master limited partnerships. Similar to regular limited partnerships, but MLPs shares are traded on the major exchanges, making for a much more liquid investment. Although limited-partnership losses are considered passive, income from an MLP is considered investment income rather than passive income. That means passive losses can't be used to shelter MLP income.

Material participation. The test used to determine whether you are involved enough in a business to avoid the passive-loss rules. To be considered a material participant, you must be involved on a "regular, continuous and substantial basis." One way to pass the test is to participate in the business for more than 500 hours during the year.

Medicare tax. A new levy that applies for the first time in 1989 to taxpayers who qualify for medicare's part-A hospital benefits. In 1989, it amounts to a 15% surtax that will cost $22.50 for every $150 of federal income-tax liability. Also known as a supplemental premium, the surtax is scheduled to rise annually at least until 1993, when it will be 28% of federal tax liability per $150 of tax owed.

Midmonth convention. The rule that treats certain kinds of property, including real estate, as though it were placed in service in the middle of the month it was first used. This somewhat simplifies the depreciation calculation for the first year. If you buy a rental property anytime during July, for example, you would claim 5½ months' worth of depreciation the first year.

Midquarter convention. In general, business property is depreciated under a half-year rule that gives you half a year's depreciation for the first year, whether you bought the property in January or December. However, if you buy more than 40% of the personal property you put into service for the year during the fourth quarter, the midquarter convention takes over. With it, you depreciate each piece of property as though it were placed into service in the middle of the calendar quarter in which it was purchased. You could claim just six weeks' worth of depreciation for property put in service during the final quarter.

Midyear convention. See above.

Mortgage interest. A term often used to refer to interest paid on debt that qualifies as acquisition indebtedness or home-equity debt.

Multiple-support agreement. An agreement under which two or more taxpayers who together provide more than half the support for someone else agree that one will claim that person as a dependent and the others will not.

Original issue discount (OID). The amount by which the face value of a bond exceeds its issue price. Part of the discount on taxable bonds must be reported as taxable interest income each year you own the securities.

Passive-loss rules. Passive activities are investments in which you do not materially participate. Losses from such investments can be used only to offset income from similarly passive investments. Passive losses generally can't be deducted against other kinds of income, such as salary or income from interest, dividends or capital gains. Generally, all real estate and limited-partnership investments are considered passive activities, but there is a limited exception for rental real estate in which you actively participate. Losses you can't use because you have no passive income to offset can be carried over to future years.

Personal exemption. See exemption.

Personal interest. Basically, this is interest that doesn't qualify as mortgage, business or investment interest. Included is interest you pay on credit cards, car loans, student loans, life insurance loans and any other personal borrowing not secured by your home. Personal interest deductions are gradually being phased out. In 1988, 40% of personal interest can be deducted. The deductible portion falls to 20% in 1989 and 10% in 1990. After that, there will be no deduction for personal interest.

Points. Charges connected with getting a mortgage. Each point is equal to 1% of the mortgage amount. Points paid on a mortgage to buy or improve your principal residence are generally fully deductible in the year you pay them. Points paid to refinance a principal home or to buy any other property must be deducted over the life of the loan.

Preference items. Tax benefits allowable under the regular income tax but not under the alternative minimum tax. Certain tax-exempt interest and appreciation on property given to charity are not taxed under the regular tax, for example, but are taxed under the AMT.

Qualified plan. An employee benefit plan—such as a pension or profit-sharing plan—that meets IRS requirements designed to protect employees' interests.

Rollover. The tax-free transfer of funds from one individual retirement account or Keogh plan to another. You can also use a rollover to transfer funds from a company plan—when you receive a lump-sum distribution at retirement, for example—to an IRA. If you complete the rollover within 60 days of the time you receive the funds, there is no tax on the distribution. Distributions from the IRA are taxed as you withdraw funds.

S corporation. A corporation that generally pays no tax because all profits and losses are passed on and taxed to the shareholders.

Section 179 deduction. See expensing.

Self-employment tax. The social security tax due on self-employment income. For 1988, the rate is 13.02% on the first $45,000 of self-employment and wage income.

Short-term gains and losses. See holding period.

Standard deduction. See deductions.

Standard mileage rate. The deductible amount you can claim for each mile you use your car for business, charitable or medical purposes without having to keep track of the actual cost. The rates are announced by the IRS in the fall of each year.

Taxable income. Income that is taxable (such as wages, interest and dividends) rather than tax-exempt (such as the interest on municipal bonds). On tax returns, it is your income after subtracting all adjustments, deductions and exemptions—that is, the amount on which your tax bill is computed.

Tax bracket. Each tax bracket encompasses a certain amount of taxable income. Currently there are four tax brackets for each filing status: 15%, 28%, 33% and 28%.

Tax-exempt interest. Interest paid on bonds issued by states or municipalities that is exempt from the federal income tax.

Ten-year averaging. A special tax-computation method for lump-sum distributions from pension and profit-sharing plans, available only to taxpayers born before January 1, 1936. They may choose between ten- and five-year averaging, the method available to younger taxpayers. Taxpayers may opt to use neither method and roll the distribution into an IRA.

Unearned income. Income from investments, such as interest, dividends and capital gains. See earned income.

Wash sale. The sale of a stock or bond for a loss when, within 30 days before or after that sale, you buy the same or substantially similar securities. Wash-sale rules prevent you from deducting the loss on such a sale.

Withholding. The amount held back from your wages each payday to pay your income and social security taxes for the year. The amount of income withheld is determined by the Form W-4 you file with your employer.

INDEX

A

Accelerated Cost Recovery
System (ACRS), *146*
Accelerated depreciation, *see*
Depreciation
Accountants, *72, 364, 365,
366-367*
Accrual accounting, *61-62*
Acquisition expenses, *70*
Acquisition indebtedness, *76,
77-79, 436, 443*
Active participation, *132, 150, 443*
Acupuncture, *263*
Adjusted basis, *70, 80-81, 83, 84,
86, 151, 294, 297, 443-444*
see also Basis
Adjusted gross income (AGI), *11,
12, 95, 149, 150, 158,
165-167, 170, 186, 207,
209, 235, 244, 252, 256,
280-281, 306, 312, 327,
427, 444*
Advertising expenses, *148*
Alcoholics Anonymous, *261*
Alimony, *17, 18, 55-59, 158, 315,
336, 340, 345, 355, 418,
444*
Alternative minimum tax (AMT),
*93, 124, 130, 135, 268,
287, 316, 388-396, 444, 451*
AMT credit, *393-396*
AMT exemption, *392-393*
AMT income (AMTI),
389-392
Amended tax returns, *86-87,
370-371*
Annuities, *17, 19, 138-140, 158,
435*
as retirement plans, *164, 171,*

172, 173, 180, 196-199, 343
Applicable federal rates (AFR),
52, 155
Appraisal fees, *70, 290, 295-296,
300*
Appreciated property, *12, 47,
207, 280-281, 286-288, 320,
395*
Appreciation, *59, 432*
Artificial limbs, *263*
Art works, *see* Collectibles
Assessments, *72-73*
Athletic club dues, *236-237*
Audits, *234, 295, 371-378, 379,
444*
repetitive, *378*
Auto expenses, *210-221, 270-271,
301*
actual-cost method, *211-215*
auto-club membership, *211*
depreciation, *210, 211,
212-216, 218-219*
for handicapped, *263, 318*
insurance, *211*
leasing, *216-218, 219*
luxury-car rule, *215-216, 326,
449*
parking expenses, *30, 211,
220*
record keeping, *210, 212,
216, 219-220, 379*
standard mileage rate,
210-211, 451
Auto loans, *12, 75, 272, 278,
414-415*
Auto rebates, *426*
Averaging, *see* Five-year
averaging, Ten-year
averaging

454

B

Bad debts, *53, 293, 371, 433*
Bankruptcy, *53*
Bargain-rate loans, *27*
Bargain sales to charity, *288-289,*
    444
Bargain stock purchases, *27*
Basis, *59, 142, 286, 297, 379-380*
    of automobiles, *212-215*
    of bonds, *114, 115, 117, 118,*
    119, 436
    of IRAs, *168-169*
    of mutual funds, *127,*
    128-129, 435
    of real estate, *68, 70–75,*
    80-81, 83, 84, 85, 86, 89,
    91, 92, 146, 147, 151, 152,
    153, 154, 155, 156, 230,
    270, 300, 422-423
    of stock, *108-110, 112, 113,*
    424
    see also Adjusted basis
Benefits, *see* Fringe benefits
Bonds, *13, 42, 101, 114-126, 128,*
    129, 132, 137, 139, 170,
    172, 424, 428, 452
    amortizable premium,
    118-119, 303
    basis, *114, 115, 117, 118,*
    119, 436
    convertible, *119*
    discount, *115-117, 449*
    municipal, *118, 121-124, 131,*
    207, 208, 277, 435
    original-issue-discount (OID),
    115-116, 450
    premiums, *118-119, 444*
    private purpose, *124, 130*
    record keeping, *117*
    swaps, *125-126, 323-324*
    tax-exempt, *121-125, 127,*
    277, 352, 391-392
    zero-coupon, *117-118, 170*

    see also Savings bonds
Bonuses, *18, 158*
Braille, *262, 263*
Bunching deductions, *10, 255,*
    320-321
Business expenses, *24, 48, 77,*
    186, 209-252, 301, 325-330,
    373
    automobiles, *see* Auto
    expenses
    business equipment, *221-225,*
    230, 234
    casualty/theft losses, *298*
    clothing, *251, 301*
    computers, *221-225*
    entertainment expenses,
    235-243, 375
    health insurance, *250, 325*
    home offices, *84-85, 225-234,*
    301, 380
    interest, *272, 414-415*
    miscellaneous expenses,
    250-252
    physical examination, *251*
    record keeping, *17, 225,*
    234-235, 249, 251
    subscriptions, *252, 301*
    tools, *251, 301, 320*
    travel expenses, *see* Travel
    expenses
Bypass trusts, *407, 408, 409*

C

Capital distributions, *113, 127*
Capital expenditures, *444*
Capital gain property, *287, 288,*
    289
Capital gains, *xi, 12-13, 43, 46,*
    53, 81, 101-103, 115, 120,
    125, 127, 128, 129, 131,
    141, 145, 153, 154, 155,
    171, 199, 202-203, 205,
    287, 288, 293, 310, 321,

P

Paper routes, *44, 432*
Parking expenses, *30, 211, 220*
Passive activities, *14, 132,*
133-136, 140-141, 149-150,
272, 273, 327-329, 449, 450
Passive income generators
(PIGs), *135, 328*
Passive losses, *1, 34, 50, 90, 94,*
96, 132-136, 141, 149-150,
153, 327-329, 356, 380,
391, 443, 449, 450
Penalties
from audits, *377*
early withdrawal, *see* Early
withdrawal penalties
estimated tax underpayment,
346-347, 348, 350
failure-to-pay, *368, 369*
late payment, *433, 436*
negligence, *433*
prepayment, *80, 279, 319*
underpayment, *350*
Pension plans, *see*
Retirement/pension plans
Personal exemption, *see*
Exemptions, personal
Personal interest, *12, 27, 51,*
75-76, 78, 92, 96, 97, 98,
278-279, 368, 389, 415,
421, 450-451
table, phaseout of
deductibility, *272*
Points, *68-70, 79-80, 81, 93, 319,*
414, 451
Political contributions, *305*
Precious metals, *171, 172*
Preference items, *451*
Premiums
bond, *118-119, 444*
health insurance, *257*
life insurance, *20, 113,*
136-137, 138

stock, *111, 113*
Prepaid interest, *68-71, 275-276,*
319
see also Points
Prepayment penalties, *80, 279,*
319
Prescription drugs, *see* Medical
expenses
Prizes, *19, 345, 425-426*
Probate, *408*
Professional dues, *12, 252, 301,*
320
Professional journals, *see*
Subscriptions
Profit-sharing plans, *193-196,*
343-344, 398
early distribution penalties,
195
plan loans, *196*
qualified, *451*
vesting, *194-195*
Property inspection fees, *70*
Property settlements, *56, 58, 59*
see also Divorce
Property tax, *xii, 11, 49, 65-67,*
70-71, 93, 94, 97, 99, 148,
229, 232, 233, 269-271,
318, 327, 340, 423
Psychoanalysis, *264*

Q

Qualified terminable interest
property (QTIP) trust,
407-408

R

Raffles, *19, 282*
see also Gambling
Real estate, *xi, xii, 13, 14, 49,*
101, 286, 398, 448
basis, *see* Basis
depreciation of, *14, 90, 91-92,*